Style
Is Not
a Size

LOOKING AND
FEELING GREAT
IN THE BODY
YOU HAVE

Style Is Not a Size

Hara Estroff Marano

Illustrations by Durell Godfrey

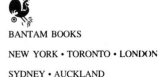

BANTAM BOOKS

NEW YORK · TORONTO · LONDON

SYDNEY · AUCKLAND

STYLE IS NOT A SIZE

A Bantam Book / May 1991

Copyright © 1991 by Hara Estroff Marano.
Cover photo copyright © 1991 by Phyllis Cuington.
Book design by Beth Tondreau Design / Mary A. Wirth

LIBRARY OF CONGRESS CATALOGING-IN-PUBLICATION DATA
Marano, Hara Estroff.
    Style is not a size : looking and feeling great in the body you
    have / Hara Estroff Marano.
        p.   cm.
    Includes index.
    ISBN 0-553-35270-9 (paper)
    1. Beauty, Personal.   2. Clothing and dress.   3. Fashion.
I. Title.
    RA778.M3274   1991
646'.34—dc20   *90-14444*
                                                                       CIP

Published simultaneously in the United States and Canada

Bantam Books are published by Bantam Books, a division of
Bantam Doubleday Dell Publishing Group, Inc. Its trademark,
consisting of the words "Bantam Books" and the portrayal of
a rooster, is Registered in U.S. Patent and Trademark Office
and in other countries. Marca Registrada. Bantam Books,
666 Fifth Avenue, New York, New York 10103.

PRINTED IN THE UNITED STATES OF AMERICA

RRH   0 9 8 7 6 5 4 3 2 1

Contents

v

"Fashion, we have been brought up to believe (and generations of writers in a myriad of journals have contributed to this belief), is a mysterious goddess, whose decrees it is our duty to obey rather than to understand. . . . It is our task to approach the goddess without fear or rancor, and to study, so far as we are able, with unbiased judgment and unclouded vision, her origin, her essence, and her edicts."
JOHN CARL FLUGEL, 1931, in The Psychology of Clothes

"If I should be allowed to choose one out of all the books that will be published in a hundred years after my death, do you know which I would take? I would take, my friend, a fashion magazine, to see how the women were dressing a century after my decease. Their fripperies would tell me more about the society of that future day than all the philosophers, novelists, preachers and savants."
ANATOLE FRANCE

Introduction

*S*omething exciting is happening. A new woman is stepping into the fashion spotlight. She is active and intelligent, fabulous and fascinating, demanding and discriminating. She is proud of herself and of her accomplishments.

She does not, however, look like a mannequin. Yet she, too, has chosen to be beautiful.

Now, perhaps for the first time in her life, fashion is catching up to her.

Who is she? She is one of the 35 million American women who wear size 14 or over.

Suddenly, it seems, leading fashion names, traditional fashion houses, and a whole new breed of designers are creating up-to-the-minute clothes for the full-figured woman. There is a new attitude dawning: You can be fashionable and look attractive no matter what size you wear.

Suddenly there is a proliferation of colors and fabrics and designs that turns upside down all the old-fashioned rules about who can wear what.

There is a whole new crop of specialty stores springing up around the country to meet the fashion needs of the full-figured woman on her own terms. And many leading department stores are creating attractive new departments for this customer.

Suddenly there's an array of looks from which the large-size woman can put together her own distinctive style. It is time for the large-size woman to feel attractive. She needs and deserves to look her best in the many roles all women find themselves in these days.

Style, however, doesn't begin with clothes, with fashion. If I had to invent a quick recipe for style, I'd say style is, for starters, one part identity: self-knowledge, security of self, feeling at home in one's body—physically and mentally. It's also one part spirit: verve, attitude, wit, inventiveness—the confidence to express whatever mood one wishes, and the understanding that such variability is not only necessary but a reflection of a person's unique complexity as a human being. Lastly, I'd have to admit, style is one part fashion. Fashion is, in a sense, the least of it. It is possible to have lots of clothes and not an ounce of style. But it is also possible to have very few clothes and lots of style. Yes, fashion is the means through which we express style. But it takes much less in the way of clothes to express style than you probably imagine. Very often, it's the most unassuming dress that lends itself most to style, that allows itself to be transformed by inventiveness. The dress of flattering cut that's a blank slate. That's why generations of women have coveted the little black dress, the dress so right in line and proportion but so beguilingly simple on its own that it is the perfect foil for excursions into self-expression.

In the past fifteen years or so, Americans have made the sudden "discovery" that people often judge other people based on the way they dress, and that in business life, with which we are all now consumed, such judgments have important economic consequences. In a typically American way, a whole new industry has sprung up to capitalize on this fact—the image biz. Barely a year ago, image consulting got the stamp of social approval—its own listing in the yellow pages. What I loathe about the concept of "image" used this way is the notion that all that's required for success is to manipulate appearance, regardless of what's behind it.

As I see it, style, in order to work, must reflect the real self, the character and personality of the individual. Not all of one's individuality at one time—that would hardly be the delight we know style to be. Style captivates because it captures a bit of someone's spirit—and intrigues us about the rest. Intrigue is its very essence.

For full-figured women, the fashion part is getting easier by the minute. For women of substance as well as all other American women, the hard part is the security in identity, the body confidence. That's where we get into trouble right away. For a variety of reasons, American culture has put serious barriers between women and their bodies and elaborated an ideal of female attractiveness that hinges almost exclusively on thinness to a degree that does not come naturally to most women.

One result is a fixation on perfection—and in this you can be sure, we all fall short. By definition. Any single ideal of attractiveness—to say nothing of the oppressively thin ideal that currently holds sway—ignores the fact that people normally exist in a healthy, and beautiful, variety of shapes and sizes.

We also wind up too focused on ourselves. Everyday cultural forces—every newspaper we read, every magazine we open, virtually every television show and movie we watch—operate to keep us preoccupied with ourselves and our shortcomings. While this book is especially aimed at full-figured women, it explores attitudes and contains information that are of interest to all women. All women are harmed by the existence of an ideal of feminine attractiveness that is so narrowly prescribed as to make us all doubt our self-worth and so ubiquitously presented as to make its impact inescapable. To be a woman in America today means to be preoccupied with yourself and ashamed of your body. Two greater cripplers of style could not be imagined.

For larger women, the wounding of the style instinct can go even deeper. Because in all the images of the good life and the beautiful life to which we are constantly exposed, full-figured women are never present. Totally excluded. They are invisible. They do not exist. The media appear to be totally unaware of the devastating psychological impact such invisibility has on self-esteem. If we do not see a reflection of ourselves, we may come to doubt that we have the right to exist. Certainly, it is hard for us to know ourselves, let alone like ourselves. We are made to feel unfeminine and unattractive, when in fact we are not.

Miraculously, there are full-figured women who, on their own, have managed to escape the punishing effects of America's infatuation with thinness. Perhaps they have seen through the many myths, especially about health and weight, that help prop up the ideal. Perhaps they are women with an unshakable sense of confidence that comes from the many other achievements in their lives. Perhaps they are surrounded by loved ones who see them, and have always seen them, as beautiful. Whether they started out in life large, or got there along the way, particularly after pregnancy and childbirth, perhaps early on they developed such a sure sense of self and of style that even official invisibility and difficulties in finding clothes could not shake it from them.

In any case, they are in many ways the leading edge of a revolution in attitude that is slowly surfacing in America. An attitude that would restore a refreshing sense of reality to the vision of fantasy that has pervaded so much of American public life in the past thirty years. The go-go years, they have been called. The fantasy version of life, which reached its apotheosis in the 1980s with the junk bond, is totally disconnected from solid substance. It enshrines endless getting and spending on everything, including clothes. You try to have something else, be someone else; you pursue symbols and labels and worship celebrities. In the reality-based version of life, you are not living someone else's image of life; you are living your own life, taking solid nourishment from its substance. You do your most inspired, alluring, imaginative, mysterious, spontaneous, whimsical, adventurous, glamorous best with what you are. It is a time of style.

There is a crucial difference between fashion and style. Though it has long been in eclipse, style thrives on the fact of individual difference and always decrees that "you are perfect for you."

It is fashionable in some quarters to trivialize the subject of style. American women, on the whole, are terribly ambivalent about style. They spend a great deal of money in the hope of bagging such elusive quarry on the one hand but, on the other, develop a series of rationales for believing it is not important, that it doesn't count.

Actually, many feel intimidated by it, or at least the mystique surrounding it. There are all these rules to be learned, aren't there? Even worse, beauty is presumed to be one of the admission requirements. To be well-dressed is one thing. To be stylish is another. To actively make a bid for style is to put oneself at risk of being judged by a different, higher standard, and it is an admission that style counts. It's much safer to maintain that it doesn't, but inwardly covet it. Which women do.

Style is in fact a powerful facet of our lives. Through clothes, we invent ourselves every time we get dressed. Clothes make public our inner vision of ourselves; they are the means by which we make visible—not only to others but to ourselves—our sense of self. Some of us, of course, do it better than others. Style is an individual's distinguishing mark. And from it, all kinds of judgments are made by other people.

Deep down, we suspect this; we make judgments ourselves about others. Perhaps what we immediately apprehend, in the first moments of viewing someone, is the clarity, or lack of it, with which that person sees him- or herself. We may also note the accuracy of that person's vision. Further, most of us are very adept at interpreting the many and ever-changing references to standing and status and confidence encoded in dress and manner of self-presentation. Yet we have all been provided with a set of intellectual rationales and clichés to divert us from the truth, to protect us from the fact that such surface matters count, that style matters. On a conscious level, we have been persuaded to think appearance is unimportant (skin deep, etc.). We have sought this kind of protection probably because we feel it is unjust—undemocratic, to say nothing of anti-intellectual and thus, ho hum, unworthy of our time—to admit that appearances count. After all, because it is visited on a favored few, beauty constitutes an unfair advantage; it is alien to the idea of merit that pervades our democracy.

A great deal of criticism of fashion and the fashion world is earned; but a lot of it isn't. Much of it is, I think, the defensive response of women who feel they haven't been invited to the party. But as this book explains, attractiveness is terribly misunderstood; it is not a label that falls out of the heavens on a select few, but an active achievement, and anyone qualifies (see Chapter 6). And the only style rules that count are the principles of aesthetics, none of which start with "Don't!" These are the same principles that underlie all art in the Western World, and to which we are all more or less exposed since birth. Maybe that's part of the problem right there, that we are not exposed enough to aesthetic knowledge.

As this book makes clear, attractiveness is more a matter of how you present yourself. A personal focus that highlights genuine strengths rather than real or imagined shortcomings is a sine qua non. Good grooming, based on a very realistic appraisal of strengths and weaknesses, counts far more than genuine beauty. No one knows this better than the society matrons. Come a certain time and they tote their daughters off oh-so-discreetly to someone wise in such matters, where they learn how to present themselves, how to groom, how to dress, if they haven't already picked up the fine points during the course of their upbringing. There is no reason why every woman shouldn't take advantage of what the few know. To get the same information and present ourselves just as well is to democratize the process.

By learning this process, we come to shape the impression we make. And that has a distinct advantage for women who are larger than (or in any way different from) the cultural ideal. We *can* direct the impression we make on all other people, despite society's stereotyped image of us.

This book is written with the aim of giving full-figured women what they need most—the freedom and the information to feel beautiful, to be and be seen as the women they really are. It will show women how to make the new fashion choices work fabulously for them. It will examine the relationship between feminine self-worth and the enjoyment of style. This book addresses many of the unspoken assumptions we operate on about people and the way they present themselves. By examining these assumptions (and admitting their influence instead of denying them), we can be in control of them—and use them to advantage.

This book is divided into two parts. The first part examines the inner elements of style, the ways and means of self-confidence and body-confidence, the very basic foundation for style. Style, in my view, makes no judgments of the body, unlike fashion. I trace the way the real human body has, literally and figuratively, fallen out of fashion (Chapter 1), and the terrible consequences that has had for those people who do have three-dimensional bodies. I look at how all women today have been made to feel so bad about their bodies: the current cultural beliefs about bodies, how they are delivered to us (Chapter 2), and how they affect us so negatively (Chapters 3 and 4). It is only by examining these carefully that we can nullify their power over us and then go about restoring self-esteem (Chapter 5) and maintaining the esteem of others (Chapter 6).

The second part focuses on the material elements of style. For the most part, clothes. What goes into them, that is, getting them to fit, which ones work best and for whom, what goes under them, what to look for, how to put them together to express something about yourself, how to build a wardrobe, and how to hold it together despite the inevitable convulsions of fashion.

Look at it this way. You have to get dressed every day of your life. You might as well do it in a way that flatters you, pleases you, reveals something interesting about you—and delights everyone around you. That's style.

I

Developing Confidence

1

Attractiveness Is an Attitude

STYLE IS NOT IN FASHION

Fashion is one thing. Style is altogether different. Many women are fashionable; few women have style. All of us want it. Style goes way beyond fashion; it is an inimitable way of putting oneself together. It is what women really mean when they say they want to be fashionable. They want to find that distinctive way of sorting through the world of things and make choices so that they present themselves distinctively and truly, so that their presentation expresses something of the inner truth about them, captures their spirit, their essence.

Fashion is clothes, accessible to anyone with a bank account or a credit card. The past thirty years has witnessed an extraordinary expansion of the consumer culture, during which time the fashion world has grown mightily in size and complexity. Women's magazines featuring fashion have multiplied in size and number. The explosion in marketable goods and our infatuation with them has, by definition, emphasized fashion—merchandise—at the expense of style. Style has virtually gone out of style.

FASHION'S NARROW-MINDEDNESS

For all their abundance, the profusion of clothes has been primarily pitched to a narrow—literally and figuratively—and narrowing base of women: those who represent what is widely depicted as the feminine ideal, the tall, thin body pictured in all those ads that have been created to sell all those clothes and other goods. These depictions, as we shall see, do their own kind of damage. At the same time, the best fashion is restricted to those who fit an idealized image of women as uniformly slim and young. The fashion designers and purveyors did not invent this ideal—it runs much deeper in the culture. They have merely sewn up the job of enforcing it, limiting the choicest clothes to those who wear size 12 or less.

The current thin ideal—or any one ideal, the proposition that there is one perfect way for women to look—is too exclusionary for anyone's good. Its underpinning is the assumption that women have value primarily for their looks. In this case it also tyrannizes women to conform to a look that is unnatural for most, attainable only at a very high cost. The existence of such an impossible ideal sets women up for failure. As if that weren't bad enough, it also fosters the mistaken notion that women are all poured into the same mold.

It artificially constricts the market for fashion. Several top retail analysts with major Wall Street investment houses, examining the inconsistent financial performance of the women's fashion retailers, have been pointing out for several years now that the fashion houses continue making clothes for an ideal of woman that is increasingly at odds with the reality of women. In 1989, Joseph H. Ellis, a partner in Goldman Sachs & Co., told a fashion industry forum that "the malls of America are still full of youth-oriented women's apparel stores" while the new majority of female customers are age 30 to 40. Not only does this lead to "a mismatch between the age and fashion focus of most apparel stores," he says, but a failure to "accommodate the increasing divergence of size and shape as we move from our 20s into our 30s and 40s." This woman wants not what is new and hot but something "sophisticated, tasteful, flattering, reasonably high in quality—in short, something that is smart."

It turns women against themselves in profound ways. The lack of clothes for real bodies and the ubiquity of an ideal image of woman invalidate all those who do not measure up. Because size has come to mean so much, and images of women have an especially powerful effect on us all, those who do not fit into size 12 are made to feel they don't fit into life. Or have no right to. Internalizing the disdain of a fat-phobic society, women who do not fit the ideal become collaborators in their own inferiority: They learn to hate themselves, and shun the right to present themselves as attractive, accomplished people. Others, perhaps braver or crazier, having rejected the cultural standard, still have had to surmount enormous obstacles—within themselves and within the marketplace—just to find decent clothes to present themselves stylishly.

The inability to find clothes is itself a powerful force of estrangement. For one thing, it leaves a person incomplete. Dress is instrumental in helping organize the personality of the individual. We complete ourselves through clothes. Clothes also help make a person a functioning member of society.

And the reign of the thin ideal turns shopping and dressing—and even some of life's most enjoyable activities, such as going to the beach—into grim rituals of self-confrontation rather than lighthearted excursions into self-discovery and pleasure. Three years ago, the nation's bathing suit manufacturers set up an industry panel to explore why bathing suit sales are so sluggish (the average woman buys only one every few years) and what to do about it. Any sane American female over the age of 25 could have saved them a lot of money and told them, free, what the experience of shopping for a swimsuit does to a woman.

"First," she would have said, "all those ads showing all those cute young things frolicking on the beach have led us to conclude that swimsuits are made only for cute young things. Second, all those Cheryl Tiegs types have led us to believe that bodily perfection is a requirement for a) buying a swimsuit and b) stepping on the sand." Third, she would have pointed out, "there don't seem to be many made-for-swimming, reasonably styled swimsuits that actually flatter figures; the choice is between overexposure teenybopper-style and camouflage behind frumpy skirts that billow in the water. All we want is a little support where it's needed, a little bareness, and a little thought about women's bodies."

And, "Oh yes," she would have added, "those fitting rooms! After all, we come in to buy a swimsuit in the middle of winter or spring, when we are not used to seeing so much of ourselves unclad. Suddenly, we're stripping down to the flesh in a barren little box of a room where there is nothing to distract us from ourselves. That is rude enough; then the fluorescent lighting doesn't do a thing for the pale and dimpled thighs that now loom so large. And the mirror is, as all mirrors are, anxiety-provoking. Honestly, guys, I've never counted how many women solve the problem simply by avoiding confrontation with the mirror and wearing last year's swimsuit, but if my friends are any indication, I know why the swimsuit industry is in trouble."

As women increasingly build their self-esteem from their own accomplishments rather than taking *all* their value from what they look like, the ideal loses its grip on them, and they feel less need to sacrifice themselves to it. Similarly, as people age and gather experience and confidence, they become less willing and less able to match society's highly arbitrary ideal; biology asserts its claim. The new respect for modern women and the aging of the population are thus helping to make the world safe for women of all sizes.

However, full-figured women still bear some stigmata from their fashion ostracism—the persistence of all sorts of myths about them. That they are poor, have no taste, have no need for terrific clothes. In short, that they most likely loaf around the house all day and wolf down anything at hand—the consumer society version of the great unwashed.

The truth is that their incomes are somewhat above average and, in fact, they are overrepresented in high-income groups. They indeed have taste; when a woman evolves from a size 12 to, say, a size 16 or 20, she doesn't lose the ability to distinguish, say, cashmere from polyester. Her size just gets bigger. Full-figured women date, go dancing, and have lovers, if that can be taken as an index of appeal. More of them are married, and they have children. Not only do men find full-figured women appealing; as much as other women, they like to flaunt their assets. These women do everything everyone else does: they ski, they swim, they bike, they play tennis. They are, in other words, vital, active, successful, attractive, modern women just like other women—because they are every other woman.

FASHION AT LARGE—AT LAST!

Gradually, perhaps too slowly for many women, fashion has been changing over the past decade. It is now actually possible for a woman larger than a size 14 to buy a silk dress, a wool crepe suit, a suede jacket, a cashmere sweater, a linen skirt, gabardine slacks—and if she's really lucky, she may even have choices in all these categories.

FACTS OF LIFE

First and foremost, the fashion industry has begun responding to the demographic facts of life—that over a third of the female population above age 18 wears a size 14 or larger. In fact, the median size of the American woman is 12–14. As many women wear a size 18 as wear size 8. While the size range of the population has not changed dramatically in recent years, the clothing needs of women have indeed.

WOMEN AT WORK

The massive participation of women of all ages in the labor force has created a huge demand for career clothes. Large-size women, like their smaller sisters, are filling multiple roles these days. They need clothes for the office, clothes for lounging, clothes for casual wear. But their most pressing demand is for quality clothes that will give them a polished image in the office and beyond.

While women themselves have been changing, the retail landscape in America has also been shifting. The last decade marked the enormous growth of specialty stores and specialty catalogues. A whole new crop of specialty stores has developed to cater to the fashion needs of the large-size woman on her own terms. These stores have collectively advanced the offerings in large sizes and have, with their significant purchasing power, given manufacturers the impetus to cut better fashions in large sizes.

In addition, the fashion industry is making large-size fashion more psychologically accessible to consumers. Recently the industry agreed to abandon confusing and erratic size designations in favor of standardized size terms that relate to the way women see themselves. Clothes are now labeled size 14 and up, an extension of the Misses size range. Before, if a size 14 woman gained ten pounds, she might jump to a size 32 skirt, a size 38 blouse, a size 16½ suit—an enormous psychological barrier separating her from other women, making her feel unattractive and diminishing her incentive to shop for nice clothes (if she could find them). The new size designation reinforces the notion that a size 16 woman is no different from a size 8 woman, only larger.

The arrival of fashion for women of all sizes is most welcome and long overdue. But it falls short of completely redressing the problem because it maintains an artificial division between women. The fashion industry for larger women is essentially a parallel fashion industry in a separate size range, sold in separate stores or in a separate department from the "fashion departments." Many of the manufacturers in this industry make clothes only in large size. While that gives the best of them a chance to perfect the fit, some are often guided by common stereotypes about what large-size women should wear. For women, having to go to a different place for clothes suggests that there is something different, therefore inferior, about them. The fact that the styling of the clothes is not uniformly wonderful, or that the whole large-size industry lacks a top tier in quality of design and manufacture, only reinforces the idea.

EVERYONE IS ATTRACTIVE

After years of walking about in tatters of self-esteem, women do not always find it easy to make use of fashion newly available in all sizes. Some women don't know how to salvage self-esteem—having been deprived of it for so long.

Yet every woman needs to clothe and present herself well. And all women have the right, the need to feel attractive. Although few women are born beautiful, every woman can aspire to attractiveness. It is, ultimately, far more interesting. Exciting. Attractiveness is, above all, an active stance toward the world, a way of projecting oneself with confidence and flair. It is a direct reflection of how a woman feels about herself, which is the strongest cue others use in forming an impression about her. Style—the imprint of personality on dress and every other aspect of one's personal environment—is a vital element of attractiveness.

Having been deprived of beautiful clothes for so long, many women have grown too comfortable using clothes as camouflage to give it up with ease. Many are just plain timid about clothes. And many, having had no use for them for so long, just do not know the principles of dressing well.

WHAT DO WOMEN WANT?

In the many discussions I have had with large-size women, and in the fashion surveys I have conducted, several themes have cropped up with regularity.

- They don't buy the stereotyped notion that large women should dress inconspicuously, preferably in overtailored clothes, to fade into the background.
- They want to wear the same "looks" as all other women, but scaled for their bodies.
- They want to know how to use fashion to portray themselves, the many aspects of themselves: sophisticated, serious, playful—and sexy, definitely sexy.
- They want to be able to dress for the many roles they enjoy—working woman, wife, mother, woman of the world.
- They want to know how to combine the elements of fashion so that they look "pulled together" at all times.
- They want to dress in ways that respect their status.
- They want to be able to build a wardrobe with some basic items of quality, then learn to "play" with additions.
- They want to boost their fashion confidence.
- They want to be and be seen as women of quality and taste.
- They want to take the frustration and the effort out of finding clothes that make them look good.
- They want to be able to find the clothes they need and like, and then, having dressed the way they like, forget about the clothes, so that they may enjoy the occasion and the company without self-consciousness.
- They want to put the fun back into fashion.

In other words, they want style.

STYLE VS. FASHION

The long dry spell in clothes of any kind for large-size women, coupled with the consumer culture infatuation with fashion over the past decades, has obscured an important point—style is not a size. Nor is it a price. Or an age. And it can be learned.

Style is self-knowledge and self-confidence. It is, in other words, an attitude. A life-affirming expression of one's character and spirit. A conviction that you are worthwhile, worth knowing and worth looking at, and can present yourself magnificently. It is knowing your strengths and your weaknesses, so that you can accentuate your strengths.

Feeling good about oneself is a sine qua non of looking good. No woman will ever look good or feel good about herself if her main fashion aim is to hide her body. Yet that is what large-size women have been taught to do, and what many large-size fashions are still designed to do. The secret to looking good is to develop body confidence, a positive body image, in which a woman learns to play on her genuine strengths, not on real or imagined shortcomings. She must know her body, so she can accentuate the positive. A woman who focuses her energy on hiding what she doesn't like creates the basis for perpetual self-consciousness, one of the surest enemies of style.

The thirty-year reign of fashion for fashion's sake is coming to an end. It is time to usher in a new period of style. While fashion is synonymous with clothes, style is something else altogether, although it is often expressed through what one wears. Fashion is in the clothes, style in the wearer. The distinction between fashion and style could not, therefore, be more important:

FASHION stuns. STYLE delights.
FASHION costs. STYLE is priceless.
FASHION is mindless. STYLE is intelligent.
FASHION is fascistic. STYLE is individualistic.
FASHION changes. STYLE evolves.
FASHION is matter. STYLE is spirit.
FASHION comes from outside. STYLE comes from within.
FASHION is self-conscious. STYLE is self-assured.
FASHION glares. STYLE glows.
FASHION is slavery. STYLE is mastery.
FASHION is literal. STYLE is original.
FASHION declares. STYLE insinuates.
FASHION is serious. STYLE is ironic.
FASHION is reproducible. STYLE is inimitable.
FASHION is safety. STYLE is courage.
FASHION is clothes. STYLE is character.
FASHION is this minute. STYLE is forever.
FASHION restricts. STYLE liberates.
FASHION is rigid. STYLE is spontaneous.
FASHION is surface. STYLE is substance.

Size is no impediment to style.

"Fashion is absolutely tacky." This comes, no less, from the mouth of a designer, Italy's Franco Moschino, one of fashion's enfant terribles because he never hesitates to point out the absurdity of the fashion system. "Fashion is over. . . . Fashion kills people. It is fascism. As a designer, I have to convince you to change—to cut your hair, to change the frames of your glasses. You're a creature of the fashion system, a Muppet, not yourself."

Style is nothing if not a celebration of individuality, of individual variability. It glorifies the fact that we all are different. It exposes as preposterous the notion that there is an ideal body, an ideal woman—that there is only one perfect way to look, that any one way is perfect for all women. Style dismisses the very concept of perfection. Style always delights because it is a revelation that the possibilities for originality are limitless. Style, in that sense, connects us with the infinite, with grandness.

Style makes no a priori assumptions about body size, about body type, or about what is "right." There is no prior "right" with style, because style is the ultimate proof that each woman's existence is right for her.

Style rejects ideals. Therefore, it mocks as unenlightened and slavish all attempts to conform to them. Style goes its own way. In fact, style is nothing if not a triumph of the unusual.

Style is democratic. It assumes that every woman has the potential to create an identity that's unique and to express it through how she carries herself, how she grooms herself, what she wears.

Yet style is aristocratic. It sets those who have it apart from those whose dress is merely functional, utilitarian. It announces to the world that the wearer has a sense of herself and has assumed command of herself.

Style is intelligent, because it requires self-knowledge.

Although it is neither solemn nor earnest in its declaration, style is true. This is because it is subverted most easily by self-consciousness, by the existence of any gaps between what one is and what one appears to be. In fact, the presence of a gap between what one is and what one appears to be immediately transforms what one wears into costume. Style hugs the self closely, even though it never represents the whole self at any one time. The self is too complex to be represented in toto by any one way of dressing.

Style is optimistic; it is optimism made visible. Style presumes that you are a person of interest, that the world is a place of interest, that life is worth making the effort for.

Style is experimentation. There is no style without taking risks, without exploring new sides of the self, without saving what works and discarding the errors. Style, then, is a springboard for personal growth.

Style is even environmentally correct. Clothes are an essential tie between us and our environment; the right clothes enable us to make use of, to enjoy our environment safely, comfortably. In this sense, the function of a business suit is the same as a bush jacket. Style helps our bodies do their work. It frees us to enjoy the activity and the surroundings without having to focus on ourselves—whether the activity is taking a walk in the woods or a spin around the dance floor.

Social critics recoiling at the rampant materialism of the last decade have leveled noteworthy criticism at the concept of style. The "style" that they are criticizing, however, is the decorative equivalent of the auto industry's planned obsolescence, a media-mediated turn of taste that renders last year's peplumed suit socially unacceptable today. In other words, trendiness, or fashion. "High consumption capitalism requires a ceaseless transformation in style," argues one sociologist. Style, insofar as it refers to changes in the appearance of goods merely for change's sake, in order to stoke the purchases that a consumer economy requires—that is definitely not the "style" that is the subject of this book.

Indeed, style is one individual's distinctive way of sorting through stuff, of sorting through the crowded marketplace. It is a way of avoiding the clutter of stuff, a way of selecting, of making choices, influenced not so much by outside pressures, including advertising, but by internal considerations. It is a connection with human spirit, the sign of an interior life. This style no more requires change from season to season than does a person's character. But neither is it completely static. Ideally, it should evolve over time, as character does. Style is really self-knowledge applied selectively—and selectivity is its essence—to the material world.

Style, in this sense, is even morally responsible. Consumption isn't promiscuous or random, at the whim of the marketplace or the urging of marketers. Rather it is focused on what is intrinsically useful and personally suitable and expressive. It is not a surface creation, but the reflection of an intelligence or attitude that gives meaning to life.

THE SEVENTH AVENUE FACTOR

How did size get to mean everything in the world of fashion in the first place? The preoccupation with size, the confusion of style with size, comes about not just from the cultural infatuation with an unrealistic ideal of slimness. It is also the outgrowth of specific alterations in the ways clothes are now designed and produced. Since the mode of design influences the clothes designed, being a designer today means having a built-in bias toward the creation of fashion for bodies that make no demands on clothes. Three-dimensional bodies, for the most part, no longer intrude on the process of creation of clothes.

NEW MEANING OF "PENCIL SLIM"

American fashion has gotten away with being preoccupied with the impossibly slim because it is designed for bodies that do not exist. Fashion's favorite bodies are strictly products of the imagination rather than reality—they come into being from sketches. The designer is free to invent whatever body proportions he or she wishes.

Not long ago, clothes were created as a dressmaker draped fabric on a form. A swirl of silk lit the imagination; a design suggested itself in the process. As a method of fashion creativity, this has distinct advantages for bodies. It automatically incorporates the mass of the human form into clothing designs. It allows for the creation of garments that are flattering to bodies. And it makes use of a fabric's basic qualities in the design. A style flows organically from a fabric's inherent attributes on a body mass. In this method of designing, fabric and form are givens structured into the creative process.

But over the past decades, draping as a technique of fashion design has virtually disappeared. It takes time. It takes money (in yard goods). It is barely taught at all any longer in the schools of fashion design. Today, clothes are designed almost totally by sketch. A sketch, of course, is by definition an abstraction, a two-dimensional fiction of body and dress, subject to distortion by the pencil, limited only by the designer's fantasy. The invented body bends to the pencil of the illustrator; real bodies do not. In fact, says Sharon Lee Tate, author of *the* textbook of fashion design, *Inside Fashion Design,* "designers who are able to drape and make their own patterns frequently find that the design they have imagined is altered as they drape it, because working with fabric on the human form suggests added design dimensions." Trouble is, few designers drape their patterns.

Removing design from the human form diminishes respect for the human body. The eye that adjusts to seeing by pencil can develop a true intolerance for the reality of the flesh. And when something clearly doesn't work, it is

In this typical example of contemporary fashion illustration, the female body is impossibly tall and slender.

(Copyright © 1990 by the New York Times Company. Reprinted by permission.)

In a leading textbook of fashion design, the misses figure is all angles, dynamism, and excitement, if unreal in its proportions. Such sketches train designers to regard such figures as normal—and to make clothes to suit such improbable bodies.
(Sketches from Inside Fashion Design *3rd ed. by Sharon Lee Tate. Copyright © 1989 by Sharon Lee Tate. Reprinted by permission of Harper-Collins Publishers.)*

the body that comes to threaten the integrity of a design, never the failure of a design to meet the needs of a body.

The change in mode of design does not even acknowledge the existence of the body as a three-dimensional reality. The body with mass is not considered in fashion design. The styles created are visualized flat, so they have most life when flat. And they are translated into flat patterns. It's a two-dimensional process almost all the way.

Sketches can be exciting pieces of art, but they are hardly stand-ins for the human body. The needs of real bodies thus never intrude on the design elements of a garment conceived by sketch. Clothes are designed and made for bodies distorted in the direction of the ideal. And that is the problem with the process of design by sketch: A body has to fit the design, not vice versa.

There is more to being pencil slim than any of us ever imagined!

CLOTHES FOR NO BODIES

A style that originates in a pencil sketch often progresses all the way to finished garment without ever having met a living, breathing, moving, three-dimensional human form, or even a muslin-covered stand-in. And it's not likely to meet one until after the point of no return. A manufacturer will solicit all orders on the basis of a sample garment, crude in measurement but precise in surface detail, made up directly from a sketch; in fact, many manufacturers employ a sample maker specifically to make the direct and speedy translation from sketch to garment. By the time the orders are in from the retailers around the country, before the garment has ever been tried on, the manufacturer has a great deal invested in a style, too much, in fact, to even consider dropping from production a garment that might not work right when it does meet a body.

The method is so universally accepted and practiced—despite the built-in limits on the body suitability of the product—that those involved in the process can not see its shortcomings. The method can be extremely wasteful—a great many manufactured garments never really fit right—but the cost of this wastefulness is discounted, quite literally, because it is absorbed by retailers.

Its great advantage is that it fits an industry in which fashion showrooms are at a major distance from manufacturing plants. A sketch is flat and therefore can be transmitted via facsimile machine. It can flow from designer's pencil to Hong Kong factory in a few electronic seconds. Sketching also works in the fashion showroom, where a store buyer may invest hundreds of thousands of dollars of a retailer's money in a group of garments presented only on "boards," by sketch with attractive fabric swatches attached. It doesn't seem to bother anybody that the body in the sketch bears little resemblance to standard human proportions.

But the dependence on sketching transforms the fitting of garments on bodies into something extraneous to the design process. Manufacturers view it as an extra step, an extra expense. An inconvenience. One result is that manufacturers are thus discouraged from introducing large-size lines; there is more variability of body shape in larger bodies, and getting the clothes to fit involves additional expenses and uncertainties. At the same time, manufacturers who think they can turn a fast buck by jumping into the large-size market, and who don't make the investment in fit, soon stumble over their mistake. However, the manufacturer is most likely to ascribe the failure to a deficiency among potential customers rather than see it as one created by the manufacturer. The news of such failure only discourages other manufacturers from entering the large-size market. This is one reason the large-size fashion offerings are frequently chaotic.

THE LADY WITH GREAT FORM

Virtually the sole surviving practitioner of design by draping in the United States is Pauline Trigere. A darling of the fashion press (but not *Women's Wear Daily*) because she is highly opinionated and deliciously outspoken, she is nevertheless viewed as an anomaly, a quaint reminder of the way things were when designers were really designers and fashion acknowledged and even respected the variability of the human form. Not long ago, on the subject of perfection of cut, Trigere decreed: "In France, where I come from, the couturier never sketched. Mme. Lanvin, Mlle. Chanel—*non*. Molyneux, Patou, no one ever sketched. Today the young designers will sketch a garment, but how do they know how it will ever come out? They hand the sketches to an assistant designer, who makes the garment for them."

"Time, it's a matter of time why designers today can't drape," a professor of fashion design explained to me. "Trigere does it. But it is not possible

By contrast, the large-size woman—who actually measures nearer to the ideal proportions set forth by the Greeks—gets a dress that's boxy, frumpy, and dowdy—and terrible posture, too. These two sketches convey the values of the fashion world, discouraging designers from seeing full-figured women as attractive.

today with mass production. There is not enough time or money for a designer to work clothes out in fabric first. When a designer sketches, he knows who is going to be wearing his clothes. He takes an educated guess that a design will fit and look good—that's what it comes down to. Whether something has been lost in the process is for Seventh Avenue to decide."

SIZISM

Along with changes in the mode of fashion design, size labeling itself has not been a broadening experience for women. It certainly helped push women of substance to the fringes of the fashion world. The potential for size discrimination was woven into the very fabric of fashion with introduction of ready-made garments for women around the turn of the century. The first thing that was needed was a system of size terminology, if not size specifications, or standard measurements. (Size specifications have always been a matter of controversy in the women's fashion industry; attempts to introduce standardized measurements have always met with failure. Every manufacturer has evolved its own size measurements and standardized patterns based on its own beliefs about body proportion. Systematic measurements of actual adult women have never figured into the standards.)

Contrary to popular belief, size—at least the Misses size range now applicable to adult women—does not "arbitrarily assign number codes for each size." There was, once, a meaning to the numbers. In the beginning, size was not a size at all, but an age. A size 12 was meant for a "miss" of age 12.

From the start of ready-made fashion, several figure types were recognized, and size ranges set. "Ladies" and "women's" were interchangeable labels for the size range *then* applicable to adult women over the age of 21. Adult women were presumed to have well-developed, "mature figures" with low hiplines and bustlines, both significantly larger than waistlines, although the place of the bustline and hipline shifted dramatically over the twentieth century. ("Mature" was not then semantic skirting around "old"; it simply meant adult in form, fully developed.) For adult women, clothes were sold based on bust measure, generally 34 to 42 inches. In the early catalogues of the major retailers, larger sizes could easily be custom-ordered, usually at a 20% surcharge. In addition, a ready-made "stout" or "extra size" range catered to those women who had bustlines bigger than 42 inches but met the manufacturer's set of standardized proportions.

"Misses" sizes were designed pure and simple for misses, or adolescent girls, and the fashions were typically designated 12 or 14 to 20. These, however, referred to age, not to size. As the 1901 Sears, Roebuck catalogue advised: "When ordering: always state age, number of inches around bust, and color. . . . A misses garment, while measuring 34 or 36 inches around the bust, will not fit a well-developed woman measuring the same, as they are cut on different patterns." The misses garment, intended for an adolescent body, was cut straighter through the torso, with less of an indentation for waist, less pronounced hips, than the women's sizes.

When the concept of "misses" sizes was later extended to all adult women, one basic fact went along on the garment rack: In early maturity, for which misses sizes were originally intended, there is far less variation in shape and proportion of the human figure than later in life. Indeed, between the ages of 15 and 19, 90% of people can fit standard sizes for those ages, Paul Nystrom, Ph.D., explained in *The Economics of Fashion* in 1928. But by 20 to 24 years, only about half the adults can be cared for with standard sizes. And from the age of 45 up, only a third can be fitted with standard sizes. Average body measurements have changed somewhat (no one is sure how much, since no major anthropometric studies have been conducted) since 1928, but not so much that they nullify the point. Today's system of fashion has a built-in bias toward youth that makes figure variability an oddity, instead of recognizing it as the prevailing biological fact that it is.

With quaint candor, in 1883 the Boston-based retailer Jordan Marsh acknowledged the constraints of size standards of ready-made fashion. In what is one of the earliest—and possibly wordiest—advertisements for factory-made suits, the retailer proclaimed: "Our ready-made dresses and garments cannot, of course, be expected to fit in every instance, which is not at all strange, when it is considered that no two persons are exactly alike in form; but in the main, they are right, and often-times with the slightest amount of alteration—a change that any lady can easily make—they will fit as well, and perhaps better, than the same article of dress custom made, and which cost twice as much." Perhaps what is most strange about the statement is its recognition of and tolerance for diversity of the human form, a tolerance since sacrificed in the worship of size label.

It is ironic that the top size in top-of-the-line designer clothes today is typically a 12. The first standardized size 12s were intended for a 12-year-old miss, a young girl whose body had not yet fully matured to that of a woman. Today, almost the entire ladies' fashion industry, led by high fashion clothes, is geared for a body most like that of a 12-year-old miss—which goes a long way to explaining why so many people have felt left out. And why every woman in Atlanta, despite evidence to the contrary, claims to be no more than a size 12.

"America is very '10'-oriented; you have to have the perfect body, perfect skin, the perfect smile, perfect everything. In Europe, people have different views. There, women carry themselves with flair whether they are beautiful or not."
MODEL PAULINA PORIZKOVA, 1987

"How dare you profess to know what the 'perfect' face is, or, more to the point, that there is a perfect face? What we need today are more articles contending that the individuality of a person's looks is beautiful rather than giving us a set of qualifications (in the form of the perfect face) for beauty."
LETTER TO THE EDITOR, Vogue magazine, January 1990

You Ought to Be in Pictures

We are surrounded by images of women. Yet they look, at least from the neck down, remarkably alike. The culture bombards us all with an ideal image of female attractiveness that is almost universally unattainable and unrealistic. The prevailing images of women in the media are slim and young, while real women are not. In this environment, it is difficult for any woman to develop a consistently positive view of herself. A positive view of self is not only essential for style, it is essential for functioning, period.

FAT IS A FEMINIZING TISSUE

To a degree only now being medically recognized, body size and shape are influenced more by genetic and metabolic endowment than by the exercise of willpower. Females start out in life with more body fat than males do, and they acquire more along the way. In women, in distinction to men, sexual maturity is accompanied by an increase in body fat. The depositing of

The Venus of Willandorf, a prehistoric stone statue now in the Museum of Vienna, embodies the very necessary relationship of body fat to female fertility.
(*The Bettman Archive, Inc.*)

fat—in areas, patterns, and to a lesser degree amounts, controlled by heredity and hormones—is an intrinsic part of the process of sexual reproduction. All the hormonal milestones of female life—puberty, pregnancy, menopause—are associated with increased deposits of fat in the female.

"Ever since the Stone Age, symbols of female fertility have been fat, particularly in the breasts, hips, thighs and buttocks—places where estrogen, the female sex hormone, promotes fat storage," says Rose Frisch, Ph.D., a physiologist at Harvard University known for her pioneering research of female infertility. "This historical linking of fatness and fertility actually makes biological sense." In fact, she says, "body fat, or adipose tissue, has a regulatory role in reproduction."

Take away the body fat deposits and you take away the ability to reproduce. Medical researchers and practitioners have long known that reproduction capability falters when body fat levels drop low enough; Frisch is researching how this is accomplished. Under normal conditions, the female body is 28% fat—nearly double the fat level of the male (the figure for men is about 15%). Women whose body fat levels drop even a small amount typically experience difficulty conceiving (as do women with extremely high body fat levels). Dr. Frisch has found that girls on the threshold of puberty do not begin to menstruate unless they attain a minimum degree of fatness—over 17%.

Frisch believes that loss of fat creates changes in estrogen, and these estrogen changes signal the brain area that acts as a control center for the cascade of hormonal events leading to ovulation. "How can fat make a difference to estrogen?" she asks rhetorically. "Adipose tissue was once thought to be inert and to merely insulate and cushion the body. It is now known to be quite active in the turnover of fuels in the body. It also stores sex hormones and influences the amount and potency of estrogen circulating in the blood."

Fat phobia, says one researcher, may be today's purest expression of woman-phobia.

Despite the contribution of biology to morphology, or body shape, cultural beliefs about what our bodies should look like are strongly shaped by images in the media. And the notion, however false, has taken hold that women can choose their own body type, presumably the idealized body type—if only they work out hard enough, diet strenuously enough, or suppress their appetite enough.

VARIABILITY DENIED

The trouble is, women's bodies naturally come in a variety of shapes and sizes, while the images of women that saturate the media do not. The prevailing images of women express the currently accepted standard of beauty. But standards of beauty endorse and empower only certain sets of human variation, despite the fact that there are many configurations the human form naturally takes. Any standard of beauty, then, represents a certain arbitrariness, physiologically speaking (if not culturally speaking; see Chapter 3). And the natural range of human variability, normal and healthy though it may be, is consigned to the realm of medicine to contend with, as if it were pathology.

Today's standard of beauty widely pictured in the media is a slim, elongated figure that is not even physiologically possible for the vast majority of women. In fact, say two prominent medical researchers, C. Peter Herman, M.D. and Janet Polivy, Ph.D., of the University of Toronto, the ideal of attractiveness widely broadcast is actually a state of "ruddy-cheeked emaciation." What is pictured as the ideal is realistic only for a small percentage of the population—no more than 5% to 10%—genetically endowed for leanness. For most others, attempts to reshape the body by willpower are doomed to failure, with its attendant feelings of failure and self-dissatisfaction, no matter how undeserved.

The average height of the American woman now stands at 5′4½″. By contrast, Paulina, a model who regularly represents the current ideal of beauty in magazines, is 5′10½″, placing her at an extreme of height shared by less than 1% of the female population. There is no degree of thinness that will allow most women to look as willowy as Paulina looks naturally.

THE IMPLAUSIBLE YOU

The human dimensions currently sanctioned and idealized as beautiful are so consistently implausible that they often cannot be represented by real people, not even those selected from the furthest extremes of human variation. For example, the operative definition of "petite" is a height of 5′4″ or under. But when petite women are depicted in images for the media, they are usually represented by models who are not petite at all. Most "petite" models are 5′6″ or more—who happen to have small-scale features. In the spring of 1989 I received in the mail a catalogue of petite fashions from a major Fifth

Avenue department store—and recognized a featured model as one whose actual height is well known to be 6′1″. She was photographed against a white backdrop, so there was no scale visible against which the reader might notice this deception. In measuring themselves against the ideal, women always come up short—in every sense of the word.

Whatever corporeal endowments the current standard of female attractiveness lacks, it is certainly endowed with high status in our culture. The result is that women throughout the United States are suffering what O. Wayne Wooley, Ph.D., a psychologist who cofounded and directs the Eating Disorders Clinic at the University of Cincinnati medical center, calls a "crisis in body image." Defining body image as "one's private assessment of how others evaluate one's body," Wooley finds that "most women are dissatisfied with their bodies, and this is caused by the prominence of idealized images of women," despite the prevalence in our everyday experience of women with real bodies.

HIPS: COLOR THEM RED

Large numbers of researchers have documented that as high as 94% of women are dissatisfied with their bodies. Wooley, who has created a novel nonverbal measure of body satisfaction called the Color a Person Test, finds that men are always more satisfied with their body parts than women are. When women rate their bodies, they are rating its utility in terms of interpersonal physical attractiveness—in other words, the body's social desirability. Men rate their bodies in terms of its strength and function.

And women are always most dissatisfied with their abdomen, hips, buttocks, and thighs—the parts that puberty pads in females. The lower torso, he finds, is invariably the focus of women's discontent, "suggesting a rejection of the curvaceous characteristics of what used to be considered the normal female body." The fear and loathing of the body parts feminized by fat is quite specific; almost all women like their face.

Time was when such padding was considered not only essential—nature's scheme for assuring sustenance for and survival of the next generation, bred in the belly and fed at the breast—but exquisite. Perhaps it will be again, when the culture can more comfortably come to terms with the facts of female difference. But over the past three decades, as the influence of women in the culture has broadened, the ideal image of female attractiveness has narrowed. And more and more women seeking cultural approval have had to wage unwavering war with biology, most, of course, ultimately losing and surrendering their self-esteem.

In Wooley's studies, not only were the vast majority of normal and "overweight" women dissatisfied with their body, but fully 45% of women who were underweight felt too fat. In a survey he analyzed for *Glamour* magazine, which drew 13,000 responses, "Almost no one felt too thin," he reported at a meeting of the American Psychological Association. The only people more concerned with how the body functions than how it looks were those who had experienced serious physical jolts—cardiac patients and the elderly. And across the board, blacks turned out to like their bodies more than whites. Wooley found that a white woman had to weigh as little as 117 pounds to like her body as much as a black woman weighing a more comfortable 145 pounds.

THE INCREDIBLE SHRINKING IMAGE

Body dissatisfaction among women has actually intensified over the past decades. Not coincidentally, the images of women in the media, the so-called public images of women, have actually narrowed, increasing the gap between the real and the ideal. When *Psychology Today* surveyed men and women in 1972, it found that 48% of women were dissatisfied with their weight, 49% with hips and upper thighs, and 50% with the abdomen. By 1986, 55% of women were unhappy about their weight, 57% with their mid-torso, and 50% with the lower torso.

Over that time, Wooley found, women's physiques displayed in magazines actually got skinnier. He measured the ratio of shoulder width to waist width and hips. He calculated height and width ratios. And over time, he concluded, women's physiques in magazines have come to resemble that of the adolescent male—elongated, with minimal curvature, and especially narrow of hip. (The biologic implausibility of public images of the female form has recently been updated; for models, this season's mutilation of choice is the surgical implantation of silicone baggies for breasts, leading plastic surgeons attest.) In a culture that has devalued the feminine, the natural female body, with its natural variability, has become unfashionable. And fat, which gives shape to the female body, has become intolerable.

Current representations of the female form bear an uncanny resemblance to representations of the female form during the medieval period, a time of ascetic experiment, a time when Western culture cut itself off from the body, deeming it a source of humiliation and shame. The Gothic image of woman is narrowed and elongated. She is stretched out in the middle. Art historian Sir Kenneth Clark, in his celebrated work *The Nude,* points out that this "Northern mannerism" stands in marked contrast to the classical representations of women, such as during the Renaissance. These are guided by a more natural sense of proportion in which the distance between the breasts is roughly equal to the distance between breasts and the navel. In the Gothic construction of the body, the distance between breast and navel is doubled. In its own way, American culture today has equally cut itself off from biological reality.

FROM QUEST TO OBSESSION

Because of its very biological implausibility, its unattainability, the resulting quest for thinness has turned into an obsession. The effort must be mounted over and over again, in the hope, this time, of success. Dieting becomes our perpetual duty. If diets worked in the long run—if only one diet worked reasonably well at all—there would not need to be so many of them. But dieting fails 95% of the time. Nevertheless, it is a rare magazine that doesn't regard it as a sacred obligation to remind readers of the Need to Diet—and rush into print the new Miracle Diet of the month.

TAKING THE STEAM OUT OF SELF-ESTEEM

Very few people escape the destructive effects of America's obsession with thinness, an obsession that subtly undermines the fabric of public and private life, one that has serious medical and psychological consequences. The most widespread effect, undoubtedly, is self-preoccupation culminating in dissatisfaction with oneself and loss of self-esteem. Of the great numbers of American women dissatisfied with themselves and the way they look, some go to great lengths and great expense—to say nothing of great risk—to reshape their bodies in the hope that doing so will improve whatever is wrong in their lives.

In addition to disorders of self-esteem, the worship of a thin physique has led to widespread disturbances in eating behavior. Numerous studies have documented that at any one time in America today, most women are dieting. Dieting is now considered "normal" behavior for women; it is, in fact, expected of women. However, dieting suspends the body's own deeply rooted ability to regulate food intake—and thus makes eating especially prone to disruptions of many kinds, particularly under conditions of stress. As a result, America is in the throes of an epidemic of eating disorders. The incidence of anorexia, or voluntary starvation, and bulimia, the binge-purge disorder, has reached unprecedented proportions. These pathological attempts to curtail body size are, sadly, a monstrous measure of the violence it takes to beat the body into submission to an unnatural ideal.

According to a wide variety of sources, anorexia and bulimia (some call it part-time anorexia) now afflict millions. One recent study reported that 25% of all college women suffer from bulimia. While adolescent women have received considerable attention for being at risk, the boundaries of affliction are extending in almost every direction. Women who are no longer in their teens or 20s have been developing maturity-onset eating disorders in increasing numbers. Alarmingly, so have children; pediatricians report they now commonly see intense weight preoccupation with disordered eating patterns in children—children of both sexes—as young as eight. And in what is a particularly pernicious evolution of the disorder, the 1980s brought what one researcher on body image, Yale's Judith Rodin, Ph.D., calls a "striking increase in body preoccupation among men." For men, the suffering brought on by eating disorders is compounded by the shame of having a condition intimately linked to women—and the inability to talk about it.

What happens to people who suffer from eating disorders? Psychically, they are totally preoccupied with thoughts of food, of binging and purging. Their bodies are thrown into metabolic and developmental disarray. Harvard graduate Caroline Adams Miller has written about her hellish life in the grip of bulimia: "I consider myself lucky to have escaped from my seven years of bulimia with only a handful of medical complications: heartbeat irregularities, dental problems, digestive disturbance, and menstrual and hormonal difficulties. Others I know have suffered ruptured esophagi, goiters, ovarian destruction, intestinal ulcers, and completely eroded teeth." Those who develop eating disorders during critical periods of body development such as adolescence may never recover the ability to grow normally or reach full sexual development.

HIDDEN HURT

No one has yet put a price tag on the cost of these disorders to society, but it is staggering. Eating disorders remain well hidden. Hidden by the shame of sufferers, each of whom is certain that he or she is the only person with such a bizarre affliction. Hidden by the privacy of the pathology; purging is not exactly a party game. And hidden by the appearance of sufferers; the vast majority of bulimics look normal. Most victims, when confronted, deny they have a problem. After all, weight control is expected behavior. And emaciation is the reigning ideal.

This crisis in body image is now openly talked about and has been making great copy in magazines since the mid-1980s. Rare is the women's magazine that has not weighed in on the subject and attempted to measure women's body dissatisfaction. Under the heading "Body Image Blues," *Family Circle* in 1990 published its own survey indicating that 78% of all women see themselves as overweight. Whether *Family Circle*'s 78% represents a difference from other findings is not clear at all. The use of widely different survey methods makes direct comparison impossible. Still, by any reckoning, the number of women who are miserable about their body is substantial.

As such magazines daily remind us and commiserate, feeling fat exacts a high psychic cost. It subverts our sex lives, our social activities, and permeates everyday routines. It inhibits us in the office, in bed, and everywhere else. It keeps us from enjoying the beach, or going at all. It makes us shun attractive clothes. It keeps us from participating in athletic activities, even from seeing friends. It keeps us from enjoying ourselves and our lives. No wonder women work hard—if futilely—to avoid the feeling.

Cultural credos about body size have been usurping so much of women's energy and exhausting their self-respect for so long now that women of all sizes are beginning to catch on to the impossibility of thin thighs in thirty days, or ninety days, or—God forbid!—ever. "I have had my battles with weight, as have most American women," one woman wrote to me. "From the time I was eight years old I have been on and off diets—with no permanent success. Exercise has put me in great shape, but I'm still 5'2" and 168 pounds, a weight my body continues to return to again and again.

"Slowly but surely more and more American women have experienced the same thing I have and have stopped dieting and begun to get on with their lives. My own attempts to reduce my body size led to bouts with amphetamine addiction (my parents still take them), a bulimic daughter, and the list of horrors goes on and on. Two years ago I stopped the whole thing, let my body become the size it wanted to become, and after a good deal of work and therapy I'm finally able to accept the fact that this—not a size six—seems to be the body and metabolism I've been dealt."

"WE CAN'T MEASURE UP"

Slowly but perceptibly, women seem to be recognizing the futility of waging unwavering war with biology, and are searching for ways to mitigate the cultural forces that push them into body preoccupation and body hatred (see Chapter 5). A more forgiving cultural attitude to problems of addiction and dependence have encouraged brave and articulate women like Caroline Adams Miller to seek help for eating disorders and to speak up about them—and the tyranny of valuing women (and men) by their weight.

And they are beginning to guess what the remedy is. "I'm tired of the 'perfect woman' represented through TV, movies, and magazines," one woman told *Family Circle.* "Because we can't measure up—an impossible expectation—we're made to feel we've somehow failed ourselves, our families, and society." This feeling may be quite generalized. According to the *New York Times,* "sociologists are finding that ideal depictions of life are being viewed with increasing skepticism and that consumers thus react more intensely to people like themselves—people with freckles, bald spots and moles." They could have added "thick thighs."

WORDS VS IMAGES

It may be safe to talk openly about the problem of body image, but it is not yet safe to display the obvious solution, or even to suggest it—a different image of women, a more realistic image of women, better yet, more varied images of women. Why not depict a broader variety of women or restore what Sir Kenneth Clark calls "the antique balance between truth and the ideal"? Only in part is it because the media depend on advertising that still regards ultrathinness as a fashionable ideal. No one has yet been willing to make the first dent in what is really a widely shared cultural value, no matter how much misery it causes women. The other part is, I believe, that the media do not understand their own power in perpetuating the problem.

As a result, it has become a common if schizophrenic practice in the media to discuss the body-image problem, the psychic cost of not matching an unrealistic ideal—only to wind up reinforcing it through use of the same kinds of images that create the problem in the first place. When one prominent health magazine discussed "the thinness mania" in 1988, and implored readers to "make friends with your body," it then went about lavishing its lens on, and proposing as "today's ideal woman," a model who stands six feet tall, has a 37-inch bust and 36-inch hips—measurements closer to those of an adolescent male than a sexually mature female.

The words go in one direction but the illustrations show the same impossibly and uniformly thin women that have always been shown. (Sometimes there's an added wrinkle; the model may be genuinely muscular. This is the same problem in its most intensified guise—it is still the tyranny of one ideal way to look. But it is a sign that it is not even enough to be skinny; whatever body tissue there is must be lean tissue—and muscles are the proof. And, of course, the same old diet articles crowd the other pages.) The catch, however, is an important one: In matters of perception, the image has primacy over the word. It reaches us first and carries more weight. It makes a more lasting impression.

So powerfully endorsed are the images of women we see all around us, so saturated is our culture with these images, that their cumulative effect is to discredit the reality of women. "The [natural] human body is not the basis of these rhythms, but their victim," observed Sir Kenneth Clark about the "nudes of fantastic slenderness and elongation," with their "remoteness from ordinary experience," produced under the gothic influence. He could just as easily have been talking about the bodies depicted everywhere today. The startling fact is that the image has more power than reality to shape the way women feel about themselves and their bodies.

MORE REEL THAN REALITY

This is because women compare themselves to the women in images more than to women in real life. And so positively sanctioned is the look of the ideal that, in evaluations of self, how a woman measures up against the ideal in body size carries more importance than almost all other facts about her. Achievement, accomplishment, these are pallid predictors of self-esteem compared with feelings about body size, as the experience of Oprah Winfrey reminds us. Beautiful, accomplished, and at the pinnacle of her profession, Oprah Winfrey nevertheless turned her own confessional style against herself for not matching the ideal, and on prime-time TV berated herself for weighing too much. She then went on the world's most publicized diet. Even the unanimous verdict of the press—that she looked better bigger—didn't satisfy her, until she gained back the weight. (Confidential to Oprah: Don't pick on yourself again; it hurt just watching. There's no psychological defect that unconsciously subverts your willpower; some women were just made to be bigger than others. Accept the fact that you're wonderful as you are.)

Our body image becomes our primary index of health and happiness, of the good, the true, and the beautiful, of our sense of self-competence, and of all else we value highly. So closely tied to feelings about their whole selves are women's private assessments of body size that "body image" and "self-esteem" have become virtually interchangeable terms. Our self-esteem has come to depend almost exclusively on what we think of our bodies. It becomes the core of identity, the axis on which the self turns.

This is not just a semantic ellipsis. Sadly it says that only one aspect of woman—body size, an attribute we have less control of than popular medical myths admit—is accorded disproportionate value over the whole of what we are, we do, we accomplish. In this way, women are abbreviated—and never finished. Because perfection requires eternal vigilance. Through such a set of values, the culture channels the efforts of women who seek social approval to a pursuit, endless by definition, of body perfection and self-preoccupation. What a waste of talent and energy!

"At this point in time it seems to me that women are pinning their self-esteem on the degree that they conform to the look of a de-sexified model," one perceptive reader wrote to me after seeing in *Vogue* magazine the first edition of "Fashion Plus," a special section I produced about large-size fashions. A woman can be a successful wife, mother, worker, intellectual, achiever, creator and still feel inadequate because she isn't thin and young! Her feelings are daily underscored by advertising which *totally* excludes the heavy and older women from all media. We simply are not worthy enough to be shown—that is the message.

"We should be ashamed, so we are told by the fact that every brochure that comes to my mailbox only shows clothing up to size 14! We who don't fit in don't exist," she told me.

The very nature of the way we learn compels us to draw these conclusions from pictures. For we visualize ourselves based on external images. The images around us, in photographs in magazines and advertising, in brochures, movies, and television—these are our primary textbooks of human appearance, on how to look.

OUT OF THE PICTURE

The picture becomes the standard by which we appraise ourselves directly. Our mental self-images are conceived with the help of external images, which are our reference points. "People inwardly model themselves on pictures, and on other people, who also look like pictures, because they are doing it, too," Anne Hollander explains in *Seeing Through Clothes*. Pictures, then, frame our vision of reality. Seeing is believing. Images in this sense leave too much to the imagination: What we don't see doesn't exist. If we are not in the picture, not in *any* of the many pictures of women, then we don't exist. What a blow to self-esteem! And to be excluded from the picture is to be deprived of a way of learning about oneself.

Images have always served mankind this way—to reflect ourselves, to provide images of people on whom we inwardly model ourselves. This was true when images were primarily prints and engravings and paintings. Now that representational art comes to us primarily in the form of the camera image, the photograph, it is even *more* true. For photographs have a kind of power other forms of art never had in representing us to ourselves.

We believe photographs to be true. "The objective nature of photography confers on it a quality of credibility absent from all other picture-making," filmmaker Andre Bazin has said on the "ontology of the photographic image." This is so because "the photographic image is the object itself, the object freed from the conditions of time and space that govern it."

INVASION OF THE BODY SNATCHERS

Camera vision carries with it, then, a sense of truth other forms of art do not share. Camera vision, Anne Hollander says, asserts total graphic authority, and through this authority has become "the ultimate reference for everyone's sense of visual truth." So much is this the case, she contends, that "dressing is an act usually undertaken with reference to pictures—mental pictures, which are personally edited versions of actual ones. . . . Such images in art are acceptable as models because they are offered to us not as models at all but as renderings of the truth." Unable to discredit the photographs, women who don't look like the ideal end up by discrediting themselves.

It is not just those women who don't match the ideal who are harmed by the pervasiveness of one highly unrealistic portrayal of women. All women are diminished and victimized. Their view of what is acceptable for women is equally distorted. They know the boundaries for their own behavior are equally circumscribed by such images, they are potentially equally threatened with censure, even if they have been favored by nature—at least for the time being—with bodies that hew close to the ideal. As one size 10–12 woman wrote from Birmingham, Alabama, "I want to congratulate you on your larger woman section, or should I say NORMAL woman. I loved every page because that 'larger' lady is my friend, my neighbor, the lady at church and at school. She's our doctor, our tennis coach, our decorator. She's Ms. America, and she's on every corner in this country and in every country club. She's in the Junior League and in the supermarket. She's everyone, including me."

A MODEST PROPOSAL

Leaving some people out of the picture—all pictures—has disastrous consequences for physical and mental health and self-esteem. Those who are not there do not exist, and the culture would consign them either to a life of reshaping their bodies—by any possible means—or to paying the psychic costs of feeling invisible.

But the nature of the way we learn from and use images, and the impact of camera vision demand the culture recognize another solution is needed—providing pictures more representative of the truth about women, more representative of the real and natural diversity of women. Indeed, the power of images imposes on the media a *responsibility* to provide certain kinds of balance in the visual messages they transmit. It creates a special need for sensitivity on the part of the media. We believe not only that the images are real, but that they represent the culturally approved view of life. Apparently the culture is engaged in the mass fantasy that women look that way. But this very image selectivity is what harms.

Magazines and television could create some mechanism for reviewing images of women with sensitivity to the need for diversity of appearance. This, admittedly, is easier said than done, because the problem does not lie in any single image. It is not a sin of commission. It is a sin of omission. No one image does harm. The trouble arises only from the collective exclusion of women in their normal and natural diversity. That exclusion is not a neutral fact; it is not interpreted benignly.

To fail to portray the fact that women naturally come in a variety of shapes and sizes that are healthy and beautiful, to represent women as uniformly slim, is to misrepresent us to ourselves. We are only beginning to understand the private suffering this public portrait causes. The conclusion women draw is that they are not otherwise worthy of being seen. Bombarding readers and viewers with essentially one uniform image of woman, excluding all but the slimmest of women, has a cumulative effect on all viewers and readers. The danger of this image is not that a few women can identify with what is shown, but that so many cannot identify—and are invalidated or psychically annihilated by the process.

The media now screen advertising messages and editorial content with a sensitivity to other elements they believe to be of harm. Why not also review them with some sensitivity to the cumulative effects of one uniform way of representing women? Why not ameliorate the devastating effects their restrictive representations of women actually have by seeing that some physical variety is introduced into the portrayal or depiction of women?

Introducing diversity into the portrayal of women validates the existence of all women. It liberates self-esteem. It frees women to trust their own individuality. And it is a powerful way of restoring health and balance to what has become nothing less than a national obsession.

THE "FASHION PLUS" EXPERIENCE

In March of 1986, I coproduced the first of several sections on large-size fashions that appeared in America's leading fashion magazine, *Vogue.* So radical did this idea seem to so many people, that this 32-page insert, showing beautiful clothes on beautiful women, all of whom wore size 16, made news in itself. Well before publication of the first edition of "Fashion Plus," when it was in the early stages of production, it stimulated a run of newspaper articles on the growth of the large-size fashion industry. The subject was so untapped that at the *Wall Street Journal,* two reporters on two different beats vied for the right to report the development.

Upon publication, "Fashion Plus" reaped a huge reader response, all of it totally supportive, from readers of all sizes. Not all of the response came from women. "Fashion Plus" inspired a column by Russell Baker, America's reigning pundit, that was at once charming and perceptive about America's infatuation with a thin ideal. Baker, seeing "an alarming quantity of bone lying under tautly stretched skin," lamented that "Flesh was out of style. . . . The fashion industry, which acts as enforcer in these matters, made things miserable for women with genes for curvaceous thighs." He saw Fashion Plus as "good news. . . . *Vogue* has just published a hefty advertising supplement asserting it is no longer disgraceful to be curvaceous."

Liz Dillon is an elegant and beautiful woman who is not only a plus-size model but also a freelance fashion coordinator and fashion-show commentator based in New York.

(photo by Phyllis Cuington)

One thing these 32 pages definitely demonstrated—the power of images to profoundly affect the way we feel about ourselves and others' perception of us. It validated the existence of many women.

> *For so long,* wrote one woman from Stratford, Connecticut, *the only sizes shown in fashion magazines have been petite, small, and smaller. It is refreshing to finally see the full-sized woman included in fashionable magazines,* **letting the world know that we are people, too.** (emphasis added)

The refrain was phrased in many ways.

> *I had wished for some evidence that we women who are not tall and slim were considered to be of some value. . . . Please let us know you care . . . for those of us with less than ideal figures.*

I would like to congratulate your magazine for writing about the "forgotten women." . . . I am a tall size 14, and consider myself an elegant woman with very refined taste. I am a perfectly healthy person with a well-built body who refuses to get into the diet hysteria.

Putting this section in Vogue *magazine has really helped show, just because we are a little bigger, we can be beautiful and stylish. People of our size crave anything that . . . may improve our image or self-esteem. . . . You've made me feel proud.*

Thank you for your wonderful section on larger women. It is very tasteful, the women are beautiful, and the fashions magnificent and elegant. . . . Thank you so much for making me feel tremendous, so to speak; you lifted my spirits.

There are many practical benefits to showing a more representative picture of women. It educates women's eyes about how to look good at the same time it informs about fashion choices that are flattering and suitable. "I have always been somewhat intimidated seeing constant pictures of models clad in size 7–9 outfits," wrote one reader. "I have ranged from size 10 to size 16 throughout my life. I am now a size 12, but very much enjoyed seeing heavier models draped in beautiful, stylish clothes. I hope the fleshier model is here to stay. These features will sell more magazines, promote heavier women to dress nicer, and make a lot more readers of fashion magazines happier."

NOT JUST A FASHION ISSUE

This, of course, is not just a fashion issue. Fashion magazines may present the most images reflecting the current ideal. Still, all the pictures in the culture, not just those in the fashion magazines, present the same image of woman. Witness the woman in the ad for the ultimate new driving machine, the woman in the credit card advertisement, the woman pictured having fun on the beach of the new resort, the woman using the bar of soap, the woman feeding her kids calcium supplements, the woman admiring her husband's new suit, baking brownies, putting on body lotion, applying deodorant, taking a bath in the new home spa. It's the woman in the ad for life insurance, for financial planning—for all the components of the good life. And it's the woman smoking the cigarette. Especially the woman smoking the cigarette! (See Chapter 3.)

The exclusion of larger women from images, and the invalidation of such women that results, the omnipresence of slim-slimmer-slimmest women— all this has happened under the banner of fashion, although these values are not limited to the fashion world. In the name of fashion, idealized images of women have become ubiquitous in the media, they are paraded before all women. In the name of fashion, clothes are made that conform to the idealized image of women; other women therefore can not even publicly present themselves as well-dressed with the same ease of opportunity. We now know this is a source of injury to self-esteem and self-empowerment. The insult is that all of this transpires under the name of fashion.

Pretending that this is an issue restricted to fashion obscures the real locus of the problem (it's in the culture at large, not in the women's clothes department, and definitely not in individuals). It trivializes concern about the issue—after all, if this is just a fashion issue and, as conventional thinking holds, fashion is so trivial, my dear, then how can an intelligent woman even waste her time thinking about this?

It trivializes the terrible injury to women, the bodies battered by diet and failure, or by eating disorders, and the psyches tattered by loss of self-esteem. After all, if fashion is so trivial, how can it possibly influence the way women feel about themselves at the very core?

And it diverts attention from possible remedies. The prevalence of "body-image blues," of body-image disturbances, and of eating disorders stems not from fashion but from a set of values widespread in and shared by every department of the culture. Body image is a private construct but it is built by reflections off shared ideals of attractiveness conveyed in all the images all around us.

Nor can image disturbances and eating disorders be written off—as the American mental health establishment has treated them—as reflections of individual pathology. They manifest themselves in individuals because body image is privately constructed. But it is built from public values. Eating disorders and body-image disturbances are collisions of societal values, conveyed in every picture of every woman, with biological reality.

DRIVEN TO ABSTRACTION

Perhaps sometime in the future, when cultural historians can look back on the twentieth century and put our popular images in a context that has not yet revealed itself to us, they will see the distorted and overidealized depictions of women as emblematic of a generalized loss of faith in nature, a lack of belief in the natural order of the universe, and thus a lack of value in the natural human body. Perhaps these images are closest not to fashion but to the cubist compositions and other abstract renderings of the human body that have dominated twentieth-century art.

In a century that has seen the massive destruction of two world wars and a forty-year cold war; discovered black holes, imploding stars, exploding atoms; and can envision the whole human race slowly, painfully overtaking our resources or choking to extinction on our own exhaust, to say nothing of instant vaporization in a mushroom cloud, or subversion by fat-filled arteries or mysterious growths called cancer, perhaps there is even ample reason for losing faith in nature. Could this be the reason for the "savage metamorphosis," to use Sir Kenneth Clark's phrase, that Picasso made of the visible world? The idealized images of women our culture has created may make sense only if we view them as personifying a sinister cynicism, our hearts of darkness—an expression of our worst selves, certainly not a vision of our best selves.

NO APOLOGIES NEEDED

If by some chance a woman suspects that the parade of images that go by in the name of fashion is more than a show of dress, she is forced into a defensive, apologetic stance. "It seems strange that in the midst of world turmoil and nuclear threats, that I am taking time to write about a small, and in contrast to the severities of world-wide issues, petty consideration," one extraordinary woman wrote from San Francisco.

"But I am so furious about the place we women have allowed ourselves to be shoved into," the San Franciscan continued, "that I write you to applaud your marketing focus: This niche that you are addressing is significant because it recognizes that we are here in a wondrous variety of shapes, and because it suggests that we who are heavier than the so-called norm have a place in the world. This, as you probably are aware of, is more than a fashion issue. It is really a question that goes right to the heart of the feminine self-worth concept."

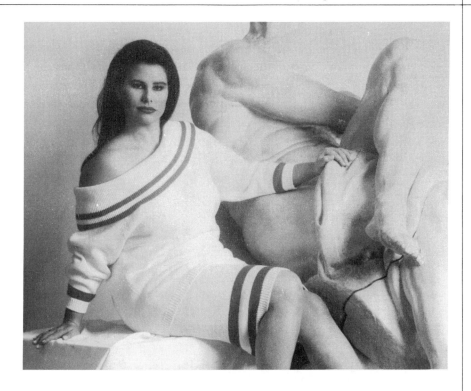

(Palma Kolansky)

Given the power of images and their relationship to the ultimate source of human power, a sense of self-worth, no, it is not strange at all that "in the midst of world turmoil and nuclear threats" someone would write about "the place we women have allowed ourselves to be shoved into." What is strange is the apologetic stance needed to defend bringing up the subject at all. As every woman knows, by calling the subject trivial, the culture attempts to invalidate beforehand the discontent with inferior treatment women sooner or later develop.

ANOTHER IMAGE

Of the thousands of letters "Fashion Plus" received, one arrived from the wilderness. It came from a woman who had trekked to a remote spot in Canada to see the salmon run, spawn, and die. The fish had yet to perform their miracle of nature when she got there. But the time of waiting produced its own surprise—a group of adventurous women in the middle of nowhere sharing their excitement over the special "Fashion Plus" large-size section in *Vogue*. And so she wrote, "never underestimate the power of the written word and great photography."

The power of good photographs—the images we select and construct of ourselves—continually impresses. The images usually displayed in the media offer one culturally approved view of the world. Because images are so important, it is time to restore some sanity, some balance, some reality to public images of women. As the accompanying images demonstrate, beautiful women come in more than one size and shape. This alternative image goes right to the heart of self-worth. And that is where the enjoyment of style begins.

(Photo by Garbin)

"The hobble skirt achieved its temporary vogue by appealing to the ideal of slimness—an ideal that was itself associated with the growing importance of youth and the corresponding growth of a youthful ideal. . . . The short skirt was something in the nature of a triumphant gesture of freedom on the part of women and, at the same time, represented the final apotheosis of the youthful ideal. . . . It has not been elegance but youth, freedom and activity that have been the dominant ideals of these post-war years."
JOHN CARL FLUGEL *in* The Psychology of Fashion—1931!

"Scholars have only recently discovered that the human body itself has a history. Not only has it been perceived, interpreted and represented differently in different epochs, but it has also been lived differently . . . subjected to various means of control, and incorporated into different rhythms of production and consumption, pleasure and pain."
CATHERINE GALLAGHER AND THOMAS LAQUEUR
in The Making of the Modern Body, 1987

Thin Wasn't Always In (and How It Got to Be That Way)

*T*hin was not always in.

Bodies are created as much by culture as by biology. How we see and experience our bodies—what we do or permit to be done to them—is always a matter of time and place. In various cultures around the globe, bodies are scarified and mutilated. They are fattened. They are stretched. They are deformed. They are tattooed and they are dyed. All in the name of beauty.

Every culture has its own ideas about what makes a body "right." For people as diverse as the Polynesians and the Eskimos, it is a substantial amount of body fat. All cultures have their own notions about how the body properly should be shaped and sized and decorated.

"The images of what a good body should look like are unbelievably varied," says Seymour Fisher, Ph.D., in *Development and Structure of the Body*

The female form idealized by the Greeks, as in this sculpture of Aphrodite, goddess of love and beauty, has a satisfying solidity, a generous arc of hip, and thighs that not only meet but overlap.
(*The Metropolitan Museum of Art*)

Image. And the amount of energy devoted to polishing and strengthening bodies should not be at all surprising. After all, the human body represents an individual's unique base of operations in the world.

In fact, it is one of the primary duties of culture to regulate how and how much bodies consume, how they shall be decorated, how they produce and reproduce, how they relate to one another. Western culture, for example, has spun its own history of sumptuary laws governing the cut of clothes, the materials from which they could be made, and how much fabric men and women could buy and wear—even specifying how long the train of a dress could be.

The meaning a culture gives to bodies changes over time and determines not just how we clothe and feed them, but also how we heal them and protect them. It shapes how we allow them to assert their needs, what disorders we will recognize. Like the brain, the body is an instrument we use to make sense of the world. How we conceive of our bodies influences not just what we permit them to do and what we may allow done to them, but how we interpret the world and what actions we take in it—our world view.

For the Greeks, whose vision of the body set the standard for Western culture, the body expressed a sense of human wholeness and summed up their confidence in a world yielding to understanding. Theirs was the body of measurable proportion and comfortable breadth that was turned into art unequaled and established a tradition of the human form as the central subject of art.

It is the fusion of sensuality and geometry that so distinguishes antique Greek renditions of the human body from all others, Sir Kenneth Clark maintains. As a tribute to the very solid geometry of the human form, Greek art still pleases, intrigues, informs us.

The body that the Greeks idealized was free of fat, but of comfortable form and substantial mass. The Greek body has volume, occupies space with a definiteness that is psychologically satisfying just to behold. The females in Greek statuary have thighs that press against each other, rippling three-dimensional abdomens, and hips that describe generous arcs. They are at once luxuriant and compact, constructed of "large and calm planes." And never, ever do their bones show.

The Greeks established a canon of proportion in which the parts had measurable relation not only to each other but to the whole. In this "full and fruitful rhythm," a body was seven heads high. The measure between the breasts was the same as the measure between breast and navel and again between navel and pubis—one head.

With the Christian era came a fashion for asceticism that rendered the human form, by itself, an unfit subject for art for centuries. When we do discern the female figure, it is flat and formless, lacking in "likeness of physiology," and usually cloaked in yards of heavy fabric. But what

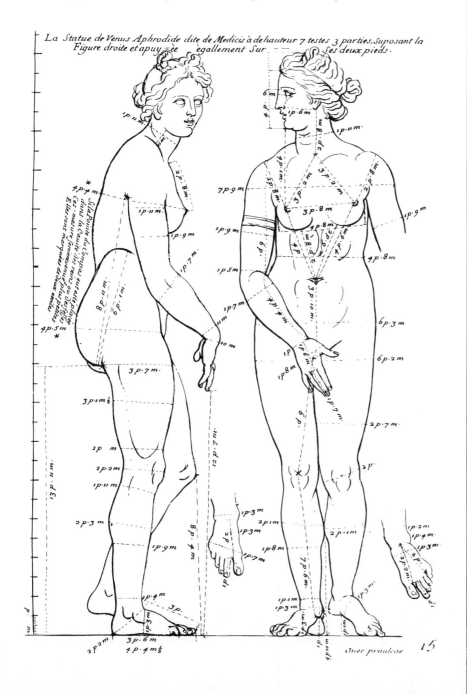

In Les Proportions du Corps Humain *Gerard Audran detailed the proportions of the female figure idealized by the ancient Greeks. The basic rhythm is a body approximately 7½ heads high.*
(The New York Public Library)

(Above) The Gothic ideal of woman, exemplified in the Venus *by Lucas Cranach, is, like the modern ideal, distorted through elongation.*
(Alinari-Scala)

(Right) In Venus and Adonis, *Rubens' joy in an abundant love goddess reflects the Renaissance faith in the natural order.*
(The Metropolitan Museum of Art)

distinguishes the medieval figure most is its shape. The preferred body style is thin and its torso is elongated—the distance between breast and navel now measures two heads. And its center of focus is clearly the abdomen. The curve of hip that was the dominating rhythm of the antique body has been replaced by a curve of stomach. This is not the structural curve of the Greek body, but a bulblike protrusion.

The Gothic body ideal, carrying all its weight in the belly, is, for all its asceticism, a figure of fecundity. Here, says Sir Kenneth Clark, is the image of the body reduced to the shame of its "vegetable existence."

Renaissance sensibility liberated the human form and returned to it the patterns of perfection established by the Greeks—balanced, prosperous, and confident. If Michelangelo was the supreme articulator of the new ideal of male form, then Rubens was the Michelangelo of the female form.

Through the "large arc of a hip," "the shining expanse of a stomach," and visible, unabashed joy in abundance, Rubens gave expression to the Renaissance faith in the natural order. What made his expression so

In Titian's Venus and the Lute Player, *one of the glories of the Renaissance sensibility, the human form resumes its position as the front-and-center subject of art.* (The Metropolitan Museum of Art)

transcendent was his concern with flesh and the texture of skin, its color, its wrinkles, its puckers, its fleshiness. Rubens revealed to the world the "invigorating luster" of the solid sculptural form. In the unselfconscious acceptance of their nudity, Rubens's women are very Greek and desport in an "antique balance between truth and the ideal."

This heritage was passed almost directly to Renoir. And although his nudes are plumper than the classical norm, they still fit the classical ideal in their "acceptance of the physical life as capable of its own tranquil nobility."

AN OBJECT OF DESIRE

But by the late eighteenth century, the roseate dawn of the Romantic era, a new aesthetic, largely confined to British culture, began to mold the arts. Call it decadence. The vision of the human form as whole, robust, trustworthy, and healthy began to give way to a new imagination in which pallor and thinness supplanted sexual vigor and fleshiness, rapture overtook reason, and revolution did away with order.

"A woman should never be seen eating," Byron decreed.

Renoir's Nude Bathers in the Sun, *resplendent in their folds of flesh, hark back to classical ideals not only in the proportions of beauty but in the underlying belief that the physical life is capable of its own nobility.*

(The Bettman Archive, Inc.)

The Romantic vision began to flourish at a time of material wealth and stable food supply. Under these conditions, fertility was no longer the chancy proposition it was through most of human history, when nutrition was far more marginal. Indeed, fertility was now becoming a burden. With the development of a prosperous economy, sexual desire thus was no longer chained to the service of sexual reproduction. Loosed from its biological moorings, sexual desire was now free to be subjugated to social needs.

Just in time. Because marriage had become a bond between two individuals rather than a merger of clans, and erotic attraction made a potent new glue. This domestic transformation held out the ecstatic promise of sexual satisfaction, but for that possibility women sacrificed their own destinies. "Given away" by their families of origin to their husbands, women now derived all their economic status and power from success in the marriage market. And from the uncertainty bred of the growing dependence on an open and highly competitive marriage market came a new burden of anxiety for women. In the service of these new domestic arrangements, sexual desirability, or attractiveness, has come to determine, more or less, the total value of women.

For the decadent Romantics, suffering of any kind was spiritually noble, heroic, but it was too good a secret to keep. An excess of spiritual energy had to have its corporeal sign, and thinness was its mark. Gauntness now acquired a new cultural meaning—it bore the suggestion of exhaustion through ecstasy or anxiety.

By the end of the nineteenth century, the reverence for nature that had dominated European culture and suffused its art at the start of the century had totally eroded. The growing view was that nature is not benign; at best, amoral. This view was sped along by such developments as the Malthusian population predictions, Darwin's concepts, notably survival of the fittest, and the dominance of scientific medicine with its orientation to pathology, particularly to those agents lurking in the world around us that infect the body and undermine it.

Nature was deemed no longer worth imitating in art. And it was held not worth heeding in any domain. Eventually, the body was seen as not even to be trustworthy enough to manage itself.

Advancing over the course of the nineteenth century, the new aesthetic—"the look of sickness, the look of poverty, the look of nervous exhaustion," as Anne Hollander puts it—was completely entrenched in art by 1910. Gone, at least from Anglo-American culture, was the body essentially set forth by the Greeks and upheld for 2,500 years by Western taste. The body was no longer seen as a balance of proportions, an expression of order, of harmony of form, of wholeness. It was looked on not to visually satisfy but to arouse; it was now completely an object of desire. "Accidents of the flesh" were "refined" away; the new visual standard decreed thin was in.

THE 100 YEARS WAR

The new taste for thinness, combined with the new distrust of nature, ushered in nearly a hundred years in which women have been waging war with their bodies. In the beginning, the imperative to diet did not involve an appeal to health; that is only a recent wrinkle. The early appeals to diet played primarily on women's mounting social insecurities, a theme that continues to this day, alongside many others. In the nineteenth century, dieting gradually became a form of insurance for success in the marriage market. Later, in the confusing calculus of twentieth-century sexuality, less body came to equal more woman. Thinness has become the requirement not just for beauty but for femininity as well.

For the Victorians, obsessed with decorum, it was sufficient that dieting got rid of lowly flesh. Flesh was rude and indecorous—it implied all sorts of bodily functions—and was totally lacking in spirituality. Under the elaborate structure of Victorian finery, women had their corsets to help rein it in. Eventually, however, clothing became simplified, and its underpinnings, too.

The paring down of bodies, at first, was part of a paring down of fashion for the modern age. The silhouette narrowed into the Edwardian hobble skirt, but it was still elaborately trussed. Then, as women rediscovered freedom of movement, as sport became possible and even fashionable, clothing simplified completely and, in fits and starts between 1915 and 1965, corsets capitulated completely to diets.

ESCHEWING THE FAT

By the 1980s, women were spending $20 billion a year on diets and diet products. Their pound of flesh has bought the grapefruit diet, the rice diet. The high-carbohydrate diet. The high-protein diet. Liquid diets. The Scarsdale diet. The Beverly Hills diet. The I Love New York diet. The Southampton diet. The names and the details scarcely matter, although diets almost always carry upscale addresses to drive home the social value of thinness. Yet more than 90% of dieters regain most or all the weight they lose by dieting.

THE END OF APPETITE

The trouble with dieting is it suspends the body's own superior ability to regulate food intake. For the body regulates hunger and satiety automatically, to maintain a steady body weight, through a complex system of physiologic controls. Dieting does to appetite what an adequate food supply does to sexuality—it frees it from longstanding automatic biological controls. The biological logic of appetite is undermined.

Unhooked from hunger by restrained eating, appetite is placed under the control of conscious, cognitive faculties. As a result, eating is subject to disruption by anything that influences conscious control. Emotions. Stress of any kind. Feeling deprived. Or overindulging in something—anything. Eating is thus easily thrown into chaos by anything that breaks one's concentration on control. Unhinged from hunger, appetite is left to the mercy of social and emotional needs, subject to the pressure of fashion—and whatever meaning of appetite the culture might try to force down our throats.

BIRTH OF EMACIATION

Indeed, the eating disorder that is the apotheosis of dieting, anorexia nervosa, a form of almost complete denial of appetite, is an example of just how powerful and bizarre a social and emotional instrument appetite could become in the right circumstances. For social historian Joan Jacobs Brumberg, Ph.D., of Cornell University, the right circumstances were the close confines of the middle-class Victorian nuclear family, where the children become "emotionally priceless at the same time they become economically useless."

Lacking economic and social value unless they were married off, adolescent Victorian daughters moved their mothers to considerable anxiety over their future in the marriage market. As pressures escalated on daughters to maintain a "dainty" body size, the body became the battleground between mothers and daughters. For young women struggling to hold on to themselves, appetite became a meaningful voice—and anorexia was born.

"It is that pushing and pulling that is at the heart of the disorder," says Brumberg. At stake is control over the body. The anorexic is a "good girl" in an "emotionally charged and materially privileged family environment" engaged in a passive method of defiance. That the domestic rebellion is conducted in obedience to the ideal of female beauty is just one of the many contradictions of anorexia. Like dieting itself, anorexia is a form of self-denial that exacts complete self-preoccupation—preoccupation with what one eats, what one looks like, how much one weighs.

SLIMNESS CARRIES TONS MORE SYMBOLIC WEIGHT

Even by the late nineteenth century, Brumberg has found, food and femininity were "linked in such a way as to promote restrictive eating among privileged adolescent women." A well-off society was making food choice a form of self-expression and the Romantics had already designated wasting the expression of a spiritual, therefore feminine, nature. "Food and eating presented obvious difficulties [in Victorian popular culture] because they implied digestion and elimination as well as sexuality." This was also partly a legacy of the Puritan Revolution that sought to subdue desire by body regulation, through dieting, fasting, and other routines of body function control.

Well before the end of the nineteenth century, thinness had become an emblem of social status. Like foot-binding in China, thinness in the United States and England became a badge of the leisure class, a sign that a woman had no need for productive work. How a body looked—body image—carried more weight than how it functioned. Ever since, social aspirations have made "social X rays" out of the newly wealthy.

Slimness already suggested feminine beauty and moral achievement when the twentieth century began, but over the past nine decades, the pressures for thinness have intensified and the suggestions have been articulated into statement. Ever since the Victorian era, our culture has been progressively narrowing the definition of beauty to a solitary dimension—slimness.

The introduction of factory-made women's clothes in standardized sizes was one added pressure. Clothing design was detached from actual bodies and became an abstraction unto itself; bodies were now expected to conform to a preset shape. What's more, the new system established a narrow range of tolerable variation for women, and it did so absolutely arbitrarily—that is, in the absence of any systematic knowledge (which continues to this day) about the normal variation of the adult female form. Nevertheless, dress size provided a visible way of restricting access to participation in life to those who measured up.

SLIM GETS SLIMMER

In the 1960s, things intensified still further; the definition of slim itself got slimmer—Twiggylike, adolescently slim. Sometime around 1965, as the leading edge of the baby boom was rocking through teendom with an unprecedented amount of change in its pockets, our culture began the outright worship of things youthful. Including bodies. Not long after she was widowed, the newly marriageable Jackie Kennedy made headlines when she dieted down from a size 12 to a 10. "You can't be too rich or too thin," has reigned as a cultural credo ever since.

In recent years, as health consciousness became a social virtue, slimness has taken on even more meaning. Slimness is not enough; slimness must be leanness—there must be no signs of fat on the body. Losing weight has come to signify not merely becoming thinner or more beautiful, but being a better person, more in control of life. In a culture that emphasizes achievement—coinciding with an era of unprecedented concern about appearance—weight has become a quick index of mastery. Dieting is seen as a form of body management, self-discipline, a visible symbol of accomplishment. All kinds of benefits—social and professional success, self-esteem, pride of accomplishment—are presumed to accrue to those who achieve thinness.

The materialist binge of the 1980s has added the moral stamp of approval on such visible "accomplishments." A bulge is not just an aesthetic flaw but a character defect. And exercise is now the only necessary work of the leisure class.

"Indeed," says Judith Rodin, Ph.D., professor of psychiatry and medicine at Yale University, "changing one's body may be the most tangible and readily accessible form of accomplishment under anyone's control at the present time. It is certainly the most visible means of showing the world how well we have done, on a par with professional success, but presumably more available to anyone."

FEMININITY'S LAST STAND

Changing role expectations for women have perhaps added the most to the cultural meaning of thinness. Today's ideal body type for women is closer to a masculine physique, reflecting the emulation of such traditionally male values as independence, achievement, and self-discipline. But ever since the Romantics, dieting has also been a way to demonstrate female frailty and spirituality, a trait thereafter regarded as feminine. The convergence of male and female sex roles in the past two decades has made thinness a visible badge of femininity, a way to uphold a distinction between the sexes. "Aspiring to thinness may be a way for women in traditionally male occupations to maintain a feminine identity," says Rodin. In that sense, "the current female body ideal may be the last bastion of femininity" as women struggle to be strong and independent.

The irony is that women now have broadened choices in careers—but not in appearance. In fact, many women pursue thinness like a career. It is their second career.

In addition to the generalized pressure for thinness, there are more intimate ones. The young women of today are the first generation to be raised by mothers who are rejecting of their own bodies. Theirs is a "heritage of anxiety and self-loathing," says Susan Wooley, Ph.D., cofounder and director of the Eating Disorders Clinic at the University of Cincinnati. They do not know there's another way to regard oneself. And while dieting was once the province of more mature women, it has now become a major concern among adolescents and even younger children.

Perhaps because we live in an entrepreneurial age, the kind that finds ways to celebrate the self-made man (or woman), Americans currently cherish the belief that almost everything is a matter of personal control. Such as illness. Or body shape. But the truth is, hormones, heredity, and history play far greater roles than willpower in determining body shape.

DIETING MAKES PEOPLE FAT

Slowly, science is revealing the irrationality of beliefs about dieting. There is evidence from the lab that dieting actually makes people fat. Studies show that losing weight by dieting is overwhelmingly bound to fail in the long run; the grim statistics are about 95% at two years. Worse, research now confirms that repeated cycles of weight loss and regain actually increase the body's ability to turn food into fat—and its inclination to do so.

Dieting by restricting food intake is counterproductive because it induces a compensatory slowdown in metabolism. According to one group of experts, the reduction in metabolic rate is not insignificant—it ranges from 15% to 30%. The net effect is an increase in the body's ability to put on fat from a normal amount of food. While lost weight consists of both fat and muscle, the regained weight is largely fat. This, in turn, makes it more difficult to lose weight the next time around. Fat tissue needs less energy to sustain itself than muscle tissue does, so the body, changed in composition, requires even fewer calories just to stay the same weight.

DIFFERENT METABOLIC DRUMS

Two women who eat and exercise exactly the same can have radically different body shapes because genes program the way bodies handle food and activity. Studies of adults who had been adopted as infants show that their "body mass index"—that is, their degree of fatness—correlates more with that of their biological parents than with their adoptive families. Researchers find that by age 42, genetic factors are more assertive than environmental ones on body mass.

And what is widely pictured in the media as the ideal body is realistic only for the small percentage of the population genetically endowed for leanness. By definition, less than 10% of the population, according to the laws of distribution that govern such things, are naturally endowed with the thin physique that our culture makes the other 90% pine for.

SURVIVAL OF THE FATTEST

In the cultural milieu that regards dieting as healthy, the risks of being overweight are, inevitably, greatly exaggerated. This should come as no surprise. In every age, cultural ideals always masquerade as "facts of nature." The men and women working in the scientific branch of the culture are no freer from the biases of the culture at large than anyone else.

Nevertheless, scientists are now "discovering" that moderate degrees of fatness actually endow women with a survival advantage. Ruben Andres, M.D., clinical director of the National Institute of Aging and a leading expert on women, weight, and longevity, has made it virtually a mission to speak the facts about women's weight despite a cultural climate of disbelief. "There's no question that a heavy woman can be healthy," says Andres. "The best body weight, especially in terms of survival, increases as a woman gets older. For women a progressive increase in weight through adult life is preferable."

One of the enduring myths about body weight is that "overweight" people eat more than those of "normal" weight. But study upon study has shown they often eat less. What makes their bodies different is that, metabolically speaking, they are in some ways extra-efficient. They burn calories at a lower rate—the inheritance of an evolutionary past when food supplies were uncertain and genes for thrifty consumption of energy conferred a survival advantage. It is becoming clear that people normally vary in the efficiency with which they store fuel as fat and the speed at which they burn fuel up. In sum, we do not march in metabolic lockstep.

In an interesting set of studies, psychologist Janet Polivy, Ph.D., of the University of Toronto, has demonstrated that dieters of any body size eat more than nondieters. The researcher fed a high-calorie snack to groups of dieters and groups of nondieters shortly before they were scheduled for a regular meal. The nondieters, no matter their body weight, ate the snack then automatically compensated by eating little of their regular meal. The dieters, on the other hand, not only downed the snack, but went ahead and ate the whole meal, too. What happened, she believes, is that long-term dieting overrides the innate physiologic signals of hunger and satiety, so that dieters lose the ability to detect when they are full and when they are hungry. Without the natural controls on satiety, the dieters went ahead and ate essentially two meals—because they were there. This interference with the perception of normal hunger and satiety signals is probably the most insidious effect of dieting. When the dieter finishes a diet, she has no built-in sense of satiety, and doesn't know when to stop. Indeed, there is reason for dieters to fear ending a diet.

What's more, dieting itself sets the dieter up for bingeing. The dieters start out by setting certain limits to how much they will eat. But such is the fragility of cognitive control of appetite that if the consciously set limit gets surpassed, either through overconsumption, such as a pre-meal snack, or is forgotten under the sway of emotional upset or the influence of alcohol, dieters eat more than nondieters. This happens even when the nondieters are subject to the same stresses and pre-meal snacks. This pattern, she points out, is "physiologically perverse. A dispassionate view suggests that perhaps dieting is the disorder we should be attempting to cure."

A CRI DU CORPS

The pressure to be thin in our culture falls disproportionately on women because the traditional female role has always placed more emphasis on appearance than on action. In addition, appetite, obsession with the body, obsession with food have become sanctioned forms of self-expression for women; traditional sex-role definitions specify these as sources for status for women only. If appetite is a means of expression, then diet madness, bulimia, and anorexia have become a cri du corps, painful evidence that appetite and body concerns comprise far too restrictive a stage for women's identity. The meaning of the cry is clear—women need a far broader theater of operations than their own bodies, a broader basis for self-esteem. So confining and conflicting is the traditional way of viewing women that it has forced them to feed upon themselves.

The push to be thin sets up such contradictory forces of deprivation and chronic hunger that dieting drives sane women to do the craziest things. "Diets are still a mystery to me," one reader wrote *Glamour* magazine in 1989. "At the height of my most recent diet craziness, I was so frantic that I actually ate potato chips while standing on the scale. Maybe I should forget my weight and start worrying about something global—it would be more constructive and I could eat again without feeling guilty."

Or, like Oprah Winfrey, they embark on a misbegotten search for the source of the "hidden" problems that make them eat, the devils that undermine their resolve.

MAGICAL THINKING

The peculiarly Anglo-American idea that an admirable body is a requirement for the female role can be such an assault on self-esteem it ultimately leads women into what psychologists call "magical thinking." They believe that transforming the body, such as by dieting, will improve the inner self and solve their life problems. That's because having the perfect body in shape and size has come to carry so much symbolic weight. Dieting is our modern fantasy of redemption—we believe that improved bodies bring us improved lives, that the correct body size guarantees success and human connectedness. As a metaphor for spiritual purification, dieting is our ongoing moral crusade. With their special regimens of compulsiveness toward exercise and rigorous if attractive denial of food, spas have become our shrines along the way.

THE INCREDIBLE BEING OF LIGHTNESS

Dieting doesn't work—it can't work—because it makes contradictory demands on the body. It is a case of cultural beliefs conflicting with the facts of physiology. Dieting represents a whole catalogue of contradictions of Western culture played out on women's bodies. Among the many contradictions embodied in dieting:

- Slimness has become the dominant norm of feminine attractiveness, but slimness is a denial of feminine physique.
- Dieting is a means of control over the body, of its appetites, of passions, of sexuality, of self, but the mastery is illusory; dieting is enslavement to an external ideal, an external set of values.
- In dieting, the body is most powerful when it is weakest, deprived of food.

- Dieting is engaged in as a form of self-denial, but it demands total self-preoccupation—with what one eats, with what one weighs.
- Dieting is embraced as a demonstration of female frailty but current demographic facts clearly prove that women are the hardier sex; they outlive men by at least eight years, on average.
- Dieting is an effort to bridge the gap between self and ideal, but it only heightens attention to the body and enhances concern with shortcomings.
- Dieting is thus an unwinnable war. Like all wars, it carries a very high price.

THE BENIGN BODY

The modern American compulsion to be thin by dieting is thwarted at every turn of physiology by nature's determination to prevent us from starving to death. That is because the body can not tell a man-made diet from a natural disaster, a fast from a famine.

To generations of obesophobic Americans who have grown up with the physiologically perverse idea that dieting is a perfectly normal way to rein in appetite, it is difficult to imagine, let alone accept as fact, that the body, left to its own devices, can actually manage to keep appetite from going haywire. We harbor the deep suspicion that the body is not benign enough to manage its own affairs. It is this very suspicion of nature that actually undermines us. For by putting under conscious control what our bodies have managed on their own since life began, we must be ever vigilant, absorbed with what we eat, what we look like. But even vigilance is never enough in the presence of unrequited hunger or feelings of deprivation.

"For every individual there appears to be a natural weight which can be maintained by spontaneous eating," explains Susan Wooley. "This 'set point' is probably primarily genetic, perhaps influenced by prenatal or early feeding, and is defended by physiological changes. If, through dieting, weight is pushed below set point, two changes occur: appetite increases and metabolic rate decreases. If weight rises above set point, appetite decreases and metabolic rate increases."

One consequence of the set point is that under normal conditions, there is a natural limit to weight gain. Another is that an unnaturally low body weight requires a permanently lowered food intake and produces chronic hunger. In the face of chronic hunger, the imposed deprivation encourages bulimia.

Dieting upsets the balance of nature. "In fact," says Toronto's Dr. Polivy, "the sorts of disinhibited eating that the dieter fears actually arise from dieting itself."

Maintaining a body weight artificially, that is, if not in the cards dealt by heredity, consumes an enormous amount of energy. Many larger women are recognizing that there are simply much better and more productive ways to expend their energy.

There is such stridency to the thin ideal in America because thinness throughout the life span can be maintained only at a fevered pitch—by continual sacrifice, continual admonishment, and intense self-absorption. It is hard, if not impossible, work that demands constant vigilance against all that fat lurking out there. One must be ever in control. For that very reason, the large-size woman is often in a highly ambivalent position with her thin friends.

To them she represents a woman out of control, and thus evokes a degree of fear. In truth, the difference may simply be that she never bought into the thin ideal in the first place, or rejected it somewhere along the way, her struggles with weight having given her insight into the irrationality of the thin ideal. After all, with the possible exception of Rio de Janiero, the rest of the world is filled with women—beautiful women who feel themselves to be beautiful—who have never subscribed to the thin ideal. The best reminder is a brief walk along a Mediterranean beach, where women of all sizes and shapes happily toast and dip their barely clad bodies, to the delight and pleasure of their children, their mates, and all other onlookers. Or a walk through any major European city, northern or southern, where women of all sizes are not deprived of access to chic. For them, body perfection is not salvation or any remotely interesting goal.

A SMOKE SCREEN FOR SLIM

Thin is so in here, however, that slimness has become the primary sales pitch for some brands of cigarettes. Virginia Slims tells us we've come a long way, but its pitch, like its name, is a calculated and cynical address to our enslavement to the ideal of thinness—one of the last frontiers of liberation for women. First, Philip Morris came up with "Virginia Slims" as a name for cigarettes; recently it began marketing a brand named "Superslims" (something that would never have made it past an adjective twenty years ago). The cigarettes are long and thin. The model in the ad is long and thin, with one long and thin leg kicking out from under her long and thin strapless dress. The clear implication is that if you smoke them, you will be long and slim, too: slim by association, or perhaps more correctly, slim by asphyxiation.

The visual message is reinforced by a verbal statement that would, under normal circumstances, provoke moral outrage—but the American view of thinness cannot by any stretch of the imagination be called normal circumstances. By means of a semantic sleight, the ad copy is startlingly explicit—"It took Virginia Slims to create a great tasting ultra thin cigarette that gives you more than a sleek shape." Smoking, we are told by way of deftly ambiguous grammar, is a way to control weight. There is in fact scientific evidence that nicotine suppresses appetite and raises the rate at which metabolism burns calories. Leave it to Philip Morris, arguably the nation's most sophisticated advertiser, to drive home the association in women's minds as a way to promote cigarette smoking.

It is not accidental that these cigarettes are packaged, named, and pitched exclusively to women. They bear the trademark of late twentieth-century American women's most obsessive concern—their weight. They reinforce women's anxiety about weight, so that what they say with one side of the mouth—"you've come a long way, baby"—they quietly take away with the other. The fact that women have not reacted with anger to the promotional campaign indicates the degree to which the culture acquiesces in the continuing belief that no price is too high to pay for thinness.

4

> *"These are models who, when challenged, can throw their hips off center or step aside in a way calculated to steal the show. The best of them earn more than $2000 a show. But for that they walk twenty miles a day, moving from one show to the next where their hair will be pulled and teased, their faces painted with yet more makeup, **their bodies twisted and tortured into clothes that no one else could wear** and then pushed out onto a new runway for two minutes."*
>
> JOHN FAIRCHILD, DESCRIBING A COUTURE FASHION SHOW, in Chic Savages, *1989 (emphasis added)*

Images Amok

The American ideal of thinness, unreal and unnatural as it is, didn't just happen. Nor was it inflicted on us surreptitiously by outside forces. Contrary to the thinking of many, it is not the result of a conspiracy by the fashion industry. It is much too pervasive in the culture. Besides, anyone who has done time in the fashion industry knows it is impossible to get two companies to agree on anything, let alone a few thousand companies to agree on something as abstract as an ideal of anything. The fashion world deals in concrete phenomena—yard goods, garments—not concepts. To hold the fashion industry solely responsible is to confuse the perpetrators of an ideal with its most visible exploiters. No, the plain truth is that we, the American public, appointed the ideal ourselves. It came to us, originally and still, not as an abstraction of Woman. It glided into the culture, barely noticed at first, in the form of the fashion model.

ENTER THE MANNEQUIN

They were mere shop girls in the Paris couture houses—ordinary girls with extraordinary qualities—elegance and grace of movement as well as slimness.

57

Introduced at the turn of the century as a way of animating "frocks" to enliven their sales potential, mannequins, as they were then universally called, quickly became the means for launching the new creations of the couture houses, then indisputably the reigning arbiters of fashion. Eventually, as the uses and value of mannequins expanded, their roles were divided in two: In America, "mannequins" are now the lifeless forms on which clothes are hung for display in store windows and elsewhere, while "models" are the real live creatures who animate clothes on runways, in showrooms, and in photography.

In 1905, when fashion modeling was new, and still a European phenomenon, *Cosmopolitan* magazine explained the practice to American women: "The custom [in Paris] is to exhibit the latest creations of the [dressmaking] firm by means of living models, those tall, graceful, long-waisted girls who know not only how to wear a dress well, but how to move about with ease and elegance. A particular style of dress, as seen in this seductive way, will take the fancy of the client."

IN THE WORLD BUT NOT OF IT

By 1915, modeling had arrived in the U.S., and *Vogue* magazine caught on that something different was in the air—a fashion force divorced from substance in a new way. As the "embodiment of the mode," the mannequin is "slender, supple, and supersmart," cooed *Vogue*. However, she is "in the fashionable world but not of it." Interpreting the mode, she "must be more elegant than the *elegant,* capable of assuming more demureness than the debutante or more dignity than the dowager." Unlike "the picturesque beauties of other nations," the American mannequin was often just a "vivacious slip of girlhood," "slender and boyish."

Performing "live" demanded that a model be a bit of the actress and a bit of the duchess. But that was all that was demanded of her at first. By the 1970s, however, it could easily if not comfortably be said that the mannequin, or by then, the model, came to embody not simply "the mode," but the American ideal of beauty, which is to say, thinness. She is our icon of emaciation. She embodies the disembodiment of fashion today.

This is a heavy symbolic load for any mortal to carry, and it was not heaped on the model all at once. To carry all of this symbolic weight, the fashion model, at least in America, has had to be relieved of just about all of her own corporeal weight and elevated to media star. It took sixty years for America to endow models with enough virtue, glamour, status, and celebrity to be worthy of upholding this unnatural, impossible, disembodied ideal.

In their remarkable odyssey through twentieth-century culture, they started out as anonymous coat hangers, but they eventually became personalities in their own right. They later became paragons of perfection. Anointed secular saints, they transcended the fleshiness of real women. And despite their shrinking waistlines and their detachment from material reality, they became the most striking symbol of the expanding consumer culture.

From the start, models were available to take on some meaning—any meaning the culture might bestow on them. Even the earliest observers and admirers were struck by their glaring vacuity. "I observed the odd, set expression of their faces—many times the expression was a smile, but such a smile as one might see on the face of bisque dolls, devoid of any meaning," an early *Vogue* editor reported. The very characteristic that made them objects of interest in fashion shows also made them the perfect vehicle for personifying an abstract, feminine perfection. That was the very detached demeanor of the model herself. Their very blankness made them the perfect repository for our developing idealization of the fleshless female form.

As early as 1913, at least one astute observer, viewing a department store fashion show in New York, detected the inherent potential of models to personify an abstraction. "As with slow, proud motion, apparently oblivious of the audience, the model moved away from the steps—it was excellently done and somehow removed her from the same category as a chorus girl or a saleswoman or an artist's model, and made her into an abstract fashion-plate. . . . Like a group of proud and painted peacocks curiously removed from humanity, the models moved back and forth on the winding platform. . . ." And the very presence of models in the department store suggested the extraordinarily important role that models were to play in American mass culture.

TAILOR-MADE FOR THE U.S.

The fashion model may have been born in Europe, but she was tailor-made for America. In Paris, the mannequin represented the world of couture and had one function—to stand in for the great ladies of society and stage, who set the fashions of the times but who were rapidly diminishing in importance. "Paris knows [the mannequin] well, and adores her," *Vogue* touted. "In Paris, her reed-like grace lends a picturesque quality to the boulevards and cafes, to the race-courses and the theater."

But in the U.S., she went down an altogether different runway. Her direction was set by the very different role fashion was playing in this culture. Here, as in Paris, the model worked in custom salons, but while that was the most of it in Paris, that was the least of it here. She also worked in the wholesale market of Seventh Avenue, displaying dresses, coats, and suits to out-of-town buyers, and she worked in retail stores in New York and around the country. In the U.S. she found unprecedented opportunity for rapid advancement with the burgeoning ready-made women's clothing industry, just getting off the ground in the early 1900s when the model made her debut. While the Parisian mannequin was out hobnobbing with society, the New York mannequin had her hands full avoiding the sweaty advances of the store buyers, then predominantly men, who flocked to the manufacturers' showrooms on Seventh Avenue to order the fashions that Everywoman could buy in Hometown, U.S.A.

A STAND-IN FOR EVERYWOMAN

On the far side of the Atlantic, where fashion emanated from couture salons and styles were set by the leisure classes, the model became a convenient and attractive but not terribly important substitute for the duchess at the racecourse. By contrast, in America, she was the stand-in for Everywoman, the rank and file woman, the working woman, the woman of the twentieth century. This was the same hardworking woman who, with her meager paychecks, was financing the growth of the indigenous American fashion industry. It, in turn, concentrated on turning out the simple cotton shirtwaists (blouses) and skirts (as popularized by the Gibson Girl) well suited to the pocketbook of the new working girl, who needed only a few simple cotton "waists" and a skirt or two to give the appearance of having a whole wardrobe.

Unlike in France, fashion in the New World was no longer set by a few leaders in society. As the *New Republic* announced, American fashions "are determined by the purchases of several million working women." And the model was poised to rise with them, by them, as them.

CULTURAL EXCHANGE

This was neither a one-sided nor completely unconscious process. There was a clear if implicit exchange of benefits between models and us, the women they supposedly represented. Over the years, we increasingly bestowed status and meaning on models and modeling. As the consumer economy bulged, we projected our values and dreams onto models. In return, we took their bodies. In this cultural exchange, they became much more than mobile coat hangers. And we were all expected to have the bodies of models, or sacrifice ourselves toward that goal.

MODELS R US

To make the veneration of the model complete, to make models worthy enough for mass emulation, the public opinion of models and modeling had to be overhauled, and modeling itself had to move into public view. Right up through the 1940s, modeling was a morally suspect endeavor, where girls were presumed to honor the after-hours invitations of out-of-town buyers with thick wallets. In 1930, *Collier's* magazine made a nod to prevailing public opinion when it reported, direct from the cultural front, that "these modern mannequins . . . are very, very nice but not very naughty." It was one of a tide of articles in the 1920s and 1930s that helped convince the public that, despite stereotypes, modeling was a respectable trade.

"I want to say right now that I have never been insulted by any man and I have never seen any other girl insulted, unless she stepped right up and asked for it," Nellie the Beautiful Cloak Model revealed in a 1923 issue of the *Saturday Evening Post*. Such an aura of disreputability hovered over modeling into the 1940s that Eileen Ford, a former model and a new parent, rose to preeminence as an agent by setting up shop in a businesslike but family-oriented way, making mothers and fathers feel secure about sending her their nubile daughters.

To hear the popular magazines tell it, models were wholesome, ordinary girls—just like us. The "new type of manikin," said *Literary Digest* in 1928, "is essentially a business girl, who is expected to go about her work in a business-like way." She is so much like us that . . . Why, even you, too, could be a model. "How is it done? How can the average woman benefit from the model's technique? How can the well-figured young girl get into the glamorous field of professional modeling?" *Literary Digest* asked in 1937, and proceeded to give advice from a new how-to book, *Modeling for Money*. "The challenge of turning a sweet country girl into a stunning high-fashion beauty is not confined to playwrights," *Cosmopolitan* reported even as late as 1960 in an article about "Modern Pygmalions." If models weren't us, they were, at the very least, the girl next door. And to prove the point, modeling schools were opening all over the country, to fulfill the dreams of every girl next door.

Not to worry, models weren't even a different breed, the beauty. "You can get by without beauty," a leading fashion model assured America in 1931. By way of telling women "What It Takes To Be a Model," model agent Harry Conover in 1947 publicized his latest discovery: "She had none of that vital bang that makes you say, 'Holy smoke, what a stunning girl!' She wasn't brimming over with sex appeal. She was an old-fashioned New England youngster with a smile that was genuine and warm, never an artificial grin. She was not a raving beauty, but she had an expressive face. . . ."

The girl next door or not, beautiful or not, models were always thin. "The average girl inducted into the Ford [Model] sorority," *McCall's* explained in 1955, "finds that her weight, her posture, her makeup and her dress are all in need of drastic reconstruction. 'Whatever a girl weighs,' says Eileen Ford, 'the camera always adds ten pounds. A girl who isn't thin just doesn't look right in the clothes. Clothes look best on a woman with a small waist, flat hips, and a small, well-placed bosom.'" And if we hadn't noticed before then that models had, as one photographer said, "a hard, bony look to set off the clothes," we certainly caught on in the 1960s, when the thoroughly modern model burst with highly picturesque new force upon the scene.

The new breed of model startled us with her lankiness. We laughed— nervously—at Twiggy's thinness. But she was just the shape of things to come. Today, her linear descendants are everywhere, no longer gawked at. They are what we are feverishly striving to look like. They are us, America's women.

It started in the fashion magazines in the 1960s, and legendary *Vogue* fashion editor Diana Vreeland claimed the credit. But it is now commonplace in all magazines to see fashion display articles and even advertising in which the model is not a professional model at all but an "ordinary" woman, commonly a working woman, like us, although most often she is drawn from the ranks of those who make it their job to be style-setters—those who, in the 1960s, we dubbed the Beautiful People. "The line between professional mannequin and female Beautiful Person is already blurry," Anne Hollander noted in 1978. Today that line is virtually nonexistent.

PRINTS OF PERFECTION

Models would never have been able to rise so far and so fast without a means for disseminating images of them and information about them. The rise of the model is inseparable from the phenomenal expansion of fashion photography and glossy editorial and advertising pages in magazines over the twentieth century, both to accommodate and to further spur the growth of the ladies' garment and beauty industries.

At the turn of the century, and to a considerable degree right up until the 1950s, fashion reporting was largely a verbal affair. Magazines, even fashion magazines, were meant to be read. Words, not pictures, were used to convey fashion. Verbal description was the mode. Occasionally, a hand-drawn illustration would accompany the wordy text. These were not what we would today regard as sketches, a much looser and more impressionistic form. The early illustrations had about as much spontaneity as etchings, which in fact they were, given the methods of print reproduction available at the time. The careful detail in the engravings of these early "fashion plates" not only limited their use but made them highly static images.

As the fashion industry grew, magazines expanded and developed more eye-catching ways to report and ultimately display news of it. Magazines bulged with pages paid for by advertisers who needed to promote all the merchandise that now had to be sold. In the process, fashion coverage was transformed from a verbal to a visual mode. Where words once stood, only the female form would now suffice. Fashion photography, which came into its own in the 1950s, virtually exploded in the 1960s, when thinness took on added dimensions in American culture. It is hard to overstate the power of the impression models have made on us since the 1960s; American women are still living in their thrall.

A PUBLIC OCCUPATION

During the 1950s, as magazines became visually slick affairs, the epicenter of modeling moved from the salon and showroom to the colorful printed page. With unprecedented impact, the ground under America's models shifted from private to public space. Models no longer were seen only by the relatively few well-to-do women who went to fancy stores. Their newly slimmed-down and revved-up images confronted every woman who opened up a newspaper or magazine, or turned on a television set. You didn't even have to leave the house to come in contact—over and over again—with the new image of woman.

Modeling was now quickly taking on great lustre, excitement, and high visibility as an occupation, and models acquired a larger-than-life reputation for their smaller-than-life dimensions. We were not only getting to know them by name—Jean Shrimpton, Twiggy, Veruschka, Penelope Tree—they were becoming national and international celebrities as fashion photography heated up like a hyperactive strobe. "Bones have names," was the way *Time* magazine put it in 1961, in an article about models' new celebrity.

When Diana Vreeland took over as *Vogue*'s editor in 1960, she was responsible for some of the most striking images of women ever to hit the printed page. What she did was dramatize—brilliantly—changes already under way. She completed the disembodiment of the female form: She banished flesh—she "discovered" Twiggy and billboarded Cher—and even did away with clothes. Her very theatrical photographs are most memorable for showing models nude or seminude—a breast wearing a champagne glass, topless bathing suits, painted bodies. Vreeland had photographers manipulate and photograph the fleshless body as if it were a piece of abstract art, which, in a very true sense, it now was.

DISTORTED VISION

Thinness was a requirement of models from the beginning. In 1923, under the banner "An Almost Perfect Thirty-Four," Nellie the Beautiful Cloak Model confided that by classical standards, "I hadn't a good figure; too tall and thin. But judged by the standards of the New York modistes, I was great. That's why I refer to myself as an almost perfect thirty-four." There it was, the ugly specter of physical perfection, that idea that there was one perfect way for women to look, the terrible tyranny of an ideal.

Even then the outlines of thinness were rapidly shrinking. As Nellie made clear, "the famous perfect thirty-six of fifteen years ago would be considered a monstrosity today. So would Venus de Milo, for that matter. Her ankles are impossible." The majority of shops, she reported, were hiring "very tall, very slender girls, on whom they could just hang their creations." There needed to be no body to get in the way of the clothes.

Thinness took on added emphasis as the camera usurped other forms of fashion display and came to dominate the representations of women. The need for exaggerated thinness arose first from the distortion created by the machinery used to bring models to us—the camera. As Eileen Ford was quick to realize, the camera lens adds ten to fifteen pounds to bodies.

The need for thinness was exaggerated still more by the new meaning of photography: It captured a moment and allowed us to understand the accelerating action of modern life, the new dynamic of virtually every aspect of life. The camera both symbolized and recorded the increasing possibilities for action and movement—freedom—newly available to women. In doing so, camera vision changed the requirements for models (lose ten pounds or else) and it changed what we got out of images (a way to comprehend the new dynamic of society). If still fashion photography imposed the need for unusual degrees of thinness, then motion photography, from the movies to television, upped the ante.

SUBTRACTION FOR ACTION

For action—even the possibility for action, which is inherent in a single photograph or snapshot—enlarges the visual space the body takes up. "The actual physical size of a human body is made apparently larger by its movements. . . . Even if a body is perceived at a motionless instant, the possibility of enlargement by movement is implicit in the image," Anne Hollander explains in *Seeing Through Clothes*. Before the era of photography, bodies could be visually enlarged in beautiful ways by portrayals of voluminous clothing or even the artistic addition of layers of fat to the body. "But a body that is perceived to be about to move must apparently replace those layers with layers of possible space to move in," Hollander points out. "The camera eye seems to fatten the figure. Human eyes, trained by camera vision, demand that it be thin to start with, to allow for the same effect in direct perception." The new potential for action adds to the impact of the thin female body; it increases its weight, as it were. Therefore, we must subtract for that effect.

When all that models did was to slowly, elegantly parade around a private showroom, salon, or fashion show—that is, when they were mostly seen in the flesh—they routinely wore size 12 or 14; some even wore—horror of horrors—size 16. In 1931, a leading model revealed that "in most wholesale houses, 16 and 18 are the desirable sizes. And the model has to be only average height—say, five feet five, or five feet six." This was so that the hordes of store buyers might better "visualize a given style on the person of Miss Average Figure of Raleigh, North Carolina, or Mason City, Iowa." Most retail mannequins, on the other hand, "are excessively tall and slender . . . 14 is the favorite size and five feet eight is a popular height." Clearly what is excessively tall and slender has been considerably slenderized since then.

Today, models routinely wear sizes that were not even manufactured thirty years ago, sizes 2, 4, 6. In a mid-1989 article about terribly thin and terribly rich designer Carolyn Roehm, whose life (including husband Henry Kravis, the leveraged buyout specialist) is emblematic of the chic excesses of the 1980s, *Vogue* magazine dared to observe that customers complain that Roehm dresses only her own body—a narrow 5'9½". The designer shrugged off the criticism by suggesting her body was the only body worth dressing. "I have size 6 to 8 shoulders, and a 4 body. It's close enough to most models." Roehm is the prototype of the ultrathins Tom Wolfe designated "social X rays" in *The Bonfire of the Vanities*.

If the dominance of the lens made increasing degrees of thinness a requirement for models, so did it put on a push for perfection. "Today, models must be nearer to perfection than ever before if they hope to succeed," model impresario Walter Thornton told the *Saturday Evening Post* in 1937. "The rapid increase in the use of photographic illustrations is responsible for more exacting requirements. . . . The lens of the camera is a cold and sometimes cruel auditor of debits and credits of face and figure."

CRUEL COMPARISONS

As modeling became more photographic and more public, and the images of models in the media became ubiquitous, what was originally a standard imposed by the lens on a few women became the standard for all women. Not merely because models were stand-ins for us in clothes, not because we now identified with models, but because we also all draw our sense of what we should look like from the pictures around us. We compare ourselves to them. They are all around us. They are more real than reality. They are inescapable.

The model was tangible proof—after all, seeing is believing—that "perfection" was not superhuman or a figment of the imagination. The incredible fact that the model was physically atypical, chosen from the absolute extreme of human variability for tallness and thinness, was forgotten. The average American woman, at 5'4", is fully six inches shorter than the average model, who is 5'10"—and growing. The fact that the model was a real human being served as living, irrefutable proof that "perfection" was attainable by real women. For all the centuries before the advent of the model, the "ideal" woman was a hypothetical construct, one that always tantalized artists; it was a product of the artistic imagination. The ubiquitous model was proof that the ideal could be flesh and bones—well, bones, anyway. The model made the ideal real and photography made it binding.

"In an important sense," *Time* magazine astutely observed (though in a typically male chauvinist way) in 1949, as the revolution in fashion photography was getting under way, the model "exercises an unsettling influence by making men and women dissatisfied with reality. She proclaims that homeliness is a sin and unnecessary. Her every image assures men [and women] that women look like goddesses, while their experience tells them that women look only like women." What has since become clear is that every image assures women that they must look like goddesses, while their experience is invalidated. The representation of the female body is more credible to us than the reality of the female form. Through this process, we lose respect for our bodies.

It is cruel, it is ironic, but it is true—the ideal that women have adopted for their own reality is often an Ozlike illusion. For at almost every step of the way, from makeup to lighting to the fit of clothes, fashion photography is a triumph of illusion, despite the presumption of truth in photographs.

MERCHANTS OF VENUS

In assigning models increasing value, in venerating them, American culture has relied on their thinness and their beauty to do more of the selling. But the fashion marketplace has become crowded, and that has imposed even more distortion in the preferred style of beauty in models.

In 1920, *Vogue* magazine carried a total of 312 pages in its September issues. By fall 1989, the magazine was typically running September issues with over 700 pages of advertisements alone. Clearly a way was needed to catch the attention of the jaded reader already reeling from sensory overload. And so models are being sought out who are increasingly unusual and exotic—who more and more are even less and less like us, even though they are supposedly representative of all women. The demands of the crowded marketplace create an impetus of their own for models to become thinner and thinner, stranger and stranger. The increasing thinness of models functions as an attention-getting device in a cluttered market and an even more cluttered visual showcase.

Weightlessness, however, is only one dimension of the new exoticism of models. Where once a vivacious wholesomeness was desirable, models have become increasingly bizarre in looks. It's what gives them visibility in an era clogged with visual information. The very success of the model, her omnipresence, has forced her into new realms of exoticism.

So far have models come from their original purpose in serving as mobile mortals, so abstracted have they become, so disembodied are these symbols of allure that they have long since ceased to represent the normal, let alone the ordinary, woman at all. The discrepancy between the image of women put before women, and the reality of women, has grown so great that the very word "model" comes back at us like a slap in the face. By semantic sleight, it tricks us into thinking that models really are representations of us, as we are or as we are supposed to be. But these women can no longer be said to represent us in any physical way. They are not models of us at all. So extreme is the weightlessness of today's models that they have achieved what might be considered the ultimate contradiction—they discredit the material reality.

"A sociologist could no doubt give ready answers why embodiments of elegance should take this somewhat ridiculous shape—feet and hands too fine for honest work, bodies too thin for childbearing, and heads too small to contain a single thought." Those are the words of Sir Kenneth Clark, commenting on the surprisingly similar body distortions that characterized the late medieval Gothic style of painting and sculpture. He goes on, "One thing is certain. Chic is not natural. . . . Their very strangeness of proportion seems to invite erotic fantasies, for which the very substantial bodies of Titian leave less opportunity."

Models today are actually sought out for *not* looking like us, that is, for not being models of women at all, despite the fact that they are put before us on the pages of magazines as the representation of women. "Figures in fashion plates, like the bizarre creatures in *Vogue* photographs," Anne Hollander wrote in *Seeing Through Clothes,* "are always known to be unreal, to represent not an ideal but a grotesque and even undesirable exaggeration, which is nevertheless distorted in desirable directions."

FALSE IDOLS

Model agencies, magazine editors, and designers now actively search out women who are extremely unlike ordinary women. Karl Lagerfeld, the reigning king of designers who now runs the house of Chanel as well as his own empire, is so in need of novelty that he has begun holding Broadway-style auditions for new models every time he presents a new fashion collection. To show his designs for the fall 1989 Chanel line, he chose ten new models. Among them was Kimora, a 14-year-old American girl, half-Japanese and half-black. If she represented nothing more than the new internationalization of fashion markets, she should be applauded. But having a 14-year-old represent the beauty grown women compare themselves to winds up discrediting the very women she is paraded before. "She is fresh and gay," commented the designer, "the kind of beauty who truly represents the nineties."

Under the rubric "role models," *Elle* magazine presented a 24-page feature on "five of the most beautiful women in the world." The first one was a 6′1″ tall 21-year-old "who sweeps in looking like an oversized spy," with her "highly athletic build complete with broad shoulders and no hips." She is a frequent model of swimsuits. She has also been a featured model in a catalogue for petite women! The next model was a mere 5′11″, a 22-year-old with "endless leg" and "exotic" looks, according to the reporter. A third model was described only as a "lanky teenager" who told the reporter, "people are intimidated by the way I look." The fourth was a towering 6′3″ model who said, "in magazines I always look like some wild woman straight out of the jungle." In other words, exotic. Only one, at age 26 a "veteran in the business of looking young and lovely," bore any relation to real people. She was a mere 5′9″ and actually worked at a real job after graduating from college. Still, the article took pains to point out, her look is "exotic," even if her approach is "refreshingly down to earth."

Some copywriter is probably smiling at the innocuous cleverness of the headline, but the label "role models" actually accomplishes a significant deception. It cues us to accept the models' looks, however exotic, however bizarre, however inappropriate, however unrealistic, as the standard for our own. This is not a case of innocent word play. Just one index of the absurdity of that proposition: sixty percent of the featured models were over 6′ tall, while an infinitesimal fraction of American women reach that height. Ninety-five percent of American women stand 5′8″ or less.

The fact that models whose photographs we compare ourselves with are not and, because of the demands of a crowded marketplace, cannot be like us, has devastating effects on women. For we measure ourselves against them and come up lacking. And the ubiquity of images of women who are uniformly slim, slimmer, slimmest carries the implicit message that no one larger exists—or is worthy of existing. But the terrible irony is that even the models are not like their pictures. Most photographs of women in magazines are filled with illusions.

This is not simply a case of makeup, lighting, and camera angles being used to chisel cheeks and mold torsos. It is a matter of who is used—14-year-old girls as the standards of beauty for women in their 30s, 40s, and 50s. This kind of misrepresentation daily sends thousands of women to their doctors in the hope of repairing what are really perfectly good looks. And it is a matter of what magazines do to present an idealized image of women and what models themselves must do to maintain the image of them in magazines.

It is vitally important for women to know—although there is no pleasure to be gained from knowing—that embodying the feminine ideal takes its toll on models as well as on ordinary mortals. For them, being ten to fifteen pounds underweight is a minimum job requirement. Many beautiful girls who aspire to be models are required to lose weight before the model agency will seriously talk to them. Being unusually thin does not come naturally to all models. But their working size, along with height, shoe size, hair and eye color, is typically announced on the photo sheets that are, in effect, their business cards. Models are routinely monitored by their agencies, and if they do not meet their stated weight, they cannot work. An agency would otherwise suffer in reputation as a poor and unreliable manager of its models; business would drop. Photographers would balk at working with them. Thus there are powerful incentives to keep models at the weight stated on their cards. And that can lead to all kinds of problems.

"A psychologist who heads the eating disorders unit at a suburban hospital says she hates to look at high fashion ads these days because she almost always sees the telltale swellings at the top of the neck that show the models have achieved their emaciated looks by self-induced vomiting," the *Boston Globe* reported recently in an article on "Fashion's Famished Slaves."

It is regrettable that models choose to do such damage to themselves. But the damage is magnified manyfold because it is also done to all those who view the pictures. They develop an unrealistic picture of what women do look like, can look like, and should look like. And they believe they are seeing a representation of the truth, though they are not.

ONE IN A MILLION

The illusion, however, does not stop there. It is compounded by the fact that the images of women on display in magazines are highly selected and further that those photographs themselves are typically tampered with, violating the camera's authority and reliability as reporter. Retouching, for example, is routine, automatic. But so is a process of selection by which a magazine may find worthy of display only one image of a model out of hundreds, sometimes thousands, taken for the purpose. Put another way, what woman on earth wouldn't look terrific if she, like the most ordinary model, had at least five people (hair stylist, makeup expert, fashion stylist, photographer, and assistant) fussing over her for an hour or two before being photographed. And then, all she had to do was look good in one out of hundreds of shots.

Magazines painstakingly edit the images within. When the fashion magazine *Mirabella* was preparing its first issue in 1989, the editors revealed it took them ten photo shoot sessions to come up with a suitable cover shot. No doubt thousands of frames of film were screened to get one workable image. Even for professional models, then, it can take hundreds of shots to get a "right" one.

THE OMNIPOTENT AIRBRUSH

And then an entirely different kind of creative work begins. The photo image itself gets altered; retouching is routine. Human hands make additions and subtractions—usually subtractions—to what the camera sees. What God giveth, the airbrush taketh away. In retouching the photos that are selected, all facial detail is systematically eliminated in women. What we see is the outline of a face, with eyes, nose, mouth. All other topographical details are annihilated. The result is a face that has as much reality as that of an early bisque china doll. When *Harper's Bazaar* ran a cover photo of model Christie Brinkley holding her year-old daughter, so many facial lines and so much facial detail were airbrushed from the model that the year-old baby actually looked more wrinkled than her thirty-something mother.

Retouching of women's appearance is not limited to women's fashion magazines, where "image" has far more value than substance and thus is thought to be in need of maintenance and protection. Retouching of appearance is commonplace for images of women in major publications of all kinds—news magazines, business magazines, even so-called general-interest magazines as well as fashion and celebrity publications. We might expect some image protection in fashion and celebrity magazines. The universality of the practice only lends the images in fashion and celebrity magazines complete credibility; it validates them.

A normal face boasts such anatomical landmarks as the nasolabial fold, extending from the sides of the nose out to the edges of the lips; the

The retoucher's art (left side) banishes wrinkles, pores, all surface detail, and gray hair (right).
(Photo by Paccione)

philtrum, the vertical groove between nose and upper lip; eye sockets, laugh lines as when flesh is displaced in a smile. But these anatomical features, all of which exist on the faces of infants and which tend to be more pronounced with age, are banished from magazine pages as reliably as nudity once was. They are a source of bodily shame in the modern era.

Nor is the retouching confined to facial features. The clothes the model wears get their own brush-up. A slim silk skirt worn for half an hour by a model may develop wrinkles across the pelvis—just as in real life. But the retoucher will painstakingly splice in a smooth portion of the garment, to keep the clothes in the picture in perfect order. This is hardly innocuous. It deletes the suggestion that clothes wrinkle around bodies and establishes the fiction that clothes and bodies bear little relation to one another, when in fact clothes take all of their meaning from bodies. The result is a false picture of the way clothes fall and look on real bodies, which generates false beliefs about the way clothes are supposed to look. And women in their own lives waste time, effort, and psychic energy striving for an effect that doesn't really—but seems to—exist.

Because such photographs are so pervasive, because they are so uniform, and because photographs have so much authority in representing what we believe to be real and natural in human looks, women—and men—develop a false image of what women do look like and therefore what they should look like. And make no mistake about this—the deception is almost exclusive to women. In most photographs, men are allowed to retain ownership of their "imperfections," their laugh lines, their pores, their wrinkles, and especially their nasolabial fold. They have retained the right to look natural and normal.

DISCREDITING OURSELVES

The presence of so many false images of what women look like is a bad teacher about women to women. The problem is not just that the images are falsified—but that they are not labeled as such. We believe them true representations. Together, they undermine any notion of what constitutes a natural look, thrusting women into genuine body anxiety.

The elaborate process of image selection and the even more painstaking process of image alteration are completely hidden from view. Yet, because we believe photographs show us the world as it naturally is, and we draw conclusions based on what we see, what we don't see is not in our frame of reality and therefore doesn't really exist. Unable to discredit the fraudulent photographs we end up discrediting ourselves instead. What we can't see can—and does—harm us.

In fact, I present this backstage view not to destroy the "fantasy" element that editors maintain is essential to fashion, but to keep the fantasy benign, to keep it from destroying the reality of most women. All across America, women have drawn the mistaken conclusion that because they don't match the pictures, there is something wrong with them, that because they can't squeeze into size 10, they are not worthy of having nice clothes; that because their eyes have lines, there is something wrong with their face. In truth, there is plenty wrong with the pictures.

One upshot is evidenced in the surge in demand for plastic surgery and other treatments to alter perfectly normal, attractive facial characteristics. Women routinely seek out dermatologists and plastic surgeons wanting to get rid of, for example—I swear it—facial pores. When was the last time you ever saw pores in a close-up photograph of a woman in a magazine?

Does it all add up to a conspiracy against women? Certainly, the effect on women could not have been worse had the media, the fashion world, and all the other departments of the culture ganged up and conspired to put only one perfect image of women before us. But I doubt there has been any conspiracy of intent. For one thing, the troublesome images are not confined to the fashion world. They appear everywhere, in advertisements of cars and deodorants as well as of pantyhose and eye shadow. They populate advertisements for men, too.

The painful answer is that the media are unaware of the real power of images in influencing how women feel about themselves. Sure, they know that images of beauty, of the sanctioned style of beauty can motivate women to buy a product. But they probably do not realize that image after image has an effect in which the sum of the images is greater than—and different from—all of the parts. The perpetual presence of one style of beauty, of one brand of perfection has a cumulative impact that hobbles women's psyches, turns them against themselves if they do not match the image. That this image of beauty is not as real as it purports to be—it is essentially an illusion on top of an actual misrepresentation of us to ourselves—magnifies the injustice against women.

In part because of their pervasiveness, but also in large measure because of their subtle falseness, these images have upset what Sir Kenneth Clark calls "the antique balance between truth and the ideal." It is time to restore some balance. As I suggested in Chapter 2, this needs to be done at the cultural level, where these images are generated. But it also needs to be done at the personal level, by individual women, on whom such images have their greatest impact.

5

Climbing Out of the Body Trap

*T*he day is seared into Jeanie Person's memory. She left work early, something she rarely does. She drove straight home, locked the bedroom door, took off all her clothes, and put on some sweet music. Then she braved the full-length mirror—and started dancing. Awkwardly, tentatively, at first; then unreservedly, even raucously, before she collapsed on the bed in tears of relief. She wasn't crazy—just fed up with always feeling fat.

Jane Harper knew the feeling well. Bullied by self-hatred, she was obsessed with becoming thinner. Much thinner. Consumed with her weight, she still always found herself eating more, not less. Desperate, she took nude pictures of herself to shock her into losing weight. Only the more she stared at the pictures, the more she thought they weren't so bad. "I started looking at my body through the eyes of someone who loves me—my husband."

CASUALTIES OF WAR

Jeanie, 139 pounds, and Jane, then 200-plus pounds, are at the cutting edge of a revolution in attitude among women of every size and shape all across

America. After years of putting their lives on hold until they meet the culture's highly arbitrary ideal of bodily perfection, or spending most of their energy attempting to attain it, they are starting to make peace with the bodies they have, however lumpy they may be.

Decades of deadlock in dieting and regaining and living with the resulting self-hatred have finally convinced them, as they did Jeanie and Jane, there must be a better way—if only they could find it. Slowly, one by one, because preoccupation with one's self and the shame of failure are powerful forces of isolation, they are discovering for themselves what science has recently been recognizing—that being five, ten, or even fifty or more pounds "overweight" isn't the end of the world, that women's bodies were not born to be pencil thin, and that waging unwavering war with biology, like all other wars, has some extremely high costs. They have found their own ways out of the body war, ways that are self-invented, highly creative, and quite diverse.

JUMPING OFF THE DIETING BANDWAGON

It's hard to say when it all started, who was the first woman to realize there's more to life than thin thighs. But gradually, over the past several years, women have begun quietly climbing off the dieting bandwagon, each woman in her own way, some pushed by the frustration of going around in diet-regain cycles, some actively groping for some other hook on which to hang their self-esteem. A woman here, a woman there, in the absence of an organized movement it's easy to miss what is truly a grass-roots phenomenon. But taken together, their efforts have the power to literally reshape America.

For Jane, life's possibilities unveiled themselves as soon as she realized "It's okay to be 200 pounds." Immediately she began to dress well. Immediately people began to take her seriously. And she signed on for what she always wanted to do—learn aerobic dancing. Today a muscular 175-pound beauty, Jane teaches aerobics in Los Angeles, body capital of the Western world, where she numbers some world-class bodies among her students. They like her classes because the atmosphere is cooperative and nurturing; she focuses not on the way women look, but on how they feel about themselves. Thus she avoids the body fixation that makes so many health clubs and exercise classes unpleasant arenas of competitive thinness.

Looking back at the life she was postponing, she now says, "I didn't have a weight problem, I had an image problem."

AMBUSH AT THE MIND/BODY JUNCTION

It wasn't her weight that prompted her to put her life on hold, it was her feelings about her body. Every woman—every person—has an image of herself that is part scheme or representation of the body, part attitudes toward it, part beliefs, and part feelings about it. Body image—the ultimate mind/body junction—reflects how we perceive our bodies and how we believe others perceive them. It begins developing early in life, is strongly influenced by parental attitudes and cultural attitudes, and is subject to revision throughout life. Body image, says Marcia Germain Hutchison, Ed.D., a pioneer in body image therapy, in *Transforming Body Image,* "is the way *you* see and experience your body, not necessarily the way the world sees it—although how others experience your body can be very strongly influenced by the verbal and nonverbal messages you communicate about and through your body."

In healthy people, body image has surprisingly little to do with how they look or how much they weigh; it is more their feelings about themselves, their attitude toward their body. Studies of body image show no necessary correlation between body size and how women feel about their bodies—nor any correlation with objective ratings of attractiveness. There are women who see themselves as attractive, whether or not they are on some objective scale. In fact, how we feel about ourselves, and projecting that feeling, is probably the strongest signal others use in forming an impression of us. Feeling attractive, then, is being seen as attractive.

Because the body is our base of operations in this world, body image is an important force in behavior—some psychologists would say *the* major influence on how we react to life situations. It guides, for example, our closeness to others, how vulnerable we feel to illness, how we cover, or uncover, our bodies with clothes, whether we use them to enhance us or to hide us. It influences whether we will participate in social activities and, too often, what we talk about. It often determines whether we will participate in physical activities of any kind. Ponder this contradiction: A negative body image keeps women from moving freely and frequently, although free movement is probably the best medicine for a body image under siege.

A negative body image is probably the most powerful inhibitor of behavior that has ever existed. It's constricting in other ways as well. It creates self-consciousness and self-preoccupation, which is not only the archenemy of style but the enemy of everything, and everyone, else. Says Kenneth Vaux, theologian and professor of ethics at the University of Illinois, narcissism destroys true personhood, which is conviviality. It distracts us "from our true self, which is being for others, into our solitary self."

BODY LANGUAGE

Body image, says Ann Kearney-Cooke, Ph.D., a Cincinnati psychologist who is a leading therapist in the field, "is much more complicated than simply being unhappy with hips that might be a little too round. Because women are taught that what they'll become in life is contingent on what their bodies look like, they've developed a code language for everything that happens to them. For example, a woman might say, 'I don't have relationships because my hips are too big,' instead of 'I don't have a relationship because I'm afraid of being too intimate.'"

At a very tender age—as early as age three, some researchers say—every person soaks up the cultural biases that decree which bodies are good and which are not. All one has to do is open a magazine, turn on the television, or go to the movies to find out which body size or body shape is acceptable for women. These views clearly affect our appraisal of our own bodies. Self-esteem is so intimately linked to body satisfaction that the search for body approval can be and is a powerful motivator of behavior and a powerful incentive to conform to the ideal. For some people no cost is too high to pay for conformance to society's ideal.

Trouble is, the need for approval from others is a form of dependence on them, a surrender of body ownership, at least in part. What's more, the idea that an admirable body is essential for participation in life at all, and the major eligibility requirement for its rewards, can be such an assault on self-esteem it ultimately leads women into what psychologists call "magical thinking." They believe that transforming the body, such as by dieting, will improve the inner self and solve their life problems. That's because having the perfect body in shape and size has come to carry so much symbolic weight. And yet, changing one's looks, even by such a radical method as surgery, does not necessarily improve self-esteem.

Slimness has come to mean feminine beauty and moral achievement—and who wouldn't kill for both. "I gained five pounds, I hate myself" is a common expression of how, for many women, one aspect of life—weight—symbolizes the whole. How women feel about themselves, their mood on any given day, is tied to only one item of all the things they are and do—what the scale said this morning. What is widely pictured in the media as the ideal female body is realistic only for a few. The rest are doomed to fight a losing battle with biology, with attendant feelings of self-dissatisfaction, no matter how undeserved.

And that, Jeanie Person and many others have finally decided, is no way to live. As any number of women can attest, nothing inhibits experience more thoroughly than feeling too fat. One highly successful forty-something woman told me that, although she speaks to her parents weekly (they live in Boston, she in New York), she hasn't visited them in ten years because she always feels too fat—and fears they would agree.

Getting to love—or at least peacefully coexist with—the body one has isn't easy in today's cultural climate. But it is possible. It is a process of growth and change that requires knowing where ideology bumps up against physiology, rejecting false beliefs about body size and shape, no matter how widely held. It means rethinking personal attitudes toward the body, and understanding their source. It means recognizing the errors in thinking about our selves and bodies that we are inclined to make. It means discounting the distortions that seem to be universal human responses to seeing our own reflections. It means understanding the cultural relativity of body ideals. And it means finding ways to know one's body and experience it positively. It means, ultimately, standing on one's own individuality, on the very same spot as style.

First and foremost is the recognition that women's bodies are designed to be fatter than men's; it is a form of survival insurance for the unborn that arose during evolution, when food wasn't as regularly abundant as it is today. So purposefully does nature pad women's hips and thighs that this fat resists diet and exercise. Its loss, by starvation, as in anorexia, generally renders a woman infertile.

It is also necessary to put the cultural pressure in its place, to recognize that the current ideal of thinness is so stringent that few women escape feeling like failures. "It is almost axiomatic that being a woman today means feeling too fat," reports Judith Rodin, Ph.D., professor of medicine and psychiatry at Yale, a leading researcher on body image. Rodin and other thinkers see the ideal as shaped by the economic, agricultural, political, and even sexual values of this moment in history, many of them contradictory, particularly concerning sexual equality.

What's more, women need to reevaluate what they think men like. Study after study shows that men actually prefer fleshier women than women think men like, and that they prefer women fleshier than the ideal.

REFRAMING OURSELVES

Then too, a woman must learn to develop respect for what the body is and what it can do—and not hate it for what it isn't. It means reframing one's point of view. It leaves you less of a critic about yourself—a trap women fall into in trying to bridge the gap between self and ideal. A focus on shortcomings and blindness to strengths is one of the particularly high costs of the body wars.

In every sphere of our lives, we need to reframe our experience—not to change it in any way, but to look at it differently. We need to focus on what we can do, not on what we can't do.

We need to create a personal résumé, in which we see all the things we are and, like a professional résumé, leave out, for the time being, what we are not. A woman who puts together a job résumé doesn't declare on it she cannot operate a computer. She states what she has done, can do. We need to practice declaring ourselves to ourselves, so that we may learn more about ourselves.

Unquestionably, a healthy body image takes in the whole person. There is more to the self than hips or weight; there must be more to self-esteem. Shifting focus from real or imagined shortcomings to real strengths and life accomplishments—personal, intellectual, family, professional, the many roles women fill today—can provide refreshing perspective and multiple sources of pride. There are other ways to succeed in life than by dieting. In fact, there are attractive, successful people who are not thin—only they are rarely seen in articles or advertising.

This is not an exercise in silliness. Make a résumé, an inventory of everything you are proud of, past and present, every accomplishment. Don't overlook kind acts and tiny triumphs. Also inventory everything that you like about your self, your personality, your mind, your soul.

Lastly, list everything you like about your body and your looks. Voluptuous softness. Sensational smile. Great legs. Beautiful if big curves.

Sumptuous cleavage. Translucent skin. General vibrancy. You are surrounded by stimuli that force you to focus on yourself, and to dwell on, even imagine, shortcomings; it is an untenable position for mental health. An inventory, a resource list of real accomplishments and real facts can be called on at times of threat to self-esteem. It not only bolsters self-esteem, it keeps you anchored to reality, to now, not forced to invent some fantasy of a future in which you float through life as a wisp of a women perfect in all ways.

SLOW MOTION

Make no mistake: It is as important as ever to be healthy and fit. But the early zealotry of the fitness movement confused some facts. In sum, fitness is not the same as slimness. Eating healthful foods, being active, and relieving tension are health measures for people of every shape.

Just about every woman who whips up the courage to get past thigh anxiety has discovered that a major route to body acceptance is through body awareness. And movement is an integral part of the process; experience with the body in action is the primary way people acquire body knowledge. Whether free-form movement, as Jeanie found, or belly dancing or aerobic exercise or hiking, activity provides a means of experiencing the body in space and exploring its capabilities, essential elements in building self-confidence and a positive body image.

While these depths are largely uncharted by psychologists, women who have reshaped their own body image report that activity is especially valuable in giving them a sense that they control their own actions. This is a vital antidote to years of having actions controlled by outside forces—the feeling that those with less than perfect bodies have no right to exist and must hide them. In addition, movement generates a sense of freedom and joy. The pleasant experience of the body that comes from activity, as well as the strength and skill built by it, are crucial for turning a negative body image into a positive one, women say. Jeanie particularly relishes the grace that "comes from owning your own body."

Activity is valuable for other reasons as well. It breeds awareness of body sensations. This kinesthetic awareness fosters a certain amount of sensitivity to variations in the body's performance, something elite athletes in fact learn to rely on. The monitoring of body sensations is one of the ways by which body image is created, and the accuracy in monitoring of body sensations that activity develops may contribute to a more realistic body image. Indeed, of the many things that are wrong with dieting, one of the most significant is that dieting itself interferes with the development and functioning of an integrated body image, perhaps by overriding a person's ability to accurately monitor hunger, certainly one of the most basic of body sensations.

Many women, unfortunately, have been raised to believe that activity is not a "feminine" endeavor. If the health movement hasn't convinced them otherwise, perhaps concern for a better body image will. Alternatively, there are those who believe that activity has to be competitive, sports-oriented, win-lose. But good activity is not the health-club norm of activity—competitive, repetitive, and punitive to those who can't or don't wish to keep up. All activity is good, and any activity is better than none. Aerobic activity comes in many forms; there has never been any proof that gym workouts are better than any other kind.

On the contrary, there's much to be said for such simple unstructured activities as walking, especially in the outdoors. It's not an all or nothing situation; even a little bit is beneficial. It boosts fitness. It is a mood-lifter. There's the added pleasure of enjoying nature—it sure smells sweeter than a locker room. It is freeing to experience the body in space. There is no one determining your pace or your movements except you—you are in control of yourself. You are free to experience and enjoy yourself; no one is scrutinizing you or judging you. There is no wrong way to do it. There is no chance of boredom from repetition of movements. That is, it is an opportunity to experience the body as an instrument of pleasure and to walk away with a new sense of body competence. Further, exercising at a moderate pace such as in walking burns more fat than exercising at a more rigorous pace. And it's less punishing to your joints.

The New Age movement has spawned its own assortment of alternatives to the health-club-type workout. The Feldenkrais Method, for example, is a system of slow, gentle movements that are specifically designed to create body ease and body awareness in a positive, even playful, way. Those who teach it say it is a way of learning about the body that is self-directed, driven only by curiosity about oneself, not willpower or compulsion. Many women praise it highly not just for giving them added flexibility but for making them feel at home in their bodies for the first time in their lives. Classes in Feldenkrais tend to be staple offerings at the many "alternative" centers that now exist around the country, places far more laid-back than the garden-variety go-go health club.

Body awareness goes beyond activity. Most relaxation techniques cultivate body awareness, and defuse tension, too. Massage is another pleasurable way of experiencing the body and its contours. Touch is a way of enjoying the body that you can provide yourself. Get out some body lotion and massage it on your body. Independent of all other effects, it has a calming effect that will help you find and focus on the beauty of your own body.

RESTRAINED EATING, RESTRAINED LIVING

To get a healthy body image, giving up dieting is essential. Over the past century, dieting has become the oral accompaniment to the visual shift in body image ideal. Equally unnatural, dieting has become today's ideal eating pattern. Implicit in it, as in worship of an emaciated ideal of woman, is a rejection of self. Locked together in dog-chases-tail circularity, dieting and body image distortion are the twin offspring of conflicting cultural expectations of women and obsession with appearance. Both are physiologically implausible. And self-destructive. Trying to meet a literally impossible ideal of thinness keeps women trapped in a cycle of diet/loss of self-esteem/body shame/diet/loss of self-esteem. . . .

"The pressures to diet that made anorexia nervosa the disorder of the 1970s made bulimia the disorder of the 1980s," says Janet Polivy, Ph.D., a leading researcher on dieting, or restrained eating, and body image. What people fail to see, she says, is that dieting is the *cause* of bulimia. The deprivation involved in dieting begets bingeing. Her analysis shows that dieting, which always precedes bulimia, doesn't work because it puts hunger and satiety under the control of intellectual faculties, rather than physiologic mechanisms, which normally regulate these body sensations automatically. Eating is thus easily thrown into chaos by anything that breaks one's concentration. Say stress. Or emotions. Feeling deprived. Or overindulging in something—anything.

Polivy believes that people with low self-esteem who diet—usually in an attempt to raise self-esteem—often wind up worse than if they had not tried to improve themselves at all. Dieting lays the foundation by rendering the normal controls on appetite inoperative. But in people with low self-esteem, her studies show, eating goes totally out of control (she calls it "disinhibited") in response to anxiety or depression—to say nothing of alcohol or a forbidden snack. The out-of-control eating further lowers self-esteem, only making the dieter more susceptible to out-of-control eating in the future, in a self-perpetuating spiral. In this way, the deprivation of dieting begets bingeing. Polivy's studies suggest that low self-esteem sets up low expectations for success at dieting, and dieters with low self-esteem may expend less effort in resisting challenges to their diets.

According to Thomas Cash, Ph.D., professor of psychology at Old Dominion University in Virginia and a researcher on body image, people who diet do so "not to lessen the health risks but to shed a negative body image." However, he points out that "there are more direct and effective ways to change body image, notably through psychological change."

Gradually, the view is emerging that dieting itself is a pathological behavior, a body contradiction, a set of impossibilities constraining women—yesterday's hysteria played out on today's field of weight restriction. By itself, dieting damages body image and self-esteem. Probably because it rides roughshod over such basic body signals as hunger and satiety, dieting throws off our ability to evaluate our bodies at all.

Dieting is, too, a paradigm for failure, since it is a case of fallacies conflicting with physiology. Dieting doesn't work because it engages the body's powerful defensive maneuvers to maintain energy balance. Dieting immediately kicks off metabolic defenses to counteract reduced food intake, which the body perceives as a threat. Going off a diet, or just finishing a diet, means regaining weight more easily than before and more of it as fat, making dieting worse than staying the same size. Dieting thus sets women up to fail, which further strips them of self-esteem. It also leads women to postpone their life; some never get to live it at all—they're always on the sidelines warming up with a diet.

"People believe dieting will change their lives in innumerable ways—get them better jobs, more boyfriends, more friends," says Polivy. "But losing weight is not the best way to get a good job. Dieting is an excuse for everything that's wrong in someone's life." Most people don't have reasonable goals.

ORIGIN OF THE SPECIOUS

In her therapy program, Kearney-Cooke teaches women to reconstruct their body-image histories to find out why they feel so negatively about their bodies. These are the stories of everything that's happened to them in their life that has contributed to forming their body image. With a stream of questions, she prods women to go back as far as they can remember to their earliest childhood memories concerning the body: What did your parents expect you to be in terms of sex and looks? Did they want a boy? How has your mother's own body image influenced your perception of yourself as a woman? Did she hate her thighs or stomach? Did she want you to be small and demure? How did your father react to your body? Only by understanding where the feelings come from can women get a grip on changing them.

Because experience with the body in action is the primary way we acquire body knowledge, early experiences with activity are important in the formation of body attitudes. But not every girl is provided with the opportunity to develop awareness of her body and its functions in space. A woman who, because of illness or parental views about femininity, was admonished as a child not to be active is thus at risk for having a poorly developed body image as an adult. Similarly, children whose parents don't readily grant them control over their own body domain may acquire an overall negative body image.

In the first five years of life, says Seymour Fisher, Ph.D., perhaps the world's most indefatigable chronicler of body image, children become aware of their mirror image as a unique representation of self. They learn there is a unique and definite space the self occupies, and by dividing their body space into categories—front-back, right-left—they perceive and organize the space around them. In this way, body image becomes the framework for structuring the world around us.

By age seven, children can quite realistically estimate body size. Interestingly, Fisher finds, while females grow up more body-aware than males, they do feel more body security in one sense—they see body boundaries, the dividing line between self and nonself, with more definition. That, he says, makes them less defensive than males about their bodies—and may explain their readiness to voice dissatisfaction with their bodies. Cultural pressures on women to be outwardly attractive magnify their inclination to voice dissatisfaction.

MIND OVER MATTER

Because body image is part cognitive schema, healing body image involves repairing basic thought processes. The premise is that we constantly make errors in thinking that consistently lead to negative evaluations of body and self, and we can be trained to catch those errors. This way of bolstering body image is the outgrowth of a novel approach to depression pioneered by Aaron T. Beck, M.D., a professor of psychiatry at the University of Pennsylvania. About twenty-five years ago Beck made the then-revolutionary discovery that depression is not just a disorder of mood but a disorder of logical thought whereby people overinterpret situations and draw negative conclusions about themselves, their future, the world. What made Beck's cognitive theory so radical is that it departed from the psychoanalytic thinking then in vogue; he proposed that this illogic—not experiences buried in the unconscious and manifest in dreams—is the cause of the dysphoric mood.

In his studies, Beck noted that depressed persons expect to fail, feel deprived, and magnify trivial losses. Invariably, he found, it's a case of selective abstraction. And so he devised cognitive psychotherapy, a form of brief treatment in which he helps people find the fallacies in their thinking, actually test their negative hypotheses about themselves, and review their successes as well as their failures. He engages people in a demonstration of success, and leads them to find rational counterarguments and other strategies for dealing with life's inevitable bumps.

The same strategies that Beck devised for dysphoria others have applied to problems of self-esteem, on the grounds that the cause of a negative self-image is not, for example, looking in the mirror per se but the spin we give to what we see. What's more, no matter the cause of a depression, depression always seems to bring with it body devaluation and general negative views of oneself.

Psychologists contend that cognitive errors trap women in self-criticism and self-rejection. These errors are responsible for making us think others are highly focused on our looks when in fact they are not; for leading us to make constant—read "negative"—comparisons with others; for labeling ourselves as failures; for leading us to think, on the days we feel bad, that everyone else feels the same way about us; for magnifying the importance of small events, as in "The zipper on my skirt won't close; I can't be seen in public." In fact, cognitive errors are so common that we don't even notice when we make them. That's because they trigger irrational thoughts automatically and rest on silent assumptions that are misconceptions about love, approval, and the like.

The way to keep our thoughts from hijacking our bodies is to meet the irrational thinking head-on with specific rational counterarguments. That means when you join a group of people and they're talking about diets, you don't automatically think "They're talking about diets because I must have gained weight," which results from the cognitive error of personalizing, or interpreting events personally, and leads to constant weight comparison with others. The more rational conclusion is that people are always talking about diets. Other kinds of cognitive error include:

- Extreme thinking, splitting things into all-or-nothing categories. "Everyone's looking at me; it must be because I look fat." The more rational conclusion is that just because one or two people look at you doesn't mean everyone is gaping at you; and you really don't know what they are thinking about.
- Rejecting positives, in which you dismiss the evidence that things are fine, as in "My assistant just told me how nice I look, but that's because she wants a favor from me."
- Jumping to conclusions, whereby one small fact serves as absolute proof of a catastrophe, as in "I feel too fat, no one wants to be seen with me, so I'll just cancel the date." The more rational approach is you are great-looking and a delight to be with.
- Emotional reasoning, in which you explain public events by your private feelings. This common error leads you to think everyone sees you as "ugly" on a day when you feel "ugly." The rational approach is to admit that everyone feels better some days than others, and other people don't notice.

VISIONS OF LOVELINESS

The healthy and happy approach to one's self—and thus to life and to style—is to build an image that conforms in significant ways not to ideal standards but to reality. It takes a certain knowledge of oneself, and a periodic renewal of that knowledge, a certain familiarity with one's body, and a certain amount of courage. A realistic appraisal of one's physical characteristics is a sine qua non for knowing how to present oneself with style, which characteristics to emphasize and highlight, which to balance.

Body acceptance therefore requires visual education by way of a mirror.

You can't like yourself until you know what you look like. But be forewarned: Mirrors are not benign objects.

In transacting the image feedback, they introduce a distortion of their own—a strong negative influence on self-appraisal. Mirrors invariably make people self-conscious and self-critical. Studies show that they raise anxiety levels in everyone (as does hearing oneself on a tape recording the first time) because they magnify self-awareness. The anxiety aroused by such attentiveness to our bodies seems to warp our ability to accurately monitor them. And making us objects to ourselves seems to arouse shame over the inadequacies we thus detect.

Perhaps "the most important consequence of magnifying self-awareness through a mirror experience," Seymour Fisher contends, "is increased conformity to the prevailing standard. People who are confronted with their mirror images seem to become sensitized to whether they are deviating from the salient values or rules. They become critical of their possible deviations from the standard. Numerous studies have documented the increased conformance and moralism brought on by intensified self-awareness."

Although self-confrontation in the mirror often intensifies self-criticism, it can also lead to greater realism. Body acceptance enables a woman to view her reflection less critically, less anxiously. A woman needs to know what her body looks like unclothed, so she can clothe it to advantage. She also needs to be able to look herself in the mirror and know she has thick thighs—without jumping to the erroneous conclusion that therefore her whole body is awful or she is an unworthy human being. To do this she has to focus on the landmarks of body geography that please her most. Many women look in the mirror and see only the parts they hate.

Turning an objective eye upon one's body can be an alarming task. As motivation, you need to know it will ultimately help you see yourself more positively. So spend time in front of a full-length mirror, alone, unhurried, scanning your body to get information about yourself. Choose a time when there will be no demands on you. It would be wise to create a gentle mood by playing music you like, turning off the telephone, and seeing that the room is lit softly but well by natural light.

Slowly scan your body. Ask yourself what you are feeling as you scan each part. For every negative—ankles too thick, neck too short—counter with a positive—beautiful hands, fabulous skin.

Focus on a part of your body you like because you think it's attractive—

full breasts; sensuous, if generous, curves; graceful ankles; well-shaped legs; sun-burst smile. Indulge your admiration. And allow yourself to think of beautiful words to describe that feature, while you are looking at it.

Once desensitized to the mirror's sting, you can use mirror-looking to actually take you beyond outer physical traits to discovery and expression of the whole person. In fact, psychologists are finding that in most women today, there is another one struggling to get out; women are aching to have their bodies express other qualities that make up their "true selves"— warmth, openness, kindness.

Finding the expressiveness of the body can be done as a mirror exercise in which you create ways of moving to match these inner feeling states. Standing unclothed, or clad in underwear, in front of a full-length mirror, concentrate on feeling one state you would like to express. Experiment by moving your arms until you find a move or sequence of moves you feel expresses that state. Then try adding postural stances, and eventually whole body moves that suggest that feeling. After some practice in front of the mirror, you can re-create these movements away from the mirror. When you feel you can evoke one feeling with movement, try finding movements to match another feeling state.

Mirrors are essential for getting information about appearance. But because they have so much potential for threatening self-esteem, body-image experts often counsel women to cut down on overall mirror exposure. So use the mirror as sparingly as possible, for necessary check-ups only, not search-and-destroy missions for flaws. Cut down on the number of times you look at yourself in the mirror. Shorten the length of time you spend at the mirror during each exposure. And eliminate some mirrors altogether.

WORDS OF WORTH

Just as controlling mirror exposure is a way of restoring balance to visual situations that negatively influence body image and self-esteem, there are simple ways to mitigate verbal situations that foster self-criticism. Avoid, for example, conversations about bodies and weight with women who feel that an extra five or ten pounds is a major tragedy; the world would be a better place without such talk.

Don't get involved in extended conversations with women who are obsessed by their weight; find something else to do for the duration. These women have a rapidly spreading body-image virus. The degree of insecurity they experience with their own bodies contaminates their perception of the bodies of others; they find defects you never knew you had. Spend more time with friends who have other interests.

In his studies, Dr. Thomas Cash has found that the women who most consistently overestimate their own body width, and the body width of others, are women who are in actuality underweight. "Perhaps," he explains, "women who have internalized the thin societal standard of feminine attractiveness are apt to believe that they appear bigger than average and appraise others in a similar light, and have negative feelings about their own failure to meet the standard."

Words count in other ways, says Cincinnati's Kearney-Cooke, who finds that the code language women use for their bodies is far too limited. "We need to re-examine our bodies and develop a richer vocabulary for them. To consider our imperfections as eccentricities instead of ugly drawbacks helps each of us appreciate our uniqueness. And when you're unique, how can you be anything less than a '10'?"

THE INDIVISIBLE INDIVIDUAL

Ultimately, getting past thigh anxiety means depending on oneself for approval, not some outside source, particularly not the prevailing cultural attitude toward body perfection. Many women find it difficult to challenge convention in any way—even though, ironically, the self-assurance that doing so implies tends to command the admiration of others. Indeed, self-acceptance, the affirmation of one's individuality, is a developmental achievement that is a hallmark of the healthy personality.

DELIVERANCE DILEMMA

Still, accepting oneself in this way puts a woman at subtle odds with the culture. Western culture in general, and America's in particular, puts its faith in perpetual progress. Self-improvement has nearly the status of a moral obligation. But high self-esteem, which permits a person to think she's okay as she is, suggests no compelling need to improve. Jane has come to terms with the dilemma in her own private way. "I've learned to accept myself without becoming complacent about myself," she says.

WOMAN TO WOMAN

For every woman who is salvaging self-esteem and climbing out of the body trap, there are probably several more who want to, but can't do it on their own. Nancy Barron, Ph.D., a psychologist whose Portland (Oregon) State University course in body image is increasingly popular, says that part of their problem is that body image solidifies in the preteen years—a time the body is at its plumpest. It is also a phase of development so touchy for most women, with hurts, rejections, and body uncertainties that reverberate for decades, that women frequently remain emotionally raw about that period throughout their adult years. Indeed, body image researchers find that adolescence, with its radical body transformations, is a time of heightened feelings of body vulnerability. With body feelings too painful to face, if even to reject, such women continually promise to be "good" by trying . . . one more diet.

What they need instead, Barron has found, is the help of other women. She would like to see women around the country develop support groups focused on body image. Individuals would not only learn they are not alone, their private revelations would be turned into public strengths. This would give even more women the necessary courage to make permanent peace with their bodies—and get on with their lives.

Do You Need an Image Consultant?

There's a whole new breed of people out there who are not only willing but eager to help you appear perfect. For a fee, of course. They call themselves image consultants. Do you need one? Could one help you? Are they worth it?

What image consultants do and how they do it is whatever and however they want. There's no standard job description for "image consultant." Some image consultants basically "do" color analysis (beware!). Some are wardrobe analysts, who try to get a more perfect fit between you, your life-style, and your clothes. Some are personal shoppers who are well versed in what to find in which store or from which manufacturer (they often get a "cut" from manufacturers for bringing clients by). Some are more like public speaking coaches—verbal communications consultants is the term they prefer. Some specialize in etiquette, which, they say, mothers are too busy to teach these days. And some—like political advisor Roger Ailes—defy description by being all these and much more, not only well versed in all the nuances of appearance before various kinds of audiences but also with the means to mold public perception of their clients, with or without regard to substance. None of them knows you like you know yourself, although some very few are shrewd observers of people and can help you see yourself more objectively, and thus help you express yourself well in clothing.

There is no course of training that image consultants undergo. Not only does "image consulting" mean different things to different image consultants, there is no specific set of skills that is called on. One image consultant may be a great stylist, with a perfect eye for assessing you and dressing you the way you've always wanted to be, helping you realize your own inner style. Another image consultant, perhaps a one-time soldier in a corporate culture, may be more interested in giving you a generic brand of polish suitable for standard business purposes.

If you need help presenting yourself for public speaking, you may want to make use of a coach if you feel at all unsure of yourself. A coach, who may or may not use the designation "image consultant," will work with you visually and verbally so that you feel at ease. The approach is problem-oriented and the investment is frequently worth it. But it can't solve all problems. Once, because of an interesting article I had written about subtle dangers of cosmetics, I was to be a featured interviewee on a major national TV-magazine show. I was unusually nervous about the prospect and enlisted the aid of one such consultant. But no matter how hard we worked, the advice never calmed my nervousness. At heart, I knew it had real outside cause—my article. It implied what was impolitic for me to say. Despite an understanding beforehand about what the discussion could comfortably cover, the TV host wound up pressing me to say what I couldn't say. The segment, needless to say, was a disaster, and it never aired.

If an image consultant urges you to "have your colors done," resist the impulse and go buy a colorful scarf instead. Color is a great spirit lifter. But there is absolutely nothing a color consultant can tell you that you couldn't get from trying swatches of color against your face. And do remember that what looks like a great lift around the face might not look so great covering your whole body, either in any one style or in some particular styles. There is absolutely no scientific basis for sorting people into color "seasons." If you are aware of the "training" many color consultants get, perhaps you'd trust your own judgment on the matter more.

Sure, some colors look better than others for different complexions, but there's more to color use than that. What looks good on your whole body is different from what looks good on your face. Much depends on the style of a garment, and where it will be worn. Large expanses of color are sometimes, well, expansive. Do you look better in colors combined with high contrast value—many full-figured women do—or in softer colors? Can you or anyone else reduce your ability to work with color to a formula? Not all blocks of even the same color have the same "weight" on a perfect body, let alone a body whose proportions need thoughtful visual balancing. Nor should color be the only determinant of what you wear; line and drape are more important almost any day. Besides, there are many ways to express the excitement of personality through color in a wardrobe—for example, with tops under sober suits, blouses, shawls, scarves, and other accessories.

The color-everything-beautiful movement has, on the whole, had a positive effect despite its debatable foundation. Like the "dress for effect" movement before it, it has helped make women aware that how they dress has an impact on their own and others' attitude toward them. It has helped many women become more open-minded about fashion in general. Because it is so common and accessible, color has been a good first step in starting women to think about style and self-presentation. It certainly isn't the only, or even most important, step, although, because it is so visible, it may be the step most observers comment about.

If what you really want is someone who can immediately understand and remedy what you mean when you say you never feel pulled together, or when you fling open a crammed-closet door and insist you haven't a thing to wear, then what you want is a wardrobe consultant, who may or may not call herself an image consultant. There are a handful of good ones—like New York's Emily Cho, who single-handedly invented the calling, and Annie Brumbaugh—among others.

The best of them will look at the total you, assess your hair and makeup style as well as your clothing concerns. They will want to know how you see yourself, what your professional and social needs are, your life-style requirements, your available time for getting dressed and taking care of yourself. They will go through everything in your closet with you, to see what doesn't work and why, what could work with the right accessories, or a different hemline, a slight taper, or shoulder pads, and so on. Don't worry—they also know that sometimes we all have to walk the dog.

What the good ones are really good at is listening to what you say—and hearing what you don't say. They don't just take you at face value. Often the most buttoned-up clothes types are expressing a desire to be freer in clothes, to develop a more open style, to appear less conservative, more dynamic. Lisa Cunningham, a wardrobe consultant in New York City, says, "There's always a subtext to what clients tell me. I have to listen between the lines. Often they are looking for permission to dress more expressively. They want to know that it's okay to do it. My job is to ferret out how comfortable they really are about it."

But even the best of them are limited by the large-size offerings in your area. Manhattan, New York City's chicest borough, is crammed with thousands of great stores, but has fewer than a dozen offering quality large sizes. You probably know more about what's available in your size than the best image consultants do. Further, because their experience with larger women is limited, some may still subscribe to general rules—often outdated myths—about what large-size women can/can't or should/shouldn't wear. These are the same myths you're trying to break free of.

If you grow faint at just the idea of shopping and you need clothes—who doesn't need to get dressed?—a top-notch wardrobe consultant could be the best investment you'll ever make. She'll run around to stores to preselect items that meet your needs in your size—and have the goodies waiting for you when you get there to try them on. Because of her extensive knowledge of what is in the market, she may well know of other stores, besides the large-size ones, that have clothes that would work on your body. And she will know which things from here and there work together. She may know which shirts at the Gap will fit you perfectly. She may decide that what you need most is a simple "little" dress that doesn't exist in your size—but knows the right dressmaker to run it up for you, in gossamer navy wool crepe for spring and jade cotton gabardine for summer. You can get a great deal of expertise wrapped up in one day of well-directed dashing about town. And the effects will be lasting. The experience can permanently open you up to new ways of looking at and finding clothes that work.

There are image consultants who specialize in dealing with large-size women. Think twice about the idea. At the very least, you want someone whose general expertise has made her aware of all garments that would work, regardless of size range or label. I own many items—including a Karl Lagerfeld dress, two timeless Geoffrey Beene dresses, some Anne Klein II tops, a Calvin Klein coat, several cotton resort-style dresses, and more—all of which came from regular-size stores. I doubt the image consultants who specialize in large sizes get around to enough places to have known about these items, all of which fit perfectly.

In the long run, provided you are not store-phobic, if you give yourself enough time to look at yourself, to go into stores, to try on new styles and colors of clothes, you can do just as well on your own.

A Few Wonderful Things to Do to Remind Yourself What a Sensuous Creature You Are Even When You Don't Feel Wonderful

1. Give your feet a massage. After all, they work hard for you. Maybe this is the real secret of Frenchwomen. They keep their fingernails short and lightly polished but regularly go in for pedicures. There is nothing like a pedicure, even a home-style one, to make you feel more beautiful all over, certainly sexier.

First, soak your feet, or totally immerse them during a bath or shower. With a pumice stone, gently rub the skin at the outer edge of the heels and along the whole bottom surface of the foot and toes.

Run your toes and feet under the water spout at full throttle and wiggle your toes around. You might want to start with warm water and work up to cold water.

With a well-soaped nail brush or even bath brush, scrub the top and bottom surface of your toes, and rinse.

Immediately after you emerge from the water, trim your toenails and clean around them with an orange stick.

Then sit down on a bed, and before your feet are completely dry, massage in a richly emollient cream, making sure to work it into your heels and between and behind your toes. Gently knead each toe starting at the base and working outward, then back again.

When you finish, luxuriate a few moments with your feet elevated—put them up on the headboard or even prop them against the wall. Rest for five minutes before resuming your activities.

2. Always carry a fresh linen handkerchief, preferably one with a pretty lace border. It's a lot more chic than a wad of tissue stuffed into your pocketbook somewhere. Even blowing your nose becomes an act of elegance and a cold is a lot more endurable.

3. In warm weather, change your usual scent to one that makes you—and everyone else around you—feel cool, calm, and collected. In the heat of summer, that's what sexiness truly is. Many well-dressed women who scrap Chanel this or Fancy that for Jean Naté, fresh and lemony—and extremely inexpensive. If the after-bath splash is too drying for your skin, opt instead for the concentrated spray cologne. Do get a package of the scented moist towelettes and stash a few in your purse, your desk, and your glove compartment. Apply whenever you need refreshing—but don't throw away the used towelette. Fold it up and stuff it down the center of your bra. That's right, into the cleavage. And smile.

4. Save an everyday suit—and yourself—from boredom with a touch of well-placed whimsy. Invest in a good-size animal pin with loads of charm, perhaps a silver iguana, a marcasite frog. Nothing too elaborate or too serious, a little offbeat. Pin the critter of your choice climbing from your lapel to your shoulder. The unexpected touch will amuse everyone you meet face to face, and the enchantment will be returned to you.

6

*"It is only shallow people who
do not judge by appearance."*
OSCAR WILDE

The Power of
Good Grooming

*I*mpressions. We all have them. We all make them. They are the vivid evidence that we take in an enormous amount of information and expend a great deal of energy to sort the world and make sense of it, process the "data" our senses take in.

Impressions are socially useful. We quickly "size people up" so that we can respond to them appropriately. Impressions even have life-and-death value. We run from possible danger when we see people whose moves, in the absence of any other information about them, appear menacing. We use impressions in deciding, for example, whom to stop to ask for directions. Psychologists find that impressions tend to have a great deal of validity as well as value; they call the process of impression formation "social cognition," giving it an intellectual legitimacy the rest of us have been taught to distrust. Nevertheless, impressions are part of our ongoing information-gathering attempts to make sense of the noisy, moving, ever-changing world around us.

FROM SELF- TO SOCIAL ESTEEM

It is one of the extraordinary facts of social life that how we perceive ourselves influences how others perceive us; self-acceptance is the foundation for social acceptance. Self-confidence, however, is only one of many elements we use in perceiving people. We categorize people—man/woman, big/little, good/ bad, like/dislike—as a way of sorting information, so that we can reduce the strangeness and therefore the anxiety of new social encounters.

IT'S OUR CALL

Just as we make sense of other people, they are taking our measure. **But we are not innocent bystanders or hapless victims in the processes by which other people perceive us. We actually play the most important role in determining how others perceive us.** We make a presentation of ourselves and are perceived and evaluated by others every time we set forth into the world, into the office, into a room. Our movements, our gestures, our voices, our facial expressions, our attitude toward ourselves and the way we dress communicate our intentions, our emotional state, our character, our status, and many other qualities about us. And they often determine whether our goals will be accomplished—or whether we will be listened to at all. It is, of course, up to each of us whether we choose to recognize this fact and thus to be in command of the way we present ourselves.

The prospect of being judged in public life, of having one's self-concept put to the test, can stir a great amount of fear—and defensive actions. Those who feel they are in danger of being judged negatively are apt to engage a variety of defenses to maintain their self-concept in the face of social scrutiny. The most rational and liberating response—and the one this book is dedicated to—is to learn the ways of making a great presentation of self in any situation. Just because we've been presenting ourselves all our lives doesn't mean we all do it equally well or that our own knowledge about how to do it serves us best.

Some people respond to the prospect of being judged by associating only with those few people who already have bestowed their social approval. This is a sure way to constrict activity and range of friendship and experience. But the most self-destructive approach is to believe that none of this counts, to devalue the importance of presenting oneself well. In presenting ourselves knowingly and well, the world takes our measure—but on terms we dictate.

Not only do appearances count, they contain a great deal of information about our selves. Indeed, it is only the ignorant or unconscious who do not gather information from appearances.

Bettina Hawthorne* is a highly visible executive assistant on Capitol Hill. In this job, she is personal ambassador for one of the more outspoken senators when the senator is not personally available. She takes all calls and greets all visitors to the highly feisty lawmaker she serves. On any given day, she could be face to face with the commander of the armed forces, any number of other senators, scores of visiting dignitaries. Her appearance, therefore, is vitally important.

When I first met her, Hawthorne, a large-size woman in her early 40s, was wearing a simply cut suit—in bright turquoise. The colorful but tasteful suit is symbolic of the fact that Hawthorne is not only in command of herself, she uses her obvious self-confidence to put others at ease. She explains: "You make a statement with everything you put on. The only question is whether or not you choose to pay attention to the statement. The basic style of the clothes I wear communicates confidence. I use color and jewelry accents to let people know I am not so serious about myself that I can't laugh or have fun. By being who I am and by what I wear, I take people by surprise. They perhaps expect someone in black or navy blue. I, on the other hand, might be wearing black, but with royal blue hose and royal blue suede shoes." She does not believe that clothes make the woman, "but I do believe that the right clothes make a good woman even better."

ALL THE WORLD'S A STAGE

In the process of being understood in social situations, there are elements contributed by us, such as how we carry ourselves, how we groom ourselves. These are totally under our control, and we heed these elements or risk evaluation at the mercy of the wind, the moon, and the stars. The best way to view social encounters, according to one widely respected theory, is as a theatrical performance in which a person presents himself much the way an actor presents a character in a play.

"When an individual enters the presence of others," explains Erving Goffman, Ph.D., in his classic work, *The Presentation of Self in Everyday Life,* "they commonly seek to acquire information about him. . . . They will be interested in his general socioeconomic status, his conception of self, his

---

*Names have been changed to protect privacy.

attitude toward them, his competence, his trustworthiness, etc. . . . . Information about the individual helps define the situation, enabling others to know in advance what he will expect of them and what they may expect of him. . . . The others will [then] know how best to act. . . . If unacquainted with the individual, observers can glean clues from his conduct and appearance." This, said Goffman, is the "documentary evidence" we provide as to who and what we are. As actors, we attempt to guide the impressions others form of us.

The "audience" brings something to our "performances," too—their own prior experiences, their own views of life, their own prejudices, their own mental flexibility, their own social ease, their aspirations. These all influence how they see us. It would be foolish—to say nothing of futile—to try to gather enough information about others so as to know all the nuances of presenting ourselves acceptably to each social group that exists. What's more, we would deny ourselves the very thing that makes us of interest to others—our individuality; it would be subordinated to others' expectations and standards, and we would be robbed not only of self-esteem but of avenues to self-esteem.

Yet we can make the audience see us on our very own terms by how we present ourselves—and our self-confidence is the point on which the plot makes this critical turn. Self-confidence, as it happens, actually cues other people on how to regard us. By recognizing what the elements are that people use in "sizing people up," in making sense of other people, we can understand well how to make the best presentation of ourselves, a presentation that is in harmony with the way we see ourselves and that also pleases those we make contact with.

PRIME TIME

It's clear: Impressions count. What's more, first impressions count more than information we later take in; they have what psychologists call a "primacy effect." We form an immediate point of view, and that has staying power. It biases all the other information about the person that we then take in. We tend to gather further information selectively attuned to that point of view, looking for evidence consistent with that point of view, and incorporate it in such a way as to uphold that point of view. It takes a great deal of negative evidence to undo a good first impression—or an extraordinary amount of positive evidence to overcome a bad one.

Impressions start forming immediately, and coalesce, psychologists estimate, in as little as thirty seconds. There are a few dimensions of "people perception" that are instantaneous, or relatively automatic—we don't think about them, we just "know." One is what people look like, an assessment of their physical characteristics—a quick overall vision. Another is gender.

First impressions, then, are formed largely on the basis of outward appearances. This is because visual stimuli are the first we receive and are more powerful than all others. In our first impressions, we see a person as a total package. Further, we make an overall moral assessment as to whether the person is "good" or "bad," roughly translatable to likable or unlikable.

What signals do we all pay attention to in making sense of people? There are physical characteristics, such as body size and shape, gender, attractiveness, facial expressions, and clothing. There are personality elements, such as animation and energy level. And there is self-confidence. Clothing is obviously a way that unites perceived to perceiver, a way for them to identify with each other, which smooths social passage. Personality is clearly a way by which people link themselves to those around them. But self-confidence turns out to forge the strongest ties between "actor" and "audience," because it unites people in a way that makes everyone feel more comfortable, more able to enjoy themselves.

Self-Confidence

Think of self-confidence as the Krazy Glue of social life; it comes from within us but has a powerful positive effect on how others perceive us and relate to us. It works both directly and indirectly.

First, it operates directly by defining and establishing the way that others should feel about and treat you. Second, because self-image is built upon the reflections of others, self-confidence suggests to the world that you have spent your whole life basking in the approval of others. It implies a history of success, of high status. It cues people to fall into line with their approval of you.

Our self-confidence has its own halo effect. It generates acceptance in social situations. And self-confidence invites the confidence of others; it gives others a precedent, a reason to judge our abilities and other attributes in a favorable way. They like us, they extend this positive judgment to our other abilities and characteristics.

Above all, self-confidence, by gently directing people how to feel about you, makes others comfortable in new circumstances. New situations, including meeting new people, generate some anxiety in everyone—this is the way our species seems to be built. We differ greatly in how much anxiety we bring to social situations, based on our individual experience, personal history and upbringing, to say nothing of the timbre of the nervous system we start out with. But self-confidence begets social acceptance by revealing to others how you are to be regarded, which relieves them of their own uncertainty about you. Unburdened of their social anxiety, they are better able to enjoy themselves. People like—and like to be around—people who make them more themselves.

Clothing

Clothes are the visual part of the self, the self made visible. We use clothes to complete ourselves, to discover ourselves, to construct ourselves, to communicate ourselves. Our wardrobe is our vocabulary. Style is our distinctive pattern of speech, our individual poetry.

"Clothes are separated from all other objects by being inseparable from the self," says Anne Hollander. "They give a visual aspect to consciousness itself. . . . They produce its look as seen from within." Getting dressed is more than putting clothes on. We invent ourselves through clothing. Like the society around us, each of us is constantly refining our ideas about what it is to be a person, a woman, a worker, a parent, a participant in a life that we change and that changes us as we go along. By careful selection of our clothes, we decide which features to call attention to and emphasize. We use clothes to enhance our self-image. Clothing thus provides other people with clues to our personality, and the clues tend to be fairly valid when they are seen as consistent with all the other clues about us. The strongest argument for style is that it projects our personality so clearly. That is why all the remaining chapters of this book are devoted to discussion and display of the elements of style.

This is one reason why clothes play an important part in helping us establish new social roles—the "coming out" dress, the wedding dress, for example. It helps us to assume the part if we "dress the part." We use clothing to proclaim mastery of the qualities and skills that are necessary for accomplishing tasks.

Body Size

In person perception, the basic body types seem to have some universal meaning and stir universal responses. The mesomorph is the typical athletic body with a hard muscular build. People rate it most highly, perhaps because of a historical association with success in the hunt for food. The ectomorph has a long, slender body shape; in American culture today, this shape has come to stand for femininity. The endomorph, with a round body contour and soft body tissue, is viewed least favorably.

It appears to be a fact of person perception that people focus their attention more on anyone who stands out for any reason, including size. Whatever they do may be observed more carefully than what anyone else does—and it will be negatively interpreted. In a room full of ectomorphs, an endomorph stands out.

But anatomy isn't destiny. It just makes more of a case for you to present yourself well each time out and let your confidence carry you.

Attractiveness

Beauty counts. Not only do people like good-looking people better than unattractive people, they attribute all kinds of other positive qualities to beautiful people. By this so-called halo effect, good-looking people are also judged to be more intelligent, more likable, more friendly, more morally worthy.

What, in the long run, is beauty? Within any cultural definition of beauty—and the definition varies from culture to culture—there is surprising general agreement on what is beautiful. There seems to be a set of standards we all recognize. But there doesn't seem to be complete agreement; we don't all find equally appealing all those generally agreed to be beautiful. Not all gentlemen prefer blondes. Further, researchers find that being of average good looks—that is, not being ugly—brings almost as many rewards as being beautiful.

And when they examine more closely just what is good looking, they find that the impression of how beautiful we are depends primarily on good grooming as well as on self-esteem and personality. Self-esteem and personality, in turn, are elements of style; style is the visible expression of personality cloaked in self-esteem. So in a world where individualism is of increasing importance, to be seen as stylish is to be seen as beautiful. The beauty of style is that it defines its own rules of attractiveness.

GROOMING If clothes are the self made visible, then grooming is self-esteem and self-confidence made visible. Grooming—the word choice is deliberate. Men groom. Women "fix themselves up"—as if there is damage to repair. Grooming is simply putting a glow on what we have, however "perfect" or "imperfect" it may be by some arbitrary standard. It is presenting yourself as if you alone defined the standard and made it a law unto itself—because that turns out to be the way it really happens.

HERE COMES THE GROOMING   This is the wave of the future; slowly, the definition of beauty seems to be growing more individualistic. Sure, the *New York Times* reported in 1989, there are still lots of women who choose to sacrifice themselves to the fantasy that they could be Cheryl Tiegs. But up and coming are the realists, those who, able to look reality in the eye, prefer instead to feel they're doing the most with what they have.

Good grooming, then, is based on a realistic assessment of features, knowing your good points and your weak features, putting emphasis on the strong ones, and balancing them all in an original way that makes sense for your features. It is this balancing of individualistic features that creates a harmonious whole, a vision that announces its own standard of what is attractive, one that can be far more interesting than simple beauty.

THE FEATURE STORY   Think of Paloma Picasso. Arch eyebrows. A nose that is far from demure. Vivid lips that naturally arrange themselves into an emphatic pout. Only a fool could call these imperfections when presented as boldly, as artfully, as carefully stage-managed as they are. Set against the backdrop of pale skin and the sleek and "clean" (unfussy) lines of her hairstyle, such features are so dramatic they rivet our attention. There is nothing to distract us from them, or to camouflage them. They do not appear accidental or second rate at all, but the result of firm intention. The unusual features are presented clearly and distinctively—the lips enhanced with bright red lipstick—balanced by strong eyebrows and dark hair. Their owner did not subdue their obvious difference from some arbitrary standard, and she has made them the focal point of her unique, and immediately identifiable, look.

This should serve as a model for an evolving view of beauty in which "imperfections" are turned into assets, in which features that do not fit the norm make the norm look vapid. Instead of trying to reduce them to average—applying lipstick to a portion of the lips in an effort to recontour them into some "average" shape—the wise woman plays them up and uses them as focal points. In other words, you establish your own face as uncommon—and using knowledge of balance and proportion write your own rules of attractiveness for it.

THE IMPECCABLE YOU   Good grooming demands impeccable neatness, an appearance with a "clean" overall look—uncluttered, unfussy, composed of strong lines and an obvious focal point. This is in part because—oh, bitter truth—larger women are judged, at least initially, on a harsher standard than most other women. But more important, we must look like we care about ourselves. Grooming by itself has aesthetic value; it is attractive. But it also has symbolic value: it conveys self-esteem; it gives the impression that you care about you. This is probably the single most important cue others use in forming an impression about us. Carrying yourself and presenting yourself to the world as if you found yourself attractive convinces other people that you indeed are. Displaying an appreciation of yourself begets an appreciation of yourself.

Impeccable neatness is certainly one of the major elements of grooming; it makes the fit, as well as the care and the upkeep, of clothing crucial to how you are perceived. Wearing clothes that are too large at any one point is, on this account, as bad as wearing clothes that are too small at any one point. Ill-fitting clothes call attention to the difficulty of fitting the body; they advertise size. Neatness in clothing fit also helps counteract the negative stereotype of large women as sloppy. Keeping clothes clean and well-pressed helps them maintain their line when worn on the body. Rumpled and wrinkled clothes call attention to the way a body puts stress on clothes; they emphasize size when you may not wish to do so.

No matter how effortless some people make it look, appearing well groomed takes a certain amount of behind-the-scene planning. But the time is always well worth it.

MAKEUP   If you think of makeup as the polish you put on your appearance, then you will immediately understand the three most important things about it. One, it is a vital element in giving you a finished, put-together look. Two, it immediately communicates that you care about yourself, that you believe yourself to be attractive, worthy of attention. And three, it must be done with a very light hand. It isn't a mask; it is *polish*.

Like clothes, makeup isn't something extraneous to how you put yourself together. It is a way of demonstrating that you believe yourself to be attractive. In this, the effort to be beautiful has as much value as being beautiful—because it rests on the belief that you are indeed attractive. And makeup is part of your total look; it completes what you wear yet it reveals your individuality. You use it—always subtly—to put the emphasis on your best features, to bring all your features into a working relationship with each other and with your overall proportions. Of course, makeup isn't the only way you bring attention to yourself, and so there is no need to overdo it.

The enemy of style is self-consciousness. Makeup that needs constant attention, that demands constant primping or repairs—in other words, makeup that aims to conceal some features—undermines all attempts at style. The best makeup approach is a minimal makeup approach, one that, by capitalizing on your best features, requires minimum upkeep.

Subtlety is the watchword in makeup for several reasons. To begin with, styles in makeup change, and today's style is definitely gentle—women want and need to be seen for themselves; professionally, it is expected of them. What's more, unusual features—don't think of them as imperfections but as marks of distinction—no longer have to be toned down or tamed, brought into line with some arbitrary, and very boring, norm. They can, and should, be used as focal points for establishing individuality—the Paloma Picasso Effect. And not unrelated, artifice in presenting ourselves always backfires; by suggesting there is something defective underneath, it calls attention to what we are trying to hide.

The necessary foundation for makeup, then, is not just a healthy self-image, but healthy skin with healthy tone. There is no way to fake healthy skin tone. It takes good general health, with regular moderate exercise, and a diet rich in complex carbohydrates. And it takes a comfortable routine of skin care that encompasses complete cleansing, adequate moisturizing, and protection during sun exposure.

The basics of makeup application are really a lot simpler than some would have you believe. There's no need to be intimidated by makeup. More words and more pictures in magazines are devoted to makeup than probably any other subject after dieting. So much advice is proffered with each issue, and changes each month, along with a new palette, that some women have turned away from it altogether—it just seems too complicated. Actually, the basic guidelines to makeup use are quite simple, and you needn't turn over your whole medicine chest to makeup supplies. One well-known makeup artist suggests that women with even skin tone need nothing more for daytime than lip gloss and a wave of the mascara wand along the eyelashes to add a bit of intensity to the eyes. What you do for the office and what you do for evening are two different things—but not that different.

"I don't do anything different for larger women," says Rick Teal, a top makeup artist based in New York who often works with large-size models.

"I make them as pretty as other women. A lot of people have fancy theories about contouring the face to make it look thinner, but I think it just looks silly and freakish and calls more attention to what you're trying to hide." A firm believer in "soft, pretty makeup" for everyone, Teal's approach is to accentuate the positive. For him, the most important facial features are eyebrows and lips. See the makeup advice culled from leading experts that ends this chapter.

HAIR APPARENT   In balancing facial features as part of a total picture, hair is an essential element. A good hairstyle doesn't just frame the face; it contributes to the sense of total body proportion. With hair, as with all other elements of appearance, simple hairstyles with clear and definite lines are better than complicated hairstyles with convoluted or indefinite lines. A good style streamlines your overall look. Definite lines give a clear boundary to silhouette. They lead the eye and help it find a resting point. They are easy to manage. What is more, they are a fine counterpoint to roundness and softness, and in their own right suggest energy.

Hair, like makeup and clothes, is part of your overall look. It is not a thing apart. The foundation of hair care is a great basic cut that gives you many possibilities for varying your hairstyle with your attitude. Remember this: Your femininity is not in the length of your hair.

OVERDOING IS UNDERACHIEVING   Many large-size women need to rethink their approach to makeup and hairstyle, which often cap an approach to themselves that is in need of overhaul, of simplification, of modernization. Ava Wolf is a former large-size model who has been running her own casting agency and large-size model agency. In the course of searching for models, she early on discovered that photogenic looks are not the sole criterion. "I found that attitudes were all wrong. Many larger women fall prey to overcompensating. They wear too much makeup. Their nails are too long. Their hair is too overdone. They are generally too overdone. I want models who are and who look like they are comfortable with themselves."

An overly elaborate and overly ornate hairstyle, or just overly long hair, is one way larger women often try to compensate for their feelings of inadequacy as women, generated by the culture of thinness. To this way of thinking, masses of hair, especially if elaborately curled, are feminine. But adherence to this view prevents a woman from exploring and finding the best hairstyle for her features and her overall proportions. It keeps her from looking modern. It keeps her from looking in tune with the rest of herself. For many larger women, a hairstyle that shows off the face with clarity and that exposes and thereby lengthens the neck is going to be most attractive. Hairstyles are discussed in detail in Chapter 8.

Posture

Few aspects of ourselves convey as much information about us in as little time as posture does. It is an instant index of self-value, and thus an instant cue to others about how to feel about us. We presume at a glance that a woman whose shoulders are hunched forward is trying to hide herself, to make herself smaller. We may even draw more inferences about her from her stance, because we interpret it as a defensive posture. Good posture commands respect, because it is a sign of self-respect. That is why we always associate dignity with erect posture. We hold ourselves up because we believe we are worth holding up. And others understand we think well of ourselves, and heed the suggestion contained in our body language. Even when we have our doubts about ourselves—everyone gets them, sometimes—good posture, on its own, works as a tonic; it seems to beget the response that helps us respect ourselves.

Besides, good posture makes us look taller and more linear. It is more aesthetically pleasing. And clothes simply look better on us when we are straighter; no parts are thrust into protrusion; we do not look as if we are about to cave in or topple over. But that is only part of it. Functionally speaking, good posture balances our weight; we move with more ease. Movement looks and feels more graceful. Further, we look well balanced. Good posture gives us equipoise.

There is no secret to good posture. The chin goes up, off the chest. The shoulders get squared, but never hunched into a square. The spine must be straight. For those who do not have the habit—and it is a habit—an exercise can help establish it.

Most important, straighten out the whole spine from the top down. Standing comfortably straight, with shoulders back but relaxed, aim to touch your head to the ceiling. Feel the lift all along your spine as it uncrimps upward. Do not pull your shoulders up; allow them to go along for the ride as your spine unfurls upward. Do this anywhere, any time, even while you are sitting down, until it is literally uncomfortable for you to hold yourself any other way. In the process, you will be strengthening all the skeletal muscles. In the meantime, practice walking and moving in this posture, your shoulders always aiming straight ahead. Add a smile and you can enter any room and be instantly approachable.

Personality

Vivacity. Animation. Liveliness. These are all aspects of personality that are instantly identifiable and communicated through gesture and movement, posture, speech pattern, and, of course, style. Style is nothing if not a visible declaration of liveliness, spirit transformed into substance. These are traits that are universally appealing in themselves. Animated people make everyone feel livelier, more exciting, and make every situation more enjoyable for everyone. But for large-size women, revealing such aspects of personality serves an additional purpose, for they specifically counteract the negative stereotype of big women (sloppy and lazy) that exists in our culture.

Like all other aspects of our selves, the personality we display must be ours truly, not an artificial contrivance. Because in presenting our self, any incongruity between what we are and what we appear to be suggests artifice—if not outright deception—and it always boomerangs into a negative reaction.

BEAUTY REDEFINED

Something unexpected has happened in the course of examining how impressions are made; we discover that beauty is not what we have been taught it was. The conclusion is inevitable: Beauty is not a designation that falls out of the sky on a favored few, preferably blonde of hair and blue of eye to say nothing of slim of figure. It is a way of actively shaping how people perceive us. The fact that self-confidence and style and posture and animation influence the way people see us transforms attractiveness from a passive attribute—an approval conferred by and at the mercy of others—to an active stance, a judgment we lead people to by our manner of self-presentation. Beauty, it turns out, is something that any woman can create herself, on her terms, built around her own distinctiveness, conveying it by confidence and calling attention to it with style.

It's about time! We American women have long been in need of a way of looking at attractiveness that recognizes the fact of variability and individuality, that allows us to see ourselves as beautiful even if we do not all fit into the same mold. We need a way of looking at beauty that doesn't foreclose us, that gives us credit for being able to present our own attributes, if we choose to. We have needed a definition of beauty that is aligned with women's changed role in life, that respects our passage from passive to active participants in the world. Our fate as women is no longer selected for us; we create it ourselves. So it is with beauty.

The new view of beauty doesn't pretend that beauty doesn't count—we all know it does. It simply changes the expectation that beauty is a passive attribute to the recognition that beauty is an active accomplishment. We now know: We influence the way others view us. And we can all master the essentials of presenting ourselves well.

SO LONG, STEREOTYPES

Stereotyping, unfortunately, is a fact of life. It results from the basic process of categorizing people by physical characteristics; people pay attention to those whose appearance is physically distinctive—redheads, cripples, the small, the large. Not only do people look more at physically distinctive people, they tend to overly notice them in any activity that's subject to a negative interpretation. And they attribute to the distinctive the ability to make trouble; distinctive people, by virtue of their distinctiveness, are lightning rods for blame. As a result, there develops an illusion that certain negative characteristics—say, sloppiness—are always correlated with certain categories of people, such as those whose weight is greater than average. Stereotyped expectations have ways of becoming self-fulfilling prophecies, because the stereotyped are treated as if the stereotype were true, and the leeway in behavior that is accorded others is not extended to them.

Whether you want to be or not, you are often in situations where you are up against stereotyped expectations of you as a large woman; they hover in the culture at large. There is no point in panicking. Or in accepting, or even thinking about, the judgment. Or in attempting a deliberate point for point refutation of the stereotype. For on their own, the elements of self-presentation—good grooming, fine posture, self-confidence, and style—give the lie to stereotypes. Self-confidence assures others that you are worth being noticed, and style guarantees the experience will be a delight. Style by definition defies all expectations; it fascinates; and it is enviable. As a mark of self-respect, it invites the respect of others. As a triumph of individual spirit, it wins the admiration of others. The art of self-presentation creates its own exciting impressions that leave negative stereotypes in the dust.

Here's how casting agent Ava Wolf sums it up.

I am a fanatic about grooming. I take good care of my skin and hair. I keep my body clean and my skin healthy. I know that when I walk into a room full of strangers, I must overcome their initial resistance to me as a large-size woman. So I feel it's important to glow with energy. And radiate confidence. Indeed, people are drawn to me.

Being heavy is not the first thing I think about myself. I am not ashamed of my size and I never apologize for it. I walk tall and dress well. It truly makes a difference in the way people treat you. There's no reason for anyone to say I look terrible—because I don't.

Makeup Demystified

The natural topography of the face, enhanced here, subdued there, is your best makeup guide. You always want to work with it, not against it. Your aim is not to camouflage, but to accentuate your assets and put all your features in proportion to each other. A strong mouth can take a strong brow, and vice versa—and strong brows are now acceptable, even desirable. (Take a look at Brooke Shields; strong brows take her face beyond beautiful to truly interesting.)

- In general, makeup should always enhance. And it should always enhance your eyes. They are the most expressive part of your face, and will always reflect your vitality. You don't want to weigh your eyes down with lines and wads of makeup, however. Your best look lies in using the frames nature has already provided—your eyebrows.
- At all times, makeup should look uncontrived, not forced. The difference between night and day is drama—depending on where you will spend your evening, you can afford a little more emphasis overall on your features. That translates as lipstick a shade brighter, eyes a bit more intense.
- The mouth looks best when it is gently polished at all times. Daytime takes a neutral shade of lipstick or a simple gloss. You can go to a stronger red only a) if it is a clear shade and b) only if your eyes and brows naturally balance such strong lip color.
- "I like lips soft," says Rick Teal. "I put a small amount of color on a lip brush, then apply it to the lips, and then lightly

- If you have a small face in proportion to your body, you can, for evening, sparingly use a highlighter under foundation, especially on forehead and chin; this will reflect more light and make your face appear larger.

- Powder, says Rick Teal, is a must, and particularly if you are being photographed, because the camera appears to enlarge what is highly reflective. Working with loose powder and a puff, Teal first pours a little powder into the lid of the container and dips an edge of the puff into it. Then he presses the puff into skin in a rolling motion across the face. This, he says, really "mashes" the powder in and sets the makeup so that it lasts longer. Reapply when the going gets warm. Teal, who says he has tried every kind of powder there is, says the best comes from Shu Uemara—"It's very fine"—in the color camel, a yellowish tone.

- Sheer powder, lightly applied on top of a sheer matte foundation, can be used to "smooth out" fine wrinkles in older skin. The combination helps skin reflect light evenly, making fine lines seemingly disappear.

- Lighten up on makeup in the summer months; you can do without foundation altogether, especially if you have a light tan. For an instant makeup freshener, always carry pressed powder leaves to blot excess oil and remove the shininess.

- Eye shadow is just that—shadow. By definition, it should be subtle, in a soft neutral color applied lightly to the top lid. Evenings can take smokier, duskier colors, applied equally subtly. Powder shadows tend to last longer and produce a more subtle effect; they work better in warmer weather or on skin that sweats easily.

- Don't aim to match eye shadow to the colors of your clothes. The actual color of eye shadow should not be obvious or immediately discernible. Rick Teal lightly applies a rust or ochre shadow—"It's flattering to most skin and eye colors"— from lash to brow. Then he applies a darker brown to the outer corner, and blends it in. "I might highlight the brow bone with yellow powder," says Teal. "It looks especially pretty in summer." It all gets blended with a clean sponge.

- If you want to bring out deep-set eyes, a light colored matte pastel shadow on the lid and into the crease will help. If you smudge it so you don't see a sharp edge. A little gloss can then go on the middle."

- The stronger the shade of lipstick, the more necessary it is to sharply define the lip line. Use a brush to outline the lips; and if your lipstick tends to "bleed," try a product expressly designed to prevent it—or switch to a softer color. For long-lasting results, apply lipstick, blot, lightly powder your lips, then apply another coat of lipstick.

- For a more natural hint of lip color, first apply lip gloss or Vaseline. Then dab a small amount of powder blush on the center of each lip. Smooth it across your lips, then finish with a scant touch of gloss.

- Foundation is used to smooth out skin tone. Not everyone needs it, and even those who need it sometimes don't need it all the time. When used, it goes on sparingly, with a light touch. Foundation color should be carefully matched to skin tone at the jawline, which it should never go beyond. Apply foundation only where you need it—remember, its purpose is to even out skin tone, not create a mask.

- Most American makeups are on the pink side, while most skin tones have some yellow in them; you may have to search for a good foundation color, or have one custom-blended. Then, buy the lightest oil-free formulation you can find; you can always add a drop of moisturizer to help foundation glide on smoothly, especially in winter. The best way to apply foundation is with a dampened sponge brush.

- Before putting makeup on, "wake up" your skin with a splash of cold water. This helps tighten the skin for smooth application of makeup. And leave a light film of water on your face for use with foundation.

- Rick Teal recommends applying a little foundation just under the eyes, to cover any dark tones. Then he suggests you take a damp sponge over the face to even out its color. That, he says, is enough foundation.

- In general, it is wise for large women to stay away from frosted makeup foundation. It looks garish. It shows up lines around the eyes and mouth. And because it is so highly light-reflective, it makes cheeks look sweaty and fuller and rounder than they are.

want to make your eyes more prominent, try a light neutral shade on the top lid; also, draw a line in the crease of the lid with a fine brush dampened with water and dipped in the shadow. If you want to minimize fleshy lids, use a pale eye shadow in a cool tone. To widen your eyes, apply shadow only to the outer half of the lids.

- Mascara adds emphasis to eyes in a softer manner than eyeliner. Teal's advice: Apply mascara to top lashes only. Let them dry thoroughly between coats, or else they will clump together. Dust lashes lightly with powder between coats, then comb them to separate them. Rick Teal prefers black mascara for brunettes, brown for redheads and blondes. "I don't recommend mascara under the eye; it drags the eye down."

- If you have an addiction to eyeliner, at least give up black liner in favor of medium brown. And never apply it beyond the natural corner of the eye: Wings of mascara at the eye corners are too artificial for today's way of thinking about beauty.

- Eyebrows are part of the basic structure of your face. They are, in fact, your most important feature. Don't even try to reshape them. If you do anything to them at all, just lightly pluck them—from underneath only—until their shape is clean. In fact, very often they need emphasis; after all, they are the frames of the eyes. Especially if you have a double chin, enhancing eyebrows draws attention upward on your face.

- Brush eyebrows up, then outward, into their natural line. If they need more: When the brows are brushed up, use a pencil (brown is best) in light feather strokes on the skin between the hairs, or apply brow powder with a firm, slanted brush used expressly for that purpose; then brush them outward.

- Blush clarifies the eyes while it sweetens cheeks. But it is tricky to place correctly on the face; many women wear it too wide on the face, which only broadens the face; others wear it like a large bright polka dot. Blush looks best brushed onto your face in feathered upward strokes so that it blends unnoticeably into your skin tone or foundation. As for color, you are better off applying several strokes of a paler shade than using a deep-tone blush.

- Blush belongs under, not on, the cheekbones. You don't normally blush *on* your cheekbones. Rick Teal recommends a pale pink or peach, even for dark skin. "Brush it on from the bottom, under the cheekbone." This works as shading that subtly contours your cheeks at the same time it colors them. "It thins the face and adds a glow."

- Always remove all makeup thoroughly before going to sleep.

- These makeup hints are general guidelines. The way to really learn which features to emphasize and how, exactly where on your face to apply makeup, is to park yourself in front of a mirror, analyze your features, and experiment. Just as you get to know your body, you need to know your face. Never, ever rely on makeup "experts" in the department store—they are there to sell products, not to find your best look. Where they often can help is in recognizing the best shade of foundation for your skin tone.

- Faces change with time. At the very least, rethink your approach to makeup—its placement, the best colors, manner of adding emphasis—every five years. Styles in makeup change, too. Few things make a woman more unattractive than a style of makeup from another era; she looks inflexible and mentally unbalanced, stuck in a time warp and rigidly heeding an inappropriate standard.

- Hands are very important to your overall look. They should always appear polished, although that doesn't necessarily mean highly colored. And nails should be kept in trim. A gentle oval shape extending just past the fingertip is most flattering. Longer nails don't lengthen short hands—they look just plain out-of-proportion silly and are ridiculously nonfunctional.

- It is a rare woman who looks good in strong color nail polish. A softer, more neutral color is more flattering to most hands and far more suitable professionally, despite the popularity of deep tones in the hard-edge eighties. Don't even think of strong colors if you have hands or fingers that are short or stubby; they only accentuate the plumpness of the hand. Go instead for soft pink-browns, which are closer to most skin tones and look better for a longer time, or a no-color polish.

II

The Elements of Style

7

Fit to Be Tried

Ypou have done it. You have espied the dress of your dreams. The style is made for you. The color is just what you wanted. The fabric is gorgeous. You are slouching toward the dressing room. You want the dress to make you look . . . well, taller and more slender. Every woman wants to look taller and more slender. But you hope the designer hasn't let his/her fantasy carry him/her too far astray; you pray he/she has created a garment to fit real women, not the imaginary women of the design board. You want the dress—every dress, every garment, in fact—to silently recognize and work around your figure "facts," then go about its main job of flattering you and your body. But first, it must get past your hips.

It not only must go over the body, it must do so with a certain amount of ease, the amount depending on the style. You don't expect a tailored suit to fit the same as a blouson jacket and skirt. It must give you room to breathe, and room to move in. (Who doesn't own a pair of pants—perhaps jeans—that look perfectly gorgeous on, but are hostage to the possibility that a shoelace might work itself loose, or a piece of paper fly out of your hand?) And then its parts must hit the corresponding parts of your body the right way.

The right way depends on the style of the garment and differs from style to style. A dolman sleeve, particularly on a wedge-shaped dress, can give a dramatic line that's very flattering to a top-heavy body, but the armhole must be just so. Too narrow and it is confining, too deep and the sleeve can actually add bulk to the torso and bust. More exact are the requirements for a fabulous jacket. You've probably heard a million times that a double-breasted blazer is a major no-no for the fuller figure. But if the shoulders are cut true enough, and the jacket is longer rather than shorter, it could be more of a yes-yes than any garden-variety single-breasted jacket.

Precision of fit is crucial in large sizes, and rarer than most women are willing to admit. The most obvious reason is that clothes are not designed three-dimensionally to start with, while bodies are. Developing a sense of style means learning to take some risks—but fit is the one place in fashion where you can't afford to take risks. That's good enough; there are plenty of other ways to put snap and presence into dressing.

A TRYING EXCHANGE

Getting garments to fit is a balancing act for designers. They want a dress to look good on the body, yet they want it to have "hanger appeal"—look so good on the rack it will leap into your arms and say "try me." Often the two are mutually exclusive. The dress that looks lifeless and droopy on the hanger may well be a sensation on the body. And the garment that looks so perky on the hanger may be too rigidly two-dimensional, more like a dress for a paper doll than for a live woman.

It's safe to say that designers could afford to learn something about bodies and customers would do well to know more about the fit of clothes. Women need to know that the best-fitting clothes are not always going to look the best on the hanger. A dress cut for a three-dimensional figure in a fabric that will skim all curves is going to look mighty droopy until filled out by a human form. Skirts and slips cut on the bias have a grace any goddess would envy, but you'd be hard-pressed to see it on a hanger, which only makes them look a bit tired.

At the same time, I wish someone would make an anatomy course mandatory for designers. If fine artists feel they need to learn anatomy, why not the artists who work as designers—those whose artwork actually has to be hung on the body? After all, clothes designers are in a sense sculptors; they create soft sculptures to fit the form of the human body. Maybe some forward-thinking fashion-school dean can come up with a "life design" class, in which each session each student or team of students has to quick-drape and create a design for a live model, and each session of the class features a model of differing anatomical proportions. I also wish designers would, all the way through design school, be taught how to create on a replica of the body, rather than on a sketch pad. That way they would acquire respect for the human form and the ability to think three-dimensionally. Once they graduate, they can work by sketch, too, but at least by then, thinking about fashion in the third dimension would have become second nature to first-rate designers. And I would hope design schools would teach students to admire variation in the female form, or any form, and to look on it as an inspiration, a test of design skill, not as an icky poo aberration from some idealized dimensions.

Unfortunately, things seem to be going in the opposite direction. When I called the West Coast's leading fashion design school, I was told that students there learn to translate a sketch to a flat pattern without ever draping their design on a human form or a replica of one. "We're way ahead of you people on the East Coast." Way ahead??!!

Fit is not something that can be patched on to design at the last moment of production. Fit derives from harmony between the shape of the garment, the fabric type and the way it is cut, the way seams are placed and sewn, the size of the parts of a garment, such as the sleeves. The aim isn't merely to cover a body—otherwise we'd all be walking around in sacks—but to have the fabric lie right and to have the parts of the garment correspond to body parts in aesthetically pleasing and functional ways. You want as much precision in conforming to the shape of body parts as a style and comfort allow. And at some body parts, such as at the sleeves or the hemline, you can afford nothing less than exact conformance with a high degree of precision.

Fit not only gives coverage, it is what flatters. Extra fabric in an exaggerated dolman sleeve is undesirable not only because it looks droopy and sloppy, but because it adds bulk. Your body looks bigger. Even your movement is compromised because of the extra fabric (try to pick up a child). At the other extreme, too little fabric in a garment is always unflattering. It always emphasizes size and calls attention to what you prefer not to advertise. And it makes the wearer self-conscious; nothing subverts style faster.

How clothes fit is a crucial element of grooming. Precision of fit gives you finish. It makes you look neat. It adds polish. It contributes to the impression that your body is a perfectly ordinary size and it was meant to be that size.

How do you get a precise fit? For starters, there are size guides. Clothes in larger sizes now come in two size ranges—regular, or Women's sizes, generally fitting women above a size 14 who are 5'4" and over, and Women's Petites, for women over size 14 who are shorter than 5'4".

Women's Petites are what, in former times, would have been called "half sizes." But there's a big difference between the new range of Women's Petites and the old category of half sizes, and that has to do with changes in women themselves. Fifty years ago, women were more or less retired to the sidelines of life as they got older. They became inactive. And as they got older, they shrank in height. Their vertebrae became compressed while they stayed the same, or even got a bit larger, in width. Today it is clear that the height shrinkage that usually comes with age is at least in part due to inactivity, and preventable with activity and exercise. For any number of reasons, adult women today are much more active than they were fifty years ago.

As women maintain their adult height and activity patterns longer into age, the need for matronly styled half sizes has diminished. Today the vast majority of women who are short and full-figured are younger women who happen to enter adulthood on the short side. After all, the average height of American women is 5'4". So the market for half sizes as little-old-lady clothes is shrinking, while the demand for large-size petite clothes for younger women is growing. A new generation of women is making its needs felt in younger fashion styling, and the new size designation is a nod to that change.

WOMEN'S SIZES
for women 5'4" and over

Clothes size designation	14W	16W	18W	20W	22W	24W	26W
Bust, in inches	39	41	43	45	47	49	51
Waist	30	32	34	36	38	40	42
Hips	40	42	44	46	48	50	52
Former size designation							
Tops	34	36	38	40	42	44	46
Bottoms	28	30	32	34	36	38	40
Lingerie size	Misses L	1X	1X	2X	2X	3X	4X

WOMEN'S PETITE SIZES
for women 5' to 5'4"
short waist

Clothes size designation	14WP	16WP	18WP	20WP	22WP	24WP	26WP
Bust, in inches	39	41	43	45	47	49	51
Waist	31	33	35	37	39	41	43
Hips	40	42	44	46	48	50	52
Former size designation	14½	16½	18½	20½	22½	24½	26½

AT HOME ON THE RANGE

The operative word here is "guide." No size chart is exact. This is a rough approximation of which clothes sizes you should look for to accommodate which body measurements. There's great variability in the cut and fit of clothes of different fabrics, even of the same style. Even color can change the fit of a garment; the same fabric takes up different dyes in different ways, and some dyes change the arrangement of fibers in a fabric's weave. It's hard enough to find clothes that look terrific. Don't ever let a size label stand between you and the right stuff.

Besides, if style is your goal, you are not going to confine yourself to a designated size range. You will be on the alert for things in other size ranges, in menswear, in unisex clothes, in unsized garments, in garments from other countries sized who-knows-how. You need to be able to judge any garment with your own eyes to determine whether it will fit and look good.

When you are strolling along the open-air market in Firenze and spot a colorful gauzy shirt you'd love to commit to your wardrobe, the number on the label will have almost no meaning to you. You must be able to quickly "size it up" for fit. (Quick check—the width, the length, the drape of the fabric, the placement of the shoulder, the drop of the armhole, the type of sleeve, darts or other allowance for dimension, the size of the neck, the placement of details.)

FIT CHECKPOINTS

Clothes that pull anywhere, regardless of the size marked on the label, do not fit. The pulling of fabric interrupts the drape and introduces a horizontal line—doubly emphasizing what you wish to cover and calling attention to size. Do not wear clothes that pull. Your best course is to retire clothes that pull from your wardrobe until you fit them better, or have them altered to fit. Be sure that hemlines do not rise even one iota anywhere as a result of widthwise pulling.

These are the points you need to pay attention to for correct fit.

Neck

The neckline of a garment does more than preserve (or dash) your modesty; it has to impart a sense of finish to any outfit. Then why, women want to know, are necklines so often afterthoughts on large-size tops or dresses?

Most of us know that a neckline opening that's too small makes a garment unwearable. A dress or top that hugs the neck closely also throws off the body proportions. But a neck opening can suffer in the opposite direction as well, and be too big and nondescript.

If you wear them at all—and short women would do better avoiding them—round, or jewel, or crew, necklines should lie flat on the shoulder and look best when the neckline is relaxed a good finger's width away from the neck itself. Otherwise, they call attention to the width of the neck and the roundness of the face and body. Enlarging a round neckline of a blouse or dress is possible, if costly; entrust the task to an experienced seamstress, and be sure that the seams are carefully finished to lie flat.

At the other extreme, you also need to avoid the round neckline that's neither here nor there. A jewel neckline can be cut so big that it leaves too much of an expanse of skin yet the style doesn't call for a scarf. You wind up looking unfinished. And even a piece of bold jewelry would be out of place between the neck and the garment. A nondescript neckline throws off a garment's proportions, and it makes your body appear shapeless when you usually need all the definition and finish you can get.

Even vee necklines, always flattering to all larger women, need a crispness of form. They, too, can suffer from being too wide, or too rounded at the vee, particularly on a collarless dress. More sharply cut deep vees are terrific; always make sure that the sides of the vee lie close to the neck on the sides but not so close that they ride up it; otherwise, the beauty of the line is lost.

Bareness at the neckline is another proposition entirely, and a law unto itself. There are no rules—except use it only in the right time or place.

Shoulder

The shoulder is a critical point for fit. A garment must fit at the shoulders for it to work well anywhere else. One of the secrets of great body fit is to buy your clothes so they hang properly from the shoulders; then they drape down the body, giving you a long line and a look of elegance. A small amount of width extension at the shoulder—the reason why you always need shoulder pads—is vital in balancing the width of the hips.

Shoulders should be roomy enough for comfort and for balancing your proportions, but not so big that they look sloppy or bulky. That means shoulders on tailored clothes should not fall below your natural shoulder line. Yet, for some reason, a great many clothes in large sizes are made with dropped shoulders. In general, dropped shoulders add a horizontal line, widen the whole upper body, and shorten the body, while normal shoulders are cut vertically and maintain a balance of proportions. A perfect shoulder fit is critical for conveying a neat and professional appearance and for the impression that the clothes you are wearing are ideal for you. Even on casual clothes, dropped shoulders are seldom more flattering, just more common. Shoulders that are too broad or droop by no more than an inch can be lifted into place if the sleeve length allows. This is definitely work for an experienced seamstress. And every shoulder needs the lift and balance of a shoulder pad.

There are three basic types of shoulders, their popularity varies through cycles of fashion, and each fits in a distinctive way. The most common shoulder is the **set-in** sleeve. In this case, the garment looks most flattering when the shoulder extends no more than a half inch past your natural shoulder and the sleeve falls straight from there. It goes without saying that the shoulder should be supported with a pad that also extends just past the natural shoulder. Not a big airplane-landing-strip type of pad, but a pad nonetheless, to lift the shoulder and sleeve area. Lifting the shoulder gives the impression of added body height. Designed with care, the set-in sleeve can also accommodate a large bust and provide ease of movement. One excellent way is for the underarm seam to be lowered slightly—slightly is the key word here—which enlarges the armhole, or armseye, but maintains a precise vertical line at the shoulder.

Raglan sleeves attach not to the shoulder seam but to the neckline with a diagonal line that can add drama and flattery. The line leads directly to the face, a primary asset for most of us. Raglan sleeves have the great advantage of affording a generous bust a comfortable amount of space. But the slope of the sleeve can be lethal to shoulders that are not naturally broad and square, and the drape of a garment can quickly turn into a droop. The solution, as you may have already guessed, is shoulder pads—not the same pads you put in your suit jacket, but pads expressly designed for raglan sleeves. These are smaller, ovoid, and they gently cup the edge of the shoulder. Take time to place the pads properly in clothes; it's very much an individual matter, but never extend the raglan pad beyond your natural shoulder.

Dolman sleeves are cut so that the bodice, shoulder, and sleeve are all of one unseamed piece. Freedom of movement is very limited—raise your arms above the shoulder line and the rest of the dress goes along for the ride—unless there is a gusset added to the underarm seam in the armpit area. Because they only vaguely conform to the chest, dolman sleeves are often sought by big-busted women. Indeed, dolman sleeves of well-controlled proportions can look terrific, especially on a wedge-shaped dress in a fluid fabric, where they suggest a slinky glamour. Because the fit is neither practical nor crisp enough, dolman sleeves are not suited to professional type clothes. They are also hard fits under jackets and coats, unless the outer garments are themselves similarly shaped, or you opt for a cape.

Armseye

The armseye is the circular hole for a set-in sleeve at the shoulder junction. It needs to be wide enough to permit movement and to accommodate a fleshy arm—but not so big that it destroys definition of parts and drags the line of the garment down.

An ideal way to get a good sleeve fit while maintaining all-important precision of fit at the shoulder is to look for sleeves in which the armseye is deepened slightly—but not obviously—under the arm. Too much drop and the look is too matronly. Just the right drop—say, up to an inch on the vertical—gives fleshy arms room and also tends to accommodate a large bust. Inexplicably, manufacturers who deepen the armseye sometimes fail to lengthen the underarm seam of the sleeve; you go to extend your arm and find your sleeve cuff stops you short. So before you buy, check first by extending your arms.

Sleeve

A sleeve should hit just below the wrist bone, never longer. If it falls on your hand, it always looks sloppy and calls attention to the poor fit; it seems always to suggest you had to buy it so much larger in order to get it to cover your body. Rolling up sleeves is not a solution. It is appropriate only for the most relaxed of clothes, and even then it can add unflattering and unwanted bulk, assuming the sleeve is finished for the purpose. More often than not, sleeves of blouses and jackets need adjustment—and the alteration is always, repeat always, worth it, for the finish it affords and the precision of fit.

Sleeves must fit not just in length but in width. A sleeve that's too narrow will keep you from moving freely. If it's too wide, you will look matronly and broader than need be. Look for sleeves that fit with just a slight amount of ease. For women whose arms are not fleshy, sleeve options are many and fit isn't an issue. Very slim slinky sleeves, especially on fine-gauge dressy knits, can be extremely flattering and oh-so-soigné. Slim sheer sleeves are another delicious option on dressier clothes. What you do have to watch out for is short sleeves that are cut too wide—they make you look boxy—or long sleeves cut full all the way down, even if they are held tight to the wrist with a cuff. Too much fabric in a sleeve adds bulk to the body line.

If your upper arms are fleshy, you don't have to avoid set-in sleeves; search for sleeve treatments that are naturally accommodating at the arm top—dropped armseyes, sleeves slightly gathered (but not puffed!) at the armseye. Because you don't want width all the way down the sleeve, look for sleeves that start out wider and taper toward the wrist, especially those without a cuff—your arms will look longer and narrower. Raglan sleeves also often work well. For you, short sleeves are not out of the question, it's just that in your case short means never shorter than just above the elbow, and then always with a tapered, not boxy, fit.

Bust

One reason we all have so much trouble here is that clothes are not generally conceived of for bodies with three dimensions. Darts have not been seen in a whole generation. And if you really want to weep, the latest edition of the leading textbook of fashion design does not even have an index entry for "bust," "bustline," or "chest." Is further proof needed that busts are out of fashion, in every sense of the word?

Complaints exist on both ends of the spectrum. Those small of bust find too many clothes too roomy across the top. And those with big busts—the majority of larger women—don't find enough styling well enough thought out for them.

Bustline fit is absolutely critical. And the first step to good fit of blouses and sweaters is the right bra. Don't laugh; I can say with the certainty that comes from surveying thousands of women that most full-figured women are not satisfied or comfortable with the fit of their bra, and the bra fit throws off the fit of clothes. So jump to Chapter 12 and read about bra fit before going further.

The same problem that afflicts most bras also afflicts tops, be they blouses, sweaters, jackets, or dresses. Namely, to attempt fit of the chest, which is really three dimensional, clothes come too wide or too droopy at the shoulders. Instead, what you need is more exactitude of cut—a bodice trim at the shoulder, but wider under the arm and down. Hold a garment out flat to test for this kind of shape. Or look for clothes with darts. Fall in love again with princess seams. All will give you room at the bust without sacrificing sleekness of line.

Sometimes, bustline fit problems can be solved in a snap. Literally. Particularly in lower price clothes, a front-closing blouse may have enough width but the closure gaps at bust level. The problem is buttons that are too widely spaced (as a cost-saving measure). Only if it can't be seen from the outside, attach a snap. Attach it to a facing only if the facing is stitched down; otherwise it will pull open the facing and betray your solution.

And that brings up another common problem full-figured women face. Though not strictly one of fit, it is closely related. Jackets (also shirts worn over tees and turtlenecks) with facings that are not stitched down to a placket or trim, or held down with tacking, or attached to a lining, are potential troublemakers for women with big and well-shaped busts. Worn closed, such a jacket appears to be fine. But try to wear it unbuttoned and the facing catches on your bust and splays open over it. E-m-b-a-r-r-a-s-s-i-n-g! It doesn't call attention to your bust—it rivets attention on it.

The solution is not to always wear your jacket closed; you need more options than that. Do look for jackets with the facing stitched down to the lining. However, not all jackets were meant to be lined, certainly not summer-weight ones. In that case, search out jackets with bound edges, stitched-on borders, or placket closures. If there's no structural solution in sight, the remedy of last resort is to tack the jacket facing to the inside of the jacket body at strategic points, or lightly hemstitch the two together without letting your handiwork show through (you're in luck if there are breast pockets). You may prefer to enlist the expert touch of a tailor.

Don't ever rely on stretch to make knit tops fit. Knits should fit without stretching to cover you. In fact, to get the right fit, you should generally approach knits in a size larger than your dress size. If you are buying cotton knit tops that you will toss into the washing machine, don't even hesitate—buy a size larger. Very often, you will need to go a size larger in sweaters, too. If you usually wear tops in a 2X, look for sweaters in a 3X, provided they are not too long in the sleeve or too wide in the shoulder.

Another factor in bust fit is fabric. Stiff fabrics—thick tweeds, lower grades of linen, even fine organza—tend to gap. Supple fabrics will drape better over the bust contours. You will want fabrics that are supple enough to skim your contours but that have enough body so that they don't cling. Instead of cotton-polyester knit combinations, for example, look for cotton-rayon combinations. Choose fine-grain linen rather than coarse linen, wool crepe over tweed, cotton gabardine over poplin or canvas.

Bodice

This is the part of the garment between the waist and the shoulders, and a garment must fit here in width and in length before you can consider purchasing it. If it is too tight or too short, don't buy it; it really won't fit any better next week or next month, and you will only feel guilty for having spent the money. If it is too tight, try a larger size; you need clothes that look good now, not some hypothetical time in the future. Don't ever let vanity keep you from trying a larger size; size labels are guidelines; there is normally too much variation in garment manufacture for size to have any absolute value. And on a practical note, no one sees the nasty size label in the first place except you. I personally feel there are enough impediments to getting great clothes in larger sizes; you can't afford to let the size label be another one of them.

If the bodice is too short, you are probably long-waisted and need to look for clothes that are longer in the torso, or for styles with less defined horizontal divisions. If the bodice is too long, then you may be what was once called—please forgive me—half sizes. A designation now rightly in disgrace for past crimes of dowdiness, frumpiness, and bulletproof polyester, yesterday's half sizes are today's Women's Petites. This is a new size range for the short or short-waisted full-figured woman. A very few manufacturers specialize in making these. Look for labels that say 16 or 20 WP. Barring that, use your own eyes to gauge which styles seem short-waisted, and try those. Or ask a saleswoman if she knows which ones run short in the waist.

The traditional way of making a bodice fit the three-dimensional body is with front and back darts from bosom level to waist or any other area along the garment edge. Because darts make fit rather precise, large-size manufacturers often use other ways to build ease as well as line into a bodice. Instead of being sewn into a dart, the excess fabric may be gathered and shirred into a waist seam. Especially if there is enough extra fabric in length to slightly blouse the bodice, this is a superb way for a woman with a full figure to get the appearance of a fitted dress yet all the comfort and coverage a full midriff needs. Princess seams, extending down from the shoulder or the armhole, are especially flattering bodice treatments for fuller figures. A surplice wrap bodice with gathers or loose pleats of fabric for ease might rank as the all-time great for flattery and fit in bodice construction for the fuller figure, especially for women with a large bust.

Bodices that get their ease of fit from gathers released from a neck or shoulder yoke can be awfully tricky on a full figure. What is gained in fit can be lost in frumpiness. Unless the shoulder yoke is just below the shoulder ridge or the neck yoke cut in a deep vee shape, a yoke cuts across the figure. And the splaying of the gathers puffs out a big bosom and makes it look downright dowdy. In addition, yokes tend to restrict movement across the shoulders. Beware: This bodice style tends to be widely available in large sizes, especially in blouses, "float" style dresses, and loungewear.

Waistline

A waistline is a lot like greatness. Some women are born with it. Some achieve it. And some have one thrust upon them.

If you're not born with one and have never achieved one, waistlines on garments still don't have to be thought of as something you'd rather not have thrust upon you. You can look good and feel comfortable in clothes that do have waistlines; you don't have to consign yourself to a waistless sack every day of your life. You may not want to make your waistline the focal point of your outfit, but you will welcome the expanded fashion option of waisted clothes, provided they are done right. The trick is softness—clothes that are gently bloused at the waist imply shape.

If you are short-waisted and big busted, life doesn't always have to be lived in separates; if you know what to look for, you can wear dresses with waistlines, too. Waistlines on dresses will tend to fall in the natural position on your body—at least from the front. From the back, there will usually be an excess of fabric at the waist. A small amount is often rather flattering and adds a certain blousiness to the look. A large amount, on the other hand, means the line of the dress top will be thrown off too much, and you'll be better off looking for a dress with a wider and shorter bodice that comes exactly to the waistline all around, or a longer one that blouses more evenly all around, or a dress with a dropped waist. Although every rule book will advise you to wear them, totally straight dresses are not the solution—they tend to make you look pregnant. Better a sheath lightly darted in the right places to give a suggestion of shape.

All waistbands can be approached in two ways—rigid and elasticized. As far as rigid waists go, the all-time best for most full-figured women is bandless. It sits at the natural waist, on top of the hips. There is no waistband to get caught in the squeeze between tummy and midriff when you sit down, or to visually chop you in half. Of all the rigid waists, this is easily the most flattering on the body to all figure types, since it defines the waist without belaboring the point. It also lends itself nicely to bloused tops. Unfortunately, skirts with bandless waists are rare species; many women say they wish more manufacturers would turn out skirts this way.

A styled waistband is unbeatable for polish when you wear blouses and shirts tucked in. Too much styling, though, adds bulk and too much detail can make the waist seem larger. Narrow waistbands are most comfortable and stay neat. Those that are more than an inch high should be approached with extreme caution. They are only for those who are long-waisted and trim in the midriff; otherwise, they seem to cut the body in half.

Elasticized waists are simply de rigueur for comfort on some clothes, and if done with thought, need never sacrifice polish. All-elastic waistbands, especially narrow ones, are ideal for those women whose hips are high, that is, they reach their widest point just below the waist.

The best waistline for most women, especially for tailored clothes, is a waistband that's no more than an inch high, styled simply in front, and elasticized in back. This maintains a neat appearance yet allows for the fact that women vary greatly in waist size.

But there's elastic and there's elastic. Most ideal is a back waistband that is of a piece with the garment body, or a traditionally turned waistband with a band of elastic inserted and multi-stitched in place. The resulting skirt or pants waistband always looks neat and holds its shape. You get a smooth line, the skirt or pants drapes well, and the waist always stretches the full width of the garment.

A waistband elasticized by virtue of a piece of elastic tunneled through it often collapses in just a few wearings, making the waistband mangled and bulky. Since all-elasticized tunnel waistbands are often necessary on knits, do make sure that the elastic is at least anchored upright to the waistband at both side seams; this will minimize waistband roll. In one terrific variation, lingerie-type zig-zag stitching is applied over the tunnel-elastic waist; this adds both polish and practicality—it keeps the waistband from rolling and eliminates the need for a belt. The design team Hino and Malee typically creates clothes with this kind of waistband.

Least desirable is a separate elasticized waistband sewn on as one unit with one seam; it adds bulk and a ridge of discomfort. Sometimes, the waistband does not stretch the full width of the garment. Be sure to test before you buy.

Hips

In general, slim skirts should look slim. They should cover hips, thighs, tummy, and derriere smoothly, with no wrinkling or bunching—and there should be enough room so that when you sit down, you can do so comfortably. Always be sure there is a chair in the fitting room when you try on a slim skirt, so you can test it sitting down.

Women whose hips are very high usually look their best in slim skirts, but getting a slim skirt to fit the high hip, ironically enough, can be a bit difficult. The reason is, most slim skirts are darted at the waist and release their full width gradually, while the drop, or difference in measurement, between the waist and the hip requires a quick and complete release of fullness. Slim skirts with all-elastic waistbands are often the most ideal not because of the waist ease (although it may certainly be welcome) but because such construction accommodates a sudden drop, and releases the skirt's full width immediately to the hip, if need be. Modified dirndl skirts also work well, for the same reason. Having reached their fullness high on the hip, however, the same skirts usually need to be tapered in gently from just below the hips, and made suitable for walking with a slit or generous walking pleat. If not tapered, they will tend to look not like slim skirts but like A-line skirts, a most unflattering silhouette. Trouser skirts and pants with front pleats also work well, provided the pleats release fully from the waistband and are not partially stitched down.

Derriere

Any skirt, jacket, or sweater that cups in, out, and then around your derriere is a size too small. Period, end of discussion. The solution is simple—go for the next larger size.

If your derriere is your most prominent body part, then save yourself a lot of disappointment and fit all your bottoms to those measurements. Even if you can get away with size 12 in full skirts. For knit skirts, slim skirts, and all pants, you will look best if you go one size larger than in other skirts. This will not only prevent unflattering cling but preserve the life of the garment by keeping it from being stretched out of shape by sitting. With pants, at all costs, avoid a tight crotch fit, even though a high crotch fit will give you a taller look by lengthening the appearance of your legs. An eased and generous—but not droopy—fit over the derriere and thigh will add elegance, which more than compensates for what you lose in leg length. If you ever have to question whether the fit of pants is too tight, the answer is always yes; go for the next size. And face the fact that you are going to be darting the waist of skirts and pants that have rigid waistbands. Your alternative, not always as satisfactory, is to look for well-made elasticized-waist bottoms. Be sure to test all pants sitting down and in a rearview mirror; you want to make sure that they don't bind or cut anywhere, and that the waistband isn't pulled down onto your backside, especially if you've opted for elasticized waists.

Thighs

If your hips are low, here's where you probably need the most careful fit. If your hips are high, here's where the taper generally begins. In either case, the thigh area should be eased, but not baggy. Slim skirts should skim the body without being tight. Watch out for European clothes—they are often too tight where American bodies are a bit wider. On the other hand, American skirts, especially from very traditional companies, may be too wide from the thigh down and look downright stodgy and unflattering.

On pleated skirts, pleats lie flat and closed when the fit is correct. The beauty is the way they dance to your movements. For a trim look, you should seek pleated skirts with the pleats stitched down over the hips. But whether the pleats are stitched down or not, a pleated skirt is always too tight if the pleats splay out when you are standing still. Rather, the pleats should hang down in a straight line and stay close to the body when you walk. To get the right fit on a pleated skirt, you may need to go one size larger. The finished look will be worth it.

Dress Hemline

In general, the best hemline is one that flatters your leg most. For starters, that's going to be below the knee. You can take it as an invariable rule that a skirt should never be shorter than it is wide, no matter how great your legs are. Hemlines will also vary depending on the style of the garment. Because of the extra width they add to the body, full skirts and pleated skirts always need to be longer than a slim skirt. No matter where the hemline falls, however, there are two rules to keep in mind. It should fall at a flattering part of the leg; above the curve of the calf (if it's a slim skirt and your legs are shapely) or below it (pleated or full skirts, thick legs) but never at the widest part of the calf. And the hemline should always be straight as an arrow all the way around you.

In practice, this often means that a skirt—even one of the right length—will have to be rehemmed. On women with full figures, hemlines tend to fall unevenly: They rise on the sides or the back, and need adjusting accordingly. Sometimes the hemline distortion is compensated for in the manufacture; a skirt hangs on the rack with its back looking longer than its front. But most often, manufacturers do not make the hemline correction. Unless you do, your hemline will be a walking advertisement about your size, and call attention to size when you do not wish to.

If you try on a full skirt and the hem rises at the rear or sides by one or more inches, which is often the case, then before you buy the outfit, have the front pinned up to even the line—and check the mirror to make sure it is a flattering length in front. If you find it too short, check the original hem allowance to see whether there is enough there for letting out to even the skirt out all around. If not, it's time to look for a different skirt. Even on full shorts, the hemline tends to rise at rear. In all cases, unless the whole hemline is adjusted to the shortest point, you will be calling attention to size.

It is therefore vital that you always check the hemline of everything you try on, from the rear in a three-way mirror. If adjustment is necessary—and it is more often than not—then you may be best off making your purchases at a store that includes free alterations and always has a fitter on hand. Stores that provide free alterations on men's clothing now also are required to do so on women's clothing.

Pants Rise

Trousers should fit neatly between crotch and waist. They should fit close enough at the crotch to give you the longest possible leg line, but not so close they are revealing. The rise must cover tummy and derriere comfortably, and a woman with a short vertical distance between crotch and waist but a large belly will need a pant with a relatively long rise. The pants must also fit comfortably when you are sitting, so be sure to try them seated. If the back of the pant pulls in any way or actually descends below your waist, you need to look for pants with a longer rise.

Pants Hips

A woman with high hips in a pair of pants cut for women with low hips will usually find the crotch too long and the seat and thighs too baggy. No amount of alteration will make them fit well or look good. Look instead for pants with a shorter rise and possibly front pleats that are not stitched down, so that they release their fullness immediately. The pleats should not appear to pull at any time, neither over the tummy nor over the thighs. Elastic-waist pull-on pants, in the right silhouette, could also work. And knit pants, provided the fabric has enough drape and the style is gently tapered toward the ankle, will fit well. Stirrup pants are excellent.

There are those who say that the full, low-hipped woman should not wear pants. I disagree. But you can't wear any old pants. You need pants that skim the body where you are wide and skim the body where you are narrow. In most cases, this is not a matter of wearing bulky pants in the hope that thick thighs will be lost in the mass of fabric, or getting the right size in traditional style trousers; you will look your best in pants whose silhouette loosely parallels the shape of your body. You are the woman "baggies" were invented for. Baggies are cut to curve out on the hips and thigh and gradually taper in on the lower leg, coming to a trim halt below the ankle bone. Often, this style is cut with a smooth, fitted hip yoke—a good combination for the pear-shaped woman. There are some excellent jeans and casual pants cut for this figure. **Lee's** baggies are famous for their fit, and you can always count on **Gitano** to offer several styles for this basic figure shape. Fine-wale corduroy and cotton twills are also easy to find in this style, and **Lane Bryant** and **Spiegel For You** almost always carry some.

Tailored pants are not the best style for this body type, because the outer thigh forms an arc, while the pants depend on falling straight from the hip to the ankle, without clinging at any point. And although you will certainly find knit pants that cover you, be sure they are not overstressed anywhere. They should provide enough ease on the thigh, taper gently toward the ankle, and never bag in length, which will only make legs look shorter and wider.

Never, ever buy pants without trying them sitting down. If you look like a stuffed sausage in the thigh area, even though the pants have some ease when you stand, you will be better off, look more attractive and more elegant, and feel more comfortable, in pants created with more thigh ease.

Pants Legs

The aim is for the longest sleekest line. And straightest; pants legs should fit with unbroken ease from the top down. However, pants legs that are full at the ankle are hard for most women to wear and especially unflattering to all full-figured women, regardless of body type; they shorten and square the body. That means all pants legs should taper somewhat toward the ankle, to provide a flattering line, even on "straight leg" pants. How much taper is relative—more in seasons when narrower legs are in style; a little less when wide legs are the mode.

If you happen to be wide and short, and you have to cut off the bottom of pants legs to get them short enough, then you will also have to have the entire legs reshaped correctly. What's the correct taper? One that leaves plenty of room for movement and that is gentle enough to give the appearance of straight lines.

Slacks and trousers should fall in a smooth line just to the top of your instep, or, for tapered baggies, to just below the ankle bone. Any longer and they will look sloppy and destroy the smoothness of line you need. Any shorter and they interrupt linearity by creating a gap between pants and shoe. Even slacks that are almost but not quite the right length emphasize width more than length.

THE CASE FOR QUALITY

It is not possible to talk about fit without talking about quality. You need quality in your clothes. They must be as well made as you can possibly afford. You *wear* clothes, give them a run for their money, make them earn their keep. You need to make sure they will perform for you, and one way is to see that they are constructed of quality materials in a lasting manner. Always examine your prospective purchases inside and out to check the workmanship before you buy.

Buy the best quality clothes you can possibly afford. It is always better to have one good item of quality than two items of lesser manufacture. That doesn't mean you have to buy designer clothes. There's lots of quality around in lower price ranges, and in the absence of a label or other clue, you need to be able to evaluate a garment on your own to determine its true value.

If you come across the same style by two manufacturers of differing price range, you will always notice that both strive for the same "look" or silhouette, but the lower-price one does it with less fabric so as to cut the cost. The fit is remarkably different; all of the ease is gone. There's less for you to draw on when you move. The garment looks skimpy. It's not cut to get the best grain of the fabric, just to approximate the look of the design. Skimpy clothes are unbecoming clothes on fuller figures.

Not only will the amount of fabric differ, but type of fabric will, too. Fabrics will be coarser and stiffer in the less expensive garment; therefore they will add bulk by their lack of drape. You can buy a blouse made of polyester and the same style blouse made of silk. But they will not perform the same way on the body. Polyester—though the color may be rich and the pattern identical—won't drape the same way or feel the same. Because the yarn has less weight, the fabric generally (there are some high-quality polyesters around) has little body and doesn't hang; you may find that it clings to your body. And it may make you feel warmer because of its synthetic properties and its tendency to cling to skin.

The better the fabric of a garment, the better the line and drape of garment. And drape is ease and line and elegance. What's more, the better the fabric, often the longer the life of the garment. This is especially true of slacks in wool, which can wear through at the inner thigh within a few wearings unless the fabric is fine textured in fine quality.

A pair of trousers in fine-quality wool gabardine will drape well and fall in a smooth, trim line, hold a slimming leg crease well, and move gracefully with you. But you may be reluctant to spend the money for them because you are sure the fabric will wear through in no time. In truth, a fine gabardine is so smooth and its yarn so surface-finished that it is extremely durable and almost never wears through at the thighs. On the other hand, the same style slacks in an inexpensive flannel with surface nap will add bulk to the body, tailor less well, release a crease sooner, and wear through from friction in a few wearings. Better fabrics tend to add flattery and long life to a garment, saving you money in the long run and giving you clothes you enjoy wearing again and again because they look good.

Some General Principles of Buying Clothes

1. Just because it's there doesn't mean it's right.

Corollary A: If an article of clothing doesn't fit, that doesn't mean there is something wrong with you and your body, that it is your fault and you should feel ashamed. In many instances, a large-size item has not been thought out or styled correctly for a body of three dimensions.

Corollary B: When something doesn't fit or doesn't work for some reason, be sure to tell the salesperson or store manager, and be sure to tell her to tell the store buyer. If you can't find anyone, write the manufacturer that there's a problem with the fit. In the long run, you'll be helping yourself. Many manufacturers introduce a collection of garments without perfecting the fit first. If the clothes are at all expensive, or colorful, or different in any way, but do not sell well because of fit, the store and manufacturer may conclude—I know of many instances where this has happened—that full-figured women are not "ready" for the styling (or color or price, etc.) when what is really wrong is the fit. When something doesn't work, consider it your job to educate retailers and manufacturers.

2. Buy only what looks good on the body.

You are better off buying a dress because it looks good than because you need something new to wear to a wedding, or a party, or whatever. You will find yourself putting on what looks good over and over, and finding a million excuses for not wearing the new dress you bought because you thought you needed a new dress.

Corollary A: What looks good on, no matter how old it is, or how much it cost, always looks better than anything bought simply because it is new, no matter how expensive it is.

Corollary B: One flattering dress (or slacks or skirt or jacket) is worth more than a closet full of any other kind of dress (or slacks, etc.). It is always worth its price.

3. Always buy quality. It always looks better. It always lasts longer.

Quality Time

How can you detect quality? Price alone is not a reliable guide, although generally speaking better clothes cost more. Besides, there are many inexpensive items, particularly imports, that are very well made. In the absence of a label, you should be able to tell whether any garment is well enough made to look good. Here are some checkpoints for quality:

- The fabric should be of good quality; have a good "hand," or feel; drape well; and hang fluidly, not stiffly.
- The seams are flat and smooth, with no broken stitches and no puckering; all edges are oversewn or bound for finish; and there are no loose or hanging threads.
- Hems are generous, sewn in thread (not filament or plastic) the color of the garment, and not visible on the right side.
- Zippers are concealed in a placket, match the fabric color, are of appropriate weight for the fabric, do not pucker, and slide easily.
- Lines of plaids and checks match at front closing, on pockets, and at all seams.
- All openings align perfectly when closed, especially necklines.
- Buttons are appropriate in color and "feel" for the style, and are firmly and properly anchored in thread of the same color as the garment. On coats, there may be a small button anchor on the

inside, and the visible button is attached with a twist of thread so that it does not lie flush with the surface of the coat; otherwise, it will not accommodate the thickness of the coat when closed. A spare button is often provided, sewn into an inner seam or in an accompanying packet threaded to a visible button.

- Buttonholes are completely finished, with no loose threads, and are neither too big nor too small for the buttons provided.
- Sleeves are set and sewn evenly and smoothly all around.
- Linings lie flat, are not visible from sleeves or hemline, and are made of fabrics that enhance the function of the garment fabric. A dress made of almost sheer chiffon needs an opaque slip in a silky fabric that glides gently over your curves; a slip of stiff taffeta would add bulk to your visible silhouette and detract from the fluidity of the chiffon.

The Ten Biggest Fashion Mistakes Women Make

1. **You wear your clothes too tight.**

   Maybe it's a holdover from the days when there were no decent clothes in large sizes and so you got used to pouring yourself into things. Maybe it's a failure of vision, an inability to see oneself clearly, due to years of feeling so ambivalent about your body you couldn't bear to face a mirror (self-knowledge requires a mirror). Maybe it's nothing more than an inability to part with some gorgeous garment from a slimmer past. Whatever the reason you wear them, you should know that tight clothes only emphasize size. Trust me, you'll look better—okay, slimmer, sleeker—in a larger garment. There should always be ease between you and your clothes. This lets clothes drape in their natural line on the body. A body that interrupts the natural fall of a fabric calls attention to itself. Readjust your comfort and vision to an eased fit. Give away all those things, however beautiful, that are one or more sizes too tight. You will look a lot smaller in larger clothes, and you will not call attention to your weight. Honest.

2. **Your skirts are too boxy.**

A slim skirt on a larger woman works only if it is tapered ever so slightly from below hips to hemline. The adjustment may be minimal, but you can't afford to make the mistake of thinking it's too minimal to bother with. A skirt that falls in an A or even a plumb line from hips to hem—as most slim skirts do—broadens your silhouette. A skirt that tapers gently keeps the viewer's eye traveling in a more vertical than horizontal direction. It's not until you pin a skirt into a slight taper that you see the difference. In fact, to the eye, the tapered skirt will appear attractively straight and keep you from looking dowdy and dumpy.

The taper, of course, should never be so much that it looks tarty. Unfortunately, you can't just take in the skirt from the sides by some preset amount. To taper a skirt correctly, first open the hem and press out the crease (when you're finished with the taper, the hem will take a slightly different course on the sides). Begin to take in the side seams gradually, starting just below the widest part of your hips and working down to the hem. Aim to take in two inches per side at the hemline, if it's well below the knee. But trial pinning, however tedious it may be, will yield the best line for you and your clothes. Only after you have permanently stitched newly tapered side seams, and pressed the seam flat, can you approach a straight hemline.

3. **You are too overdone in general.**

Stop overcompensating. You know what I mean. Long red fingernails. Complicated hairdos, or overly long masses of curly hair. Clothes that come with lots of decoration on them—daytime clothes with fringe, fluff, beads, appliqués of many fabrics. It's easy to ridicule such taste as unsophisticated. But I have a more sympathetic view. I understand why you dress that "hyperfeminine" way. Our culture, with its peculiar attitude about women and body size, strips women of substance of the right to feel feminine. You grasp society's view of you as not fully feminine. And you attempt—mistakenly—to reassert your femininity in frills and furbelows, ruffles and gewgaws. (Indeed, overdecorated clothes make up an unusually large share of the fashion offerings in large sizes.) After all, body decoration is part of the accepted female role, and it's a visible badge of femininity. But overdecorating is the wrong approach to femininity. Femininity isn't an accessory; it isn't something you put on. Besides, frills and ruffles don't work well on big-busted bodies, which are intricate enough. They add too much bulk, too much detail. They divert attention from line. There are much more attractive and flattering ways to underline femininity: sleekness, raciness, elegance, softness of silhouette, color. A plain black straight dress in silk or rayon crepe with long sheer sleeves is one hundred times more alluring, more modern, more interesting, and more flattering than a doohickied sweater. Simple clothes of fluid fabrics with graceful lines and movement also come across as extremely feminine—and much more flattering.

4. You confuse casual with sloppy.

The bad news is that there are stereotypes about women of substance. Frequently we are presumed to be sloppy, lazy, etc. The good news is we can completely control the impression we make, first and foremost by impeccable grooming. Even casual clothes must fit precisely at key points. Crisp sleeve lengths and leg bottoms. Well-defined necklines and shoulders that make us look proud and tall. Hemlines that are straight as an arrow all around, not hiked up in back. You can't look good and you can't possibly feel good about yourself when your pants bottoms are dragging on the ground. If you ever have to stop and think whether you can get away with something a little on the sloppy side, the answer is usually no. Attending to the details of fit and neatness will have a payoff worth the effort.

5. You over-rely on knits for fit.

You like them because they are not only comfortable but stretchy. And you make use of that stretch. But coverage is not the same as fit; think body-skimming ease when you think of fit.

Very often in knits, you have to go up a size to get the ease knits need to look good on the body.

Most knits, especially for warmer seasons, are made of polyester/cotton interlock, and you have to go a long way to find a more difficult fabric for fuller figures, especially in the fabric's lighter-weight versions. It clings where it should drape. It has a high loft—it doesn't lie flat. It has almost no built-in body or shapability. You're much better off, if you insist on knits, with a true jersey, especially in cotton. Or knits with some rayon, for body and drape. Also, reacquaint yourself with other kinds of fabrics. There are highly comfortable woven garments with such built-in comfort features as elastic waistbands. Especially if you want to project a polished professional image, choose knits very selectively.

6. **You wear clothes that are too tailored, usually made from fabrics that are too stiff and bulky.**

Somewhere it is written—I know where, because I was called on to update that section of a well-known etiquette book—that large women should wear tailored clothes. Don't believe it . . . unless you are truly the tailored type. These clothes can be mannish and forbidding. You need clothes with lines that are fluid and graceful.

7. **You lack enough experience to know what looks good or works well on you.**

You have taste, and you buy attractive outfits. But somehow when you go to put them on, you can't quite say why, but you feel they do not suit you. Problem is, you don't try on enough in stores to honestly assess, to experiment. Your eye needs to practice, at the same time you need to see for yourself that there are enough good looking items for you to feel safe passing some by. We all try on outfits we love, but it takes a great deal of experience to put aside one if it doesn't look good. It also takes the possibility of choice—that there will be something else if this doesn't work out. Fortunately, that is increasingly the case. Don't be ashamed to go into a store and try many things on. That's why God made fitting rooms. In fact, it's wise to plan some nonbuying shopping trips.

8. You dress to camouflage.

"Tents are for campgrounds and floats are for parades" a very articulate large-size fashion designer once remarked. She was right. Tents, bubbles, dolmans—you buy them to hide behind the fabric. The trick to looking and feeling good is to dress to accentuate your assets—and don't worry, you have them. Dressing to camouflage flaws only brings attention to what you are trying to hide. Dress to highlight your face, your curviness, your legs. If you highlight your strong points, no one will notice your weaker points. Look for silhouettes with less fabric and more purposeful design.

9. You wear jackets too short.

They stop at the widest part of your body, just at the height of your hips. This is especially true of short women. The conventional wisdom is that a short woman takes a short jacket because it will make her look taller through the visual contrast of a short bodice and a long expanse of skirt. Short, however, is strictly a matter of proportion. What is short on a woman of 5'6" is a lot longer on a woman of 5'2", and most fashions are designed for women of about 5'6". The secret of proportion is the relationship of parts to the whole. No matter how you slice it, a "short" jacket that hits mid-hip cuts the body almost exactly in half and widens it. A jacket or other garment that stops at your widest body part always emphasizes width at the expense of proportion.

10. You think discomfort is a way of fashion life.

Again, the result of limited fashion choices in the past. But there really is no fashion in discomfort. One secret of style is to choose clothes that, once on the body, allow you to completely forget about them, and focus on the life around you. Make sure your clothes have ease and drape built into them, so you don't always have to be on the ready to readjust them. Fidgeting and fussing with clothes, again, calls attention to exactly that which you are most uncomfortable about. Choose clothes that fit, fabrics that do not cling. Keep styles clean and unfussy.

8

You Are the Perfect Size—for You

*T*he aesthetic claim on the human imagination is very strong and very deep. Beauty craves a certain amount of organization; it is an expression of the basic human need for order and stability, without which all is chaos and experience can have no meaning because everything is competing for the attention of the nervous system. What appeals to the eye, because it pleases the brain, is some sort of harmony, the combination of elements in a satisfying way.

Of all organizing principles, none is more primal than balance, the equal distribution of weight around a central point. But not too equal. Balance that is static in its equilibrium is essentially boring. The eye—and the mind—loses interest very quickly. There is nothing to stimulate the imagination. Somewhere, somehow—and the ways are as varied as your wit and inventiveness—you have to add a frisson of excitement. The need for order, then, must be itself carefully balanced against a need for stimulation. Vivacity is everything.

Within the area of space occupied by the body, **how the elements are**

145

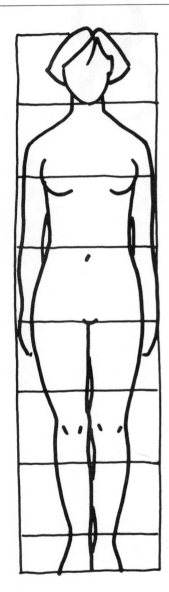

combined is more important than how big the elements are. For we visually comprehend the dimensions of a part in comparison with the others and the whole. The shapes that make up the basic parts of the human figure must have enough variety to keep the eye interested but need to relate to each other in a pleasing way—we call this proportion.

The way still regarded as most pleasing was defined by the Greeks in the laws of proportion, in which we interpret length in relation to width. In the classic scheme, the whole body is the height of seven and a half heads, the head measured from chin to crown (top of head, not top of hair). This is the ideal; relax—**no one measures up exactly.** Through the imprinting of Western culture, through the training of our eyes, we expect the body to be several times longer than it is wide, by a margin that is readily apparent. In the world of proportion, the **measurements per se are not as important as the visual proportion,** the perception of apparent dimension of width and height.

That leads to the single most important aesthetic concept for dressing; you might say, the single most important incentive to getting dressed at all: **A figure of any height can appear to be in good proportion.** Clothing affords us the means to rearrange the proportions of our bodies so that they can be aesthetically satisfying. This is the good side of having been expelled from the Garden of Eden.

Imagine the body as generally occupying a rectangular space. The parts of the body that must visually relate well to each other include the size of the head, the distance to the waist, the length of the torso, and the length of the legs. Those are the important vertical space divisions affecting the perception of height of a figure. In a figure of average height standing with hands at sides, the fullest part of the hip (about seven inches below the waist) aligns with the wrist, dividing the body roughly into two equal halves.

In addition, the placement and width of the body's natural horizontal lines—the shoulders, the bust, the waist, and the hips—strongly influence the perception of space. When you add clothes, count the hemline as one more major horizontal. This is one reason why, when skirt hemlines rise in a cycle of fashion—potentially cutting the perceived length of the body—other proportions change, too. Jackets usually lengthen (a long unbroken line restores the perception of height). This explains why shoulders that slope even slightly drastically shorten the apparent height of the body, increasing the perception of width.

In addition to the space divisions of the body, the perception of balance in shape of the whole is determined by scale. Scale relates the size of the details of a garment to the whole garment and to the wearer. Proportion decrees, for example, that if an item of clothing is made wider to suit a larger body, it also should be made a bit longer, and the wider the skirt—as in a pleated or full skirt—the longer it must be to balance the volume of fabric. Scale decrees that the details be subtly—the emphasis is on subtly—related to that size; to maintain the integrity of the design, the lapels, the pockets, the size of the buttons must be slightly enlarged. The size of accessories also falls into the domain of scale, and they are one of the major means by which integrity of scale is achieved.

The laws of proportion and scale in perception of body size have these major consequences:

- The size of the head is one of the most important elements in determining the visual height of the body. A small head increases the apparent span of the body. (This, by the way, is one reason most high-fashion models have small heads.) Of two women identical in height but having different face lengths, the woman with the shorter face will appear taller.
- Because the brain sees the shape and size and color of a part in relation to the whole, in relation to all elements in the field of vision, perceptions of size and shape depend not only on the part in question but on juxtaposed elements. That makes judgments of size and shape subject to the effect of illusion— thank heavens!
- By skillfully deploying the visual components of clothes and their design—namely line, texture, color, and emphasis— we can create the way we want the body perceived.

THE NEW LAW OF RELATIVITY

Because judgments about the shape and size of body parts are made in relation to the entire figure, or perceptual "field," as the psychologists call it, **your body sets its own standards for itself. It is a frame of reference complete unto itself.** It creates its own logic—which answers only to itself. Just as style dismisses the concept of external standards of perfection, the principles of aesthetics give you a chance to prove it. If style is the spirit, then knowledge of aesthetic principles is the means—both assume you have the potential to create an identity that's unique and attractive and to express it through what you wear. **By applying the laws of proportion to ensure** that the body parts arrive at a pleasing visual balance, and seeing that the details are in scale to you, you can use clothes to create the impression that you are the perfect size—for you. This may be the single most important element of fashion savvy; it transcends all fashion trends and applies at all times. **It means that there is no reason why you can't look at least as terrific in clothes as any other woman.**

However lumpy you may be, however large you may be, however top-heavy or bottom-heavy you may be is a matter strictly between you and the mirror. You're not finished until you are dressed. Dressing thoughtfully can put your proportions in beautiful balance and let you put the focus where you want it.

Proportion means that the way to handle parts of the body that look too big is not to cut them off—I know, you've been tempted—but to put them in balance with the smaller parts by judiciously adding to the smaller parts. I'm sure you're thinking: "She must be crazy. My problem is I'm too big and she's talking about adding more."

Don't panic. I know it's a completely different way of thinking from what you have been conditioned to. But adding to a part that is small in proportion has an effect that pleases the eye. It balances the body parts—it satisfies. And remember, it's the disproportion in body parts that really calls attention to size. Anyway, creating balance among body parts implies that there are at least two ways to work: While you are adding to the part that appears relatively too small, you will also be applying the elements of design—such as line and color—to the part that's too big, attempting to put *it* in proportion with the smaller parts.

FROM DON'TS TO DOS

Learning how to dress by the principles of balance and proportion and scale isn't difficult. You probably know some of the principles already (long jackets are flattering because their vertical lines influence the perception of height), although it is a safe bet that most of the fashion rules that you do know begin with a very loud DON'T. They are prohibitions more than style principles. And even the few DOs that you do know a) don't tell you why and b) don't even give you a clue as to what else also creates the same effect. Nor will they indicate when and why a long jacket may not be flattering (if it's cut wide on top, especially for the pear-shaped figure; because it broadens the narrowest part of the body to the width of the widest part, fostering the perception of all-over width. A more fit-and-flare shaped jacket design would allow the whole body to appear as trim as the top part).

Even the commonly stated imperative that large women should wear tailored clothes is absurd because it has no basis whatsoever in design principles of balance and proportion. That so-called rule sounds awfully punitive to me—being banished to man-tailored clothes for not being thin (read: feminine). Not only can tailored clothes be very unflattering (the cardboard fabrics they're usually made from add bulk; and the shapes they're usually cut in can ride roughshod over your good proportions without even noticing), there is absolutely no reason on earth why any woman has to always confine herself to one style, let alone one that may not even come close to representing her true style spirit. To think of all those beautiful clothes you may have been avoiding because of such a groundless imperative!

BODIES BY DESIGN

What *Style Is Not a Size* has done instead is to outline general principles of good design in fashion—which apply to all bodies at all times. By understanding these, it is a simple step to applying the general principles to the specifics of your own body, however well-proportioned it may or may not be.

This approach assumes you have some intelligence and it completely demystifies dressing. Dressing is not something you can leave to "the experts"—you are the expert on you. No more being at the mercy of other people's opinions, or not knowing why something you put on just doesn't look right. You become the best fashion decision-maker for you. You can put on a skirt and understand why it isn't helping you look good. Knowing the principles of design helps you understand what you are doing and why, so that you can always make informed and intelligent fashion choices. There are times when you will probably want to violate one or another design principle—you simply have to have that short black leather skirt—in favor of some other important principle (say, unadulterated trashiness). But at least you are making a choice and know what the downside risk is. (And you will know to cover your legs in opaque black stockings; that way you will not only lengthen the body line but look chic, too.) Not to worry: Fashion isn't the most important thing in life, and anyway life is nothing if not a series of risk-versus-benefit trade-offs. And style is nothing if not the judicious and delicious taking of risks.

This approach is invaluable for another reason. It returns ownership of your body to you. Women in general and full-figured women in particular have rarely been allowed to inhabit their own bodies freely. The culture has truly estranged us from our own bodies. For full-figured women, the world of fashion has been, in the past, made daunting enough just by the search for clothes. The existence of so many prohibitions has made fashion far more intimidating than it really is and undoubtedly turned many women away from enjoying what should be at least a pleasurable part of their lives. Framing style guidelines in the general rules of proportion will also help you understand that these are principles of design as applied to all other bodies, and to all other objects in life as well as to bodies. They do not single you out. And they will help you judge the aesthetic value of other objects in your life.

Nor will these guidelines inhibit you. They won't keep you focused on your shortcomings because most of them are presented in terms of what you want to accent. And there are always choices; there isn't just one way to counterbalance the fact of width with the perception of height. You can wear a certain silhouette, you can add shoulder width, you can add hemline length and taper the hem, you can add details that throw the emphasis on your face. Besides, you are doing something positive: You are not learning a list of don'ts . . . you are taking Aesthetics 101. And every single one of the guidelines has only one goal—to help you find the most exciting, attractive, sexy, terrific, and chic way to dress every day, all day—and night.

PRINCIPLES OF BODIES BY DESIGN

If you are like most women, you want to use clothes to balance body proportions, to maximize the perception of height, to minimize attention to width. Here are some of the most important implications of aesthetic principles applied to clothes design. You will want to familiarize yourself with them so that you can easily make clothing choices that flatter. And remember, fashions in clothing may change, but the aesthetic principles do not. Whether jackets are trapeze or slim, hemlines longer or shorter, a flattering line is always a flattering line.

LINE AND FORM

Line defines form and contours. In clothes, line can be in the outer shape or cut of the clothes, the seams, jacket edges, hemlines, details like topstitching and trim and button placement, as well as patterns such as stripes. If there is a guiding principle to the use of line on an object, it's that you don't use line to repeat the dimension (in bodies it's usually width) you prefer to de-emphasize. If you'd rather not announce to people that your hips are big (let the suckers figure it out for themselves, if they have to know), you won't use horizontal lines across the hip zone, whether they are style lines (such as a jacket bands) or pattern lines (such as stripes).

- The dominant line of a piece of clothing is its outline, or silhouette, its cut and outer shape. The silhouette line—which is where fashion works its changes—should complement the shape of the body, so that it appears as a natural elaboration of body lines.
- Because the eye tends to follow a line, lines on garments should be used to guide the eye visually to an area to be emphasized.
- Straight vertical lines—seams, trim, details—create length, as they keep the eye moving upward, and suggest strength. They also divide the figure, making it appear thinner. A vertical line appears longer than a horizontal line of the same length.
- Horizontal lines keep the eye from moving upward and magnify the impression of width. They imply the pull of gravity—and repose. At the top of the body, horizontal lines make narrow shoulders appear wider—which makes wide hips appear narrower, provided the bottom hem is kept slim for contrast. Off-the-shoulder, square, and boat necklines emphasize width and can make a short woman seem shorter. Bands or seams across the hips will make the hips seem broader.

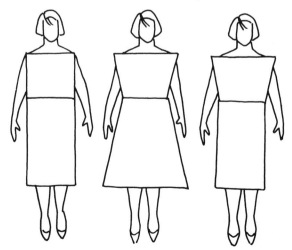

In this most basic of perceptual illusions, a vertical line typically appears longer than a horizontal line of the same length.

- Diagonal lines suggest movement; they are dynamic and sophisticated and attract attention to one detail as they lead the eye upward. Provided the angle is not too abrupt, diagonal lines tend to slenderize a garment even more than vertical lines do. Slim vee necklines lengthen the overall figure and lengthen a round or square face.

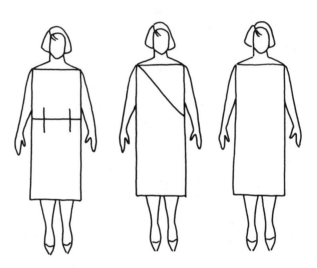

- Oblique lines look short next to wide horizontals, but they emphasize length when put next to narrower horizontals—the best argument in the world for tapering straight skirts; it reinforces the verticality of a shape.
- Curved lines that are gentle and restrained in their curve but strong in their presentation—princess seams, for example, or contrast trim—are graceful and feminine. Because they lead the eye in a fluid motion, they create the impression of a smooth figure. Extreme curves are fussy and exaggerate size because it takes longer for the eye to negotiate them.
- Large, unbroken spaces seem larger than equal areas divided into segments. Divided into vertical segments, the perception of height is increased.
- Asymmetric divisions of vertical space, especially when combined with diagonals, are powerful ways to balance the body.

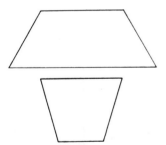

Even though oblique lines are the same length in top and bottom figures, and top horizontals are same width, top figure appears much wider. No better argument exists for tapering slim skirts.

VALUE

In addition to the direction of line, the value of spaces influences perception of size.

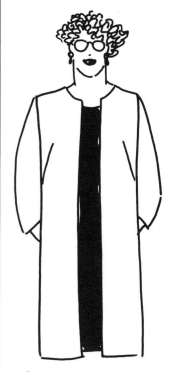

When a space is divided into vertical segments, the perception of height is increased.

- Spaces evenly divided horizontally emphasize a shape's squareness and shorten and widen the body. Using clothes to divide the body horizontally into uneven areas lengthens the body. The eye automatically compares the smaller area to the larger segment, making the whole appear longer and thinner. The most satisfying effect is created by dividing a garment into two parts, one of a third to a half, the other between a half to two thirds. The greater the difference between the length of the bodice and the length of a skirt, the taller the body will appear.
- Very conveniently, the waistline normally creates a body segment shorter than half and is safe to use as a stopping point for maintaining balance of body proportions. Clothes that stop at the hip—slightly dropped torso dresses, hip-length jackets—cut the figure into two halves, give it a boxy appearance, and call attention to the widest part of the body. For this reason, a short jacket does not always increase the height of a short woman.

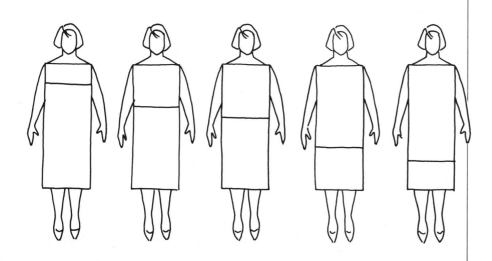

- Colors differ in value, the property by which they are seen as light or dark. Because the eye travels to light areas first, they stand out, making those areas seem larger, particularly when contrasted to dark areas, which recede visually. Unequal areas of dark and light are more satisfying than equal areas. Using a darker color value below the waist makes the hips appear smaller and the figure taller.
- In general, figures in which the width of the hip and the width of the bust do not appear equal, that is, they are not balanced horizontally, can be brought into balance through the use of colors or style lines that maximize the smaller body part and minimize the larger one.
- Detail and ornamentation function like color value in balancing figure proportions; they enlarge an area, and therefore should be used in areas that need to be visually enlarged. The pear-shaped figure, for example, carries ornamentation best when it is above the waist.

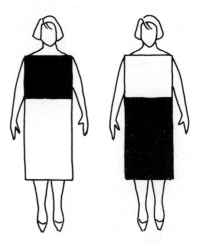

TEXTURE

The surface qualities of a fabric give it character and influence the way it feels—its hand—and the way it falls, or drapes. A fabric that drapes falls softly and smoothly into straight lines and moves fluidly. The character of the fabric should determine the type and silhouette of clothes it can be made into. Texture is seen as well as felt because lustrous fabrics and smooth surfaces reflect more light than matte surfaces and rough textures, which absorb light.

- Obvious texture tends to expand the space it covers.
- Shiny textures, by virtue of the shading effects of their sharp highlights, increase size and emphasize even minute protruberances underneath; matte textures minimize size and contour.
- Soft pile fabrics, such as velvet, velour, terrycloth, chenille, and corduroy, absorb light in their deep folds but at the surface reflect a great deal of light, making a garment and body appear larger.
- Rough-textured fabrics, and stiff or crisp ones, tend to increase the size of the body by adding bulk. But because they also can ignore the lumps and bumps of body contours underneath, and create forms independent of the body, they have their value. They are best confined to clothes in simple, predominantly vertical shapes, particularly jackets and outerwear.
- Pliable fabrics that cling to the body emphasize its contours.

PATTERN

- Space filled with pattern is seen as larger than "unfilled" space, particularly when the pattern or print is widely spaced—big polka dots, wide stripes, even vertical ones.

Filled space appears greater than unfilled space. The greater the space between stripes, the wider the whole appears.

- Patterns—plaids, checks, and prints—look best when they are in scale with the body. Medium-size patterns of related rather than contrasting colors are most becoming to all body types. Huge prints, even on a large figure, emphasize size.
- Plaids are highly flattering when cut on the bias; they create diagonal lines that lead to the face.
- Vertical stripes carry the eye quickly upward and make a figure appear taller and slimmer—unless they have to negotiate contours; then the pattern bows, usually calling attention to the widest part of the body. They work best, then, on clothes that fall in a very straight line either because of the drape of the fabric or the ease of the silhouette.
- The more commanding or complicated a print, the simpler the line of dress should be.
- Beware border prints. By adding horizontal detail to the widest part of the design—the hem—they stop the eye and cut the figure, making it appear wider.

COLOR

After line, color is the most important element of design for creating flattering perceptions.

- A garment in one color makes the body appear longer.
- Darker colors visually recede; a body dressed in dark colors takes up less visual space, looks smaller. A woman who has a large bust but narrow hips can equalize her figure proportions by wearing a dark top and light-colored bottom.
- Bright colors compel attention, but the eye reads them as closer, therefore larger. Still, use them to call attention to an area of the body you want to highlight.
- Light colors, when contrasted to dark ones, also attract attention, and are particularly suitable for collars and necklines because they call attention to the face.
- Warm colors (red, yellow, orange) advance, and attract the eye; they maximize size.

- Cool colors (blue, green, violet), because they recede, minimize size.
- Because clarity of skin is vital in conveying a healthy appearance, skin color is generally more important in determining flattering colors of dress than are hair or eye color—unless those happen to be your most outstanding features. If your hair is bright red, it will certainly claim attention first; select colors accordingly.
- Black or other dark colors improve the clarity of light skin.
- Complexions, regardless of skin color, are either cool (blue-pink undertones) or warm (yellow undertones); choosing clothes that complement basic skin tones (assuming they are not masked by makeup) generally creates the most flattering effect.

THE OTHER PRINCIPLES OF DESIGN

In addition to proportion and balance, clothes should impart to your body a sense of **unity**. All of the parts must work together to create an attractive visual effect. And in this case, a whole is definitely more than the sum of its parts. A dress of sharp straight lines, for example, doesn't work with a rounded cocoon-shaped jacket, even though each one may be beautifully designed in itself. Lines and shapes have expressive qualities as well as aesthetic ones, and all go together to create an effect. A coat of restrained curves is seen as more feminine than one whose lines are straight or diagonal.

Unity also demands that the style lines and seam lines on clothing covering the top of the body align with those on the bottom, whether the items are bought separately or not. Jogs in lines stop the eye and emphasize width. In addition, all areas of a dress should reflect the same shapes; if collars and cuffs are curved, then pocket lines should be, too.

The lines and design features should be organized with **rhythm**, graceful, flowing movement that leads the eye from line to line to create patterns— and to keep clothes from looking static and disjointed. Rhythmic use of design features gives clothing orderly, related movement, and should lead the eye toward a feature you want emphasized.

And there should always be the power of **emphasis**. Emphasis creates a center of interest—and there should never be more than one center of interest in an outfit—so that the eye can come to a rest. Emphasis stops the eye. It focuses attention on the most important part of the design or the feature you are most interested in accenting. Emphasis also implies that one kind of line or color dominates the others in an outfit. A favorite ploy of designers is to place detail so that it directs the eye to the face. It works well for you.

BODY TYPES

You are doubtlessly more than familiar with the fact that not all bodies have the same proportions and that all large women are not large in the same way. The body naturally falls into one of several patterns of weight distribution and shape. These are not good and bad bodies, or right and wrong ones; these are natural and common variations in women's body proportions.

The body type you are generally influences the fashion silhouettes that look best on your body. Because aesthetic values are built in, when the integral style lines align loosely with your body's shape, they automatically rebalance contours using the minimum amount of fabric. The fit and flare shape on a semifitted princess coatdress, for example, is a classically beautiful silhouette that happens to be the most flattering item of clothing a bottom-heavy woman could wear. Because the built-in flare accommodates the hips as part of its unbroken course, without calling attention to them, the silhouette implies that the body is as narrow all over as at the semifitted top. And if the vertical lines of the dress are given some visibility—a line of buttons down the front, perhaps princess seams—the lines will carry the eye swiftly up and down to enhance the perception of height, as opposed to width. And nowhere do we have to talk about hiding hips, or camouflaging them, because the style lines allow for hips.

Of course, to dress your body well, you need to understand your body. You have probably already at least tried to get on friendly new terms with it via the mirror. This is important for establishing a positive body image, as outlined in Chapter 5. But using the same techniques, you also need to study it to see its shape. Think of it as a fact-finding mission, not a search-and-destroy mission for finding flaws. In fact, you can dismiss the concept of body flaws; you are looking for body facts. You are approaching yourself with a healthy realism. What are the curves, where are they, how large are they in relation to the waist? Are your hips just below your waist? Or are they lower? Is the top of your body broad and square? Note curves, contours, proportions, general shape, from the front and from the back.

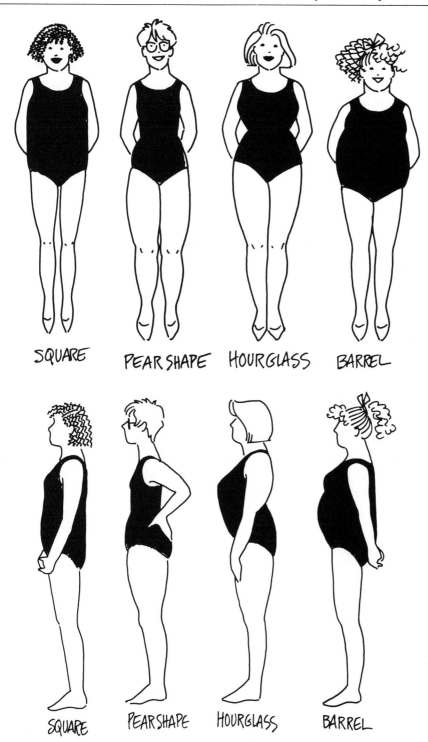

SQUARE PEAR SHAPE HOURGLASS BARREL

SQUARE PEAR SHAPE HOURGLASS BARREL

ASK THE MIRROR

Choosing a private time when you won't be rushed or interrupted, put on a leotard, get out pencil and paper, and stand in front of your mirror. These are some basic questions you should answer as you look at your body:

- Is your face short from chin to hairline, or is it long?
- Is your face full or fleshy, or is it slim in relation to your body?
- Is your neck wide or narrow? Is it long or short?
- Are your shoulders straight? Or do they slope down?
- Are your shoulders the same width as your hips? If not, which appear wider?
- Is your upper back fleshy? The back of your neck?
- Are your arms fleshy? Your upper arms or the whole arm?
- Does your waistline visibly indent?
- Is your high hip, roughly three inches below the waist, the same or even larger than your hip, at seven inches below the waist?
- Are your hips full and rounded? Or are they more squared?
- Are your thighs wider or narrower than your hips?
- Does your body appear longer above the waist than below it?
- Does it appear broader above the waist than below it? Or narrower?
- Seen from the front, are you straight up and down?
- Are your legs slim or shapely? From the knee down? From the thighs down?

Unless you understand your body shape, getting dressed will always be more frustrating than rewarding, and going shopping for clothes will be an agony. When you are aware of your body shape, finding clothes that look good will no longer be a matter of chance, a hit-or-miss proposition. Turned loose in a store, you will know which clothes to zero in on. You will be able to look clothes over before you even try them on to assess whether they will work for your kind of body. And if you don't see what's appropriate on a rack, you will know what kind of styles to ask for. Since asking for something helps make it happen in the fashion world, asking is the next best thing to having it. Stores really want to sell clothes; they meet your needs or they don't stay in business.

Think of the body as essentially rectangular in total configuration and several times taller than it is wide. The size of the head, the width of the figure, the length to the waist, the length of the torso, and the length of the legs all affect the perception of size. It is important to know what body type you are so that you can visually balance awkward body proportions and characteristics with clothes. Clothes, of course, add graceful and other notes of their own. Full-figured bodies tend to assume one of four silhouettes.

The Figure-Eight or Hourglass Shape

BASIC CHARACTERISTICS   This is a great shape no matter the size. You have a well-defined waist and balanced shoulders and hips, although your shoulders are not very broad. Your hips are the same size or slightly larger than your bust, and they are rounded and full, curving inward at the lower hip; your low hips are wider than your high hips. Your face tends to be in proportion to your body.

IN ADDITION   Your arms are basically well-proportioned; the upper parts get flabby if you gain weight. You may have a double chin.

YOUR BEST FEATURES   You have a small waist that takes accenting. And you are proud of your generous bust and like to accent your cleavage for evening dressing. Your hips are sexy and your back is relatively trim.

YOUR LEAST FAVORITE FEATURES   You probably have thick thighs in relation to your lower legs and the rest of your body; thighs may be thick at either the inner or outer side.

YOUR FASHION AIM   You have lots of choices, since you are not dressing to correct the proportions of your shape. Basically you can let your curviness speak for itself in clothes of simple lines and semifitted shapes that fall smoothly through the torso. You can acknowledge without overemphasizing your curviness by dressing in soft, flowing fabrics, or you can downplay them with long, slim jackets over slim skirts; both lend great sophistication. To downplay your curviness, choose shirts and sweaters that are soft and loose. You look good in belts, but keep them narrow to avoid looking dumpy. You can wear prints and all color combinations, so long as the patterns don't fall in funny places and overemphasize your bust.

LOTS OF SLIMMING VERTICALS

FASHION SUGGESTIONS Slim belts and medium cummerbunds of soft fabric were made for you; they gently emphasize your trim midriff. You can wear jumpsuits especially well. Dresses with gently dropped waists balance the bustline. So do tunic styles. Raglan and dolman sleeves of controlled proportions will often simplify fit and provide a long, lean line. Cocktail dresses with softly draped low front or back necklines whisper your name. Skirts with good linearity but exciting movement are also for you—trumpet skirts, stitched-down pleats, softly pleated skirts.

WHAT TO AVOID Since your shape is frankly feminine, you need to avoid dressing in clothes that emphasize the sexiness of your curves. Go for sophisticated lines rather than fussy (ruffled and flounced), cute (little girl puffy sleeves), or detailed ones, which overcomplicate your figure and make it look larger. In bottoms, full or circle skirts are not your best look; slim or pleated skirts will be more flattering. In tops, especially for daytime dressing, avoid any design features or silhouettes that overemphasize the bust, such as large buttons or awkwardly placed pockets or pocket flaps. Your big bust can make tailored clothes, and especially boxy jackets, look very matronly.

The Pear Shape

BASIC CHARACTERISTICS You have nature's preferred—and protected—female shape. Your hips are wider than your shoulders and bustline, which appear trim and narrow. Your waist is not especially well-defined but it is definitely there, narrower than your hips. Your bust tends to be small, rather than large. Because of the relative narrowness of the top of your body, you may feel long-waisted.

IN ADDITION You may also have a thin face in relation to your body. Your neck may be slender—and long. Your legs may be significantly heavier than your arms.

YOUR BEST FEATURES "I look fine sitting at my desk." Your face, neck, bustline, midriff, waist, and arms are average and in proportion to each other.

YOUR LEAST FAVORITE FEATURES   "Bulges" is the word that first leaps to your mind. Your hips, thighs, and derriere are by far the fleshiest parts of your body; they give you a low center of gravity, and you have been planning an insurrection against them for years. Your shoulders are narrow and may slope downward. Take comfort: Scientific studies show that of all body types, yours, with its weight concentrated below the waist, is the one least prone to diabetes and heart disease.

YOUR FASHION AIM   To balance your body, you need to add width to the shoulder and upper torso area. Therefore, shoulder pads are absolutely essential. To help in the balancing, you need to de-emphasize the hip area with silhouettes that flow smoothly and gracefully over the lower body. Your waist may not be clearly defined, but it is indented, and belts will help place it and add emphasis to the top half of your body. Fit and flare silhouettes that skim the body are cut perfectly for your body type. To balance the width of your lower body, always wear slight heels—one inch for walking, no more than two inches for dress—rather than flats.

FOR THE PEAR SHAPE FIGURE

FASHION SUGGESTIONS   Skirts with soft front pleats in fabrics that have built-in drape and fluidity will skim over the hip line, then fall gracefully from there. Dropped yokes are an excellent design feature for you and are essential if you want to wear all-around pleated skirts. Bell-shaped skirts look good and provide a flatteringly tapered hemline. Look for skirts with linings, especially in knit skirts, to minimize cling. All skirts should be longer rather than shorter, to balance bottom width. You can wear light colors, bold prints, even horizontal stripes on top. Short jackets and easy cropped ones, especially in color, were made for you. So were vests. Since you will frequently find yourself dressing in separates (your top and bottom take different sizes), invest in attractive belts. You can enjoy jackets and shirts with such shoulder detail as epaulets and flanges. Cap sleeve blouses also look good on you. Cowl neck sweaters balance your top well. All tops—blouses, shirts, sweaters, jackets, coats—should have tapered wrists, to avoid the addition to width across the hip line, where wrists naturally fall. You will often be balancing your narrow top by wearing dark skirts; stock up on matching dark pantyhose in sheers and opaques; those made with spandex will help give you the firmness you may feel you need and a smooth unbroken line in clothes. You can wear leggings and stirrup pants—they lengthen your legs—provided you wear long lean tops that glide over the widest part of your hips. Be sure all your pants are long enough in the rise (distance from crotch to waist). Pants with ease from soft pleats falling from the waist or a hip yoke look terrific on you, provided they are not overly full and the legs are tapered gently toward the ankle. Go for loose raincoats rather than belted styles. And keep shoes and stockings the same color.

WHAT TO AVOID   Watch out for sloppy, oversize tops with dropped shoulders; they will make your whole body look shapeless and unnecessarily large; you will look better if you add definition to your shoulders and suggest your whole body is more along the lines of your top half. Rounded shoulder lines and raglan sleeves will not give you enough of a shoulder line. Boxy jackets that end at the hip line call attention to your widest part and broaden the whole silhouette. Stiff fabrics will not improve your contours. Circle skirts and those with all-around knife pleats falling from the waist tend to broaden your whole silhouette, too. If your weight is more in the thigh than the low hip, avoid man-tailored trousers, which need to fall straight, in favor of styles with soft front pleating or hip yokes. Long sweaters tend to cling to the hip and derriere area and emphasize it. If you like the comfort of knit skirts, avoid the slim silhouettes and opt instead for skirts with soft knit-in pleating all around, especially from a hip yoke. Avoid panty lines by wearing waist-to-toe support hose.

The Barrel Shape

BASIC CHARACTERISTICS   From shoulder to thighs, you appear round or oval, and you carry your weight in front (bust, midriff, tummy). The distinguishing feature of this shape is a waist that is either not well defined or larger than the hips below, with a pronounced midriff bulge. Your bust is also larger than your hips. You have a short neck, and your face tends to be full in relation to your body, fleshy at the jawline and in the cheeks. Because of the width at top and your high hips, you may feel short-waisted.

IN ADDITION   Women with this body type may have beautifully shaped legs from thigh to ankle, which are slim in relation to the body. You tend to have high hips and "no rear." You may have a broad, and possibly fleshy, upper back.

LEGS AND DRESS SAME COLOR

YOUR BEST FEATURES   You'd like to keep your legs and trade in the rest of your body. You'd keep your arms, too.

YOUR LEAST FAVORITE FEATURES   Your waist and midriff have always tended to thickness. You carry your weight in the upper part of your front torso; you feel your figure is top-heavy.

YOUR FASHION AIM   You need to create strong vertical lines to counterbalance the roundness. Establishing a strong shoulder with pads and wearing long lean tops in relaxed shapes that drape from there will give you the linearity you need. So will wedge-shaped dresses, as the cut perfectly accommodates and complements your shape. Dresses that drape from shoulder detail are your natural ally. You can highlight your attractive legs with skirts that stop at the knee.

FASHION SUGGESTIONS   You will find dressing easier if you look for slim skirts with elastic waistbands; they work for thick waists and allow for the sudden "drop" of a high hip. Deep vee necklines, especially those created by draped surplice bodices, were made for you. Long slim blousons keep your look very narrow since they fall between the low hips and thigh area, where your torso is narrowest. Even soft shirtwaist dresses are good. if the shoulders are lightly padded, the bodice is bloused and draped slightly, and the waist is suggested with a narrow belt, loosely drawn. Slim belts worn loosely so that they drape slightly in front will suggest the waistline you wish you had, especially when worn over long shirts outside your pants. Alternatively, tunics and other silhouettes with undefined waistlines work beautifully for you, as do straight, unfitted jackets. Provided you bolster them with shoulder pads, big sweaters worn over slim pants or tapered skirts are attractive for you. In fact, all your bottoms—pants or skirts—should always be tapered. You can wear softly pleated skirts in fabrics that drape close to the body, and they will look best when combined with jackets with slim silhouettes. Draped tops and asymmetrical cuts are very good for you. You can wear colors on top, especially as accents under jackets. Prints and patterns will work best on the bottom half of your figure. Long scarves draped over a shoulder look terrific.

WHAT TO AVOID   Set-in waists, especially high rise ones, will generally not work well for you, and will certainly be hard to fit. Jackets that stop at the waist will overemphasize it. Circle skirts will overwhelm your figure. Clothes with details (ruffles, any kind of fussiness) that emphasize the roundness of your front should be sacrificed; simple collarless jackets will look better on you—and are much more chic. Turtlenecks also tend to repeat the roundness of your shape, so avoid them.

The Rectangular Box Shape

BASIC CHARACTERISTICS   Your shape is broad all over: more or less equally wide at the shoulder, the waist, and the hips. You appear straight up and down. Your hips are square, rather than round, with your high hips and low hips of the same dimension. This is not a body that shouts "Curves Ahead." You have little or no bust. You tend to have a short neck. You have slim legs and arms in relation to your wide torso, but your upper arms and thighs may tend to fleshiness.

IN ADDITION   You may have fleshiness in the upper back and above the waist, where it may concentrate in "love handles." You may have fleshiness at the back of your neck. And your stomach has a sly tendency to protrude.

YOUR BEST FEATURES   Your legs and arms tend to be gracefully slim, and your small bustline tends to be suited to most clothes.

YOUR LEAST FAVORITE FEATURES   Your lack of curves has always made you feel a bit . . . well, unfeminine. Your straight waist and high hips have always presented problems in getting skirts to fit right, even though you look great in slim skirts and pleated skirts in supple fabrics.

YOUR FASHION AIM   You will want to relieve the straightness of your shape, but take heart: Your figure is not difficult to dress. You do not need to camouflage anything or balance proportions; you can wear most colors and silhouettes. Clothes that suggest a waistline will help give you the definition your figure needs. You will also want to wear gentle shapes and fluid lines that add a bit of softness to your body and that move gracefully—femininity without the frills.

ASYMMETRICAL HAIR, TOO

TULIP SLEEVES AND TULIP SKIRT

SLIGHTLY DROPPED WAIST

TOTALLY SOFT

FASHION SUGGESTIONS   Slim wrapped skirts are wonderful for you. Dropped-waist dresses and slim low-hip blousons add gentle curves while suggesting that there's figure definition underneath. So do semifitted tops. A softly blousing one-piece dress with an elasticized waist will also suggest a curvier middle. You can use belts, too, to help define your middle without confining it; just buckle them loosely so they drape toward the high hips. Use details and accessories to put the emphasis at your shoulders, and always wear shoulder pads. Sweaters with ease will not call attention to your fleshy back. In addition, you may find one-piece body briefers the perfect solution for back fleshiness. One-piece dresses with gentle vertical lines will emphasize your body length and add gracefulness. You also look great in trousers, especially made of fabrics with great drape, such as fine wool gabardine; worn with an unconstructed jacket, the look will be smashingly soigné.

WHAT TO AVOID   Man-tailored, structured clothes broaden your entire silhouette and make you look mannish and forbidding. Avoid bulky sweaters; they add width to your torso. Boxy jackets will make you look boxy on top, as will tops with horizontal patterns or style lines, such as low shoulder yokes.

FOR ANY BODY

Other proportions count, too.

- A long neck, all by itself, makes the entire body appear longer. It is definitely a fashion asset. And it is the single most important reason why keeping necklines free of encumbrances—hair fairly short—is important for most full-figured women. Keeping the neck area "clean" gets the maximum mileage from the neck; it increases the perception of height.
- Long legs always make a body look taller and thinner. Slim lower legs on a body of any height will also make a whole body appear taller and thinner provided hemlines are not wide. They also tolerate a greater variability of hemline length.
- Straight, broad shoulders, while acting as a strong horizontal, are perhaps the greatest fashion plus for the larger woman. First, by sharply delineating the upper-body space, they create

the perception of upper-body height, which, if emphasized, the eye interprets as whole-body height. In addition, they make the hips appear narrower by contrast. And it doesn't hurt that straight, broad shoulders provide a platform from which clothes can drape gracefully, skimming over the body.

- Hemlines and the width of the skirt or pants at the hem are the other great factors affecting visual height for the larger woman. Manipulating the hemline and paying attention to skirt width and pants width at the hem are not fashion details for you—they are absolute necessities for visually balancing the proportions of your body.

HAIR—THE BEST-TRESSED LIST

By now, you already know what's coming. If head size goes a long way to influencing the perception of your body proportions, then how you wear your hair can make or break the way you look in clothes.

Remember all those rules about hairstyles you learned while growing up? They categorized faces into about four shapes and dictated which style of hair goes with which face. If you had a heart-shaped face you were locked into a pageboy for life. Styles of living and working could change, needs could change, attitudes could change, moods could come and go, hair color could wane, bodies could change, but you walked away from your hairstyle at the risk of abandoning your face.

Today it's different. There are no such formulas.

Hair is no longer viewed as having to be tamed into submission to a small range of suitable styles. What's acceptable today is not defined by some external code as it was in the 1950s. It's what you do to create the sense that it is right on you, that it is an integral part of your structure and an integral part of your overall style, that it captures your individuality and looks as dynamic as you do.

Nor is it seen as a final touch, an accessory, an afterthought, something apart from your body or your spirit. It completes your whole look. It is an element that is indispensible in balancing your overall proportions and capping your particular style. The thinking about hairstyles today is not which "do" goes with which face—wearing your hair full and curly to "soften" a square face makes no sense if the square face is attached to a body that's 5'3" or your style aspires to elegance. It's more a matter of what kinds of hairstyles create an interesting and pleasing balance with your body and are in a dynamic harmony with the overall style you aim to project. As a result, your hairstyle plays two basic roles: It plays an architectural, or structural role, shaping the character of the whole form, and it plays an aesthetic role in enhancing the attractiveness of your best features.

A haircut is not to be approached like walk-in surgery—a remedy for what's wrong with your nose (too wide, too long) or your forehead (too low, too high, etc.). A haircut works *with* your features, not against them. Let the *Style Is Not a Size* approach to clothing your body also go to your head—aim not to hide what you don't like but to accent what you do. Rachel G. is a full-figured woman on the short end of medium height. Her hair is dark and wiry. She wears it in a short asymmetrical blunt cut that rivets attention to the intensity of her eyes; it also makes her look taller by carrying an onlooker's line of vision upward and out; by the way, the people she meets are so dazzled by the drama of line no one notices her double chin or the fact that her ears protrude slightly (something I never knew until she demonstrated the fact).

THE LONG-HAIR THING

I won't say that long hair is a no-no, but I will say it's difficult to wear well. It tends to shorten the head and neck, and adds bulk to what is ideally perceived as a narrow part of the body. Still, there are those who can wear it well (we'll get to that later). But there are many more who can't. But do. And would look much better in shorter hair, or some other hairstyle.

Large women hold onto their hair when other women are willing to explore shorter styles. And the younger the full-figured woman, the more likely she is to hang on to her hanks. Why should this be so? It's puzzling why a woman wears a style that neither flatters her body nor her face. It certainly isn't from lack of time or care: These same women also tend to be well-manicured, a time-consuming ritual. It doesn't seem to be lack of knowledge, for these women often dress with a certain understanding of fashion or style, suggesting that they also know about trends in hairstyles. And how to dress themselves flatteringly. But a funny thing—they seem to see their hair as a thing apart from their body. Hair is in a separate category, for them. And indeed it is.

TOO MUCH HAIR! NECK DOESN'T SHOW ENOUGH

ASYMMETRICAL AND CURLY — LONG OR SHORT BUT OFF THE NECK AND SHOULDERS

For hair turns out to be a way of declaring "I am feminine" by a woman who has had her feminine identity stripped from her by the topsy-turvy cultural climate in which thin is feminine and full-figured is not. The culture may have switched the labels on bodies, behind our backs, but it hasn't messed with hair—yet.

Feminine identity is hard enough to get in this world that is, at best, so ambivalent about women. It's even harder to get when women's bodies are devalued and you've got a woman's body. It's certainly something no woman should have taken from her, no matter how fragile it is.

But there is more to femininity than hair. And there are more ways to express it in appearance than in hairstyle. There are soft colors, or vibrant ones, fluid lines, graceful silhouettes, revealing styles—ways of dressing and creating styles that span the range of femininity from gamine to femme fatale. So if you have been holding on to long hair without considering whether its the best style for you and your body, just remember, it's okay to let go of your hair; you won't have to let go of your femininity, too.

WHAT'S IN A GOOD HAIRSTYLE?

First, it's not what you can do for your hairstyle but what a hairstyle can do for you. Here is what you can expect of a good hairstyle:

- It allows for your individuality. The shape and proportion are cut into your hair, but with enough versatility so that you can add your own touches according to mood, occasion—or just the need for a soupçon of novelty, or fantasy, or wit. And you should always strive for some novelty. You will bore yourself to tears if you wear exactly the same hairstyle day in and evening out. While your look for day should be more natural than for evening, put a little play into your hairstyle when you can. If you usually wear your naturally wavy hair brushed up and back from your face in a short layered cut, try combing a thatch of hair forward on one side into some impertinent bangs; use a little gel for staying power, if need be. Or if you usually wear the same kind of hair side-parted in wispy bangs, try brushing the bangs back and up for a slightly spiky effect, again dipping into gel if need be. You get the idea—improvise and play a bit. You will discover new sides of yourself in the process.

- It is always easy to keep neat. You need the neatness, particularly for your work life. It is critical for projecting a polished image. Case closed. And yet, style being what it is, and the image of perfection being essentially boring, there are occasions—strictly social, perhaps intimately so—when you might want to introduce interest through a touch of disharmony; it is possible to do this with your hairstyle provided you keep all else in absolutely strictest order. So your hairstyle should be one that holds its shape neatly and naturally—and looks good slightly mussed up or shaken out, too. The best and most workable hairstyles get all their neatness, shape, and style from a terrific cut. A good cut by an experienced hand almost always has enough play in it for the "sweet disorder" in slight disarray.

- It flatters you, makes you feel beautiful. Let's face it, we are not blind to the aesthetic shortcomings of human bodies, especially full-figured ones. We all know that in real life women develop double chins—or have no chin at all. That necks come short and long, and narrow, wide, and wider, and that longer and narrower is usually closest to the aesthetic ideals of Western culture. That eyes, even beautifully intense ones, can get lost under barely ordinary eyebrows. A good hairstyle flatters you by bringing the onlooker's eye to your high points, by being interesting and attractive in its own right, and by balancing body proportions. While your hairstyle wisely ignores your "flaws," your hairstylist can not; he or she must know what they are in order to work around them. The same is true for you; after all, your hairstylist is your hairdresser only one hour a week or month—the rest of the time it's up to you.

- It brightens your look. It makes you feel alive, not dated. While the classic cuts can be perfectly fine, you don't always benefit by sticking to a tried and true bob. Modern hairstyling, because it now works with, and not against, the natural possibilities of different kinds of hair, has discovered many ways to shape hair with dynamic lines, to create interesting angles leading off from the right parts of the face. You are the woman who can let this kind of originality go to her head, because it attracts attention to facial features. It has built-in spirit without your having to change your wardrobe. And it has another advantage for you—haircuts with dynamic lines give you a modern, updated look, a perfect counterpoint to having an "old-fashioned" full figure. Such contrast is positively beguiling. And très chic.

The trick, of course, is finding a good basic hairstyle for you to work and to play with. There are a few constants that influence what you can do with your hair, such as its texture and your life-style needs. But your body proportions are definitely the driving force in the equation. However, they are not the only thing, as two acquaintances, both fashion executives, illustrate. Both have the same round body shape. Gina is of short-medium height with a body that is thickest at the waist. She does have beautifully shaped legs. Sybilla has the same body, with a bit more height, and perhaps the best legs on the East Coast. Both need a substantial, but not overwhelming, presence on their shoulders that is in scale with their substantial bodies. But Gina has a small head with delicate features—and the most baby-fine hair imaginable; its natural tendency is to hug her already small head. Sybilla, on the other hand, has a long face—and a voluptuous mane of cinnamon-colored curls, a look that would easily overwhelm any ordinary person, except that Sybilla is no ordinary person. She is a lady of high drama, and every gesture she makes and every word she utters and every dress she wears is highly dramatic. Her entire wardrobe consists of one silhouette—her best silhouette, of course—in every imaginable variation of fabric and color: dolman sleeve, wedge-shaped dresses that skim her body in one sweeping arc and come to a show-stopping halt just above her graceful knees. Sybilla's hair, on a head already well-proportioned for her body, would be too much for most women, and it's almost too much even for Sybilla, except that it is simply of a piece with her strong personality. Gina's soft features, gentler personality, and surreptitious wit, on the other hand, would be lost, and her body would look even rounder, amid even half that rococo riot of hair. Still, she needs a style that adds volume to her head, while letting her gamine nature poke through. And indeed, she has the spunkiest style for her—her straight dark hair is cut to one short length all around, just below the ears, but above the ears and on the crown her hair is feathered into shorter wisps that stand out softly but spiritedly, a sort of burnished halo at the top and sides.

HAIR TODAY

Body Proportions

The length of the face influences how tall your body seems, and the taller your body seems, the more it balances your width. So it's simple. Styles that shorten the face—say, bangs brushed over the forehead—will be aesthetically satisfying by making the body seem longer. Right? It's not quite that simple. To seem the perfect size for you, then everything about you has to have a harmonious scale. A tiny face or head on a large body is unbalanced and aesthetically unsatisfying; and the disproportion calls attention to body size.

That leads to two important ways you will consider using hairstyle.

1. To give yourself a lift. You may want a hairstyle to add actual height to the body. Where the face is small (short from chin to crown) and the body height is on the short side, it may be more important for you to create the overall impression of body height. This is especially true if your face is especially round or your cheeks are full. If your hair is curly and short, you may want to consider an upswept style.

2. To turn up the volume. A hairstyle with volume is one of the most necessary ways of balancing head and body size. (See, it's really another way of adding width in strategic places to put body parts in proportion.) Volume refers to the fullness of hair around the head, and for most full-figured women, as it was for Gina, the strategic place is on the sides, above the ears, although adding volume is not incompatible with adding height. There are few full-figured women whose whole appearance could not be improved by the simple addition of volume to the sides of the hair—not an elaborateness of style but a lifting and fluffing out of hair at the roots, from underneath. The key here is *controlled* volume. Too much volume and you can dwarf a great face *and* look overpowering; do not fool yourself into thinking "I'm a big girl, I can carry a big hairdo." A big hairdo overcomplicates your silhouette. But too little volume and your head looks like it belongs on someone else's body. Volume, by the way, has nothing to do

HAIR IS TOO FULL AND TOO ROUND FOR A ROUND FACE AND A SHORT NECK

ASYMMETRICAL AND SWINGY — A BOB THAT IS SHORTER IN BACK

with length; in fact, length *and* volume make an almost unbearable combination for full-figured women. Whether your hair is cut blunt or layered, it should have enough length so that the hair can be gently lifted outward. First, turn your head upside down and brush your hair straight out, then turn your head up and style your hair. If it won't hold the lifting on its own, you can apply a touch of mousse or gel to the roots after you style it to hold the volume. If all else fails, or you simply need hair that gets up and goes on its own, you can always get a root permanent.

Hair Texture

The general trend today is to work with your natural hair texture, not against it, whether it's curly, wavy, or straight, frizzy or shiny, thin and fine or thick and heavy. Partly that's because no self-respecting woman today has a great deal of time for elaborate maintenance rituals. And partly it's because self-respect for everyone hinges on the recognition that people differ in such matters as hair color, hair texture, and skin color (to say nothing of body size) and such differences are normal, healthy, and attractive.

TOO MUCH VOLUME

TOO LITTLE NECK!

Face Shape

A good hairstyle is the best way to complement the shape of your face. The general principle is, if your face is too round, too square, too long, too anything, you handle that by choosing a hairstyle that doesn't repeat the shape of your face. That only emphasizes what you would rather not advertise. And remember, you don't want to repeat the shape of the body in your hairstyle either.

If you have a **round** face, which is full in the cheeks and round at the chin, most likely you want to elongate it and narrow it. Style features that often aid and abet this goal include: asymmetrical styling; side part; soft, asymmetrical bangs; upswept hair; crown height.

If your face is **square**, with forehead, cheeks, and jaw appearing the same width, then you may wish to soften the angles. Styling possibilities include: side or diagonal part, asymmetrical bangs, asymmetrical cuts, crown height or fullness, forehead width, soft upsweeps, and a length that stops anywhere but at your chin line.

SHORT, FLUFFY & BEVELED

If your face is **heart-shaped**, with full cheeks narrowing sharply to a pointed chin, you may want to increase the sense of width at the jawline and balance the jaw-forehead discrepancy. Styling possibilities include: fluffed bangs, asymmetical styling, soft wisps at temples and cheek, or a cut with volume from cheek to chin.

If your face is **oblong**, longer than it is wide, you will probably want to gently widen its appearance. Styling possibilities include: bangs, volume and softness at the sides, medium length.

If your face is **triangular**, with a narrow forehead and wide jawline, you will probably want to balance the shape by widening the forehead and narrowing the jawline. Styling possibilities include: low side part, chin-length cut, asymmetrical bangs, upswept or outswept temples.

EVEN FOR A MOVIE STAR ITS TOO MUCH HAIR

LIGHTER WITH LAYERS

Facial Features

Women of style with an extravagant facial feature—an aggressive chin, a strong nose—that they face up to boldly by highlighting, rather than hiding, always seem to balance the feature with their hairstyle. And not just from the front, but in profile, too. The moral is: It isn't always wise to tone down strong facial features, but your hairstyle should be part of the overall balance with your features. Good styling approaches to common "problem" features include:

HAIR IS TOO MUCH OF A TRIANGLE FOR A TRIANGULAR FACE

FOR BALANCE— LIFT HAIR UP TO HIDE A TRIANGULAR FACE OR A BROAD JAW

- **High forehead:** long, soft bangs—unless you have the style guts of designer Mary McFadden, who has done for the high forehead what Paloma Picasso has done for the downturned mouth. But that's style—turning a "flaw" into a centerpiece of a look, and keeping everything else boldly simple. That's inspiration!
- **Weak, receding chin:** fullness at the low back of the head.
- **Large nose:** pulled-back hair with fullness at the upper back of the head.
- **Jowls:** upswept hairstyles.
- **Double chin:** upswept or outswept hairstyles, angled asymmetrical styles.
- **Dowager's hump:** short hair feathered and wispy over the nape of the neck.

OBLONG HAIR ON AN OBLONG FACE DOESN'T WORK

SHORTEN A LONG FACE WITH VOLUME AT THE SIDES AND LESS DENSE BANGS

Life-style

Every hairstyle requires some upkeep and maintenance, and some more than others. It is wise to choose a hairstyle that fits into the time you have available for such activity. Otherwise, you'll either be a slave to your hairstyle or won't get the benefit of the style; over time, or busy days—just when you need most to look good—you'll be tempted to not take the time. Better to let your life-style dictate your hairstyle, if you have a choice. In these days, when women are extraordinarily busy and active, and often have to go from office to social event with no time to stop, or straight from the health club back to the office, many women are opting for cuts with all the styling built into the cut. And women whose styles need volume or curl are forsaking curlers and getting the right look from long-lasting permanents, or root permanents, which lift hair away from the scalp.

Hair Color

A good haircut isn't the only way to balance body proportions and facial features. Hair color can give you a great visual lift—literally, since we know that light colors can visually enlarge a space. We are not talking heavy-duty changes here. But subtle highlighting or lightening of hair shade at strategic places—say the crown, or the temples—can also be used to draw the eye upward or outward, to add visual height or volume. "Highlights keep the facial features soft-looking," according to the hair experts at Glemby salons. If you routinely get your hair colored, ask your colorist about selectively lightening the shade in places. If not, seek out the colorist at your next haircut appointment; he or she may have some wonderful ideas that will work along with your haircut.

A CUT ABOVE

Some of the outstanding hairstylists in the world offer these suggestions for hair that's the tops with your body and your face.

- Short, full-figured women look best with short hair—it clarifies the verticality of the neck—and fullness at the top of the head, says Miwa, a New York–based stylist with an international reputation. Adept at makeovers—and having once made over the entire U.S. Olympic team with on-the-spot haircuts that gave new meaning to "performance"—Miwa is skilled at sizing people up instantly for their best looks. "Fullness at the sides is very important," she insists. Done at the high part of the face, she says, it brings out the cheekbones.

CLOSE HAIR MAKES THE FACE TINY

FLUFFY LIGHT AND UPLIFTING

- For full-figured women with straight hair, Miwa finds that "a chin-level bob looks good. A good, crispy blunt cut adds sharpness, which balances the roundness of the body. Bangs brushed a little to the side are better than straight bangs."

- For those with wavy, curly, or wiry hair, Miwa recommends a short cut but not one with a rounded top or with rounded sides because, by repeating face and body shape, it emphasizes it. Instead, she advises that the hair be cut bluntly and beveled upward and outward from the chin.

- "It's good to show some ear," says Miwa. "It's important for the face shape to show there's more to the face than the cheek. Showing the ear takes the emphasis away from the cheek."

- Fine, limp hair on a short, full-figured woman poses the greatest style challenge, says Miwa. The hair's natural tendency, to form a cap on the head, is an extremely efficient shortener of body height, it emphasizes body weight, and it fails to provide the above-neck balance that's needed. Her solution is to keep the hair a bit longer and layer it to add fullness and body, to style it upward and outward so that there is fullness, especially above the ears, and to expose the ears.

A MOUNTAIN OF HEAD AND SHOULDERS — COMBINED FOR TOO MUCH BULK — CENTER PART DOESN'T DO MUCH

- Full-figured women who are tall need longer hair, Miwa finds, to keep the head large. Long is to the bottom of the neck—maximum. "Short hair is not becoming to tall big women. They look like their heads are too small for their bodies, unbalanced. But long hair is very bulky looking." And if such a woman has thin straight hair, Miwa knows she needs to cut some body into the hairstyle.

TRIM TO A BOB — IT HAS A SLIGHT BEVEL

REMEMBER — DON'T LET HAIR HIT YOUR SHOULDERS

- For tall women and short women, "hair should be off the face. On the face, it rounds it. It's a mistake to try to cover a full face; it only winds up emphasizing the cheeks." But pulling the hair back into a bun is not the solution, either.

- Big hips, says Miwa, call for "balance with bigger hair, if the head is small. If the face is narrow, the hair needs fullness."

TWIST A DESIGNER SCARF AND TIE OFF CENTER ON TOP

VERY FRENCH!

- "For all full-figured women, it is important for hair to be neat and simple. Because it counteracts the impression that the body is messy."
- And she throws in this party favor. "Full-figured women look great with a tightly twisted scarf or a turban around their head and tied at the top. It adds fullness to the top. And it can be very chic and very playful."

FINISHING TOUCHES

In the end, dressing doesn't just affect how others perceive us. It comes full circle and influences how we perceive ourselves. To see ourselves well-dressed and well-groomed is to see ourselves complete. Clothing and grooming borrow the elements of art to modify—to redress—the structure of the body. Getting dressed completes our internal sense of self, our conscious selves; we define ourselves through dress. It also completes our physical selves. It is a way of redefining our bodies.

It does this not because they are essentially deficient, but because we have the chance. We have to get dressed; it might as well look good. Just making the effort has an effect on how we are taken. In this venture, all bodies are created equal—because they all face the same task, completing themselves.

9

Silhouettes That Flatter—Dresses and Coats

*I*n Spring 1990, the Italian designer Gianfranco Ferre announced he would launch a line of large-size fashions to be sold in Italy and other countries, including the U.S. Called Forma O, the line is a complete collection of clothes in "classic Ferre style adapted to the woman who is not model-thin." The line was started, said the company, because "it's hard to find elegant, refined looks in large sizes." The idea? To "revolutionize the silhouette," by "widening the shoulders and tapering the skirts." That this silhouette is flattering is hardly revolutionary to large-size women—but what is revolutionary is that a first-class designer is beginning with the body and developing suitable silhouettes in first-class fabrics and designs. Grazia, Maestro!

In redefining the appearance of the body with clothing, the most important element of dress design is the cut of the clothes, their basic outline. Let's face it, despite the perpetual novelty of fashion, and the hype of the new, there are just so many basic shapes clothes can come in—no matter how hard some designers may try to invent new ones. These so-called silhouettes show up year in and year out, season after season, on fashion's runway. The music throbs, the Nikons flash, the pulse quickens—and last year's trapeze emerges as next Spring's *pyramide*. The trapeze, the sheath, the flounce, the blouson, the princess, the wedge—the only thing that changes is their relative popularity from season to season. And their *noms de theatre*. The chemise attempts a comeback, gains some publicity, loses some length, and starts life over as . . . a slink.

It can be said, at least for the classic and traditional styles of clothing, that they have some basic affinity for the human body. Quaint as it may seem today, clothes were once designed with the real human form in mind, not a disembodied image. True, body proportions were often distorted en masse, but the distortion was in directions occasioned by one or another variant of the human shape and, unfortunately, dictated to all women of fashion regardless of their shape. However tight-laced the late Victorian costume might get, its cut—sagging bosom, lowered front waist, prominent rear—mirrored the very matronly dimensions of the aging empress. In fact, long after the Victorian silhouette died and went to fashion limbo, it lingered in (actually, it provided the very prototype *for*) fashions for the "stout," a size range created just about that time by the advent of ready-made clothing. The confusion between big and "mature" has survived to our times.

Among the generally exquisite legacy of clothing shapes invented and evolved over time and now in the public domain, some, like the princess, highlight one body part, the bodice, and make light of the others. Others accent a different feature; a surplice front puts the most graceful wrapping on a big bosom. Some, like the broad-chested styles of the Renaissance, accentuate horizontal dimensions—the Renaissance was an expansive era for mankind—while the high-waisted gowns with long trains of fabric from the late Middle Ages focus on the nearer-my-God-to-three vertical. All have been inspired by cultural infatuation with one proportion over another throughout the course of history. But all acknowledge the human body nonetheless.

You can be sure that over the course of history it occurred to one or more dressmakers that some women had bigger hips, or some lacked a well-defined middle. These women weren't banished; they were clothed—and often imitated. And the style inventions have entered the mainstream of fashion history. As with the best of inheritances, we can enjoy this bequest—and make use of those conventions of fashion shape (we call them classics) that most naturally and attractively accommodate our own endowments. You will always look best in those clothes whose integral silhouette and style lines embrace, subsume, incorporate your body's shape, skimming over its contours, while balancing its proportions. You will always do well to look for those classic clothes offering a happy confluence of style lines with body lines.

What makes this so possible—and makes today such a unique period stylewise—is that no one clothes style dominates the culture. The variety of clothing silhouettes available to a woman of fashion today is remarkably broad. We no longer march in fashion lockstep, all tucked and zipped into one prevailing shape. No one silhouette prevails because our lives are too various. And such events as the fitness revolution and the continuing advance of women in active business life have unalterably changed the relationship of women to clothes. We no longer approach clothes as strictly decorative. They must be functional; it is simply not possible to focus on one's work and on one's clothes at the same time.

Using the style lines of clothes to define the best parts of your body is hardly a new idea. Well-dressed women do it instinctively. But if you have been using clothes to hide behind, to camouflage, to cover up, what we are talking about is, admittedly, a radical change in philosophy. Still, if you can grasp the potential of accenting the positive at all, the time has come to change your entire approach to dressing. You will look so much better, you will be able to see your assets, and take pride in them, if you dress the positive.

You will definitely need a new fashion vocabulary to help you along. Forget oversize; don't look for loose or, of course, tight. The most important words in your lexicon of looks will now be **body-skimming, drape, fluid, sleek, relaxed**—as well as balance and proportion. You don't want to hide a thick waist; you want styles that either do not make an issue of the waistline or that on their own suggest waistline definition. You don't want pants to billow over thick thighs; you want styles that give them a long sleek line. Your natural allies are now silhouettes with good lines and fabrics that hang well rather than cling or go their separate way. You want the suggestion of shape, not of shapelessness. You want shape by **intimation, insinuation, implication**, not a declaration of size. This is a much more imaginative, **sexier** way of thinking about yourself. In the end, it lets you wink at the mirror.

GENERAL RULES OF SILHOUETTES

- Don't use any more fabric than a silhouette needs to make its point. The wedge dress silhouette is terrific for women whose weight is on top or in the middle. But if sleeves are too full, and the line between the sleeve and the bodice swoops and billows, the body loses all suggestion of shape, too.
- The elements of a silhouette, however flattering in themselves, have to be combined in a way that makes good design sense. Flounces and flourishes at the hem of a dress need the contrast of a fit above. It's that fanciful release of tension we find so wonderful. A shapeless dress with a flounce on the bottom doesn't provide the same attraction.
- As a general rule, almost any design that can be worn semifitted will work on a full-figured woman. The key is to think of the best silhouettes as gently relaxed or body-skimming.
- The corollary is that shapes that are too voluminous are as unattractive as shapes that are worn very fitted. Too much fabric makes you look shapeless. A silhouette that's highly fitted calls attention to size.
- There are some silhouettes that, no matter how loose, just don't work for full-figured women yet are often used. One is the dress or jacket or robe with a straight-across chest yoke.
- Dresses and coats offer the best possible opportunity for creating a long and flattering line—but it is devilishly hard to get a good fit in a dress. Partly it's because greater variability in body shape makes fit harder among larger women. But also it's because the necessary variety of dress silhouettes is generally not available. And even more so it's because clothes that are available are not always well enough thought out for larger figures—the three-dimensionality of human bodies is not well understood in the fashion world at all any more. Retailers and customers alike complain that there is a shortage of well-designed, high-quality daytime dresses—the kind of utterly simple, chic and elegant clothes that most lend themselves to a woman's own style. As a result, most full-figured women

dress most of the time in separates, even when they would prefer the simplicity of one-piece dressing.

- Sometimes the best way to find a good dress is to look in the sportswear department. Many sportswear designers now add dresses to their collections, and the dresses borrow from their sportswear soulmates the twin virtues of simplicity of silhouette and body-skimming fit that work so well for you. What makes a look modern is a strong, simple silhouette.

DRESSES

The strongest, longest, and sleekest line you can possibly get is from a dress. It is one piece that, at its best, glides over body contours and balances them in its style lines. What is true for dresses also holds true for jackets and other tops, skirts, and outerwear. So even if you rarely buy dresses, you will need to read this section to understand about dressing your body, period.

The chemise is the simplest of all dresses. It ideally skims the body with its pure, straight lines from shoulder to hem, wherever that may be . . . this year. Whether in a woven fabric or a knit one, it is often collarless and always worn beltless—giving you the longest, straightest line no matter what lies underneath. Because the chemise must fall straight, it takes shoulder pads and hips that are not the widest part of the body. A chemise should be in an utterly fabulous supple fabric, and makes a perfect dress as is or with one bold accessory, your way. In some popular versions, the chemise falls in gathers from shoulder detailing or a front yoke. However, unless the yoke is kept high on the shoulder, these are potential troublemakers for big-busted women, emphasizing both roundness and fullness on top.

One variation of this silhouette that is particularly attractive is a dropwaist panel with soft shirring set into the front of an otherwise straight chemise. It takes a longer length, but the addition adds softness and permits an otherwise narrow silhouette to be worn by those broad at the thigh or lower hip.

The longest running hit in the chemise silhouette, and a dress that simply looks wonderful on you, is the Chanel dress. Straight and narrow, gently fitted, buttoned down the front, banded in contrasting color around the collarless neckline and down the front, it is usually buttoned with crested metal buttons. It never seems to go out of style. But beware of little details

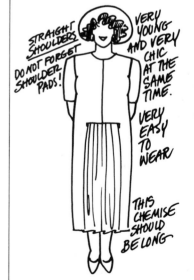

STRAIGHT SHOULDERS

DO NOT FORGET SHOULDER PADS!

VERY YOUNG AND VERY CHIC AT THE SAME TIME.

VERY EASY TO WEAR

THIS CHEMISE SHOULD BE LONG

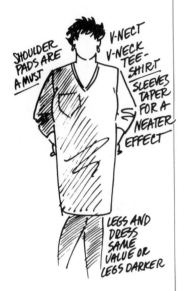

SHOULDER PADS ARE A MUST

V-NECT
V-NECK TEE-SHIRT
SLEEVES TAPER FOR A NEATER EFFECT

LEGS AND DRESS SAME VALUE OR LEGS DARKER

A REAL SHIRT SHIRTDRESS

that can derail this otherwise flattering silhouette. Sometimes there are banded-edge pockets appearing as horizontal dashes across the bust and across the hips. Just make sure they hit you in the right places and don't sidetrack the vertical flow. Easier to wear are styles where the pockets are finished only with button-through detail, rather than contrast trim.

The tee shirt dress is a linear descendent of that universal favorite. Whether in a vee neck or a crew neck, in the original jersey or a fine slide of woven silk, it is straight and simple. In a recent variation that also looks fresh, to say nothing of flattering, **Adrienne Vittadini** produced a rendition with a drawstring waist that can be bloused as much or as little as you want and placed anywhere from waist to low hip. Other, more traditional variations of the tee shirt dress include a built-in elasticized waist. This kind of dressing can be American sportswear at its sportiest best. To get the right effect from tee-shirt dressing, make sure that the dress is roomy enough to start and stays roomy enough after you toss it in the washing machine. Also, the crew neck version is hard for larger women to wear unless it is somewhat relaxed away from the neck. Both crew and vee neck editions look better if the expanse of fabric has the detail of a properly placed chest pocket, since this is not a dress that takes much in the way of accessories. And as for fabric, knits with ribs and jerseys are excellent because they drape well. But beware of interlock, which adds bulk through its high loft and holds no shape of its own. Like the chemise, this is a dress best avoided by those whose hips are their widest part.

The shirtwaist dress is also a top that grew into numerous variations, some straight of line, others with fuller skirts. Because of its front closure, the shirtwaist has a built-in linear detail that makes it great for fuller figures. The simplest shirtdress is a long shirt that falls in a straight line to a shirttail hem or a straight hem, ideally with side slits. Provided the sides are long enough, this dress has enough spunk to be dressed up or down. But it is ideally suited to summer casual wear, especially over a swimsuit. It also makes a great long jacket. A true shirtwaist is constructed more like a dress, with a button-front shirt top, a fixed waist, which may or may not be elasticized, and a full or straight bottom. When done in a fluid fabric such as silk or cotton lawn, with a softly full skirt and an elasticized waist that lets the top blouse very gently, this can be one of the most flattering silhouettes for any full-figured woman.

The princess dress with its contoured vertical seams and long unbroken lines has many virtues for larger bodies. It automatically accommodates

VERY FLUID SHIRT DRESS

SILKY SOFT FABRIC WITH SELF PATTERN

LEGS SHOULD MATCH CENTER PANEL IN VALUE

forms of three dimensions; its lines are body lengthening and slimming; it isn't even interested in a waistline—it gets its kicks elsewhere. It is an ideal body-skimming silhouette for the bottom-heavy figure type. But it can be tricky to wear in its pure form, with a jewel neck and high inset sleeves. Instead, look for dresses that get their shape from princess seams but add interest from other design features, such as interesting collars, front openings, and color blocking of the side panels. I know a pear-shaped woman who bought one several years ago in midnight blue wool crepe and loves the way it looks on her so much she wears it at least twice a week, always accessorized differently. She has already lined up a seamstress to duplicate it, for the fateful day when the dress wears out. It looks that good! Also, make sure the fabric has body but is not stiff. Princess seams on a straight coatdress are almost de rigueur for it to work well on a larger body.

The drop-waist dress creates the appearance of a long smooth torso and deals with a waistline by implication only. This makes it very popular for full-figured women. But position is everything. Don't make the mistake of thinking anyone can wear any drop-waist dress. The position of the hip yoke determines which body type can wear it; try on the wrong one and you will wonder who ever thought this silhouette could be flattering. Whatever else you do, you don't want the waist dropped to the widest part of your hip. Nor

DROP-WAIST DRESS

BUTTONS DOWN THE FRONT FOR VERTICAL LINE

BLOUSON SHIRT

ADD PADS AND A GREAT FLOWER

PLEATED SKIRT TAKES TO A BREEZE

WRAP DRESS

GREAT DIAGONALS

PLUS GATHERS CREATE VERTICAL LINES

should it be at the narrowest. In general, the higher your hip, the higher the waist. Hourglass bodies can take only slightly dropped waists. Rectangular and round bodies must wear the "waist" at a point before the hip turns inward to the thigh. Pear-shaped bodies need the longest hip yokes. Also, fabric matters, too. Stiff and crisp fabrics don't work in this silhouette; fluid knits and drapey fabrics with body do best.

The blouson is another favorite of full-figured women, and while it looks good in some proportions, it is definitely overused and frequently misused. A blouson silhouette is gently bloused from shoulder to waist—and the best and the worst thing about it is that the waist can be anywhere from the natural waistline to below the fanny. Good because it can be used to reproportion the torso to suggest it is long and shapely, and bad because the blouson has to stop somewhere, typically with a wide band and dangerous if at the wrong spot. As with the dropped-waist silhouette, the wrong spot for the blouson silhouette is different for each body type. A bloused waist caught at the natural waistline with a slim elastic waistband or a narrow belt is attractive on all full-figured women who are not long-waisted. It is a graceful way around bumpy contours. Hip-level blousons work on those whose body is rectangular or round, for whom the blouson suggests hidden shape in the middle. And then the horizontal formed by the bottom band of the blouson must fall comfortably below the widest part of the hip, but not so low it cups over the derriere. No matter where it stops, the blouson works only—repeat only—if it is slim in shape, not billowy. The blousing must be gentle, subtle, insinuate a shape beneath, not overwhelm it. The fabric can't be too droopy, but it can't be too stiff, either. When the blouson is well proportioned, it works beautifully both in dresses and suits, with the contrast of a slim skirt. The blouson top simply doesn't work with a full skirt or tiered skirts; then the dimensions are too horizontal. And the blouson silhouette is positively fabulous in a top over tapered or stirrup pants, particularly for the woman round of body.

The wrap dress has such alluring possibilities for full-figured women it should be far more widely available. What it has going for it are asymmetrical closure, a long vertical formed by the closure, often ending in a sinuous curved line to the hem, and usually more than a fair share of graceful draping. The wrap dress that Diane von Furstenburg built her reputation on, a wrapped surplice bodice with a graceful full skirt, is still an ideal silhouette for the pear-shaped and hourglass-shaped, when done in fine and medium-weight jerseys and soft silks and crepes. Wraps with more vertical emphasis, such as kimono wraps tied at the side and surplice side-draped straight dresses, are wonderful for hourglass, rectangular, and round bodies. The combination of surplice diagonal, sinuous draping, and open closure gives us exactly what we need—flattering, elegant, and sexy dressing. The silhouette is perfect not only for dresses (sometimes called a sarong dress, especially when the draped skirt is slightly tapered) but for jackets and skirts, too. And if ever a silhouette could go effortlessly from day into evening, this is it, because draping is ipso facto alluring. The only trick with wraps is fit. Any suggestion of tightness and the beauty is completely lost. The overlap must be very generous. And somewhere, for peace of mind, there must be an infallible fastener, best at waist level, and best accorded a certain amount of ease. A word from experienced wearers: look for good quality manufacture so that all edges are completely finished or secured to a lining; simple facings, unanchored on the inside, have a curious way of showing their face, and emphasizing size.

The surplice dress or top is a first cousin of the draped wrap. It has much of the beauty of a wrap with none of the anxiety because the parts are securely anchored at side seams or waist. The bottom half may be either a straight line continuation of the top (perfect for all but the pear-shaped) or a stitched-on gathered or soft-pleated skirt (ideal for the pear-shaped and other bodies except the round). Graceful drape and flattering diagonals make the surplice line so wonderful (and sexy) on fuller figures that it, too, deserves to be more widely available.

The sweater dress is fabulous when done right and can be embarrassing otherwise. Easy construction, easy fit, fluidity of knit—that's when it's done right. The most wonderful sweater dresses I've ever seen for fuller women have rib knits that add wonderful verticals while providing graceful fit. The ribbing functions like Fortuny pleating. The best knits are made of fine, smooth yarn, either merino wool or full-bodied cotton (look for the label **Michelle St. John**). My absolute favorite—and it's a staple offering at **Marimekko** (the regular large will fit up to a size 22)—is a simple long sleeve straight dress of merino wool knit with subtly graduated ribbing from shoulder to hem, the hem having a slightly fluted effect that adds a sexy flourish to movement. Sweater dresses of fluffy lambswool or mohair add too much bulk and have not a scintilla of fluidity, especially if worn body-hugging. A good sweater dress has body to the knit, and should always be folded flat when not being worn. Look for style pluses such as vee or button-front necklines and shoulder detail. Whether the sleeves are set-in, dolman, or raglan, sweater dresses need the support of shoulder pads, but the pads should be subtle and their outlines invisible.

USE
VALUE
TO
LENGTHEN

LOTS OF
CURVES
IN THIS
COAT DRESS
WHICH IS
GOOD FOR
YOUR
CURVES—
MAKE THE
HAIR SOFT
+ CURVY
TO KEEP
THE
MOOD.

The tunic dress is one of the all-around best silhouettes for full-figured women. It is at its best and most versatile when its two parts are separate units complete on their own. The tunic dress exemplifies the principle of design that states that a body divided into unequal parts always looks taller than a body divided in half. A tunic top is long and visually narrow, skimming the body, ignoring bulges, evening proportions and balancing parts. It works for all figure types, and is at its very best when the silhouette is long over short-and-slim. To work, the tunic must be narrow, not boxy. To help achieve the longest, trimmest look, tunic silhouettes demand padded shoulders (especially for the bottom-heavy).

The straight coat dress, with its closure making a clear vertical line down the front, is another great silhouette for full-figured women. The trick is getting a good fit; you need body-skimming styling that accommodates a big bust without excess fabric, and neat lines that nevertheless provide ample room for sitting without stressing the closure. As for closure, buttons need to be relatively close, so there's no gapping when you sit. Look for princess seams to give needed bust contouring and graceful style lines down the front. As with all slim-line dressing for full-figured women, the skirt needs gentle, not obvious, tapering.

The swing dress, sometimes known as the tent (Ugh!), makes its swing in and out of fashion, when it carries such modish monikers as the trapeze or the *pyramide*. Currently in fashion, the swing dress looks like it covers all bodily flaws—thick torsos, nonexistent waists, broad hips, big bottoms— and it does, with a big proviso. Unless the fabric accomplishes the feat of fluid drape, it is generally lethal on women with big busts. The bust throws off the fall of fabric so that the hem is higher in front, and the fabric stiffness sends the outline careening out from the bust. When this dress is done in fabrics that drape well, you get the benefit of one long line from neck to hem. Look for swing dresses that fall from the shoulder, best supported by good but not obvious shoulder pads. Always check that the hemline is even all around; it often has to be adjusted.

The wedge is a silhouette made in heaven for the top-heavy or round figure. Its broad shoulders are straight and strong, automatically lengthening the body and narrowing the hips, while the bodice skims the body underneath. It falls uninterrupted in a tapered line, like an inverted triangle, to the hem. It is the totally unobstructed fall of fabric and the narrowing of the hem that make the body seem to disappear inside. Often created with dolman sleeves, the wedge can actually take any kind of sleeve. Some wedges are more extreme than others, with masses of fabric in the bodice. Too much volume, however, is unattractive and counterproductive—it ruins the line of the dress, and it adds nothing but bulk to the body. Many fabrics take to the wedge.

The sheath is a narrow dress, typically with no collar and long slim sleeves, that's fitted close to the body with vertical darts and seam lines. The skirt may or may not be a separate piece; when it is, of course, the waist seam adds a major horizontal line that can be hard to wear and often needs coverage with an unobtrusive belt. It is a timeless and sexy silhouette that is always in style. Admittedly, it isn't for everyone, just those with hourglass and rectangular bodies. And getting a good fit can be difficult. But when it works, it works very well indeed, especially when all the seam lines are verticals. First, think semifitted instead of fitted, body-skimming instead of body-hugging—the same general outline only with more all-over ease. Absolutely the most stunning sheath dress for full-figured women gets all the shape it needs from short vertical darts just above the waist level. That nipping provides the necessary fit, with enough leeway to accommodate variation in body contours and stunning brevity of body contact.

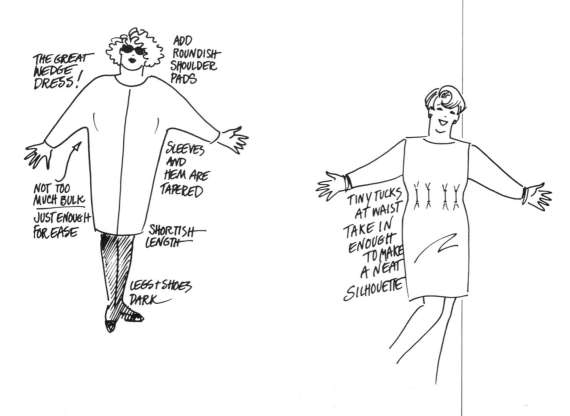

THE GREAT WEDGE DRESS!

ADD ROUNDISH SHOULDER PADS

SLEEVES AND HEM ARE TAPERED

NOT TOO MUCH BULK
JUST ENOUGH FOR EASE

SHORTISH LENGTH

LEGS & SHOES DARK

TINY TUCKS AT WAIST TAKE IN ENOUGH TO MAKE A NEAT SILHOUETTE

VERY LONG IS THE MOST EFFECTIVE

FLOATING SKIRT

The sundress can be as much a part of your wardrobe as it is for other women. Thoughtful styling—in a word, wide straps—is required. And for those who prefer not to reveal fleshy arms, so is a jacket, preferably coordinated or matching. But the bareness is a nice option that deserves to be available more often. There are several ways to get around the need for shoulder coverage over brassiere straps. First—get a bra that fits well enough in the cup and back so that it doesn't cut into your shoulders; yes, it's possible (see Chapter 12). The top options include: cutaway shoulders, which look especially good on shirtwaist-style and drop-waist sundresses; wide camisole straps, which work well on blouson, chemise, drop-waist, and swing dresses; tank-style tops; and halter backs for those who don't need a brassiere or who can find one that fits in a halter style.

The empire dress, a simple high-waisted chemise falling in Grecian folds from a band just below the bosom, is credited to the neoclassical painter Jacques-Louis David, who essentially served as costume designer for the French Revolution. An obvious contrast to the panniers and crinolines of the ancien régime, it made its official debut on Josephine, wife of Napoleon Bonaparte, at their 1804 coronation. It has flowed in and out of fashion ever since, and is almost a sure no-no for full-figured women—except that one of the most beautiful and flattering dresses I've seen was an empire dress designed with thoughtful sophistication. What the empire dress has going against it is snug fit over the bosom; so unless the fit or the line is relaxed, it is usually taboo for big-busted women. It also doesn't work at all for the round-bodied woman, or anyone with a fleshy midriff, who tends to look pregnant in this style. What it has on the plus side: a long vertical line, and the longer, the better; graceful drape of fabric from under the bust to the hem; and a youthful appearance. The clever empire dress I have encountered actually gets its ease of wearability from styling in two parts. There's a simple empire slip dress with unpressed pleats falling sinuously from the underbust seam, then it's topped with a short back-buttoned jacket that slides gracefully over the bosom and ends just below it. This is a perfect example of how eased fit and thoughtful styling can make almost any silhouette work in large sizes.

The Fortuny pleated dress is another style that owes something to classical draping. Named for the permanent irregular minipleats Venetian dressmaker Mariano Fortuny was able to induce in silks by a process whose secret died with him, this style of pleating has been revived single-handedly by dress designer Mary McFadden, working with polyester. It is extremely sensuous, extremely flattering to larger women (all those minipleats making all those verticals), and has enough give to be comfortable. Because the fabric, which takes color well, says it all, it is at its graceful and elegant best in the simplest of straight silhouettes, so that the overall effect is of a fluted Grecian column. Reserved for formal occasions, this dress looks good in simple tunic-skirt combinations, for maximum lengthening effect, or chemise styles with such detail as beading at the neck and shoulders.

tea length

SHOPPING FOR DRESSES

If fabrics are not that important to you, and you are flexible about quality, sometimes the best looks in dresses are at the more moderate price ranges. A good case in point are **Leslie Fay** dresses; among the profusion of styles, some are better executed than others, but there are usually some silhouettes that work well on each of the different body shapes. Good classic sheaths with good style lines—princess seams—are a mainstay; so are shirtwaists.

Among the sportswear manufacturers who do a few dresses but good ones, **Tamotsu** stands out; there always seems to be some simple but flattering coat dresses and thoroughbred shirtdresses for spring and summer in a range of colors and first-rate fabrics. **Harvé Benard Pour la Femme** is another sportswear maker whose dresses are few in number but outstanding—when you can find them, usually in the fall season. In flattering silhouettes and basic seasonal colors, which makes them perfect for accessorizing, they frequently have a fluidity that the separates do not.

In a class by themselves are the fall-season dresses from **Givenchy En Plus**; singularly among the dresses regularly available in large sizes, these have the mark of fine design, well-thought-out fit, precision tailoring, and superior fabrics, almost invariably from fine European makers. An occasional dress descends into stodginess. But they are at their best when they retain the classic elegance of the master, who designs the silhouettes and guides the company, a license holder, on color and fabric choices. Signature looks include tunic dresses, coatdresses, and three-piece ensembles. There is dressmaker detail to these dresses—which makes them perfect for power dressing, important luncheons, daytime weddings, and day into evening functions.

In a much more casual vein are dresses from knitwear specialists such as **Nancy Heller** and **Adrienne Vittadini**. Both regularly turn out spring-weight cotton jersey dresses with up-to-date styling. The Vittadini dresses are usually cut quite long, making them ideal for taller women.

THE HEMLINE MATTER

There are essentially four basic considerations where your best hemline is. One is your body. One is the dress or skirt style. One is your legs. And the other is fashion's dictates. The newspapers are full of reports that the designers have decreed short for this year, but that there are some longs in the best collections, and thus long is blowing in the wind. That sounds a lot like having it whatever way you want. The truth is, designers have lost their power to dictate, on the one hand, and, on the other, women with great legs will find any excuse to show them off.

Where does that leave you? Heeding your body proportions, the skirt style, your legs, and fashion's thrust. It's true that almost anything goes today. If you have shapely legs, you can go relatively short—provided the skirt is slim and tapered, just above the curve of the calf is fine. Fuller skirts always take longer lengths to balance their proportions, no matter your legs or body type. But in general, the best skirt length for women with thick legs is just below the curve of the calf. In this case, you can wear your slim skirts the same length as fuller skirts. What you always want to avoid is stopping a dress or skirt at the fullest part of the calf, which emphasizes width.

Of course, smart women always know that there are ways around the hemline issue that are chic and elegant in their own right. The longstanding way is pants. That's great if you look your most stunning in slacks and you can wear them every place you need to be. But they don't go everywhere, certainly not for every woman. Another fabulous way is with a soft-pleated split skirt, which not only goes everywhere, but is in keeping with the newly revised, which is to say newly softened, view of women. It acknowledges femininity in a way that pants do not. A split skirt has the coverage of a longish skirt, the dash of true fashion, and the comfort of pants. It takes any kind of jacket. I rest my case.

No matter the ideal length by the above criteria, one more criterion applies when you wear a skirt with boots—the skirt must cover the top of the boots. Otherwise you have a sure-fire line-up of horizontals—boot top, patch of leg, skirt hem—to make you look short and wide. Even when your boots and skirt overlap, if you are smart, you will wear opaque pantyhose the color of your boots, so that when you sit, the leg line will not be broken.

And while we're on the subject of stockings, let's pause a bit. What you are looking for is the longest line from waist down. The longest line comes from wearing skirt, hose, and shoes in the same color (say, black slim skirt, black opaque hose, black low heel shoes) or of the same color value (burgundy skirt, dark taupe sheer stockings, cordovan heels). Nude color stockings against dark clothes break up the line; better to go for darker stockings, not just in opaques, but in sheers. If you are wearing a bright color, like royal blue or red or green, forget about matching your stockings, even if they are sheer, to the hue of your clothes. Match them to black shoes, if you are wearing them. Or wear sheer black stockings or sheer dark taupe stockings anyway. They have a way of going with all except the lightest color shoes.

COATS AND RAINCOATS

If you are looking for a coat that does handstands, you are probably using the wrong strategy for buying a coat. Good cloth coats are so expensive but so necessary, and play so big a part in looking good, that what you look for in a coat should reflect the expenditure (quietly) and stand you in good stead for more than a year or two. That means your best choice should be some type of classic coat silhouette, which won't look tired and outdated in two years. Classic coats have two other hard-to-beat reasons for winning your closet space—they tend to be your most flattering silhouettes, and they have more potential for style than any other coats. They serve as a fabulous backdrop for big mufflers and giant shawls and other flings of color and panache. The reason they have persisted in the showrooms of fashion is that they are easy to wear and make women look good. Here's what you need to know about buying a coat:

- The softer or more supple the fabric, the better the coat will look and the better you will look.
- Structure is important in a coat, even a cape. Totally unstructured clothes tend to make you look shapeless. Well-placed medium size shoulder pads are truly necessary.
- The less fussy detail and trim, the better. You won't need to worry about placement of pockets, because most classic coats do not have patch pockets plastered on the front; they have welted angled pockets that reflect the coats' good lines.
- If you try on a coat in the late summer or early fall, remember the cardinal rule of coat fit: It doesn't fit unless you can wear it comfortably over a sweater or suit and move your arms about. Period.

- The more duty your coat gets, the more it has to perform over casual pants and go-to-work clothes, the more classic your coat style and the more basic the color should be. Traditional coats look rich and chic in neutrals and darks. Red is a neutral, too.
- The right coat length is an inch longer than your longest skirt. Unless you wear a seven-eighths coat or cape, which deliberately contrasts lengths and silhouettes (see "swing coats" below), all coats should cover all your skirts.
- If you find yourself wearing full skirts often, don't even think of stuffing them under a narrow coat silhouette. Go instead for a coat that's fuller on the bottom. You probably have a pear-shaped body and look best in a fit-and-flare style like the redingote.

FLIP UP THE COLLAR AND PUSH UP THE SLEEVES

The balmacaan is a roomy classic that always falls in a smooth unbroken gentle A line from raglan sleeves that fit the shoulder with precision. It is simple, sophisticated, and leans to chic, when it's in a supple enough fabric. The traditional one for this silhouette is gabardine or twill, right for the times because they are both strong and supple, sleek, travel brilliantly without wrinkling, withstand weather (it's that smooth finish), and drape down rather than extending the hemline out. And never, ever wear out. You'll really appreciate these fabrics if you spend any time at all in a car, since you can sit and drive comfortably without bulk. Get a balmacaan in wool gabardine—cotton gab for raincoats—and your grandchildren will wear it. Get it with a button-out lining (zippers throw off the line) and you have a three-season coat and raincoat to boot. The traditional style lines on this coat are in your body's favor; so is the button fly front. This coat is best in solid neutrals, including red and white as well as black, navy, and tan. Sound boring? This coat was made for all your big scarves and shawls. And if you want to look dashing, put on your tan balmacaan raincoat (over anything), spread open the top few buttons and fill the neck with a scarlet scarf, add your sunglasses, and go. **Burberry's** and **Aquascutum** always stock women's raincoats in this silhouette (up to size 20, fitting up to a 22). For winter coats, look for **Calvin Klein** (a 14 will fit a size 20 woman easily) or **Sanyo** labels. The prices will give you sticker shock, but think of a good gabardine classic as a long-term investment. My navy Calvin Klein balmacaan looks as fresh today as when I bought it four winters ago. You amortize the cost over many, many seasons.

The trench coat is an eternally favorite silhouette that is now frequently interpreted in ways that are easy for full-figured women to wear, and very flattering—long, lean, in supple fabrics like wool gab, and unlined. Invented by Burberry's for the tommies in World War I, the classic trench has shoulders bolstered with epaulets, a double-breasted front, a cape back for rain protection, and a belt with buckle (the original is hung with D rings to hold all those grenades). For all its spirit and intrigue, and despite its strong shoulders, the trench, in its strict traditional guise, has been a hard coat for full-figured women to wear; it added bulk with all its top detail and dumpiness with its wide belt; a wool lining made it virtually unworkable. But relax the silhouette and soften the fabric, and voilà, the trench is now our great ally. As for the belt, you can 1) double it and buckle it in back, and look chic with the merest intimation of waistline; 2) wear it loosely tied in front or 3) leave it completely unbuckled, turning your trench into more of a balmacaan. Worn this way, even the round-bodied woman can look good in a trench.

BIG AND SOFT REEFER COAT

The reefer has long reigned as the long, lean classic. And it does create a strong vertical—provided it is fit with enough ease to fall in an absolutely straight line unbroken by pulls or bulges. That makes it awfully hard to get a good fit. And the traditional fabrics for this coat, such as napped meltons, are on the bulky side, especially at the lower end of the price range. So, unless you're fairly tall, a reefer is not going to look as good on you as theory holds it should. What's more, this silhouette, at least in its traditional renderings, is looking a bit passé because fashion is softening up its approach to femininity-in-the-streets, and classic coats with swing and spirit now seem more in tune with the times. An unlined gabardine, however, makes a great spring reefer. But even at its best, this is not a silhouette for the bottom-heavy.

WRAP JACKET AND SHOULDER PADS!

DARK STIRRUP PANTS

The wrap is a tailored silhouette that speaks softly and carries a big allure. The key to this silhouette, both in short and long editions, is supple fabric; camel's hair and cashmere are ideal, if expensive; gabardines, wool crepes, and soft plushes are more reasonable. The strong diagonal rather than up-tight closing, the generously scaled notched lapels, the ease of the closing—all work for you provided the overlap is generous, you gently blouse the bodice into the belt, and you don't wear the belt pulled too tight. This coat is worn best by women with hourglass or rectangular bodies.

The swing coat is a classic at its best in a seven-eighths length—ideal for all full-figured women. It goes over all slim skirts and looks especially

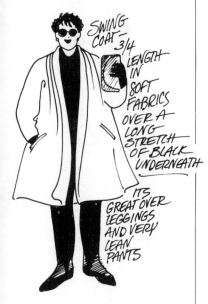

SWING COAT 3/4 LENGTH IN SOFT FABRICS OVER A LONG STRETCH OF BLACK UNDERNEATH

ITS GREAT OVER LEGGINGS AND VERY LEAN PANTS

terrific over pants; it's the contrast of big over narrow that suggests the body is trim all over. Lengthen the swing coat to just below your dress hem and you look shorter and wider; all that's visible is the broadening horizontal of the coat bottom. Shoulder fit, with pads, is essential, because this coat hangs from well-defined shoulders. Fabric is important for the swing; if it isn't supple, it doesn't move, and, as the song says, it don't mean a thing if it ain't got that swing. Gabardine is a natural. But so are soft, plush fabrics, which look luxurious. A good swing coat is in style for eons and goes over most of what you own. If your winter wear hews to dark colors like black or navy, think about a swing coat in a high color or an offbeat neutral like tobacco. You'll be surprised at how much you'll want to put on this coat. When you get tired of wearing a swing coat, don't throw it out. As with all classic silhouettes, stash it in the back of your closet and take it out again in a few years. It will look fresh.

The redingote is the quintessential fit-and-flare coat silhouette. It started life as a coat for full-skirted English ladies who wished to take in the countryside on horseback. It still has an awful lot of romance. Its distinguishing features are a fitted bodice, a back-belted fitted waist, and a skirt back descended from formal tails, with a true vent or an inverted pleat to simulate a vent. It is best worn by those whose body proportions need the fullness of skirt—the bottom heavy. Even in a tweed, this is a silhouette on the dressy side, not for going to the mall or other casual use. This coat begs to be in a red wool herringbone, with collar and cuffs of black velvet.

The duffel is a classic coat that has swung into high fashion and high colors the past few seasons. It is straight, long and narrow, has its own hood, and closes with leather toggles. Length is everything. Wear a duffel coat two inches too short and you look boxy and dumpy. Go two inches longer, and you look tall. A traditional duffel can look, well, boring, unless you are a freshperson at Yale. But get an unlined duffel, in a flashy color—royal blue, raspberry red—and you have a very versatile "odd" coat that can go a lot of places in high style. It's a supple sport coat for all casual wear and has enough zip to go over everything solid in your wardrobe, whether for everyday use or casually dressy. It's an eyecatcher, so walk tall. A classic item in an unclassic color is a classic recipe for instant style.

The sweatercoat makes a good wardrobe booster, if you should happen to stumble across one you like. A good sweatercoat can't be categorized easily, and depending on what you wear under it, can go casual, to the office, or even a bit dressy. Its great virtue is the long slim line it creates. But if the

REDINGOTE

RED WITH BLACK VELVET TRIM

knit has to stretch to make it around you at any point, the charm vanishes and you look wide. Get the next size larger, and make sure there is ease in the fit. You are best off if you stick to rib knits and flat knits. Mohairs and other fluffy yarns are warm, but bulking. Flat knits not only lay flatter, they have more body and drape better; when you need the extra warmth, put on an invisible layer underneath it all.

A DUFFLE COAT NEEDS BRIGHT COLORS!

RIBBED LEGGINGS AND SHORT BOOTS

KNIT COAT

The cape. Don't buy a cape to hide behind. Buy a cape for dash. Capes have romance. Style. Think of a cape and you think of movement. And that pretty much governs how you buy a cape. Not a thick or stiff bulky thing. But a fluid body shawl that drapes over your contours and responds to your every move. Capes make great second coats and dress coats; no matter their length they have a way of looking right with whatever hemline you're wearing. If you've tried a cape and it doesn't move you, try it again with respectable rounded-edge shoulder pads placed on your shoulders—it's astonishing how they support the right drape. (Of course, you'll tack them in at home.) The undisputed master of the cape is coat- and suitmaker **George Simonton.** His creations, on the dressy side, are now available in large sizes. For very casual wear, a cape in colorful synthetic fleece—the kind that Patagonia dubbed synchilla and is now a standard for cold-weather activewear—has its charms. It's very light, reasonably thin, totally supple, and very warm. The only problem with a cape is what to do about a pocketbook (warning: a cape can also be treacherous for driving if you don't have total freedom of arm movement). If it's for dressy wear, you can get away with traveling light and carrying a clutch bag (make sure it's slim). For casual or everyday wear, you'll probably need a shoulder bag. Get one with a very long strap—the bag must hit below the widest part of your hip, and it must lie close to the body—in the slimmest style your belongings will fit into (do you really need to carry all that stuff?). This is not the time for pouch bags, feed bags, book bags.

The down coat is making a comeback, now that fur is under assault. I don't care if it comes in your size and it fits perfectly. Unless you are six feet tall, wear it at your own risk.

The duster coat is a long straight cotton coat loaded with style, which probably stems from the fact that it has no essential purpose in life since the Stanley Steamer was dropped from production. But dusters make fabulous casual spring-fall coats over slacks, and double as robes. Their essence is long and lean. If you stumble over one and you can afford it, by all means get one.

ADD CHIFFON FOR THE BREEZE

DUSTER COAT— DASHING EVEN WHEN YOU'RE STANDING STILL!

10

Silhouettes That Flatter—Separates

JACKETS

Style-conscious women on a very limited budget often choose to put what they have into a jacket. Nothing pulls a look together more, nothing adds as much authority to a working wardrobe, and nothing has as much versatility. And when fashion changes, the new look tends to be summed up in jacket shapes (after all, how much can a straight skirt change?). A luxurious jacket upgrades everything else that's worn with it. Jackets—provided they have the right proportions—also work as figure smoothers, and can do a great deal to give a woman confidence in clothes. The right jacket can help a woman venture into a sundress or camisole blouse. But it all depends on the proportions.

- There is no middle ground with jacket length on full-figured women. A jacket comes to a straight halt either just below the waist, particularly with full skirts, or it goes to well below the fullest part of the hip. Nothing else works. That is a strong statement, but true. Your jacket length and the visible skirt length should never appear to be equal.

- The shoulder line must be impeccably defined. Sloppy shoulders will make you look sloppy all over. Neat shoulders will make you look like your clothes were custom-designed for you and you have no trouble getting clothes to fit. It is worth fussing over shoulder fit, because how the shoulder fits determines how the jacket drapes on the rest of your body, whether it stays in place when you are on the go, and whether you look well-dressed. Jackets need the lift of moderate shoulder pads, and it may take some experimenting to find the right pad to help define the shoulder. If you can't get a good shoulder fit, it is better to pass up a jacket than to try to change the shoulder line.

- The fit of the jacket on the body is critical. You need ease—but you also need trimness of fit. A shapeless jacket makes you look shapeless, while a tight one emphasizes size. What you should look for is clarity of silhouette—enough fabric to sustain the shape of the garment, but no more.

Swing jackets should flare out from trim shoulders, not hang off the body in voluminous folds.

Short jackets should be only semifitted, close enough to the body—underarm fit is key—to look straight and narrow but eased to work well. Hint: Look for styling details such as little side slits that allow a short jacket to fall smoothly to the high hip.

Long jackets must be semifitted or straight-fitting; a long boxy jacket will make you look short and wide, in a word, dumpy. Narrow the silhouette and you have a great jacket shape for smoothing out body lines and appearing tall and trim. This is the trick to making a double-breasted blazer work. A long jacket has the appeal of a tunic and should never be boxy. Beware: Stores seem to be filled with shapeless dresses accompanied by long boxy jackets that create shapelessness.

Fitted jackets and peplumed jackets will work very well on women who are hourglass-shaped or bottom heavy. But the jacket has to be long enough to cover the widest part of the hips when worn with a slim skirt, the shoulder line must be broad enough to balance the hip line (often horizontally puffed sleeves are added) and the peplum has to have more vertical than horizontal thrust.

- The wrist is another strategic point for proportion. The sleeve of your jacket must be just below your wristbone, never longer, otherwise your jacket will appear too short and you too wide. You can't count on rolling up the sleeve because sleeve width influences the all-over proportion. The trimmer the sleeve, the trimmer you will look all over.

- The jacket must have the right silhouette and proportion with what it goes over. Long jackets can only go over skirts that fit smoothly under them: slim skirts, softly pleated skirts and all-around pleated skirts that drape in a straight line, drop-waist skirts, trumpet skirts whose flare is reserved for well below the jacket, and full skirts in gossamer fabrics like chiffon (they fall straight). A long narrow jacket just doesn't work over a skirt that flares from the waist; its line will be thrown off by having to cover all that excess fabric. Shorter jackets, on the other hand, work especially well with full skirts, whether the fullness comes from soft pleats or a circle flare. Fit-and-flare jackets must cover the widest part of the hips when worn with a slim skirt.

- The jacket should have enough detailing to give it finish and polish but not so much it detracts from the line. In fact, look for smart detailing and interesting fabric texture, rather than exotic shapes, to give your jackets variety and appeal. Can't wear a peplumed jacket but love the look? Search for a semifitted jacket with a curved or cutaway front. The right buttons can do more to take a (correctly fitting) jacket from ordinary to sensational, especially if they emphasize a vertical line, such as on a simple cardigan jacket. So before you cast a good jacket out because you're tired of it, or before you decide against a good-fitting jacket because it's too dull, think about changing the buttons to simple but interesting ones. Jackets with heavy decoration are often overwhelming on full-figured women; a fringed yoke on a boxy western-inspired jacket may be trendy but it may simply be too, too much.

SINGLE BREASTED BLAZER WITH SHOULDER PADS

SLEEVES UP

TURN BACK CUFFS AND PUSH UP SLEEVES FOR A CASUAL JEANS LOOK

Jacket Shapes We Have Known and Loved

The single-breasted blazer is a wardrobe basic. It's terrific over skirts and it adds instant snap to pants, from the most tailored to a pair of jeans. The trick is finding it in the right fabric, the right proportion, and the right shape to work right. As for shape, only straight or very lightly shaped will do (that takes it out of the running for the pear-shaped). Actually, to get the look of straight usually requires some shaping of the jacket over body contours and bust, such as princess seams in front. And the blazer must be of a fabric that is not stiff nor overly tailored. Gabardine makes an excellent blazer; flannel in whisper-soft, fluid renditions is great, but lesser grades are often too bulky. Nor should the tailoring give it hard edges. As for linings, it's a toss-up. If the lining is a fabric that matches the jacket body in fluidity, fine. If it is stiffer, better to forgo it. While summer blazers need no lining, their facing definitely needs finishing to keep it from splaying open over the bosom; unless the blazer is impeccably finished, you are often better off with a lined one. A blazer with rounded corners will give you a more finished look and a softer edge than a blazer with square edges. Patch pockets and flaps will not add bulk if the fabric is right to begin with, but you will always be best off in a blazer with besom pockets, especially at the breast. If you are dressed all in one color, let a colorful pocket silk or a tiny pouf of white lace peek from the top pocket. A blazer can be worn with any skirt except a trumpet skirt or a fullskirt.

The double-breasted blazer is definitely not taboo if it is done right. The trick is a flat, supple fabric—avoid tweeds and other bulky and heavily textured fabrics. And make sure button lines are not too widely spaced, so that you get two vertical lines rather than a box shape outlined in buttons. Tiny lapels do not work any more than oversize ones, and they must lie absolutely flat. A longish double-breasted peak-lapel blazer can look terrifically chic; just add a peek of pocket scarf. Wear it with slim skirts, matching as in a suit, or contrasting, or wear it with pleated skirts. But don't wear it with full skirts or with trumpet skirts.

The cardigan, with its clean and simple straight shape, is always a winning style because of its vertical lines and classy breeding. There are basically two types of cardigan. One is the classic high-armhole, trim shoulder, Chanel-style jacket. Often outlined at collarless neck and down the front with braiding or banded trim, this jacket can look boxy on you unless it is elongated. Ever since Karl Lagerfeld took over design at Chanel, he has

DOUBLE BREASTED BLAZER A TRUE CLASSIC

SHOULDER PADS MAKE THE SHAPE WORK BEST

STRAIGHT CARDIGAN JACKET

DECORATIVE TRIM MAKES VERTICAL LINE

TOP AND SKIRT CLOSE OR THE SAME COLOR

played around with the classic look and introduced a fashionably longer jacket, so you are well within your fashion rights to want longer Chanel jackets. They always look right and they give finish to everything. Fabric, however, can be a real problem. The original purebred came, and still comes, in bulky tweeds. You look better in less bulky fabrics. Best are silks and other smooth and supple fabrics. In an unusual approach to the classic cardigan, the manufacturer **Bis** has elongated the jacket slightly, put it into familiar but thin fabrics like cotton, then shirred the whole bodice of the jacket with elastic. The inventive result is an astonishingly flattering cardigan that fits any body with ease.

The second major type of cardigan borrows the open vee neck and relaxed feeling of a man's cardigan sweater. It is delightfully easy to wear, is also stunning in its simplicity, and lends itself to the presence of interesting buttons and to fluid fabrics from silk to gabardine. Wear it over slim skirts, pleated skirts, even full skirts.

The jean jacket is a lean classic that has too much versatility to pass up. It is eminently wearable when the silhouette is relaxed into a slightly longer shape, and the bodice is body-skimming (but not blousy) rather than body-hugging. **Lane Bryant** has offered its own great-fitting version.

The blouson jacket, with its bloused effect, works with either a banded or drawstring bottom. For this jacket to look good, it must cover the widest part of your hips, and it must do so in the narrowest way possible. The idea

BUY EXTRA LONG AND ADD PADS

ROLL UP SLEEVES

A GREAT BLOUSON SHOULD END BELOW WIDEST PART OF THE HIPS

is to imply a shape beneath, not bury it. The blouson needs sleeves that are also controlled in fullness, preferably ending in a wrist cuff. And it only goes over bottoms with slim lines: slim skirts, all-around pleated skirts if they are stitched down, and all tapered pants. It is the best jacket to pair with trumpet skirts.

The shirt jacket is an automatic winner because it is extremely easy to wear (those cutaway sides help it over all hips) and its overwhelmingly vertical style lines are 200% in your favor. It's best cut in body-skimming straight lines, rather than made full with gathers, and looks especially good when the collar is worn up in back and open in front, giving your neck a long graceful line. Beware billowing shirt jackets (opt for straight instead), billowing sleeves, oversize collars, and over-large pockets; you need details scaled to your size, not exaggerating it. A shirt jacket should close fully, although you will often want to wear it open, or partly open. Make sure it is finished with a placket front rather than an open facing (which will tend to catch on your bosom). Add a shirt jacket hanging free or loosely belted over jeans or a skirt. Get one in an interesting fabric—a soft suede in a bright color if most of your clothes are neutrals, or a lush neutral if your clothes colors are often bright—and you can add a great deal of versatility and panache to your wardrobe without sacrificing comfort. A wonderful way to get the polish of a suit without the starch is to buy a shirt jacket and matching skirt, and add a simple tee shirt underneath. In the same spirit, skirt and shirt combinations can be turned into soft suits if the shirt is finished with shirt-tail hems and a placket front; it can be worn as a jacket over a tee or simple shirt. Shirt jackets work nicely with slim skirts, soft pleated skirts, and full skirts. They don't have the right attitude for knife-pleated skirts or trumpet skirts. They work with all pants.

The fitted or hacking jacket is a highly traditional style that works best for the hourglass-shaped and the pear-shaped. And even then, it takes great precision of detail and fabric. The hacking jacket, like the redingote, was born among England's horsey set and so is traditionally made in tweeds and other bulky fabrics. It is single-breasted and fitted through the bodice, then flares gently, its hem curving from front closure to a slightly longer vented back. It is this gentle curviness that gives the hacking jacket its feminine appeal, even in its most horsey tweed, and flap or besom pockets are set on an angle that further echoes the curve.

For the most part, forget tweed. But this jacket done in a superior doeskin flannel, especially when trimmed in velvet, can be smashing, both for city

SHOULDER PADS

TRY THIS SHIRT JACKET OVER A CAT SUIT!

and country wearing, especially over a midcalf challis skirt. Wear it over softly pleated skirts or split skirts, and full skirts. Also trousers or trim jeans.

The wrap jacket that you belt like a bathrobe is an elegant wardrobe addition for women with hourglass or rectangular bodies. In a fabric that drapes, it has the right touch of slouchiness to soften body lines while covering them. Whether collarless, as in a kimono, or notched- or shawl-collared, the wrap jacket needs plenty of overlap to stay securely closed when you are seated. If it's front tie, the belt loops should be perfectly placed—neither too short-waisted nor too long-waisted—to keep the jacket slightly bloused at the waist. Make sure the belt is generous. If the belt doesn't hold with a simple tie and you don't like the bulkiness of a knot to secure the front, you can always buy a trench-coat type pull-through buckle and stitch it on; it's a simple do-it-yourself addition. Wrap jackets that hitch on the side are usually fabulous for all full-figured women, not only because of their built-in drape and strong diagonal line, but because they do not create a definite waistline. The slouchier the fabric, the better; look for fabrics that blend rayon for great drapability yet good body. Wrap jackets need slim skirts, including wrap skirts, or softly draped split skirts and soft-pleat skirts. They can also be worn with trousers in supple fabrics, stirrup pants, crop pants and, of course, jeans.

The safari jacket has a way of never going out of style; sometimes it is simply more ubiquitous than others. It makes great sense for warm-weather looks. I know one woman who always dresses in black—black shirts and jersey tops, black skirts and pants—and wears only an old tan Abercrombie and Fitch safari jacket, anywhere in the world. She never looks anything less than smashing and intriguing. The right safari jacket is important, because it is easy to look boxy in one, especially if it has wide short sleeves and the fabric is too stiff. The most versatile is the traditional—long sleeves with button cuffs that can always be rolled up once or twice for extra throwaway chic and the waist as tight or as loose or as vague as you wish to define it. A workable variation is one with a drawstring waist or with side elastic slightly defining the waist. In all cases, ease is the essence of fit in a safari jacket. You need a little extra length, too, and a superb fabric. There are cottons and there are cottons. The best fabrics have body, feel soft on the skin, but hold their shape reasonably well. You don't want a limp fabric or a stiff one, nor do you want one that wrinkles if you so much as look at it. Fine twills and cotton gabardine are excellent; poplin is too stiff.

Again, details count tremendously. A safari jacket typically has four

HACKING JACKET WITH VELVET TRIM

ADD AN ASCOT FOR SWASH

CHALLIS OR SILK

A GREAT PAISLEY IN SUBTLE COLORS— VERY REFINED!

WRAP JACKET WITH CONTRAST LAPELS AND CUFFS

OVER SKINNY BOTTOMS MAYBE AN EVENING SKIRT

SAFARI JACKET WITH DIVIDED SKIRT

SHOULDER PADS TOO

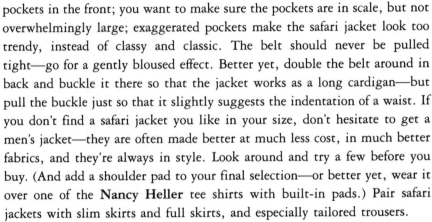

pockets in the front; you want to make sure the pockets are in scale, but not overwhelmingly large; exaggerated pockets make the safari jacket look too trendy, instead of classy and classic. The belt should never be pulled tight—go for a gently bloused effect. Better yet, double the belt around in back and buckle it there so that the jacket works as a long cardigan—but pull the buckle just so that it slightly suggests the indentation of a waist. If you don't find a safari jacket you like in your size, don't hesitate to get a men's jacket—they are often made better at much less cost, in much better fabrics, and they're always in style. Look around and try a few before you buy. (And add a shoulder pad to your final selection—or better yet, wear it over one of the **Nancy Heller** tee shirts with built-in pads.) Pair safari jackets with slim skirts and full skirts, and especially tailored trousers.

The sweater jacket, because of its basic soft construction, has some automatic pluses. But even though it is made in fabric that stretches, relying on the stretch of a knit for fit permanently disqualifies it from looking good. A sweater jacket needs controlled ease to fit well. At any length and style, a sweater jacket should follow all the rules of styling, fit, and proportion of a jacket of any other fabric. Where sweater jackets often go amiss is that they use fluffy yarns that simply add bulk to your body. Opt instead for flatter knits. And if the jacket is waist length, forgo all-over designs. **Gispa** and **Adrienne Vittadini**—leave it to the Italians—consistently turn out stylish good lookers. A good sweater jacket can go with just about any bottom.

The drawstring jacket is one of the all-time greats for larger women. With its soft construction, built-in ease, and fluid good looks, it is currently on one of its periodic swings into fashion, although it is never really out of fashion. In fact, now's the time to buy wisely for the future. Fabric is important—not too droopy, not stiff. This jacket should blouse at the waist or anywhere below—but not billow. For that reason, the narrower the line, the better. A personal favorite is a jacket that is at heart a long collarless shirt, has long slim sleeves, substantial covered buttons, and is reversible from a silky bronze matelasse to a leopard print chiffon in such a way that the reverse print forms contrast piping at neck and sleeves. I wear it as a blouse or a jacket. Drawstring jackets look terrific with slim skirts, full skirts, softly pleated and split ones, with plain pants, and drawstring pants.

The vest, with its deep vee neckline, and vertical and diagonal lines, is almost a magical top for some women. In traditional styling, silky and supple fabrics, and almost any kind of pattern and color, it's got a drapey

DRAWSTRING JACKET

ROLLED SLEEVE SHOWS CONTRAST TRIM

attitude and a totally vertical thrust when worn open. It smooths the line from bodice to hip, breaks up a wide waist, adds a lot of interest and finish to a look—without an ounce of bulk. This is not the vest that looks like it came from your father's suit; it's much less uptight, more relaxed in line.

I know a woman who has for years bought them here and there, whenever she could find them. They never go out of style. Pair them with slim skirts, full skirts, pleated skirts, trousers, jeans, baggies, and hip-yoke pants.

A PATTERNED VEST WITH RELAXED FIT

SKIRTS

There is no way to skirt the matter. Skirts are among the most important items for establishing body proportion. And they are the backbone of any serious wardrobe. There are two guiding principles for skirts.

1. A skirt should always be as slim and close to the body as a silhouette can bear, and the most important skirt for you is the slim or straight skirt. This is because a skirt hemline is one of the major horizontal lines on the dressed body. Therefore, **the wider a skirt at its hem, the shorter and wider you will look.** Categorically. No exceptions. The narrower the width at the hemline, the narrower you look. Because the width of the skirt at the hem is so vital in balancing your proportions, the fabric of a skirt becomes extremely important. Always look for skirts in fabrics that drape straight. Stiff fabrics and bulky fabrics will not serve your needs in a skirt.

2. A skirt should never be wider than it is short. No matter how wonderful your legs. It will just emphasize the fullness or roundness on top. Short skirts are riding high these days, but that doesn't mean you have to follow suit. Just below the knee is as short as your skirts should get—and that's if your legs are attractively curvy. And of course, the wider the style lines of the skirt—pleated skirts, full skirts—the longer the skirt must be.

A third principle might be that vertical detailing will make the skirt longer and slimmer—button fronts, vertical seams. Knife pleats are a special

GRADUALLY
TAPER
YOUR
SKIRT
FOR BEST
EFFECT

TAPERED
LOOKS
LONGER!
(AND THINNER!)

THE TRUMPET
SKIRT—
GETS A THIN
WAISTBAND

GODETS AT
HEM CREATE
THE FLARE

case, because while they certainly are vertical lines, a series of uniform pleats pulls the eye across, accordion style; still, they have their place in the wardrobe. Horizontal detailing—that includes patch pockets or any pocket with a horizontal opening—will stop the flow of the line.

The slim or straight skirt is the natural ally of full-figured women, whether it's a knit skirt, a simple side zip skirt, a trouser skirt with a suit, or a jean skirt for more casual wear. Not only does it have a narrow hem, the skirt is vertical in its emphasis. Even the pear-shaped woman can wear it well, providing she has the right hip-skimming top. A straight skirt that goes over full hips, even if it falls straight, tends to look like it describes a slight A line, broadening out from the hips. For that reason, **you must taper all slim skirts for them to appear straight and flattering.** The taper should not create a hobble skirt, just a slightly narrower line at the knee. Many slim skirts by better manufacturers are made with the slight taper that's needed—and a back slit for walking. If not, do the tapering yourself or have your tailor do it. The slim skirt, wide where it needs to be wide and then modestly tapered, not only can but should be worn by pear-shaped women, who often feel confined to circle skirts. The tapered slim-skirt silhouette has the effect of narrowing the whole body, for all women, while the circle skirt widens it. Although the bottom-heavy can't wear a straight dress, by breaking an outfit into two parts and wearing a long jacket, such as a swing jacket, whose natural lines admirably accommodate large hips, they can take advantage of a slim skirt.

The essence of a slim skirt is a slim, straight line. Therefore, the straight skirt cannot be worn too tight or it backfires. If, in profile, it curves in from tummy to pelvis, or cups around the derriere, it is too tight; get the next size. It is worth looking for a good one that is simple, fits well, and is well constructed so it can carry its weight as a workhorse of the wardrobe. Look for the narrowest waistband possible, or no waistband at all, a zipper or closure that always lies flat, and a walking slit or pleat. If you have high hips or a full waist, you'll do best with a trim elasticized waistband, because the drop to the hips is immediate.

The trumpet skirt never fully disappears from the fashion scene, but it definitely swings in and out. It's been in for several years, but appears to be in retreat this moment. When done right, it is a wonderful silhouette for full-figured women, sexy and ladylike at the same time. Not only does it have numerous vertical seams, but its style lines frame our body lines. It needs curviness to work right; it is one of the few skirts to make a supreme virtue of full, round hips. It then tapers to the knee before bursting into a flourish of fullness without interrupting the vertical seam lines. It is important that the trumpet skirt narrow inward before it flares out; otherwise, it's just a sloppy skirt without a defined silhouette. While the skirt needs to follow body contours, the effect is totally ruined if the skirt is too tight or too shapeless. This skirt looks better in woven fabrics than in jerseys or knits, which often can't support the sharp bottom flare. This skirt loves to go dancing! And loves a hip blouson top.

The front-close wrap skirt, provided it isn't an A line, is an ideal silhouette for full-figured women, and it's always in style, especially now, with the return of softly feminine looks for daytime. The asymmetrical close adds interest and another flattering vertical line. If the skirt is draped, there's even more elegance. A well-made true wrap skirt has a very generous overlap and is held by two fasteners (buttons, velcro, slide fasteners) at either side of the waist, or closes with a row of buttons asymmetrically placed down one side, so that when you sit, your inside story is not revealed. If you're already thinking safety pins or other added security devices, don't bother; they'll just inhibit the natural play of this silhouette. Another fabulous alternative, especially for the insecure, is a wrap skirt permanently anchored in place to a pull-on waistband.

The modified dirndl is essentially a straight skirt that makes the "drop" from waist to hips by a series of all-around, or front-only, gathers. That makes it a good choice for the woman with a tummy or with high hips. It's important for this skirt to be in fluid fabrics, otherwise the waist gathers are too bulky and the skirt stands too far away from the body.

The A-line skirt is traditionally regarded as an ideal line for the full-figured woman. It is, in fact, one of the most difficult silhouettes to wear, and one of the least attractive. What makes the A line so difficult is that its hem is always the widest part of the skirt, creating a figure-shortening and -widening horizontal. Stiff by nature, the A line lends no grace to its wearer. Why bother when there are so many other flattering skirt silhouettes to choose from?

The all-around pleated skirt is definitely a good option for full-figured women provided the size is right, the length is right, and the fabric is right. With all-around knife pleats, this skirt literally dances to movement, which always is alluring. That makes this silhouette ideal for fine, smooth fabrics that have some body. But if the pleats do not lie flat against the body at its widest part—the hip—when the skirt is not in motion, then the pleats splay

FRONT CLOSE WRAP SKIRT

NO SHORTER THAN KNEE LENGTH

TAPER THE SKIRT— IT SHOULD BE LONGER THAN IT IS WIDE!

DIRNDL MODIFIED BY SIDE POCKETS

STITCHED DOWN PLEATED SKIRT

LONG ENOUGH TO BALANCE THE STITCHED DOWN PORTION

SOFT, FLUID PLEATED SKIRT

ELASTIC BACK WAIST CONTROLS GATHERS

BUTTON FRONT ELONGATES

out and not only create a more horizontal effect, they scream "size." So if you have your heart set on an all-around pleated skirt, you may have to try one size larger than you usually wear. There are three very attractive ways to get around the problem. One is a hip yoke, from which the pleats are suspended; this limits your top options, since you have to cover the yoke. The second is to look for a skirt with pleats stitched down to the hips; this is not workable for the very short woman, who will not get enough length of unstitched pleat to make this style work. The third is to look for a skirt whose all-around pleating is knit in by virtue of fine rib-knitting; because this eases the fit and the drape, this version is superb for women with wide hips or thighs.

In any case, a pleated skirt needs well-below-knee length, and it needs an even hem. Be sure to check it all around. If the pleated skirt is a knit, it will probably be easiest to shorten from the waistband. To get pleats that lie flat and have beauty of movement, you will do best with fine, smooth fabrics. This is not the place for chunky wools; only the finest will do. Georgette holds a crisp pleat and sways with great allure in this style. Silk crepe or broadcloth is another winner in this silhouette. Whatever the fabric, look for a solid color or a small all-over print. Border prints are lethal; there is no length long enough to counteract that horizontal.

The soft-pleated skirt is one that all full-figured women, regardless of body type, can wear well, with no provisos. And this is the silhouette of choice for the dog days of summer, with enough fabric for ease, but not so much it overwhelms. What makes this skirt wonderful is its long vertical lines, the additional play of verticals from the pleats, and the softness and easy grace of movement it affords. All of the above are conditioned on one fact: The skirt works only in supple fabrics that drape well, falling close to the body in a straight line from the hips—jerseys, crepes, rayon-blend challis, georgette, lightweight linens, and cottons. The skirt takes to solids with some surface texture or to small all-over prints; it's better to avoid large prints. Styling details like button fronts or plackets add to the vertical and give you the option of more leg play. But put a border design at the hem and you kill the vertical impact. Details to look for include pleating in front and back only, not on the sides; in-seam pockets, so that the flow of line is not stopped or bulked up anywhere.

SPLIT SKIRT

SOFTLY PLEATED

DIVIDED SKIRT

The split skirt, or culotte, when done in a supple fabric with soft front pleats, is an ideal silhouette that packs tons of panache. It's got all the virtues of a soft-pleated skirt plus all the comfort of pants, and is a great warm-weather style. At a time when short skirts are popular, the split skirt is a great way to get more coverage without sacrificing an iota of chic. Besides, split skirts in fluid fabrics have more innate grace than any other bottom. Fabric is everything in this silhouette, though, and it determines just how dressy the split skirt can be. In filmy silks and beautiful crepes, it can go partying; in wool or cotton jersey or wool challis it can go to the office; and in baby-fine corduroy it is great for the country. Split skirts that are closer to trousers in their heritage are likely to be stiffer and far less flattering. The proper length for a split skirt is calf length. Check out the offerings from designer **Tamotsu**, who almost always presents a variety of split skirts in superb fabrics in every season's collection.

A GORED SKIRT— A PIECED SEMI-CIRCLE

The flared skirt, also known as a semicircle, is a good silhouette for the bottom-heavy woman, as the skirt's natural style lines encompass her body lines. As with other full skirts, the fabric must be supple and soft so the skirt doesn't widen out from the hips. Best yet is a skirt with gores; you get the addition of vertical seam lines. A flared skirt, like all full skirts, needs more length to balance out the fabric width. Wherever the best below-knee hemline is, you will probably have to even out the hemline all around, as different body parts tend to hitch the fabric up.

The gathered or dirndl skirt, which fans out from waist gathers, can be difficult to wear if the fabric is not absolutely soft and fluid. In coarse or bulky fabrics, it seems to weigh the body down. In drapey summer-weight fabrics, which do not bunch at the gathers, this skirt is at its best.

The hip-yoke skirt is a clever invention; by providing a smooth line over tummy and hips, it makes many skirt styles highly workable for the full-figured. There are many versions of the hip yoke. One is a Western style front yoke that rides diagonally over the hips and comes to a point at the skirt center; unpressed pleats are released from the yoke. Another is an all-around yoke over the hips, from which is released gathers, soft pleats, or knife pleats. What the hip yoke does is suspend the skirt body from the widest part—so that gathers and pleats fall assuredly in a straight and flattering line. There isn't a woman who can't wear this style—provided the yoke falls in the right place: just above the widest part of the hip for the bottom heavy; just below for others. The Western yoke skirt looks best worn with a tucked-in blouse. The all-around hip yoke needs an overblouse or other top to cover the horizontal seam.

HIP YOKE SKIRT WITH SOFT PLEATS AND GATHERS

The circle skirt is, sad to say, usually too much fabric for most women to wear well, except when hemlines get very long or on a very tall woman. Then, it's a good option for the bottom-heavy woman, in soft fabrics.

The flounced skirt can be considered—for dressy wear or light summer wear—only when the flounce is at the bottom of an otherwise slim silhouette, and the longer the skirt, the better. In its fuller renditions, a peasant or dirndl skirt with a bottom flounce, or a multi-tier flounce, it is better left to those who can benefit from all those ever-widening horizontal lines. It looks costumey. Leave it for Carmen Miranda.

Smart Skirt Shopping

Finding a good skirt that fits well is getting much easier than finding a good dress. Since some skirts never go out of style—a pleated skirt, a slim skirt—you can pick one up whenever and wherever you spot one to your liking. Women report that **Jones New York** is an excellent fit on different body types. In knits, **Gispa** runs beautiful and full. **Adrienne Vittadini** is up to date and cut fairly long in hip-yoke skirts; slim skirts are shaped perfectly and look terrific. If quality is important to you, you'll love the skirts (and, often, matching tops or jackets) from **Waldman De Luxe**, an English company that makes beautiful skirts in all sizes. The fabrics are always perfect and the styling right; no one makes a better stitched-down pleated skirt. Waldman skirts are a mainstay at Harrod's, a long way to travel for a skirt but worth a stop if London's on your itinerary. In the U.S., The Forgotten Woman carries this brand.

PANTS

If you have shied away from pants—and I know there are those women who have, and I know why—it's time to get reacquainted with them. In the early days of full-figured fashions, it was difficult to get a good fit in pants, and your early experience may have traumatized you. It's time to come back into the fold; pants fit much better. If you don't wear them because you think they're inappropriate, or because they wear through too quickly on the inner thigh, it's time to rethink that, too. It is possible, with some knowledge of your body, of the right pants silhouettes, and of fabrics, along with some fitting room experimentation, to look as good or better in pants as in anything else. And to get durability.

There are no women who can't wear pants. It's that categorical. The issue is finding the right pair of pants that go with your body lines. It's true, pants don't belong everywhere. In fact, if you find yourself crawling into a pair of pants day after day, surprise yourself, and everyone else, by wearing a skirt or dress now and then; you'll discover new ways to see yourself. But pants are an important part of the modern woman's wardrobe, especially the active ones. And they are at times indispensible.

If your idea of pants is polyester pull-ons, or any one type of pull-ons, you are missing a good way of looking polished. By keeping lines eased and fit relaxed, you can wear trousers that will give you a whole new take on yourself and go many more places. By looking better defined, you will look more refined.

Pants balance body proportions via their long vertical lines. Keeping the look of pants vertical, however, can take some doing. In order for pants to look good and balance width, **pants must fall with ease from waist to hem.** They can not appear tight anywhere; that will break the fall.

Pants generally encounter five points where fit is critical: 1) the abdomen-hip area, which is often wider and rounder than long, 2) the "rise," or length from waist to crotch, 3) the derriere, 4) the thigh, which needs the right amount of ease, and 5) length. Length is the easiest to remedy. Even with only four points to negotiate, plus the waist, it's easy to understand why getting pants to fit well is difficult.

What's changed is that many manufacturers have become more sophisticated in testing pants on a variety of fit models. And they have recognized that there is more than one body type when it comes to bottoms. The big jeans manufacturers—Levis, Lee, Gitano, Chic—all produce several varieties of jeans and casual pants for each of the major body types. Other manufacturers may regularly offer one or two styles of pants—some have a particular style and fit as their trademark—but have tested it on a couple of bodies. And there is enough variety among manufacturers that you will now have choices to make.

Once you find a brand of pants that fits, or design features that improve the fit, stick with it/them. The watchword in fit of pants, as with fit of everything else, is ease. The enemies, again, are tight and baggy. Tight pants call attention to size. Baggy pants at one of the five fit points make you appear wider and shorter—and sloppy. Here's what to look for:

- **Abdomen-hip**. If you have a round tummy and pants follow every contour, out, in, then down, you are wearing your pants at least one size too tight. If pockets pull, or pleats splay open, or the leg crease immediately vanishes over your belly, or you have trouble getting the zipper closed, ditto. Hey—I understand; there were eons of having to wear clothes too tight or not at all. It is time to get used to a more flattering fit. If there is ever a question of pants size, you are better off going one size larger than one size smaller—you will be surprised how a pair of pants with ease makes you look smaller all over.

- A word about **waists**. Getting pants to fit your hips is more important than getting pants to fit your waist. Altering the waist of pants with a fixed waistband is a relatively simple matter. If waist fit is always a problem—even when pants fit at the hips they are too tight in the waist—then you should look for pants that have back elastic and a tailored front. If your waist is wider than your hips, as it may be for women with rounded body shapes, then you need pants with all-elastic waists.

- **Rise**. This is the one place where women often find pants cut too big. In order to wear pants well, you don't want a rise that sags. A droopy crotch shortens the apparent length of your legs. But you don't want it curving at all into your private parts, either. It can't bear repeating too often: Clothes that are too tight only emphasize size; and they make you self-conscious, which is the enemy of style. Besides, pants that are tight in the rise will wear out quicker than you can say "thigh friction." If the rise is too long, the pants were designed for someone with a rounder tummy or a fuller derriere. There is a happy medium, and you will find it. Keep trying pants on. But not all pants should fit the same in the rise. Jeans can be worn with a higher crotch fit than tailored pants. If you are bottom heavy, you need pants with a long rise; you will take it up. And if your belly is very full, as in round-bodied women, you also tend to need a slightly longer rise.

- **Derriere**. Pants should tackle the curve of your derriere with aplomb. Once they round the bend, they should descend in a straight body-skimming line. If they turn inward and hug you—and that's standing up—go a size larger or look for a different cut or brand. Pants don't fit in the derriere until they negotiate the curve in its most extended form—sitting down. Never buy a pair of pants until you try them sitting down.

- **Upper thigh**. You probably need more room in the upper thigh than you realize because you try on pants while standing up, and the upper thigh tends to spread when sitting down. Get used to wearing pants that have ease in the upper thigh. Proper fit in the upper thigh means that the pants crease is sharply defined. This cannot be stressed too strongly: The pants crease is an important vertical line that will help add length to your proportions. It must be maintained at all times. A pants crease that is obliterated by thick thighs or poor fabric calls attention to size—and it makes you look sloppy, too. It is worth going up a size, or looking for a different brand. That is also the best argument for buying quality pants. The better a pair of pants, the better the fabric, and the better the fabric, the better it will hold a crease. This is especially true of cottons. When pants are cut with bottom-heavy women in mind, other women may find them too baggy in the derriere and upper thigh.
- **Length**. Straight-leg or slightly tapered trousers should fall straight and come to a clean stop at the top of your shoes. If they "break" over your shoes, they are too long; they will break your line, too. Other types of tapered pants can be worn a bit shorter, but always with matching-color hose or socks to maintain an unbroken line. Stirrup pants—a fabulous silhouette for full-figured women—come flush against the instep, and it is the taut line of stirrup pants that helps them look so good. If they bag at the instep, they are simply too long and will shorten you.

If you are shorter than 5'4", you are no doubt tired of having to hem your pants or having someone do it for you. Look into buying pants especially sized women's petites. You can always find a good selection in the **Spiegel For You** catalogue.

Another word about pants length. Some of us are knock-kneed, and flesh seems to love to sit on knock-knees; deposits of flesh on legs can subtly distort the hemline of pants. If your flesh is on the inside of the thigh, you have probably noticed that pants bottoms are often a bit higher on the inside than at the outside of the leg. If your weight is distributed more on the outside of your leg, that side will seem to rise. Either way, the unevenness calls attention to size, and the hem should be straight. If your pants are being altered, make sure the adjustment—at most, a half inch longer on the inside seam—is made in the hemming.

To cuff or not to cuff? The rule books say never to cuff, because cuffs are double horizontal lines. But tailored trousers look more finished if they are cuffed. You can safely cuff your pants provided 1) you are over 5'4" or under that height but relatively long-legged 2) the cuff is no more than one inch high, compared with the standard one and a half inches (be sure to tell your tailor the cuffs must be only an inch) and 3) your pants are obviously tapered. Wide legs and wide cuffs are too overwhelmingly horizontal for any full-figured woman.

Now for leg width. The wider a garment, the longer it has to be (and the softer the fabric). It holds as true for pants as it does for skirts. The wider the pants legs, the longer they must be. This is not a matter of this season's fashion; this is a matter of aesthetics, year in, year out. No pair of pants can be worn long enough to tolerate wide pants legs, or wide pants bottoms. So unless you are tall, you can't wear palazzo pants without looking dumpy. (Not only are they wide, they get wider, and they lack a crease.) Or bell bottoms. But then again, no one except lanky sailors look good in bell bottoms, and no one but models look good in palazzo pants.

Pants should be worn straight-legged or tapered. And as with slim skirts, you will often find that getting pants to look straight requires tapering them ever so slightly. There are few alterations that will make you look taller and sleeker than tapering a pair of pants. The narrower the horizontal where the eye comes to rest, the narrower all-over you will appear to be. Trousers, by contrast, are meant to fall straight. But even here, unless you are six feet tall, a slight taper will serve you well and appear "straight." Currently, most quality pants are cut with a slight taper.

The final consideration about pants legs is that old bugaboo—instant wear-through at the thigh. Don't be embarrassed. It's a real problem, and a bigger deterrent to sales of better-quality pants than many manufacturers realize. And it isn't limited to full-figured women. All women experience the problem if their thighs meet. And so do men, although men's clothes usually have a built-in solution to the problem—the right fabric. The problem, dear reader, is not really in your thighs, and not in the pants' construction. It's mostly a matter of fabric. Wear pants in a fabric that eliminates the friction of thighs meeting, like silky gabardine, and you eliminate the problem. You can wear your pants every day, walk for miles, and they will not wear through. Wear a fabric that doesn't ease the friction, like sueded silk, or increases it, like a stiff wool flannel or a nubby tweed, and your investment is gone in no time flat. (Men's clothes are usually made of worsted wools; the yarns are twisted tight and finished to a frictionless sheen.) And thigh wear-through is partly a matter of pants fit. The more eased the fit at crotch and upper thigh, the less friction there will be. The solution to the problem, then, is not to swear off pants—limiting one's options is never a good solution to anything—but to choose fabrics carefully. And to make sure they fit well in the upper leg.

Trousers are pants that have a tailored waistband and front pleats. One of the most enduring myths is that full-figured women can't wear pleated pants, that pleats enlarge a tummy. Well, yes and no. Yes if they don't fit right. And no if they do. Trousers must fall in a straight line with a straight crease to work. For that reason, they are not usually suitable for bottom-heavy women, unless they are specifically cut full in the derriere and outer thigh. For all women, a good waist fit is often accomplished by back elastic. Trousers are pants at their polished best, and are the only kinds of pants that make a suit, or go uncompromisingly to the office—that is, an office where pants are acceptable in the first place. Trousers work best in supple but strong fabrics. Probably the single best fabric for trousers is a fine wool or cotton gabardine. It drapes well, it's not too heavy, it holds a crease well, it feels great on the skin, it's virtually a year-round fabric, and its smooth, close weave eliminates wear-through from thigh friction. Smooth worsted flannels, wool crepes, silk crepe, rayon-acetate combinations, cotton twills, and cotton-polyester combinations, even full-bodied cotton jersey—all work well for trousers. So does denim. Tired of jeans? Or think you can't wear them? Get denim trousers; they can go everywhere jeans can go, plus some. Because linen wrinkles so easily, avoid linen for trousers, which need to look polished (linen works better for more relaxed pants). If you are full in the hip and thigh and want the polish of trousers, look for pants where the front pleats start not at the waist but from small, flapped watch pockets set a few inches down from the waistband. Check the **Spiegel For You** catalogue.

Plain pants are absolutely simple in shape and have a smooth front. They make good casual pants, especially if you wear long cardigans, tee shirts, or other tops over them. Otherwise, the pain front reveals all the contours of tummy and hips without an ounce of distraction or the help of pleats. They can be as casual or dressy, or as soft or tailored as you want, depending on the fabric. This is the silhouette of most pull-on knit pants and other basic bottoms. It's also a good style for dressy but simple silk evening pants.

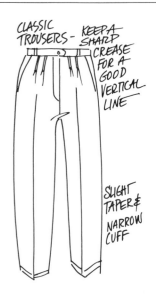

CLASSIC TROUSERS— KEEP A SHARP CREASE FOR A GOOD VERTICAL LINE

SLIGHT TAPER & NARROW CUFF

ELASTIC WAIST PANT

MUST BE TAPERED

SHOULDER PADS ARE IMPORTANT!

STIRRUP PANTS WITH AN ELONGATED BOMBER JACKET

Tapered slightly, these pants are great backdrops for all the tops and jackets in your closet, especially all those longer, slightly oversize tops falling from padded shoulders. This is by far the easiest pant to find in large sizes, and many manufacturers make a version of it.

Stirrup pants are strictly terrific on us. No matter what your body or leg shape, stirrup pants create a slim, taut line down the leg, especially from the knee down. The best way to wear stirrup pants is with a long, slightly oversize top that starts from well-defined (read: padded) shoulders. The best fabrics for stirrup pants are cotton jersey, flat wool knits, wool jersey, and anything else with a little spandex mixed in, to keep the pants in shape. **Danskin** always has a cotton-spandex stirrup pant in its line.

Crop pants are not an obvious choice for full-figured women, but they are an excellent one nevertheless, for all but the pear-shaped. Because they don't go the full length of the leg—they stop a few inches above the ankle—crop pants would theoretically seem to shorten the body. (They do for those whose weight is largely below the waist.) But if they follow the course of a normal straight or tapered pants leg, and don't widen, the eye seems to continue the line down. The exposed ankle (matching hose, please) looks narrow by comparison. Crop pants are chic and modern. They look terrific with low-heeled shoes. Because their line is essentially clean and crisp—it's that abrupt stop—be sure to wear them with tops that also have very simple shapes, either crop tops or long tops, nothing in the middle. If you want a pair of crop pants but can't find any, buy an extra pair of your favorite pants, stand in front of the mirror, mark the length that looks best, and either cut them down yourself (leave enough for a hem, no cuff) or take a trip to the tailor.

CROP JACKET WITH CROP PANTS

Jeans are the all-American classic pants, originated by Levi Strauss in indestructible serge *de Nîmes* for miners of the Gold Rush. Jeans should fit closer to the body than other pants, but if they get tight, they just emphasize size. Getting a good fit in jeans is a relatively easy matter now. Many companies, including **Levi's**, turn out variations of the standard five-pocket straight-leg jean, or one with a slightly tapered leg, well proportioned for different body types. Call me old-fashioned, but I like traditional straight-leg jeans only on those with slim limbs. And although it's again the fashion to roll up the bottoms, I think jeans look best when they are worn absolutely straight to the ankle. The neater jeans look, the better you'll look. That doesn't mean you can't go casual. Shirt-tail shirts were made to be worn outside of jeans, alone or over tee shirts or turtlenecks, loosely belted or not.

But the more deliberate, the less sloppy your assemblage, the more stylish you will look. Blazers also look great with jeans, over shirts tucked in or worn out (but shorter than the jacket).

Baggies are a shape of jeans and other pants ideal for bottom-heavy women. They accommodate the contours of that body, widening at the hips. What makes baggies work is that the silhouette eventually tapers toward the lower leg, describing a graceful arc along the side. If you are short, and you buy baggies that have to be cut down and hemmed, you also have to readjust the contours of the leg; if the baggies are cut off before the taper, you will wonder why anyone ever devised this silhouette. Look for baggies proportioned for you. **Gitano** and **Chic** jeans offer them. Also check the **Spiegel For You** catalogue. Because baggies are a bit bag-shaped, that is not an excuse for sloppy. The bagging is a very controlled, definite contour; if not, it just looks sloppy and adds to your bulk. And baggies should stop at the ankle.

Hip-yoke pants are also perfect for the bottom-heavy woman. These have a flat, vee-shaped yoke across the tummy and hips or a straight yoke all around, then unpressed pleats falling from there to provide room for hips and thighs. Like baggies, these are casual pants best done in casual fabrics. Unlike baggies, the vee-yoke versions must be worn with tucked-in tops, and look best belted. The all-around yoke pants, like any dropped yoke bottom, need a blouse or sweater that covers the horizontal seam.

Drawstring pants, like any drawstring garment, look best when they have a loose, easy fit. To keep the silhouette from being overwhelming, however, the pants can't be too full—and they can't widen out at the bottom. Provided they fit with ease elsewhere, sweatpants, with their ribbed or elastic bottoms, look terrific on fuller figures because they end on a slim note, snug at the ankle. To maintain the ease, always buy them on the big side, because they are bound to shrink with repeated washing. This silhouette takes best to lightweight fabrics; just be sure they have enough drape to hang close to the body. And if your waist is big, tie the drawstring a bit loose, so the pants appear to rest on your hips. Cotton jersey is ideal. So is cotton gauze. In one variant of drawstring pants, paper bag pants, the drawstring (or elastic) tunnel is placed about an inch down from the top edge, which forms a frill when the pants are drawn closed. This is a workable design feature only if you are long-waisted, have no midriff bulge, and have a relatively small waist; in a word, pear-shaped.

The jumpsuit is an idea whose time has come; it makes dressing so

JUMPSUITS GET PADS IMMEDIATELY!

COWBOY BOOTS

incredibly easy (no thinking, no coordinating, no stockings) and can be so body-lengthening (one long drink of fabric that tapers at the bottom) that it is worth enduring the vicissitudes of fit to find one that works. As I write these words, I am wearing a jumpsuit that is two, maybe three winters old—who knows? a good silhouette never goes out of style!—and made of satin wool gabardine by **Nancy Heller**. Mine has a fixed waist with back elastic, a zip front (a good vertical), convertible collar, covered-button cuffs, and a soft self-fabric belt with a pull-through buckle. What makes the fit perfect is a top slightly bloused into the waist seam, and tapered pants (necessary for balancing width) with unpressed inverted pleats over the tummy. It's also got great shoulder pads (for narrowing the hips). This jumpsuit never fails to get compliments, which I always appreciate. But wearing it has also convinced me jumpsuits should be the uniform of choice for anybody who needs to focus more on what she is doing than on what she is wearing—and still look chic.

Walking shorts may rank as the best way to approach legs in the summer. Their to-the-knee length looks modern, has flattering proportions provided the shorts are kept on the trim side, and does wonders for thick thighs. Woven fabrics look better than knit ones, since they hold a crease. But avoid stiff fabrics, which bulk and billow. Tailored walking shorts now even go to work in many offices; they look best in neutral colors with sheer dark hose and tailored flats. You can skip the hose for casual wear, but still opt for tailored flats.

Shopping for Pants

WALKING SHORTS SHOW OFF GREAT LEGS!

- It is worth buying pants—or at least trying them—in a large-size specialty store, where the sales staff knows the ins and outs of fit. These stores can't afford to take up space with clothes that don't fit the bodies of full-figured women. Ask an experienced salesperson which pants she suggests for your figure type. Or which brands have an excellent reputation for pants fit.
- Always try on more than one style of pants. It may be that the fit you are looking for is in a silhouette different from what you are used to wearing.
- Don't limit your search to jeans manufacturers or casual pants makers. Look at the collections of sportswear companies. They

have experimented with fit, too, and often have a pants shape that works on many figures.

- Some brands with good reputations for fit: **Le Painty, Jones New York, Regina Porter, Gitano, Chic Jeans, Levi's Dockers, Silk Club.**
- If you are short, look for pants especially proportioned for petite women. **Gitano** always offers them. The **Spiegel For You** catalogue usually has many varieties. And **Lane Bryant** stores are usually well-stocked.
- Once you find a pair of pants that fits well and looks good, examine the style features to analyze what makes them work for your figure. Then look for other pants with the same features. And, of course, look again for more pants by the same manufacturer. Because good fit is hard to achieve, manufacturers tend not to fiddle with pants design once they get it right.

TOPS

Tops are, well, tops for looking good all the time. This is probably where you get most of the variety in your wardrobe. And that's a smart approach. Sweaters and blouses and other tops in an array of colors, fabrics, and shapes, paired with a few classic, usually neutral, bottoms in your best silhouette, will give you a great deal of versatility and flexibility. A simple, cream-colored shirt in a dynamite fabric like semisheer georgette bloused gently into a plain slim black wool crepe skirt can take you to cocktails, dinner, and little evenings out. A surplice draped-front silk or polyester blouse and a swing gabardine jacket worn with the same skirt will take you smartly to the most professional of offices. And a slightly big and long but not bulky vee-neck sweater and a colorful scarf flung into the breach lets the same skirt go casual. You get the point: tops radically change the look of basic bottoms. They therefore allow you to develop a fabulous wardrobe that will always perform for you—by investing in a few beautifully tailored great-fitting classic bottoms that have years of wear built into them and a larger array of tops that add spice and personality.

If you're like many full-figured women, you know all the rules about blouses. Simple: You can wear any blouse as long as it's an overblouse. Right? Wrong, again. It's another one of those enduring myths. You don't know how wrong it is until you try tucking in a blouse. The secret to flattery is getting a fit with enough ease for blousing over the waistband, leaving the waist a bit vague. There's nothing more to it. Of course, you will want overblouses, especially for drop-waist skirts. But you are wrongly limiting your fashion options by sticking only to overblouses. Trust me; other types will flatter you as much or more. The always-an-overblouse school of thought is part of the hide-it-all mentality; it's time to ditch it.

Getting tops to fit and look right takes no more doing than getting everything else to look right. The cardinal rule for tops is the same as for other clothes. When you go shopping for tops, the images you should have in your mind are: body-skimming, sleek, drape, relaxed shaping. You always want the least amount of fabric to establish the outline of a silhouette, and no more, otherwise you'll be adding bulk and changing proportions. Big-busted women are probably no strangers to the fact that some tops will have to be bought a size larger than others. No one sees the size label. Just remember, the greater the ease in the fit of a top, the trimmer you will look.

What you should look for when shopping for tops:

- *Blousing*. Tops that get tucked in should have enough length and enough ease of fit so that they can be bloused or draped at least slightly at the waist. This is a critical element of fit for women with full midriffs or thick waists. A bloused top in a fabric that drapes fluidly smoothes the way and establishes easy elegance—in other words, it is chic.
- *Shoulder definition*. The shoulder is important for establishing the fit of the top, the proportion of the whole body, and the impression of neatness you convey. Sloppy shoulders make you look sloppy all over. A precise shoulder line, created by precision fit at the shoulder and support of the fit with shoulder pads, is thus essential. Good fit at the shoulders of tops also gives you the most versatility in coordinating jackets with your wardrobe of tops. A top that fits precisely can take almost any jacket. Sweaters are no exception to the rule that your tops should drape over your body from shoulder pads. Pads for sweaters need to be rounded, and you can either put Velcro on the pads, which will automatically anchor them to your sweaters, or you can wear pads anchored to your bra straps or other lingerie.

- *Neck fit.* Even if you buy a shirt you intend to wear with the collar open, make sure the collar fits when closed. There's no faster way to make a neck look wide; If there isn't room for a finger between collar and neck, it's too tight.
- *Bodice ease.* Whatever the silhouette or style of garment, whether sweater, tee shirt, or button-down shirt, it doesn't fit unless there is enough ease in the bodice for the top to skim over your body from neckline to hem. Blouses, shirts, and sweaters that follow the ins and outs of your body contours fit too snugly; they should fall in smooth straight lines from bust to waist or wherever the garment ends. As with all garments, it is the strength of the vertical line that balances your proportions.
- *Sleeves should be under control*—as narrow as possible for the silhouette, but never snug. And remember that no matter what lines sleeves take, you want them narrow at the wrist; your wrists rest against your hips, and too much fabric at the wrist appears to widen your hips. The only exception is when puffed sleeves are the focal point of an outfit, and then the body silhouette is kept perfectly straight and simple (and the sleeves must extend down toward the elbow).
- *Sleeves end at the wrist.* If they extend over the hand, they emphasize poor fit, call attention to size, and make you look sloppy. When trying on a shirt or blouse with button cuffs and the sleeves are too big or too long, the easy fix is to move the button over. If the sleeve is so long that it blouses over the cuff after this maneuver (naturally, you'll test it first by pinning the cuff closed in the fitting room) then it needs to be shortened; the cuff has to be taken off and the fabric removed from the sleeve end, and then the cuff replaced. This is a task only for experienced home sewers—or professional tailors—and the blouse has to warrant the expense. Folding up the end of a sleeve that's too long is fine for your most relaxed and casual clothes, provided the fabric isn't bulky. But you can do it on other tops only if the inside seams of the sleeve are finished for that purpose and the sleeve ends in a straight hem. Otherwise, it's no go; you'll be compromising your look and adding bulk. It must be shortened.

STRAIGHT SHOULDER LINE

THE MOST CLASSIC BLOUSE

DON'T FORGET THOSE SHOULDER PADS!

COLLAR SHOULD BE IN GOOD PROPORTION SCALE IS A KEY ELEMENT

TINY, OR NO CUFFS

- In looking for tops, *do break the "go with" syndrome*, as in "I need a blouse to go with my blue suit." Never buy a top just because it goes with or under something else you own. It should be able to perform on its own. And you should love it for its own style, with as much finish and detail as any other item you look for. And it should fit as well as any other top.

The Top Tops: Blouses

The classic blouse or shirt, usually with notched convertible collar and button front, is a pivotal piece in your wardrobe whether it's in silk, linen, cotton, or a synthetic crepe—or all of the above. I even have some I adore in ultrafine wool. This blouse should be of the very best quality you can possibly afford, because if you buy it at its body-skimming best, you'll be relying on it through the seasons and through the years. It's always right. And it is always flattering, given the open vee neckline and the straight shoulders. Do make sure, if there is a shoulder yoke, that it's high, on the shoulder, not low, on the chest. Raglan shoulders are fine, too, if they are lightly padded. And if it's good quality and the fabric drapes well—drape is a must on this item—it gives chic to everything else you wear. You must own this shirt in white or cream—the color will always put your face in a good light. It goes under suits, under sweaters, by itself with a simple skirt or pants. You can always pick up more in other colors you love and interesting fabrics. Polyester is not a good fabric for this shirt; in most blouse weights, it clings instead of drapes. Do give a thought to such unusual fabrics as semisheers. They go out dressy on their own but they also add instant panache and great softness to a tailored suit. In any version, don't go in for funky details, like oversize pockets or collars. The beauty of this shirt is its simple and sophisticated classicism.

The shawl collar blouse is a variation that is also good, provided the collar is scaled right. On a blouse, it could be too small, which only emphasizes size. (Too big is just as bad.) If you like shawl collars, they are usually scaled better on jackets.

The stock tie blouse, a classic that is at home under a hacking jacket, has been a predictable choice under suits in very conservative professions such as law. But because of its high neck, it isn't always the most flattering choice for larger women and, unless it's in the most obviously drapey fabric, it looks awfully schoolmarmish under a suit. Softer dressing for women is now in,

SURPLICE

and as far as I'm concerned, that's great news for us because we look better in it. If you must have a stock tie blouse, look for one in a fabric that has great drape.

The surplice blouse has your name on it. With its diagonal lines, vee neckline, and draped front, it's a natural flatterer, whether it buttons in the front (a version sometimes known as the "*L.A. Law* blouse"), hitches on the side, or slips over the head (a good bet since it can be worn as an overblouse). Need I remind you that it is also sexy (that drape does it every time, to say nothing of the minimalist approach to fastenings)? Again, drape is the essence of this silhouette, so look for fabrics that have body and hang well, and be sure shoulder pads are in place. Jerseys of any kind are sensational. Woven cotton is too crisp and might reveal more than you want when you bend. If your midriff is trim, or there is enough drape in the surplice to fudge the facts a bit, a bodysuit in this silhouette is terrific, and it does wonders for the fit of jackets.

The sailor blouse, or middy, is an ideal silhouette. It's got a deep vee neckline and a sizable collar with trimming that draws the eye vertically. It's best as a blouson or overblouse or tunic—and it always looks fresh. Men find it irresistible, and so does everyone else. I love a middy solo, but I also think it has appeal when it's worn collar-out under a collarless cardigan suit. Since this look never goes out of style, buy it where you find it. Just make sure it's not skimpy anywhere. It is a natural with pleated skirts and with crop pants, and pairs well with slim skirts, too.

The blouson is either born or made. Any blouse that's bought right can, and should, be made to blouse at the waist. The same silhouette may also be built in to tops that stop at the waist or hips. Waist blousons have a band that encircles you just below the waist. If the band is a rigid one, you could have problems getting it to fit and look right. It should lie flat all around. If not, look for a similar silhouette with a knit bottom band. Or a longer blouson. The same rules apply here as apply to blouson dresses and jackets. If you're like most women, you'll be getting plenty of wear from hip blouson tops, be they blouses or sweaters; they are that flattering. And they go over all your basic narrow bottoms. So make sure the fabrics are right (no cling, no fluff), that the fit is body-skimming and the top falls in a straight line, that there is a definite and flattering neckline (no turtlenecks), and that the shoulders are padded.

The cossack shirt is just about the only high-collared blouse you can wear easily. What reprieves it: The collar is simple and not all that high. The

SHARP SHOULDERS — THIS NEEDS PADS

MIDI BLOUSE

BLOUSON TOP NEEDS SHOULDER PADS FOR BALANCE

LEGGINGS HOSIERY AND SHOES — ALL DARK

COSSACK

AN OFF CENTER VERTICAL IS STILL A VERTICAL!

blouse is best worn as an overblouse, giving it a long line; the asymmetrical closing adds another vertical and breaks the body width. Just be sure the sleeves are under control. Pair it with slim skirts, soft-pleated skirts, drop-waist skirts, plain pants, and jeans.

The jewel-neck blouse has its place, and except when it's a blouson in an interesting and nonclingy fabric, its best place is under a cardigan or jacket with a deep vee that counteracts the horizontal effect of the neckline. And even then, self-fabric piping at the neckline gives it the finish this otherwise plain style seems to beg for. Alternatively, so does a nice chunky necklace. When the styling of this blouse is relaxed ever so slightly, and the neckline must be relaxed away from the neck a bit, it is often referred to as a tee shirt blouse. Then it can do everything a tee shirt does, including go out on its own with pants or skirts, tucked in or out. In a sharp white crepe, it looks positively fresh and chic in the summer over a black linen skirt. The relaxing of the neck makes all the difference in the world, and you can't have too many of this blouse. Go for color and small all-over prints as well as basic white or cream.

The tank top is your best way to show some skin if you are full-busted; you can wear your brassiere and bare your shoulders, too. And your neck. Fit is everything in this utterly simple silhouette—make sure the straps cover your straps, and that there is plenty of ease over the bustline. Also, check from the side, to make sure the armhole lies close to the body. Ease around the bustline will keep the drape vertical and the armhole from gapping open. Tanks go dressy—under a suit for office-to-dinner events—in luxurious fabrics such as silk charmeuse. My personal favorite is a semisheer rayon georgette printed in deep desert colors, which I wear under a relaxed shirt of the same fabric, from **BB USA**. And tanks go casual, especially in summer, when they often stand alone; or they can go under jackets to the office. Since they suggest the sun, color is wonderful, especially in a knit cotton jersey; besides, white looks too much like your father's underwear. Because every manufacturer cuts a bit differently, try on several brands if you are having trouble with sleeve gap. Avoid interlock because it doesn't hold its shape and knit polyester because it clings. And make sure there's plenty of length if you plan to wear it over pants or shorts; because it appears to start low on the chest, you need the extra length.

The tee shirt in pure white is the chicest, freshest look under a summer suit—or many another suit. If you watch the best dressed women in America or France or Italy, you'll notice that's what they wear. It's a bit unexpected,

SLINKY AND SILKY TANKS GO ANYWHERE!

therefore very appealing. To say nothing of comfortable. It's very tongue in chic about fashion. The tee shirt has a natural affinity for vee-neck cardigan sweaters and jackets, too. But not just any old tee shirt will do. Why beat around the bush—there is only one tee shirt available in large sizes that has maximum chic. It's from **Nancy Heller**, and it's a staple offering every season. It's a bit expensive if you're used to Fruit of the Loom (about $40), but I guarantee it's worth every penny. What's right is fabric, shape, and construction. It's made in a fine, flat cotton jersey that keeps its shape through many launderings. The neck is relaxed exactly to the right place, finished with a hem, then given the fillip of a sweet satin lingerie bow. The sleeves are well proportioned; the body length is long, the fit slightly oversize. And I've saved the best for last—the perfect shoulder pads are sewn in as part of the shirt, with trapunto stitching; they never lump or migrate. And they allow the shirt to drape over the body, which distinguishes it from all other tee shirts you may have tried and found wanting. This tee has enough presence to stand on its own over or tucked into anything, and makes a great bathing suit coverup. If you want to travel light, it will be half your summer wardrobe. It comes in colors.

THE PERFECT T-SHIRT WITH STITCHED IN SHOULDER PADS AND TINY BOW

Peasant blouses are impossible for any full-figured women to wear except those who are narrow and small-busted on top. And then care has to be taken to avoid an unscheduled appearance of bra straps. White with colorful embroidery is the standard, and fine linen and cottons are the ideal fabrics.

High ruffled neck blouses are so hard to wear, and there are so many other good blouse choices available, it's painful even to bring up the subject. Unless you have an unusually long and slim neck, avoid them. Between the ruffled neck, the lower shoulder yoke, and the full sleeves that usually go with this silhouette, we tend to look rather overstuffed. It's best for people who need to *add* bulk.

The camp shirt is a version of the classic shirt with short sleeves, a short boxy shape, and a finished straight hem so as to be worn in or out. Especially in crisp fabrics, this shirt when worn out can be lethally boxy. If those short sleeves don't drape down but stand out, they can seriously widen and shorten you. Still, camp shirts are cool and easy. So if the sleeves are too boxy, roll them up a bit, angling the outer edge up. Stand the collar up to lengthen your neck. And look for cottons that are soft and fine rather than crisp and hard.

The sweatshirt is as American as blue jeans and at least as comfortable. As a result of the fitness movement, the sweatshirt moved into high fashion and high fashion moved into the sweatshirt. The sweatshirt has left the gym and now comes in fashion colors and many other fabrics besides the standard fleece. Its relaxed crew neck and raglan sleeves make it easy to wear, provided it's roomy and on the long side. The problem with many sweatshirts is not the fit or shape but the fabric. Too much synthetic and the shirt is too lofty and the fleece too fluffy; it tends to look like a balloon on the body. The best sweatshirts—great with jeans for very casual wear—are still all cotton or cotton touched with rayon. Sweatshirt-style blouses and sweaters—with woven or knit bodies and rib-knit cuffs, necks, and bottom bands—are easy to wear, too. Pair with slim skirts, very soft full skirts, drop-waist skirts, pleated skirts, and all pants.

The Top Tops: Sweaters and Jerseys

The most important consideration for sweaters, besides the general rules of ease of fit outlined above, is fabric. The most flattering fabrics are always going to be flatter, smoother knits. Merino wools and fine lambswools will almost always look better than Shetlands and mohairs by providing the trimmest silhouette. Cotton is terrific, and heavier weights of cotton make sweaters that can be worn year-round.

SHOULDER PADS ARE A MUST!

CREWNECK SWEATERS WORN LONG WITH PADS OF COURSE!

Sweater length should follow all the rules of proportions for other tops and jackets. But a few points are worth emphasizing. If you wear flare skirts, your sweater needs to end above the flare, otherwise you will look too wide and the line of the sweater will be thrown off.

The cardigan has grown up since the 1950s, when it was a timid little round-neck thing in pale pink that ended high on the hips. Cardigans today beg to be long and lean with a touch of slouchiness, with or without a rib-knit bottom band, and definitely with a vee neck. That's good news for us, as they just don't work for our bodies in any other form; that midline vertical has to be long and strong. The cardigan is also no longer something you toss on just because there's a chill in the air (a shawl does that job today). It works only when it's a planned part of your look and balances the proportions of everything else you wear. Color-matched to an odd skirt, it lets you wear the skirt and a tee shirt and get the effect of a soft suit. Or color-contrasted to what's underneath, it lets you team up any bottom and top that are even closely color-related and get the effect of a suit. The shawl collar sweater is a variant of the vee neck; it just makes a fuss over its neckline. Nobody makes a cotton knit cardigan better than **Adrienne Vittadini**, and for wools or other fibers check out the offerings of **Nancy Heller, Gispa,** and **Outlander.**

The crew neck sweater has also grown up, and grown up essentially means fine knit. Short crew necks now look chic (in a preppy sort of way) tucked into trousers or a skirt (slim or pleated, and always bloused to smooth the line). They look even smarter long like a hip blouson. Either way, the neck can be hard on a full-figured body, so drape a colorful little silk scarf into and over the neck to break up the roundness and add soft interest near your face. A crew neck over a turtleneck is too neck-widening for full-figured women; if it's warmth you want, put a tee shirt or snuggie top underneath. And throw a big shawl over your shoulders. How to say this kindly: The standard catalogue crew neck sweater, whether cotton or wool, couldn't be worse proportioned for our bodies; it cuts them exactly in half. Go for longer versions when you find them.

SHOULDER PADS HELP THIS NECKLINE EVERY TIME

LONG AND NARROW

The vee neck pullover is one of the great stylemakers for French women. They wear it long and loose but not bulky—and with nothing underneath (except a bra). They wear it in black over a slim black skirt. It's got that lean-as-a-bean power and a soupçon of sex appeal. It's a great look to borrow. Not that the same vee neck couldn't go over tee shirts, turtlenecks, and blouses. It's best in heavier weights of cotton, merino wool, lambswool, or wool/acrylic blends. This sweater is also great over pleated skirts, trousers, stirrup pants, jeans, and crop pants.

The cowl neck sweater is essentially well-proportioned for full-figured women. And the cowl serves as a frame of the face. Avoid too exaggerated a cowl, though—it will tend to obscure your shoulders. And make sure the sweater is at least to the hips (to balance the cowl) and skims the body. However, raglan sleeves on this sweater can undo all the good, because unless they are propped up with properly curved shoulder pads, you get a long down-sloping line from neck to shoulder that seriously distorts your shape—you look like your flesh has slid down toward the ground, your hips seem wide by comparison, and because your shoulders seem low, your whole body looks short. Look for merino wool and other fine knits, rather than bulky yarns. And look for colors that truly complement your complexion— white is always a good choice. The bad part about cowls is figuring out what to wear over them; if the sweater is in a fine-gauge knit, you won't have trouble getting the neck under any coat. And when you get tired of looking at your cowl sweater, try pulling the cowl together in front and pinning it down with a great brooch. It certainly solves the coat problem too.

SHOULDER PADS

A COWL NECK MUST NOT BE TOO SAGGY

The turtleneck in cotton jersey is a classic that is just downright indispensible sometimes—for all winter outdoor sports—even though it really doesn't look good on thick necks or short necks or chubby chins.

CONTROL THE COWL WITH A FOLD AND A GREAT PIN

PADS ARE ESSENTIAL

FINELY RIBBED RELAXED TURTLE

However, it can be worn by full-figured women with total impunity so long as the neck is relaxed. That could be as easy as buying a regular cotton turtleneck, making sure the neck isn't fortified with spandex to keep it in shape, and stretching it out a bit. However, the relaxed neck is a modification that's getting easier and easier to find on turtlenecks, partly because it's in keeping with the general mood of relaxing the strictness of clothes. And partly because it's just a new wrinkle (literally) in fashion design. If you buy one turtleneck, make it white—that old face flatterer. If you buy two, add black. After that, go by what looks good near your face. But if the rest of your wardrobe is predominantly dark, think about brights: red, hot pink, jade. And if you want to see the most incredible transformation before your very eyes, slip small shoulder pads under your turtleneck. Suggestion: Search out a turtleneck with a zip front; then you have a good vertical line *and* a way to relieve the severity.

The sweater vest, especially when as long as a hip blouson and very lean, has a lot of chic. It is a natural ally of the pleated skirt because it doesn't add bulk to sleeves, which hover near the hips. The best way to wear a crisp white cotton shirt is under a long black or red, completely sleeveless sweater vest. (No cap sleeves, please!) You get the beauty of the sleeves and collar while the vest does damage control over the midriff, waist, and tummy. Here's where the knit is critical—only fine merino wools, the finest-gauge lambswool knits, or, if you can afford it, cashmere; mid-weight cotton knits or cotton-rayon blends. No mohair or other furs that add width. That goes for all those sweater vests that tie at the waist, too. Between the furriness and the short stop, they add more to width than they hide. Go for long lean sweater vests instead. Neat trick of the week: If you can't find it in the woman's department, get a man's extra long. And who says a sweater vest can't solo as a top, alone or under a suit jacket?

A GREAT SHAPE BUT A MENS EXTRA LONG SWEATER REALLY NEEDS SHOULDER PADS TO HOLD IT OUT!

11

The Fabric of Flattery

*F*or the very best designers, style always starts with fabric. The inherent properties of a fabric dictate the ways it can be worked, the shapes and lines it can hold, the silhouettes it is suited for, the way it will feel on the body, the way it will take color, the way it will reflect light—the character of the garment to be made from it. They get a feel for a fabric by rubbing it gently between their fingers, they scrunch it in their fist to see how it resumes its shape, they pull it in every direction to see how it can be handled and worked. And above all, they hold it up loosely to see how it will drape. In the beginning, before color, before the print, is the nature of the fabric and what it lends itself to, because a fabric must support the silhouette it is made into. If the fabric doesn't perform, the dress, or the skirt, won't perform. For real women of style, fashion starts with fabric, too, and for the very same reasons.

Why is drape so important? No less an expert on bodies than art historian Sir Kenneth Clark had this to say: "Drapery may render a form both more mysterious and more comprehensible. A section of [moving] limb as it swells and subsides may be delineated precisely or left to the imagination; parts of the body that are [aesthetically] satisfying can be emphasized; those less interesting can be concealed; and *awkward transitions can be made smooth by the flow of line.*" (emphasis added) Drape in fabric use is essential to full-figured women because it

- reveals only what you want revealed about your body.
- stimulates interest through a sense of mystery.
- creates line.
- contains grace—it makes movement appear to flow smoothly, all the while maintaining line.
- lets your clothes move with you. If they don't move with you, you feel uncomfortable and you look awkward.

Fabric is one of the great secrets of chic. Fabric contributes more to style than most women realize. Clothes are sometimes made in inappropriate fabrics. Not all fabrics suit all styles or cuts of clothes. What's more, many fabrics are not suitable for all body types, or all body parts.

You need a crisp image. But you don't get it by using stiff and crisp fabrics. You get it from precision of fit and appropriateness of styling, from the clarity of your self-image and the image that you project, from the energy you radiate, from the clarity and dynamism of the style lines of your clothes—their "cleanness."

When it comes to thinking about fabrics, consider these fabric uses you might not have appreciated:

- *Polyester.* If all you know is polyester from textured knits or cotton-poly interlock, think again. Polyester has some virtues in other forms; it makes a georgette and a crepe that have the right weight and body and movement for an all-around pleated skirt, a fine use because of its total lack of bulk.

   Fine poly charmeuse is *the* fabric for today's Fortuny pleated dresses. It takes colors deliciously and holds the crimped pleats permanently. Because poly charmeuse in its uncrimped state is supple and smooth, it is also a good fabric for colorful slips.

And while polyester woven into a thin film of fabric tends to be overused for blouses that cling rather than drape, and act as if they were designed to be hidden under jackets, poly densely woven into full-bodied broadcloth makes a terrific blouse that has enough presence to stand alone. Look for simple shirt-jacket, overblouse, and other jacket-type styling so that it can be worn on its own—and thrown into the washing machine for easy upkeep.

- *Rayon* or its upscale European twin, *viscose*. This is the fabric of the nineties, as the cost of natural fibers has escalated into the luxury range. While rayon is overused on its own, especially in challis and broadcloth, it makes a wonderful blend, because it usually adds sinuousness, body, and drape to other fibers, and it creates excellent knits. Blended with cotton, rayon turns a jersey knit from ordinary into special, and gives it more durability as well. Mixed with linen, it makes a better suiting fabric than linen alone; there are fewer wrinkles, and the fabric hangs well. Mixed with wool, it makes a challis that adds drape to wool's softness and that is far richer looking than rayon challis alone.

  On its own, rayon is incomparable in a few types of fabric. One is velvet, as soft and as smooth and as sleek as silk but with more body. Another is matte jersey, the hands-down winner in the great-drape contest and for which no other fabric comes close. **Criscione** frequently uses this extremely sensuous and flattering fabric to make wonderfully sinuous dressy dresses. But look out—they're expensive unless you get them on sale. And at the totally opposite end of the price spectrum, there is crinkled rayon, a fabric so fine and so soft that it even feels better than cotton against the skin on the hottest of summer days; check out import stores for simple summer shirts and dresses in this fabric, which is visually interesting as well. **Incognito** is one brand to look for.

- *Wool.* You know it, rightly, as a fall and winter fabric. There's no law that says it has to be woven thickly. Think of wool also as a spring and summer fabric. In a fine, lightweight gabardine, wool is actually a year-round fabric that is smooth and silky to the touch and drapes beautifully without ever clinging. It has a sleekness that makes it ever so right for the image of modern women. It's great for body-skimming dresses and skirts that go into a suitcase and come out anywhere in the world. Because this is a virtually indestructible as well as a beautiful fabric, lightweight gab makes a perfect pair of trousers; they hold a crease forever, and they never wear out on the inner thigh, which makes them definitely worth the investment. **Le Painty** makes the best gabardine trousers you can find in large sizes.

In a light to medium weight, gabardine also makes the best-looking, unbulkiest trench coat you can buy; if you get one with a button-out liner, you automatically have a sleek winter coat, spring coat, and raincoat all in one—and it will last forever, so it is more than worth the extra dollars such a fine fabric is likely to cost.

Wool gauze is a spectacular fabric that deserves to be better used for spring-summer dresses. Because, like all gauzes and crepes, the yarn is crimped before it is woven, it makes a fabric that never clings to the skin and has fabulous body. Its texture is achieved without any bulk at all and creates visual interest.

If you don't already know that wool crepe is one of the most versatile fabrics around, now's the time to find out. It drapes, it's comfortable, and it looks dressy even in tailored shapes. A simple, unadorned black wool crepe skirt can go out partying at night and to the office by day. Wool crepe goes right through spring.

- *Linen.* Like denim, linen gets better and looks better the more it is washed and pressed. It gets softer to the touch, it drapes better because it gets more supple (and thus wrinkles less), and it feels divine on the skin. So look for summer clothes of linen in simple and classic shapes—shirts, shorts, pants, skirts— that are unlined and free of complicating detail. Once there is a lining of any fabric but cotton, you're committed to dry-cleaning; so be sure your linen clothes are unlined. Toss them in the washing machine. And if you can't bear ironing them yourself, then bring them to the cleaners—for pressing only. You don't know how good linen is until it is washed, and washed, rather than dry-cleaned. And it's better for the environment, too.

- *Silk.* This once-dressy fabric has been coming out of its cocoon for several years, and it is now the hottest thing for casual clothes, especially in its washable versions. However, there's silk and there's silk. Gossamer silks are sensational for afternoon and evening dresses. For a soft-pleated skirt on the dressy side, thin silks are perfect. But they are often also made into everyday sportswear, for which they are sometimes too light-weight. They may look luscious on the rack, because silk takes color fabulously, but because they lack body, they tend to billow if you move or the air around you moves, making you look big. And they cling to the skin if you or the air stands still, making you hot in warm weather and revealing all. No item of clothing looks good if it clings to the skin, and anything that does will make you feel terribly self-conscious. So be sure to check the weight of the silk. Textile experts say that unless silk is 18 mumme weight or more (a measure of its thickness), you are likely to run into problems with sportswear.

- *Cotton.* This fabric needs no introduction, but do remember its great versatility. Cotton jersey, for example, makes more than a terrific tee shirt. In a heavyweight rendition, especially one given an interesting texture, such as ottoman, and tailored into a respectable silhouette, like a tunic and skirt, it is an excellent year-round fabric. It is also great for travel, since it never wrinkles. Because it's cotton jersey, it not only doesn't wrinkle, it never gets clammy, either, so it is also the perfect fabric for wearing on rainy days, under a raincoat, winter or summer. Remember, having on hand at all times muss-proof, fuss-proof clothes that can stand up to any weather is one of the great strategies for style. The most workable cotton jerseys for year-round wear tend to appear in stores for the season known in the clothes biz as "transitional," or clothes that look like fall but feel like summer. They are the earliest fall clothes and they come in fabrics that won't fry you if you look at them or try them on in the heat of summer. They start arriving in the better stores—are you ready for this?—even before you've got your summer wardrobe down pat, and they may linger on racks through August. But do prowl around the stores early on the lookout for year-round wearables. And to get the most mileage out of clothes in this fabric, choose clear colors like red or royal blue and anytime neutrals like khaki, black, and white, rather than the burnished shades that traditionally distinguish fall-only clothes.

Under It All—Bras

W hen it comes to the chest, this is certainly our place to shine. This is our body part, the one we, as full-figured women, truly own. This is the one part of the body where more is always . . . well, more. Where natural padding is more beautiful than the alternative. Where boniness is downright U-G-L-Y. When bones are going strong elsewhere in fashion's anatomy, we can still proudly present a full chest to the world and make heads turn. We can wow 'em. No matter the vagaries of fashion, they can't take that away from us. Let them try to defeminize us—this is where we draw the line. This is our shape at its best, and it's always in fashion. Nobody can give it its due like we can, as Liz Taylor has so often proven in her seasons of plenty. Put on a simple dress that would be boring on other bodies, let loose a button or two, flash some breast—and the world is ours for a moment, a day, a night, forever. Let others have their tiny waists, just let us bare the beauty of our breasts. Who would choose to minimize what the gods would gloriously grant us?

So how come, women want to know, we can't readily find bras that work for our bodies? Why can't we have beautiful ways to use it as a fashion asset? As one woman lamented, "Size 38D bras should be lacy, not some fortress-like thing."

What you can't see in fashion is just as vital as what you can see. How clothes look and fit, how they feel, and how they relate to the body, depend

237

on the contours of the body underneath. And that, to a great extent, depends on what you wear under your clothes. That beautifully cut tuxedo suit that now comes in your size will add a cache of chic to your whole wardrobe, but the investment won't be worth it if your bra doesn't let you bare your bosom a bit. And that sinuous jersey dress that looks so soigné and so slinky will not work if your bra doesn't collaborate in the smoothness. This is a truth so evident—often painfully evident to full-figured women—that it would hardly seem to bear a chapter's worth of repeating. But a truth so clear-cut in principle encounters an extraordinary amount of difficulty in practice.

It is a fact of nature that larger bodies vary more than smaller ones. But for full-figured women, brassieres and pantyhose seem to defy the laws of gravity. What goes up always seems to fall down, and what goes down always seems to ride up. A body at rest is never able to enjoy its rest.

The right bra is not an option for larger women as it can be for smaller women. It is vital to fashion for the definition it gives to shape, without which clothes neither fit nor hang properly on the body. It is extremely important to posture and health for the support it gives to major body parts. Further, it is essential to style for the comfort and freedom of movement it affords. For there is no style without comfort and absence of self-consciousness.

You should expect the right undergarments to support and firm your flesh. You can't expect them to remake your body—you wouldn't be able to function; we are living in the 1990s, not the 1890s. If you are lush and plush in the hips and derriere, no undergarment with any amount of control will disguise the fact and the attempt to do so will make you too self-conscious for a shot at style. The modern way of functioning leads to the two basic undergarment principles of *Style Is Not a Size:*

- You will always look your best and feel good about yourself by focusing on your strong points, enhancing and defining your assets. Your "flaws" will fade in importance; you won't be focusing on them, and neither will anyone else.
- Your undergarments are part of a total approach that includes your attitude and your clothes. Your best look will come, not from trying to hide the size of any body parts, but from the right support for clothes cut in flattering silhouettes and proportions for your shape.

THE UNDERCOVER TRUTH

Here's what you should expect of all undergarments:

- Waist definition but not waist constriction.
- Correct breast carriage; that is, the bosom as a well-defined entity in one place on the front of the chest wall, not spread all over the upper body. This is of critical importance to short women and short-waisted women of any height.
- Smooth and moderately firming coverage of abdomen, derriere, hip, and, if desired, thigh.
- Freedom of movement; no restriction at crotch, legs, arms.
- Anatomically shaped and sized undergarments that hug the body at all times and stay anchored in place while providing light, breathable support.
- Comfort that lasts all day, or all evening as the case may be.
- Fabrications, such as cotton, that are suited to the realities of functioning bodies. Always remember, no one is more of an expert on the large-size body than you, the full-figured woman. You know what fits, what feels good, what doesn't.

There is one thing more that you should expect of your lingerie. It goes without saying that full-figured women want—and need—as much luxury and fantasy and beauty in their lingerie as all other women want. Perhaps more. It may be that our lush bodies are honored more in private than in public, and beautiful intimate wear is a necessary expression of that appeal. Or that fine lingerie feels so extravagantly wonderful it keeps self-esteem in the pink. It certainly helps remind women, even those who wear the severest man-tailored uniforms by day, that they are sensuous creatures. Sure, lingerie, or at least the brassiere, has more than a decorative role. It *must* function. Without fulfilling its obligation to function, lingerie's fantasy is of no use—okay, little use. But just because we need undergarments that are functional doesn't mean they can't also be decorative or—heaven forbid—outright sexy. As one woman put it, "Larger ladies are just as feminine as slim ladies. I'd love to see more fine lingerie. I have driven hundreds of miles in the state of California for good fitting, sexy, good quality lingerie."

Great lingerie doesn't just shape your body and your clothes, it shapes the way you feel, and it shapes the way you act. Having underclothes that fit perfectly is the necessary underpinning for the confidence that your body is attractive the way it is. Underclothes that fit also permit you to move freely and so do not inhibit your actions in any way. And beautiful lingerie encourages you to feel sexy and feminine, feelings our thin-obsessed culture does not readily grant you. Wearing beautiful lingerie is a way of holding on to an important aspect of yourself as a woman.

In general, the undergarment industry has some catching up to do with us on this point. "It is impossible to look good or feel good in any fashions when undergarments are ill-fitting or look like institutional issue," one woman commented. As a major fashion executive put it not long ago in a speech to intimate wear manufacturers: "The large-size woman does not negate her sexuality. We [the apparel industry] negate it for her." Still, there are some real goodies out there—if you know where to look for them. This chapter is designed to help make the search a lot easier.

THE FIT BIT

Most—but by no means all—of the most intimate of intimate undergarments are built as if all women's bodies were created the same way and varied the same way. It is terribly difficult—though not impossible—for larger women to find an undergarment that fits properly. In all of my surveys, formal and informal, I have never, repeat never, encountered a full-figured woman—no matter how sophisticated a fashion consumer she is, including many women in the fashion industry itself—who is happy both with the fit of her bra and the fit of her pantyhose. Many are relieved to talk about the trouble they have getting a good fit—and do so in the hope that the undergarment industry will hear their concerns and heed their needs.

The complaints big-busted, or in industry parlance, full-figured, women have are always the same, no matter what their body size. What I find so surprising is that women have not made these problems better known to the industry, although I do know that many women who have written to lingerie manufacturers have never received even the courtesy of a reply (including myself). I know one woman, a petite exercise physiologist and avid runner, who couldn't get a running bra that safely accommodated her large bust. Every bra she tried not only failed to give support but often created pain and irritation to the point of bleeding. Her attempts to tell manufacturers the problems she encountered with their products and to offer suggestions for improvement were always met with absolute silence. When she couldn't even get manufacturers to listen to the experience of real women, she did the next best thing—she started her own company! The active bra her company produced was superb, made of the best, most functional materials and with intelligent and comfortable design. Unfortunately, after several years as a tiny, independent manufacturer, increasing difficulties with suppliers led her to find an easier way to make a living. Even so, her solution was hardly the path for most women. At the same time, it is fair to say that the undergarment manufacturers have not publicized their solutions to customers, and there are undergarments that do work well.

Many women, with drawers full of expensive experiments that failed, and put off by the utter disorganization of most store lingerie departments, resign themselves to less than a good fit, hoping never to be seen in their undergarments and knowing the mess will be covered by clothes. True, clothes do go over the mess, but they also always reveal it.

Full-figured women often endure not only bad fit but a great deal of physical pain from their undergarments. They tell of leg movements inhibited by pantyhose that do not stay up, or almost unbearable thigh friction, of shoulders automatically hunched to minimize bosom overhang, or shoulders carved indelibly with strap marks, or frequent underbreast rashes. The catalogue of complaints is shocking since we have all assumed that torture went out with the tight laces of Victorian corsets.

The pain from poor fit remains under wraps because women with less than ideal figures have been led to believe by the culture that the failure of things to fit is their fault for being too big. "They are too ashamed to speak up," says one pantyhose executive, queen size herself, who frequently makes store appearances to ferret out what women want. Their silence only allows manufacturers to blindly assume that the products that now exist are doing the job satisfactorily.

THE TOP OF THE LINE

Let's look at the functional aspects of bras first, and then see how we can meet both functional and aesthetic needs. If you find all this embarrassing, or somehow too inglorious for a book about style, just jump to the punchline. But you'll better understand your body, have more respect for it despite current difficulties of getting a good fit, and know how to overcome those difficulties, if you stay tuned.

Many large-size women have large breasts; some do not. Breast size is one thing; the size of the chest wall, or ribcage, or whatever you want to call the dimension that represents body girth, is another. In order to buy most bras, you have to first pretend that chest and breast are one combined thing—the bust—that varies as a single dimension. Then you have to make an estimate of cup size based on body width. The trouble is threefold. One, body girth and breast size actually vary independently of each other (otherwise all size-18 women would be 38DDs, or 42Cs, or whatever), so there is no value in combining them into one measure for any purpose, especially fit. Two, the range of cup sizes is very limited. Some bras only come in three cup sizes (A, B, C), many go to four, and a very few admit five; if you don't fit into a DD, then you are truly beyond the pale. Three, the cup dimensions, placement of shoulder straps, and other features are simply not anatomically correct. Cup depth and bra width are essentially regarded as interchangeable. So your estimate of cup size is always made from an incorrect base.

As a result, the average full-figured woman (and most full-busted women) has to make do with a bra that is too big around the back in order to come close to getting a cup that fits. A few women suffer with the opposite problem—too big a cup size in order to get the proper size around the back. "I have a small bust (44A–B) and have tremendous difficulty finding bras that don't hang," one woman complained.

But a bra that is too big around rides up in back, creating discomfort, throwing off balance, upsetting posture—and failing to give the critical support a large bust needs. You're then forced to rely on the shoulder straps. And here you encounter a whole other set of problems. In most bras, as the bra-back size increases, bra straps get placed farther apart, even though shoulders do not vary with bust size. The bra straps, which by now must carry the full weight of the breast because the back strap has abdicated, tend to fall off the shoulders. So you pull tighter on them, etching the straps deeply into the flesh. This creates more discomfort and looks so unsightly even when the bra is off that bare-shoulder dressing is unthinkable. And you feel shame, because you bear the stigma of difficult fit, and you think it's your fault things don't fit right.

There's more, women report. Because the cup doesn't usually come close to fitting, the breast is compressed against the chest wall and diffused to areas where it doesn't belong. It is sent sprawling sideways, under the arm, down under the bra against the chest wall, and over the top of the bra. This is unhealthy—it creates prime conditions for a rash on the underside of the breast, and it impedes circulation. It is uncomfortable. It distorts the fit of clothes: You wind up with a sort of monobosom that takes over the whole front of your body above your waist. It denies you the pride in a beautiful part of the anatomy. And it fails to give the very figure definition that would make clothes look so much better.

The good news is, it doesn't have to be this way. And any day now, the intimate apparel industry may catch on to the needs and desires of women with fuller figures. Sales are way down for bras in cup sizes AA, A, and B. Way up is demand for bras in D, DD, and beyond. The same is true for back sizes; demand is increasing for larger sizes.

THE SUZANNE BRA

For years, as a corsetiere, Susan Kadas pondered these problems. And a number of years ago, she came up with a solution that ranks as one of the best-kept secrets in the undergarment industry—a bra that fits and provides a beautiful contour to the breast. It fits big-breasted women of all body sizes, and it fits big women of breast sizes larger than a B cup. Called the **Suzanne Bra**, it does what no other branded American bra does—it treats back size and breast volume as two totally independent measurements, so that no matter a woman's breast size, there is a bra that totally supports the breast while totally encompassing it in a cup. And it does this without an underwire. The bra comes in ten cup sizes and back sizes from 28 to 60. Yes, this bra has a seam across the cup, but let us be realistic; it is not possible to shape a large bra cup adequately without a seam somewhere. The total look with a seam, even under knits, is more shapely and supportive than from a seamless bra.

The Suzanne Bra puts the bust back in its proper position on the body—in front, halfway between the shoulder and the elbow—which takes the stress off the back. The back of the bra, made of a fine powernet, stays anchored in place, so it can help support the breast. The midriff band, under the cups, is no more than half an inch wide. And the shoulder straps are never farther than eight inches apart (nine inches for those with highly developed pectoral muscles), so they stay on the shoulders and actually help support the breast, as does the snug-fitting back of the bra. "A woman looks taller, she breathes better, she stands better—and her body looks better," says Kadas. Supported, defined, lightly rounded at the apex, and properly placed on the chest wall, the breast needs no underwire or longline for support, Kadas insists.

For some women, the best part of the bra is that they can wear a smaller dress size. "Most women who put on a Suzanne Bra at first think it makes their busts look bigger," says Kadas. "What it's doing is giving them better definition, a better profile. They don't understand how it makes them smaller. But I tell women they'll shrink two dress or blouse sizes—and they do. Because the bra takes the breast tissue from the sides, under the arms, the back and the midriff and puts it all in one gorgeous place."

There are essentially two versions of the Suzanne Bra. Neither will win awards for sex appeal, but they aren't ugly, either. What does look sexy is the bustline in clothes. Both bras have straps that are three-quarters of an inch wide and completely of woven fabric, with no stretch inset. Both have a ribbon of felt for support partially lining the underside of the cups. And both have backs made of powernet fabric with limited stretch. One is made in all cotton cups, the other features cups of nylon lace. Both are available in nude color only—and both have six-month warranties.

The bra is available in selected stores and boutiques that have specially trained fitters Kadas insists on calling "bra-ticians." It is also available by mail order. For more information, write **Suzanne Henri, Inc.**, R.D. #3, P.O. Box 85, Blairstown, NJ 07825. Or call 1-800-634-2590.

THE CRISS-CROSS

For full-figured women, criss-cross bras in cotton and cotton blend fabrics make a certain amount of sense. The criss-cross design gives support without an underwire and it defines and separates the breasts. In theory. In practice, the criss-cross straps are almost always made of elastic, and while that feels comfortable in the fitting room, the bra quickly loses its supporting ability. The straps then have to be pulled tighter into the shoulders and around the back. A criss-cross bra with a nonstretch frame would be well worth trying.

RUNNING AND ATHLETIC BRAS

At the moment, you won't find a bra in larger sizes specifically designed for athletic purposes. That is a short and painful statement, a sad commentary on the power of the cultural stereotype to deprive fuller-figured women of their needs. Simply put, you are not presumed to be an active woman. At least one activewear manufacturer is seriously interested in developing a good sports bra for full-figured women and is working on the proper design. It's no coincidence that the executive in charge is a full-figured woman who happens to work out regularly, not to lose weight but to stay gorgeously fit.

UNDERCUP SUPPORT PANEL

CRISS-CROSS

A good bra for active use keeps bounce to an absolute minimum, stays put, and totally encompasses the breast with a sturdy, breathable fabric. Unlike conventional active bras, it should not do its job by compressing the breast against the chest. That is satisfactory only for small breasts that exert no downward pressure of their own. Over a certain size bust, that approach doesn't work and actually creates some painful problems. There is, however, a highly workable solution for women with large breasts. For active use, I suggest that you buy an extra Suzanne Bra in the plain style and reserve it for athletic wear.

LEISURE BRAS

Even though they come in only one or two cup sizes, these bras usually feel comfortable—at least, at first—because they are made of exceedingly stretchy, usually synthetic, fabrics. They accommodate; they give. Under a robe, or for use as a sleep bra, the leisure bra has its greatest justification. In those cases, your best bet is one made of all cotton. Even then it is safe to say the existence of the leisure bra is an indicator of how poorly regular bras serve larger women.

Leisure bras, if you will, are meant for hanging loose. They are not designed to be worn under daytime or evening fashions. Nevertheless, undercover agents inform me that many women treasure the comfort so much—a relief after the pain of so many other bras—they wear them whenever they can get away with it. The truth is, you can get away with it less than you think.

It is unfair to hold these bras up to standards they were never meant to meet, but for larger bosoms, these bras afford neither sufficient support nor definition for use with street clothes. They flatten the breast down against the chest wall. And thanks to the law of gravity, the stretchiness gives way very quickly and you are no better off than without a bra.

For big-busted women who have just given birth and are breastfeeding an infant, the more substantial of the leisure bras can sometimes serve as a substitute nursing bra; they certainly fit better than many nursing bras, and many open easily from the front. If you resign yourself to replacing them the minute they begin to stretch out of shape, you can solve a problem corsetieres have not even begun to address yet.

UNDERWIRES

Although the Suzanne Bra proves that doesn't have to be the case, many women feel, and the undergarment industry seems to foster the idea, that the only way to get enough support for a large bosom is with an underwire bra. There was a time when underwires were regarded as strictly heavy duty instruments and made of fabrics more akin to armor than lingerie. Even today there are underwire bras of Valkyrian attitude and fortification. But in the past ten years or so, perhaps as the undergarment industry has begun to realize that breasts aren't optional for all fashion-conscious women, underwires, certainly in D cup size, rarely in DD, have become gorgeous. Many are made of fine laces. Many have—be still, my beating heart!—daring décolleté. They often come in luscious colors. Many have stretchy cups that accommodate (although they do not necessarily flatter) larger breasts.

Many, alas, don't fit, subject to all the drawbacks noted in the beginning of this chapter. When they fit well—and that's a big if—underwires have one supreme advantage for full-figured women: They can uplift and support the breast without requiring an anchor band at the bottom of the bra that intrudes on the midriff. That is a special advantage to the short-waisted woman, who needs as much definition of body parts as possible. In practice, however, many do have a midriff band of half an inch to an inch in width. And the creation of space between the bust and the waist is negated by the lack of bust definition these bras typically afford.

In general, underwires have many drawbacks, and some of them go well beyond fashion. First, these bras almost always spread the breast sideways. Second, their shape is fixed, wired in, and the bra's contours are probably not your contours; very often, the underwire circles too low on the midriff. Or it stands away from the body at the center, a look that is sometimes terribly embarrassing; you can pretty much take it as an invariable rule: Your clothes should always move in the same direction you do. Third, they are typically made of synthetic fabrics that hold in heat, subjecting wearers to discomfort, particularly in warm weather.

They also have major portions of elastic. Around the back, these usually stretch out of shape in no time, and with them goes all support. Stretchy cups feel wonderful because, for the first time in her bra-wearing experience, a woman may actually get complete bosom coverage; however, the coverage typically comes at the expense of shape definition; stretch fabrics just simply cannot support and contour shape adequately. But perhaps most important, they are usually so constructed that the wire extends into the armpit, where it hits against lymph nodes and other structures. Is this healthy? Who knows, but why take a chance? It certainly is uncomfortable.

If you feel you must wear an underwire bra, do take the new bra to a corsetiere who can pad the side ends of the wire so they do not cut through the bra and into your armpits.

TAKING THE PLUNGE

There are many variations of the underwire bra. The ones that make the most sense fill a need no other type can—they give you enough support for wearing a revealing neckline. Underwire bras are sometimes cut up to a 42DD with a plunging front, a tiny front closure, and are made of attractive lace. These are wonderful bras for adding spice to a wardrobe, for they allow you to transform any button-front dress or blouse for evening use by leaving a button or two open. Even if the cup fit is not exactly perfect—and it often isn't—this kind of bra can work. A little extra flesh above the top of the bra can look voluptuously attractive with an exposed neckline.

PLUNGE/CONVERTIBLE WITH UNDERWIRE

PUSH-UP BRAS

If you love décolletage—and who doesn't?—these special-occasion bras are for you; big breasts, little breasts, firm breasts, soft breasts, long-waisted, short-waisted—these bras work for one and all when they're worn as they are meant to be—with bare necklines. They hold you UP, and they give you a well defined, voluptuous cleavage. Some have a contoured cup that not only pushes you up from below, it keeps it all in front. Contoured cup push-up bras tend to have widely spaced shoulder straps, a boon for cut-away necklines but hard to keep on the shoulders unless you anchor the bra strap to the dress shoulder by way of a dressmaker's tack. That will hardly hold back a woman who likes to dress daringly. The real problem is 1) finding one that fits, then 2) finding the dress to wear it with. You'll do best in the catalogues or special lingerie shops.

PUSH-UP BRA

MINIMIZERS

The aim of these bras, almost invariably of the underwire variety, is to reduce bosom projection, a concept that has suspiciously much in common with the breast binding of the 1920s. We are all smart enough to realize the flesh doesn't simply disappear; it has to go somewhere. I suppose it's a case of you-pays-your-money-and-you-takes-your choice. You can buy a bra that puts it all in one place neatly up front where it ought to be and gives shape to your body, or you can buy a bra that tends to flatten it against your chest and spread it out. That only minimizes projection; it doesn't minimize width or mass. Oh yes, it definitely minimizes shape distinctness, when you tend to need all the clarity of shape you can get.

Because these bras push flesh up toward the neck, they are generally inadvisable for full-figured women who are short or short-waisted. They create too much bulk in the neck-chest area.

Now, here comes the really Big Question: Why minimize at all? Is it shameful to have a big bosom? Is it something to hide? Besides, do you really think you can hide it? Most women are proud of their endowment and would prefer a bra that supports it well. Most, however, make do with a minimizer because 1) it's often the only kind they can find in larger sizes, 2) they don't know they would actually look better proportioned and clothes would fit better if their bust shape was well-defined, and 3) they believe a minimizer really makes them look all-over smaller. It is certainly a marketer's dream product name for our times. When in doubt, remember the guiding principle: You will both feel better and look better if you enhance and define your assets, not try to hide your size.

A LONG STORY

Once upon a time, longline bras were popular among women of all sizes. Thinking has changed, and these bras are now quite rare, although **Exquisite Form** recently introduced a front-close version in nylon tricot and lace. Strapless versions can solve a logistics problem. But health concerns (why squish all your internal organs, and why bind a large portion of your body in unbreathing fabrics?) and mobility concerns (these bras tend to inhibit movement, and you need freedom of movement) have made regular longlines largely relics of a dated way of thinking about bodies. If the aim is to better distinguish the bust from the midriff, you'll do better with a bra that gives you good bust definition. If your aim is to hide it all, remember it has to go somewhere; you'll do better with a bandeau bra and clothes cut in flattering silhouettes.

LOOK MA, NO STRAPS

Tell the truth: Is there a full-figured woman who doesn't have at least two strapless bandeaus, both unworkable, lurking in a lingerie drawer, wistful reminders of the wish to dress dreamy or sexy in the right time or place? One is probably a gorgeous little wisp of stretch lace, the other a more constructed attempt at uplift. I have encountered only one bandeau bra that can support a larger bust—**Goddess** model 389. This bra looks intimidating hanging on display, with its wiring and shape. But don't be put off; it looks very good—sexy—on the body, with lace half-cups. And it works. You could boogie all night and still feel secure. But be forewarned—the bra runs true in cup size but the back runs exceedingly small. You'll have to go up *at least* one size around the back. It comes up to 48DD.

STRAPLESS BANDEAU

Perhaps the safest way to get a strapless bra that stays up is to get a longline strapless or a merry widow. **Goddess** makes a longline strapless (model 688) up to 42DD and 44D. It features a demi cup, a low back, and a gripper bottom band to keep it from riding up. The bra is made of white nylon lace, and the bodice front is partly in sheer nylon.

STRAPLESS LONGLINE

Another possibility for bareness, if you are not going to be wearing a strapless dress. Perhaps you can get all the bareness you need from a convertible bra. There are beautiful low-cut bandeaus with adjustable straps that can be worn in three or four ways for varying types of bareness: halter, vee-back, and criss-cross back for cutaway shoulders. Look for them in catalogues.

BOOST FROM A BUSTIER

This is the full-figured woman's answer to Victoria's Secret. You look great in a bustier-type garment. You are the woman who gives it a run for its money. And considering that you'd never wear it for playing tennis, it's surprisingly comfortable as well. The supreme virtue of this garment, aside from its well-established fantasy value, is that, without straps, it can always support a large breast, whereas a bandeau cannot. Mind you, this isn't make-do straplessness; this garment gives a great line to the body, from the front and from the side. It truly supports the larger bust. Wear it under strapless or other low-cut dresses. Wear it in private. But please, despite the popularity of "the lingerie look" in daytime fashion, don't wear it as is for

STRAPLESS MERRY WIDOW

public consumption. The lingerie look works well only on those who don't need support. On anyone else it looks tarty, at best. Yes, do wear it to a costume party, if you dare. **Goddess** makes the same wonderful, old-fashioned, well-boned bustier with garters (style 711) that you probably wore to your high-school prom. The bra is currently available in sizes up to 46DD, and the manufacturer informs me that the company would go higher than 46 if there were enough requests. Be sure to ask for it if you want it.

ALL-IN-ONE

I was surprised to discover how popular these are among larger women. Women report they seek these because they give the feeling of being held in all over. Unless you are reasonably shapely already, one piece body shapers tend to just push the flesh somewhere else. They also detract from definition. They encase a large portion of the body in an unbreathable fabric. And if finding a good fit in a bra is difficult, then the chances of finding a good fit in an item that combines bra, midriff, torso length, and panty is even more difficult. Again, the general principle should prevail: You can't camouflage it; it's better to give up the illusion of all-over control for separate undergarment pieces that define you and clothes that are cut for and flatter your body type.

That said, it would be unfair if I did not tell you about several body briefs that have devoted followings. All three are made principally of nylon and spandex, offering what one manufacturer calls "updated control." These are a far cry from the near-inflexible powernet of days gone by.

Modern all-in-one body briefers are flexible and mobile, silky to the touch, and support without an underwire. Popular ones are made by **Va Bien**, by **Flexees**, and by **Tara**, in both brief and longer leg versions. The Tara body briefer is especially designed for women of average to full hips and average to long torso. Va Bien's version differs from the others in having a lace-top bra. All three come in black, beige, and white. Unfortunately, on a recent search expedition that included the world's largest store, none of these were stocked in more than a D cup. And only the Va Bien was available in back sizes over 40, and then only in scattered sizes.

Remember powernet? As one saleslady describes it: "It holds you in and turns you blue." Well it may not be the liberated woman's version of control, but it is alive and well at stores that cater to an older trade. **Lane Bryant** does a stiff business, as it were, in the longer leg **Subtract** all-in-one body

ALL-IN-ONE BODY BRIEF

HIGH CUT LEG

shaper by True Form. No one under 50 laid a hand on it. It only runs up to a D in cup size, but a well-informed saleslady suggested the cup ran so full it could fit at least a DD.

FINDING BRAS

In an ideal world, to buy your undergarments you would go to a store where you shop for your clothes. You could then try a bra on under the dress or sweater it was meant to be worn with. Actually, finding any bra—to say nothing of an attractive one—in a size larger than a 38D in any store other than **Lane Bryant** (plus **Women's World** in the West) seems to be exceedingly difficult, women report. The well-stocked corset shop is virtually a thing of the past. Department stores are disorganized, and the help generally knows less than you do; unless you know specifically what you are looking for, your search may be frustrating. Most large-size specialty stores can't stock bras in enough variety to give you a real choice.

Don't despair. You can get what you need by catalogue-shopping for bras; there is much more out there in mail order than in stores. Just make sure the items are returnable if they don't fit right, and acknowledge the probability that you will have to do a considerable amount of experimenting. Getting to do it in the privacy of your own home, under your own clothes, has its advantages. Of course, you'll have to plan well ahead. And don't take the tags off until after you've tried the garment. Some excellent offerings can be found in these catalogues besides those of Sears and J. C. Penney:

Arizona Mail Order Company:
Old Pueblo Traders, Regalia, Intimate Appeal Catalogues, P.O. Box 27800, Tucson, AZ 85726-7800: 1-602-747-5000

Comfortably Yours:
61 West Hunter Avenue, Maywood, NJ 07607: 1-201-368-0400

Lane Bryant Catalogues:
1-800-445-4299

Silhouettes:
1-800-852-2822

Spiegel For You:
Spiegel, P.O. Box 87603, Chicago, IL 60680-0603: 1-800-345-4500

Vermont Country Store:
P.O. Box 3000, Manchester Center, VT 05255 802-362-2400

TIPS FOR BUYING BRAS

- When trying on a bra, loosen the shoulder straps and slip them loosely onto your shoulders; then hook the bra in back. Bend forward from the waist and let your breasts and the tissue under the arm come forward and fall into the cups. Shake your breast tissue so it is completely in the bra cups. Before you straighten up, tighten the shoulder straps; this ensures that the breast tissue stays in the bra. Be sure the nipples are positioned in the center of the cups, and smooth the fabric all over. The straps should rest gently on your shoulders. If they make an indentation they are doing too much of the work.
- After your bra is adjusted, raise and lower your arms. You should not have to yank the bra down.
- The final check is the look of clothes over your bra. Your breasts should be well-defined with a gently rounded contour—no points, or you will look like a space alien. If there are any bulges, the bra does not fit right, and you need to look further.
- If you like the bra, ask whether it comes in other colors and fabrics, whether it is a new style, whether it is always in stock in all sizes.
- If at all possible, buy only one bra—but ask the salesperson to reserve however many more you might want in your size.
- Try out your new purchase at home for a few days under a variety of clothes. If you are happy, then call your saleswoman and have her send the reserved bras to you.
- Your color selection will probably be limited to beige, white, and on occasion, black. By all means, go for sexy black when you can, but be sure to wear it only under dark clothes. If you choose only one, a nude color is the most versatile. It is the color to wear under stark white tops (a white bra will show through) and it is excellent under dark colored clothes if you can't find a black bra in your size. You do not need a white bra.

Under It All— the Rest

Again, it's a case of women in search of a satisfying combination of fit, function, and fancy. And in general, it's getting better all the time. Still, considering the vast choices available in smaller sizes, large-size lingerie needs much more playfulness and much more of the Bimbo Factor; just because it has to do a job doesn't mean it can't make things fun, too. If there's one thing full-figured women say over and over again, it's "we aren't different from all other women, we want and need the same things."

THE BOTTOM LINE: PANTIES

Five years ago, if you wanted to buy panties in large sizes, you had little choice: It was a brief or it was nothing. About the only choice you had was whether to get it in utilitarian white cotton or in heavy-duty nude nylon tricot. Today, there are many more styles available, a greater array of colors, and many finer fabrics. There's even silk. In a perfect world, that would not be a matter for comment, let alone surprise. But this is a less than perfect world for bodies that are deemed less than perfect, and too often you are denied even the feel of luxury next to your skin. I will not guarantee you that it is easy to find silk lingerie in large sizes; in most cases it is made by small companies, often run by full-figured women, and distributed to small stores. But it is definitely out there. Seek it; it will make you feel wonderful. It is worth the price.

As you undoubtedly know from trial and error, all panties for larger women are not created equal. What you want is the perfect blend of fit, function, and flattery.

Top Drawer

HIGH CUT BRIEF

In the flattery category, the hands-down winner is the high-cut brief. This gives the longest expanse of leg and the greatest freedom of leg movement. The high diagonal cut slims legs, makes a short torso appear longer, and provides great comfort. Alas, high-cut briefs work best for those whose flesh is firm in the hips and rear. For good fit, you want to look for a well-proportioned rise, a comfortable waistband, a leg opening generously cut and body-hugging but not binding; after all, what you don't need is an indentation on your hip flesh. For function, there should be a cotton crotch. Silk or cotton would be an ideal body fabric; this is not a panty for control fabrics. Be sure to try the sexy "babycakes" briefs by **Fine and Fancy**, a lingerie company run by a full-figured woman for full-figured women. Made of nylon stretch net, they have a generous pima cotton crotch and a five-inch band of stretch lace from hip to waist. They come in sizes up to 5X. Many women swear by the all-cotton high-cut briefs made by **Jockey for Her**. They come in pastels and in brights and are ideal for summer. And with Jockey's tank top, they make a great pair of summer (or winter) pajamas.

Tap Snap

TAP PANTS

For fit and comfort, you can't top tap pants. Their sides, lapped and unseamed, often cut in an elegant, elongating, sexy curve, accommodate all varieties of hip—high, low, big, little. They are exceedingly comfortable for all except those who need crotch coverage at all times. Tap pants have, instead, a looser, boxier fit. The boxiness may work against women who are on the short side, squaring the appearance, but tap pants are otherwise generally attractive because of their drapiness. And bottom-heavy women love the thigh coverage. In silk, tap pants feel divine and make a slip unnecessary. They are ideal under split skirts and full skirts (pants and slim skirts generally need a trimmer line). Because they provide automatic air-conditioning, tap pants are great for summer use. And as far as I'm concerned, the best, the most sensuous, and the most comfortable pair of pajamas in the world, summer or winter (besides my own skin), is silk tap pants topped with a spaghetti-strap camisole. Check out the offerings of **Fine and Fancy.**

Brief Encounters

Briefs are the most versatile of panties. You almost always need them under slacks and they certainly work under all other clothes. Briefs come in the greatest variety of fabrics, including several weights of nylon tricot, cotton jerseys, cotton-nylon mixes, and firming spandex combos, with and without inset lace. The limiting factors with briefs are usually the finishing touches at waist and leg. Bottom-heavy women often find the leg bands restrictive, whether made of sewn-on ribbing or elastic; the ribbing has limited stretch, and the elastic makes its mark on flesh. For other women, briefs are standard fare.

BRIEFS

In general, they should fit and feel like a second skin, not cut into the body anywhere, or even show a line. If you are broad of backside, look for briefs with a seam down the derriere; they may be cut fuller. Panties with high elastic-lace waistbands are best left to those who do not have midriff problems.

A popular brief is **Vanity Fair**'s covered-waistband plain panty in a semi-sheer nylon tricot with a silky feel, called Ravissant. There are fancier pants, with lace insets and trim, but none lighter. Cotton-spandex combinations, such as those from **Hensen Kickernick**, provide the most comfort, the feeling of control, and a great line under clothes. They are especially ideal in summer or for workouts anytime.

Keen on Bikinis

Let's get intimate about bikini panties. We all want them, and she who wants them should have them. Where and how to wear bikini underwear is another matter entirely. Under clothes, bikinis are *only* for the well shaped *and* firm of flesh. In your private life, bikinis are between you and your fantasies; enjoy them. PS: They make great sleepwear bottoms. **Lane Bryant** always has a selection in flashy-trashy colors; the sizing, however, is often erratic and your bikini size may be a couple of sizes larger than your brief size.

BIKINI

Shopping Advice

- As a general rule, the sexier and fancier you want your panties, the more likely you are to find them in a specialty shop. The sexiest items for full-figured women tend to be made by small companies that are run by full-figured women; unfortunately, these companies come and go with dismaying frequency. You'll need to look for great lingerie both in large-size specialty shops and in lingerie shops. Even if you don't see what you want, ask for it. Small boutiques can't display all their wares but may have what you want in stock. Or they will order it. Because specialty store owners are likeliest to be responsive to your needs, asking for what you want can help make available what you'd like.
- Nude or beige color panties are the only color panties you can wear under whites, even sheer whites.
- Always try panties on in the store. There is great variation in fit from manufacturer to manufacturer, and even among panties of differing fabrics from one manufacturer.

GIRDLES

With the advent of pantyhose in various versions of control-tops, there is no need for girdles—they force your thighs together—especially those with powernet. Control-top pantyhose provide all the firming you need while allowing you free movement.

PANTYHOSE

All pantyhose is divided into two parts, and the difference couldn't be more important for you. Let us think of them as The Tube and The Cube.

The Tube is probably what you are wearing. It is all of a piece lengthwise from waist to toe. This pantyhose may be sheer from waist to toe, or all-support, or it may have a knit-in "panty" of varying degrees of control that extends to varying lengths on the thigh. The key point is that the leg and the top are essentially a continuous tubular construction, and a left tube and a right tube are joined down the center of the belly, with a small almond-shaped gusset, often cotton-lined, at the crotch; there may be an extra back panel over the derriere.

This kind of pantyhose is by far the most widely available in queen sizes; almost invariably, it is the *only* kind available. Whatever variety of texture and fabric there is in queen-size pantyhose—support, ultrasheers, pin dots, lace, opaque, colors—it is usually in pantyhose of this basic structure. Leaving aside the support versions for the moment, if the sheer versions of this pantyhose work well for anyone, it is usually for the pear-shaped, more bottom-heavy woman. In some brands, the knit-in control top extends all the way down the thighs for those really seeking to smooth out bulges.

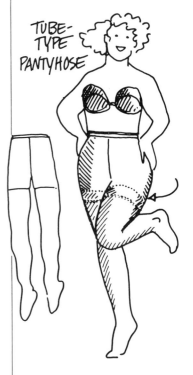

TUBE-TYPE PANTYHOSE

The trouble with tubular-type pantyhose is that it does not have an anatomically defined shape. Your body is jointed, or articulated, at the point between abdomen and thigh, and you have a crotch extending the full depth of your body, while the pantyhose does neither. Since it doesn't conform to the body at critical places, it rarely stays up on its own; most women report they must wear panties over their pantyhose to keep the crotchpiece from descending toward the knees.

But there is a far more serious problem: Because the legs of the pantyhose are not articulated, leg movement stresses the crotch gusset and inner thigh area. You go to step up onto a bus and your pantyhose gives way; the result is a tear on the inner-thigh area that sets the stage for painful skin irritation from friction over the course of the day. One fashion executive refers to this as the "poppin' fresh syndrome," where a "bubble of flesh" is forced through the pantyhose tear, making movement excruciatingly painful. In addition, the waistband on these pantyhose, which has to function as an anchor, may not stretch the full width of the hose, and only cuts into your waist.

If the knit-in panty is made with a substantial percentage of spandex, support pantyhose in tube style can work better for all body types; the spandex yarns stretch enough to provide freer movement. Still, there is a tendency for even the best of these to ride down over the course of several hours if they are not smoothed up from the ankle from time to time.

Support pantyhose come in opaques and sheers. For downright versatility, stunning (literally) color range, well-engineered fit, and range of sizes you can't beat the opaque support fashion tights made by **Danskin**. They are available in two degrees of support.

Danskin's **Too Pretty To Be Support** tights are nylon and 16% spandex from toe to waist in a matte finish. What distinguishes these further is an unusually large crotch gusset in cotton knit. The rise is ample and there's a

PANTY TOP
PANTYHOSE

full-stretch soft sewn-on elastic waistband .These two-way stretch pantyhose are ideal for women who do a lot of standing, for those who have varicose veins, or for anyone who wants an opaque pantyhose that stays in one place. In addition to a traditional footed version, these tights also come in a footless version trimmed with lace at the ankle. A-d-o-r-a-b-l-e and s-e-x-y! They are great for leisure wear, for schoolgirls who want the latest fashion look under mid-calf and short chiffon skirts, or anyone who wants lighthearted legs anytime, anywhere. Both versions come in basic colors, bright jewel tones, and seasonal fashion colors.

Danskin's **Ultra Shimmery Tights** are made of nylon and 8% spandex from toe to waist and have a shimmer finish. They also have the advantage of a large cotton-knit crotch gusset, and come in footed and footless editions. These look especially great for evening wear in any season but summer.

The Cube

The Cube has two parts united in one garment: panty and hose, joined in a fine horizontal seam at the top of the thigh. The panty can be a control-top brief with spandex, or a high-leg panty with or without control. Either way, the panty top, like traditional briefs, has a distinct cut-and-sewn crotch-piece, usually cotton-lined, that accommodates the full depth of the body. It is more three-dimensional and more anatomical, articulated where the body is articulated, at the juncture between thigh and torso.

In contrast to the more widely available tubular-type pantyhose, and for no particular reason that anybody can figure out, the cube varieties are not widely available or widely advertised. But in the experience of women who have been able to find these pantyhose in queen size, they have major advantages for full-figured women. Because they are anatomically shaped and have a horizontally positioned crotchpiece that allows for depth and width—body volume—they stay up on their own. Most important, they afford complete freedom of movement without stressing the fabric at the crotch or inner thigh area. They last longer, making any extra cost well worth the expense. However, colors and textures are limited.

There are two versions, one pure cube and one hybrid. The award for the best-kept, best-fitting secret in pantyhose unquestionably goes to **Slender-style**, a queen-size brand that has been quietly available for years in a limited number of stores, including **The Forgotten Woman**. I discovered them only because a saleswoman thrust them at me and wouldn't take no for an answer. She and the rest of the store's staff had given the brand a tryout and fallen in love with it. Recently, the original manufacturer announced he was retiring and ceasing production; devoted consumers went into a panic. The upshot is that Slenderstyle is alive and well and now made by industry giant Pennaco.

The pantyhose has a silky-smooth control top of spandex and nylon that lightly firms hips, tummies, and derrieres. The full crotch is cotton-lined, and the legs are made of a stretch sheer nylon yarn in a matte finish that is comfortable in all seasons and sheer enough for most purposes. It comes in two sizes, XL and SL, fitting women wearing up to dress size 32. You won't find tones-of-the-moment in Slenderstyle, but you won't miss them, either. There are enough pale tints and pale neutrals (off white, oatmeal, dove gray, soft pink), midtone neutrals (beiges), and darker tones—taupe is a terrific everyday color for most legs—as well as basic colors (black, navy, gunmetal), and even some downright exotic shades (a smoky gray green, for instance). You wouldn't call Slenderstyle out-and-out sexy, but it is definitely attractive, and there's even a fillip of lacy edging at the waistband. A similar type pantyhose is now also available in basic shades via the *Comfortably Yours* mail order catalogue.

For sheer sexiness, there's **Berkshire's French-Cut Scallop Panty** pantyhose. This is really a hybrid pantyhose, cut as a tube but functioning as a cube. It has a high-cut brief that, like any brief, traverses the crotch from front to back, but the brief is knit in rather than sewn on. The brief is lace-patterned with a scallop edge, and it has very sheer legs. It comes in black and beiges. The look is sexy and the fit is good. This pantyhose is especially suitable for the woman with high hips. Unfortunately, the style is much harder to find than Berkshire's other pantyhose; as so often happens, a manufacturer makes what you are dying for, but retailers don't stock it because sometimes they have very unfounded beliefs about what you want—as if what you want is different from what other women want. Here's a nice touch you don't often see—the package is beautiful. Against a white background, it shows a woman of voluptuous hip proportions, seen in soft focus from the back, nude except for the pantyhose. These are well worth the search. If you can't find these, contact the manufacturer directly: Berkshire IT FITS, IT FITS, P.O. Box 244, Wayne, NJ 07474-0244.

A Yarn

While we're on the subject, it's time to mention something about pantyhose yarns. Some are better than others, particularly for full-figured women. In sheers, there are stretch sheers, regular sheers, and silky sheers, and there are matte finishes and sheens. The very softest and most comfortable pantyhose year-round are made of two-way stretch sheer nylon yarns in a matte finish. If you have difficult-to-fit proportions—say, thin ankles and thick thighs—you will probably get the best fit in these.

Ultrasheer yarns have less stretch, which makes fit a more exact science and finding the right size a matter of great experimentation on your part. Some sheer yarns are so stiff they feel wiry to the touch; beware, they can—I swear!—make noise on the body. They rustle loudly as your legs brush against each other as you walk. You will cringe in self-consciousness, the true enemy of style.

Silky sheers have a more comfortable "hand," and often contain spandex yarn. Yarns with high sheen reflect a great deal of light and so magnify the body part they cover. Support pantyhose always have spandex yarn but that no longer means they always have more sheen; newer versions have a more flattering matte finish. The best have a very soft, silky, and supple feel.

Shopping Tips for Pantyhose

STRETCH LACE TOP SLIP

- If there isn't a display pair for you to carefully examine, ask to see an open sample of any pantyhose before you buy a pair. Be sure to examine the style, test its give, and feel the yarn, both of the panty and the hose, if they are different. Most pantyhose are prepackaged, and the package rarely shows the style of the pantyhose. So kindly wait your turn at the sales counter and sweetly but firmly insist on seeing a sample pair. You have a right to see before you buy.
- If a yarn or fabric doesn't feel soft to your hand, you can be sure it won't improve on a more tender part of the body.
- In your inspection, make sure on the tubular-type pantyhose that there is an adequate waistband to anchor the pantyhose, and be sure to test that it stretches the full width of the pantyhose.

SLIPS

I have to admit a personal bias. I have never understood the shape of slips; the skirt half is always more or less A line, which means full slips are great under full skirts but not slim ones. The cut suggests the best use for full slips—sexy sleepwear, since there's plenty of room to move around in. Most slips are made of nylon tricot, a fabric that tends to cling. Silk or fine-quality woven polyester is infinitely better—feels better, garments drape better—under clothes, especially if cut on the bias. So is cotton batiste, which is well worth the search.

Here Comes the Glide

Full slips do have their purpose—they are essential under knit dresses, the hang and the fit of the dress is greatly improved, and the silkier the slip, the better the look of the dress, the easier it glides over the body. If you get the least bit itchy from sweater fabrics, a slip will save your skin. Slips belong under very sheer dress fabrics, too, unless the sheer garment comes with its own lining.

Getting full slips to fit right is a problem for those who are short and those who are big of bust. If you are short, look for slips without bottom trim, so you can shorten them easily from the bottom. Silk styled with a lingerie top may be best, although those women large of bust will probably have to experiment to find one that fits well. The easiest fit for women with a big bust is often a stretch top, of lace or smooth spandex. Under sweaters, especially white ones, the smooth spandex version will give a smoother underline than stretch lace, which can not only cling but show through.

Half Slips

If full slips are hard to find, you could opt instead for a camisole and half slip. Particularly if you prefer fine fabrics, such as cotton batiste or silk, which function best and feel best and usually are the prettiest or sexiest, you will want a camisole and half slip. Be sure your slip is shorter than your shortest skirt. Buying two slips in different lengths, or hemming one of them, is better than rolling up a slip at the waistband. Let's be frank; none of us benefits from the extra bulk or the distortion to line that results.

If you put on a knit skirt or sheer skirt that is unlined, you *must* wear a half slip. In all other cases, if you wear pantyhose, and it's a choice between a slip showing at the bottom of a skirt or through a walking slit in a slim skirt, you are better off without a slip. Except in summer, when any unlined skirt has a tendency to stick to the underside of the body if you sit for very long. This not only looks unattractive, you don't want to lurch into a telltale

FANCY CAMISOLE AND HALF SLIP

PETTI PANTS

St. Vitus's dance to wrest the fabric away from the body. Better to skirt the problem altogether with a slip.

I can't think of anything more romantic or more practical for summer than a slip-camisole duo in white cotton batiste. You'll also find them addictively comfortable. Cotton batiste is perfectly fine all year round, too. The most attractive versions readily available come from the **Vermont Country Store** and **Comfortably Yours**, both mail-order companies you may not know of because they aren't the first to spring to mind when you think of beautiful lingerie. Both usually offer attractive lace-trimmed editions (full slips, half slips, camis in cotton batiste) by catalogue. Any number of small lingerie manufacturers in large sizes now also make attractive slips and camisoles in silk and other fine fabrics, and you can find these in specialty stores.

PETTIPANTS

For full-figured women, pettipants are sometimes the preferred insurance against ill-fitting pantyhose. Pettipants can be, well, ooh-la-la. Nylon tricot tends to the utilitarian in style; in use, it builds up too much static to be a good solution. If you like pettipants, try cotton batiste, often available with lovely lace trims. Check out the catalogues from Comfortably Yours and Vermont Country Store.

CAMISOLES, CHEMISES, AND TEDDIES

A SIMPLE CAMISOLE

As mentioned above, camisoles can be essential items under sweaters and sheer blouses and dresses. They make ideal (sexy and comfortable) pajama tops. The most attractive, the best-feeling, and the most functional come in body-skimming silk or fine polyester charmeuse, cotton batiste, or fine-gauge cotton jersey. Some are so pretty you will want to use them as lounge wear and, under open jackets, for dressy little evenings. A silk or poly charmeuse camisole, in a tank style or suspended from spaghetti straps, also functions as the ideal blouse substitute when you want to transform the right suit from office attire (buttoned up, please) to dinner dress (open if you wish). Camis never seem to go out of style, so feel free to pick one or two up when you come across an especially pretty version. **Fine and Fancy** makes a gorgeous bias-cut cami in polyester charmeuse with lace trim, and a matching half slip, in attractive colors. They also offer a more fitted camisole in black lace, and another in stretch lace.

To get proper camisole fit, you may have to shorten the straps, a very simple alteration done from the back on lingerie-style camis, or the top of the shoulder in tank-style ones. Just make sure the camisole has plenty of ease over your bust and that the slope of your bust does not hike it up under your arms. In length, it should extend no more than an inch or two below your waist. Tank-style camisoles in silk or fine polyester fit especially well when cut on the bias; cutting on the bias also adds a grace note to the bottom edge, even if it's finished with a plain hem.

TRY A TEDDY

Teddies are very sexy-looking little wisps of lingerie that have great fantasy appeal. Surely they serve no other purpose in life but to look luscious. Okay, if you need an excuse, buy one for sleeping. Getting a teddy to fit is not easy in any size; it's a real challenge for the full of figure. **Fine and Fancy** makes several editions: There's a sleeveless stretch nylon lace teddy in black and white and—catch this—the company is making a long-sleeve version for streetwear! The company also makes a jacket to go over the teddy—or out on its own. Fine and Fancy also does a teddy in soft white pima cotton trimmed with French lace and a little pink satin bow at the bosom. If teddy fit is simply too difficult to negotiate, you can duplicate the look of a teddy and enjoy perfect fit from a camisole and tap pants.

GARTER BELTS

A little silk. A little lace. And a lot of sex appeal. The question is not whether you should wear one. It's where can you find one in your size. **Fine and Fancy** makes it in silk charmeuse with imported French lace. Also, check out the offerings at **Lane Bryant**.

FANCY GARTER BELT

SLEEPWEAR

Glamour. That's what you want in a nightgown, if you wear a nightgown. It actually exists in your size. Finding any sleepwear at all expressly designed for full figures in stores can be a challenge to the hardiest shopper. A saleswoman at Macy's in New York, the world's largest store, told me the store regularly stocks large-size sleepwear, including some of its own manufacture. But on one recent expedition, early but not too early in the season, the store could produce only one shopworn long cotton gown and robe in one department, definitely in the granny gown mode, and one short gown and robe in silk charmeuse in its Fantasies lingerie department. While

ROMANTIC POET SHIRT

the silk gown was attractive and identical to a style carried in smaller sizes, finding it in a sea of merchandise required considerable determination and the help of two salespersons.

My experience exemplifies the problem real women encounter day in and day out when shopping for full-figured anything in major stores. The problem is not so much what is there—the silk charmeuse gown was indeed lovely—but what is not there. A full-figured shopper has to wade through acres and acres of every permutation of gorgeous, colorful, sexy, sensuous sleepwear in misses sizes, search high and low, and then somehow be thankful if in the forest of merchandise she locates one item designed for her. Choice of style and fabric is limited. (Whether it fits is another matter entirely; the silk charmeuse shorty gown was improperly cut for a full-figured woman with a bust.) No matter how determined she is to buy, the experience saps her enthusiasm and convinces her she is not a desired customer. Along with her enthusiasm, her self-esteem fizzles. Is it any wonder she sometimes gets downright hostile? Over and over again, this is the message full-figured women tell me they want manufacturers and retailers to understand—the experience of shopping from the customer's perspective.

As with almost all other items of lingerie, the widest selection of merchandise will be available to you through catalogues, or through small stores specializing in lingerie or in large-size fashions in general.

There are two ways to look at sleepwear. The traditional way includes short and long nightgowns, poets shirts, oversize tee shirts, and tailored shirt-and-pant pajamas, all created for sleeping. The nontraditional way gives you the additional options of full slips, camisole–tap pant combos, skivvy-brief duos and other items not expressly designed for sleeping but ideal for the purpose. Either way, you don't want sleepwear too big or billowy; it only gets tangled. But few things are as uncomfortable as sleepwear that's restrictive. Of course, there's always that other option—no sleepwear at all (except when being a houseguest).

If your shoulders and back are the thinnest part of you and you are a diehard romantic of the Victorian persuasion, you can probably find a good selection of sleepwear in the Misses sleepwear department. Just be sure to avoid anything with a baby-doll or other high puffy sleeve; it will not flatter any full-figured woman. On a recent expedition, all-cotton **poets shirts** in misses sizes from **Gilligan and O'Malley** were excellently cut with generous raglan sleeves and a full body. A Misses size M comfortably and attractively fit a size 20 woman without any compromise of line or comfort. Poets shirts, falling somewhere between the knees and mid-calf on women of average height, look good on both short and tall women, too. With all their flounciness at the top, they work best when balancing the pear-shaped figure.

LINGERIE STYLE—MOVIE STAR STUFF!

Gilligan and O'Malley also makes large-size sleepwear, but none was in evidence on a recent shopping expedition, while forests of merchandise awaited the S-M-L regular customer. Two manufacturers whose sleepwear offerings you also might want to check out are **Barbizon** and **Priamo.** Both make large sizes in addition to Misses sizes, but in both cases the Misses sizes could well fit fuller-figured women comfortably. Priamo seems to specialize in poets shirt-type sleepwear in fine cottons. If you happen to be nursing a baby, you'll be interested to know you can always count on Barbizon for some front-opening styles.

If you are big-busted, a poets shirt may not be your best look; it all depends on just how poetic the look is. The open neck of a poets shirt is fine; there just may be to much in the way of ruffles and flourishes on top for you. You also will not get the most flattery out of granny gowns or any other sleepwear with frou-frou at the top and gathers falling from a yoke that runs straight across the chest; it broadens you and exaggerates your chest out of proportion to the rest of you.

If glamour and seduction are more your style, then without question the best gown for you—and probably any full-figured woman—is a **lingerie style gown.** There is no point in being coy about this: You want the Fantasy Gown made by **Fine and Fancy,** in cotton jersey, nylon tricot, fine polyester charmeuse, or silk. Company owner Ellen Smith has been perfecting the fit of this gown over the past three years, so that it works like a dream for women who wear dress sizes 16 to 26. It's got a halter top held with spaghetti straps; it hugs and supports the bosom because it is bias cut and held by an underbosom band from which the skirt falls in graceful gathers, creating a flattering cascade of fabric that just winks at a thick waist or full abdomen. The gown is floor-length, but a new waltz-length version should make it suitable for shorter than average women as well; this version also has its bosom piece of stretch lace so that, in the words of company president Smith, "the bosom enticingly shows through." You can hunt out **Fine and Fancy** gowns in specialty stores.

SEXY BIAS CUT GOWN HUGS AND FLATTERS AT THE SAME TIME!

Another good gown for you because it drapes gracefully on the figure—if it is sized right—is a less fitted **bias-cut slip-type gown** of woven silk or

SHOULDER PADS AND SILK PAJAMAS

AND OPEN THAT EXTRA BUTTON!

fine polyester. It's simple, it's sinuous, and it's sexy, a necessary alternative to most sleepwear in large sizes, which is flouncy and bouncy. Check Macy's **Fantasies by Morgan Taylor** label for silks.

Sleepshirts, especially with embellishments of lace or other trim, are good for all figure types, although they are short on sexiness. Since they generally are made to fall just below the knee on medium height women, they can also serve shorter women and longer women without losing their proportions.

Tailored pajamas, plain except for border piping, can be anything from cuddly to soigné depending on the fabric. In cotton batiste they are delicate, in flannel quite cozy, and downright alluring in silk. For batiste and flannel, you can find them in all sizes through the **Vermont Country Store** catalogue. They work well for all figure types, although they tend to make the short figure a bit boxy. The batiste comes in summer and winter versions, with short and long sleeves and short and long pants. A pair in silk charmeuse would really be the definition of chic, especially with a jacket slightly elongated, like a tunic, for flattery.

A pajama style that is highly popular—and can do double duty for lounging—is a **knit tee shirt and bottom** combination. The top is usually big, it may have short or long sleeves depending on the season, and the pants are usually tapered pull-ons. Particularly when the knit is all cotton, the silhouette is flattering on just about all body types if the shirt is cut to below the hips. You need to make sure that the top is also cut amply enough to drape loosely; otherwise, it just doesn't work on bosomy bodies. **Lane Bryant** always seems to have some variations of this style in its stores.

Don't, however, feel you have to be limited to conventional sleepwear. You will do magnificently to sleep in a slip, a teddy, or a camisole and tap pants.

T-SHIRT PAJAMAS YES, WITH SHOULDER PADS

ROBES

Sure, a robe is for comfort, but fit is important, too. The same principles that apply to street clothes apply to robes. You will look best if the shoulders are neat. You need sleeves that end neatly at the wrist. And you don't want to sweep the floor; if you are short, you may have to take up a hem. Because robes are designed to fit loosely, most styles, if properly cut in the first place, fit most body types.

Wrap robes specifically designed for full-figured women usually have a generous enough overlap to accommodate body parts of differing sizes. A wrap robe is great for the short-waisted as well as the long-waisted; all that's required is a bit of blousing of the bodice when you tie the waist. I consider a wrap robe in silk, whether traditional cut or kimono style, a wardrobe basic. It lasts for years, since it never goes out of style. It works for all seasons. It looks and feels terrific. And it takes up no room at all in a suitcase. Another excellent—and sexy—possibility is an ankle-length wrap in a very untraditional fabric, such as semisheer rayon georgette. Cotton flannels also look good on full-figured women and feel cozy in the winter. Terrycloth can begin to get bulky, although terry with a velour finish often gives a smoother look.

SLINKY WRAP ROBES NEED SHOULDER PADS TOO! CLEAVAGE IS A GOOD IDEA TOO!

If you like **plushes** and pile fabrics, look with care; most styles easily add unnecessary bulk to a full figure. So can chenilles and quilted robes. At the very least, a robe in this type of fabric should be on the longer side, to balance the width, and must have a vee yoke or high shoulder yoke. Otherwise, a yoke across the chest chops the body down, and the gathers fan out across the bust, emphasizing width. Even a wrap robe in a plush velour would look less daunting.

For summer-weight robes, a lace-trimmed flowing cotton batiste affair with slight Victorian airs proves the frill isn't gone. A cotton kimono offers a sleeker line, if that's what is wanted.

To get a stylish and sleek look in a robe, however, you don't have to be limited to what is hanging in the robe department. In fact, you'll do much better elsewhere. **Bathing-suit coverups** are often not only more stylish and more flattering but less expensive, too. My personal favorite summer "robe" is a sleeveless, drop-waist, button front cover-up from **Wear Abouts by Sirena** in hot pink crinkle cotton, since subdued by countless washings. Every year at resort time a version of this swimsuit cover-up reemerges in stores.

VERY GAUZE-Y POET STYLE WITH LOOSE BOWS AT WRISTS AND NECK—

LEAVE THE NECK OPEN FOR GREAT CLEAVAGE!

Free-flowing, tea-length summer **dresses** in gauzy and colorful Indian cottons and crinkly rayons make ideal robes that travel well, go stylishly to the pool (especially with a big hat and sunglasses), and can even endure a hot afternoon in public (add sandals). I love them for the beach, too, because they can shield you from the sun after you've had enough and still feel airy, they look sexy catching a breeze, and they look chic back in town. They are the only dress/robe/garment of all purpose that can spend a week in a backpack and carry on immediately. Inexpensive, indestructible, and versatile, they are among the all-time bargain styles. Look for them in import stores and buy a couple.

And then God created **dusters**. You know, those long, unlined, billowy cotton coats for outings in Stanley Steamers and now seen only on the Marlboro man and the pages of the J. Crew catalogue. They are loaded with dash. Well, they were made for us. Shhh! Don't tell anyone, or they're likely to vanish from the face of the earth. They make great year-round robes, and casual spring-fall coats over slacks. And you don't even need a large size. One of my favorites is "The Big Coat" made in a heavyweight cotton gauze by **Sangam**. Just this side of slouchy, the double-breasted coat has notched lapels and closes with a set of buttons just below waist level. I like my sleeves rolled back once or twice. Every season, the duster is available in a great range of fashion colors. It flies into the washing machine and would look much too prim if it ever got a pressing.

SHORT CHIC

For very short women, there is another solution. The same heavyweight cotton gauze is usually made, by the same company, into a bigshirt of wonderful and neat proportions. On a size 20 woman of average height, the shirt comes to mid-thigh. It would make a knee-length robe (and bathing-suit cover-up) on a shorter woman, and the button-cuff sleeves are on the short side, as well. The texture and drapiness of the fabric, as well as the high colors usually available, keep the shirt from looking too tailored.

OH CAFTAN, MY CAFTAN

To caftan or not to caftan? Liz Taylor has recycled her old Halstons and, frankly, not even she gets away with it. If you want camouflage, go for the gauzy Indian cotton dresses or the duster instead. They don't look so dated, and you won't set yourself on fire if you have to put up a pot of coffee. If it's drama you want, be sure to pick the right color.

COLD COMFORT

Call them skivvies. Call them knickers. Call them snuggies, or whatever you want. There is an attractive and lightweight version of long underwear that is a must in every full-figured woman's wardrobe. It is a not-quite-body-hugging top of fine jersey, plain or rib knit, with long, short, or no sleeves at all, and a scoop, crew, or vee neck. Very European—how else to survive the seasons in all those drafty chateaux?—these come in silk, wool or cotton jersey, and innumerable combinations thereof.

Here's the beauty of them: They are of such fine gauge that they can keep you toasty under a silk dress and still be invisible. They are great for you because, aside from being sexy and feeling good on the body, they keep you warm without adding a scintilla of bulk. And if they happen to peek out from under a blouse, so much the better. Any day—many days I do it—I'd trade a layer of outerwear for one layer of this innerwear. These are the perfect solutions for cool fall days and spring days when a suit isn't quite enough but a coat might be too much; add a skivvy underlayer, even under a silk blouse, and go. Or in winter, they can be worn under a sweater with a suit—and no coat. I love the bravado of that look; add muffler and gloves. And yet, they feel comfortable when you go indoors.

It's possible to buy these in America now (**Jockey for Her** makes tank-style ones in cotton jersey), but the finest are still imported from Europe. My absolute favorites are Italian and made of a wool-silk combo, have a lace-trimmed vee neck and short sleeves. They hand-wash like a dream. In the U.S., these tend to be marketed as luxury items (read: expensive) and hard to find in large sizes. (The ones in Misses sizes run extremely small; don't even think of buying one in XL if you see one.)

If you travel to Europe, you can find them in almost any lingerie boutique or department store. But the best place to buy them is where the Europeans get them (in multiples)—humble little notions stores that have infinite varieties in endless sizes and bargain prices. These stores are often located on side streets just off the major fashion shopping thoroughfares, as well as in more residential neighborhoods. In Italy, they all look rather dingy and old-fashioned from the outside, and are called "Mercerie" (mare-chair-ree´-eh). You have probably walked past dozens of them without noticing. Do go in. You'll have a ball. And everything comes in your size (in Germany and Switzerland, too).

Standard-issue long underwear is essential for skiing or other winter outdoor activity, or for just enduring subfreezing weather on terra firma. And it is getting prettier all the time. For the best fit, you'll look for separates, rather than one-piece union suits. There are silk jersey tops and leggings in many pretty solid colors. (**Beauti-ful Skier** imports them from the Orient in large sizes and sells them by mail order.) There are also

ROLL AND ROLL THOSE SLEEVES

ADD PADS

ROLL UP EXTRA LENGTH TO SHOW OFF YOUR SOCKS!

LONG JILLS

double-thickness crew tops and bottoms (by **Duofold**) in wool-cotton jersey knit in attractive pointelle patterns.

That said, there are a few ways to have much more fun in the long-john department. Look at it this way. They go under casual clothes; you can afford to do something a little wild and let it show, especially for a weekend in the country or lounging around après ski with friends or family. Think about a union suit in bright red and loose enough to fit more like a jumpsuit. You can get it in a store that sells men's uniforms or work clothes or in the men's department of Kmart or other mass merchants. Be sure to buy it in a generous body size. If the sleeves and legs are too long, roll them up, or tuck the legs into socks. Unbutton a few buttons at the neck, add a bandana—belt it, even—and you'll look adorable. Another good source for getting a union suit that not only fits but is loose enough to have some style possibilities of its own is an army-navy store that sells new or used clothes.

14

> *"'What shall I wear?' is society's second most frequently asked question. The first is, 'Do you really love me?'"*
> JUDITH MARTIN,
> *in* Miss Manners Guide to Excruciatingly Correct Behavior

Wardrobe Strategy

*I*tem: It is that inevitable rainy day in April. The temperature is neither here nor there. You have a meeting with the boss and you want to look your polished best. But for at least forty-five minutes you'll be crammed on a bus that will verge on the tropical by the time you get off, what with the heat of all those bodies and the water, and then you'll have a five minute dash through the downpour to the office. The last thing you want is to arrive feeling like a sloppy mess, which is to say defeated, before the day begins. So you do the next best thing. You fling open the closet doors and moan, "I haven't a thing to wear."

Item: A new play has opened on a limited run. It's the hottest ticket in town, but you don't have one. At five o'clock on Saturday afternoon, your best friend calls. Her husband is giving in to his bad back for the evening, how would the two of you like to make it a girls' night out and enjoy the orchestra seats? And of course it's short notice but can we meet at the restaurant in an hour and a half? No sooner have you delivered an almost automatic yes and hung up when panic strikes. You just took your good coat to the cleaners.

Item: It's the Christmas season. A good friend from the office is getting married. Everyone has known about the afternoon wedding for months. It's going to be a very gala affair; not only is it the holiday season but the reception is the first "public" event in the swank club atop the city's newest skyscraper. You have postponed shopping because, to be honest, you expected to lose a few pounds first, although you told yourself you were really waiting for the new holiday clothes to arrive in the stores. You have done some serious browsing, but now, the week before, you are up against a closet that suddenly appears barren although it's so crammed you can't even get the door shut. You spend a day of frenzied shopping in every store in town that carries your size, but nothing knocks you out, or feels gala enough, or really looks right on you. After trying on at least seven "outfits," the last of which is a red silk charmeuse tank top/palazzo pants/cardigan jacket that even Santa Claus's mistress couldn't carry off, you thank the ever-optimistic saleswoman apologetically, and resign yourself to sitting out the event.

If you have more than half a dozen items in your closet and have ever missed a social or other occasion because you felt you didn't have the right thing to wear, then your wardrobe isn't working for you.

If you have ever stood in front of a full closet and sworn that you have nothing to wear, your wardrobe isn't performing right.

Or if this instant, you couldn't put yourself together in ten minutes for any spur of the moment event (except, perhaps, your own wedding), your wardrobe is underperforming.

If you are an alive and aware human being, you change, gradually, over the course of experience in the world. Unless you are psychically disabled, your sense of yourself evolves, too. It may be that, somewhere along the way, you and your clothes got out of synch—that is, if they ever were completely compatible with your true self. You have gone one way while most of your clothes remain stuck in an earlier view of you. Every time you open your closet, only a few of the many things you have are actually viable possibilities. In that case, it's time to reexamine how you see yourself and how you see clothes—and make sure the clothes you get can't possibly fail you.

Or perhaps you have gradually switched life-styles. And while you pride yourself on your go-to-work wardrobe, your way of going out has gone from casual evenings in friends' homes to more sophisticated entertaining in restaurants and at cultural events. Like every other woman today, you need clothes that can carry you through several roles, clothes that have chameleon-like power to work, with a change of approach and accessories, in several different types of situations.

Or perhaps you are expecting too much from clothes. You want each item of clothing to say it all for you; after all, at these prices, each piece should have drop-dead impact. If that is the case, you have made the assumption, completely mistaken, that style is in the clothes you wear, not in the way you wear them. As a result, few things in your closet work with each other. Bargain hunters beware: You can get the same effect from landing a closet full of "great finds." They're likely to leave you with a closet full of clothes that not only don't work with each other, they are not likely to represent a coherent you.

The infallible way to create a wardrobe that always comes through for you, no matter the occasion, no matter your fashion personality, is to start with a core of timeless classics, indispensable pieces every woman needs to make it through almost all situations—effortlessly. Classics are classic because their interest and appeal are enduring. They are simple and attractive. They have survived because they flatter easily. Classics have special value for full-figured women. What makes a style classic is that its shape, its silhouette, and all its design lines have been aesthetically perfected over time. And the beauty of the design is imputed to the body beneath, provided the body does not interrupt the flow of the style lines. This is the best argument for body-skimming fit in clothes. It is also a good reason why women should avoid jumping on fashion-of-the-moment bandwagons. The trendiest clothes have not undergone the process of design refinement—it comes with time and, yes, copying—that works out their aesthetic kinks and starts a contender down the long road to becoming a classic. Consequently, it is better to buy into a fashion trend on its second (or even third) season than in its first. Classics make a perfect base for any accessory, those flourishes and details that make your look distinctive. Women of real style select these essential pieces of clothing for their quality, their durability, their fit, and their ability to flatter. What's more, they choose this core of classics in only one or two solid neutral shades.

They approach dressing this way so that they have a repertoire of reliables, pieces that always look good on their own and work well with each other—and serve as the ideal backdrop for the color, flair, and personal style that come from adding accessories and special accent pieces in ways that reflect individuality and spirit. Classics, then, make up the starting point for expressing personal style and dressing well for a range of situations. Because classics remain in fashion a long time, there is no need to worry about them going out of style next season or next year, so a wardrobe can be built around them. By buying classics, you, too, can afford to invest in a few pieces that have the quality you need and the good but unobtrusive detailing that gives clothes polish.

These are pieces you can always count on to carry you through—perhaps even now, with a closet full of clothes, you find yourself relying on only a few items. These pieces are simple and flattering enough to work with little effort on your part. They are clothes that live up to you at your best, not clothes that you have to live up to. They are worth investing in whenever you find them, even if they cost a bit more than you are used to spending; they will pay you back with years of long-term use. With a wardrobe pared to flattering essentials, you have clothes you wear again and again because you love them, because they look good, and because they make you feel good when you wear them. It is more important to have a few terrific and versatile items you love than a closet full of clothes and nothing to wear.

To develop a wardrobe this way, you may have to reverse your usual priorities. You may have to stop looking for fancy clothes when you should be looking for simple chic ones. I often hear women say they want great special occasion clothes. They swear they'll "pay anything." But that could be the problem right there. They are looking for clothes that put too much into the dress; that way of thinking invests clothes with more power than they actually have; it diminishes the wearer and her contribution to style.

First, you should look for clothes that look good every day—because life is lived every day. Get used to looking great and making a great presentation of yourself every day. It will give you more fashion savvy for special occasions. And it will reduce the need for you to make special occasion dressing speak too loudly. Get used to having clothes that, because they always look good, can go anywhere, any time. Then, if you happen to stumble across a sensational dress, you can pick it up and add it to your wardrobe, secure that you're ready for that next special occasion—or capable of making any occasion special.

EIGHT EASY PIECES

Rule #1 of building a successful wardrobe is to start with a core of classics. These are the essentials, items for which there are no substitutes. But they are versatile. Therefore, you want the best you can possibly afford. The payback will be in style and reliability. Believe it or not, there are only eight basic pieces you need as the foundation of a great wardrobe sometimes referred to as a capsule wardrobe:

- a black slim skirt
- a cardigan sweater
- a suit
- a pair of jeans or khaki slacks
- a classic silk shirt
- a white tee shirt
- a large shawl (40″ to 52″ square, depending on your height)
- a signature scent

GRADUALLY TAPER YOUR SKIRT FOR BEST EFFECT

TAPERED LOOKS LONGER! (AND THINNER!)

The **black straight skirt** is the workhorse of any great wardrobe, for a woman of any age or size. It pairs with tops in any color and jackets of any silhouette. For winter, it is at its most versatile in strong and supple fabrics like lightweight wool gabardine or crepe, or wool jersey, since they not only drape well and feel good but work easily with other textures. Lightweight wool gabardine is excellent for summer use as well, along with heavyweight cotton jersey, cotton-linen blends, or viscose and linen. This skirt goes casual with every sweater you own. Or team it with a classic shirt and your basic cardigan sweater, drape a shawl over your shoulder, and you have the presence of a second suit. This skirt with any top and a shawl that picks up one color or the other has as much power as any suit. Of course, this skirt gets tapered for flattery and has a back slit for walking ease. If you can't find a simple black skirt in fine fabric that fits perfectly, and you know how to sew a straight line, this is the item to make yourself.

The **cardigan** is a sweater so versatile you can't stop at one. Its essence is long and easy, big but not oversize, and never bulky. And totally plain. Ideal cool weather fabrics are lambswool, merino wool, rayon knit, full-bodied cotton or, of course, cashmere. For warm weather, think cotton or, for delightfully slinky slouchiness, cotton-rayon jersey. No matter its color, it goes naturally with your black skirt or your jeans, over a classic shirt or over your tee. But that's just for starters. Think about your cardigan:

SHOULDER PADS ARE A MUST!

- over a lace-edged camisole or a silky tank top for "little" evenings—bareness by implication
- or backwards, over a simple skirt

A GREAT IDEA FOR AN OBLONG SCARF AND A SUIT THAT NEEDS A LITTLE KICK

CHIFFON CATCHES THE BREEZE AND LOOKS GREAT

- loosely chain-belted over a long side-slit skirt, for casual elegance at parties and for entertaining at home
- over khakis and a tee shirt, loosely belted, with a shawl flung over your shoulder, for early-fall weekend ease with a lot of panache
- and if you really want to give it panache, change plain buttons to crested metal ones.

The suit can be structured or unstructured, skirt suit or pants suit, depending on where you live and how, but it is essential for pulled-together chic. And it is versatile. More casual living takes a less structured approach to a suit. It can have a slim skirt, soft- or knife-pleated skirt, or full skirt, but its silhouette should be one whose natural style lines are most flattering to your body shape. This is a suit that is going to perform for you, so it is worth investing the time and effort to find a stylish one that looks good and matches your life-style needs, in an excellent fabric. Some choices might include:

- a dressmaker suit, which tends toward the dressier side of polish
- a double-breasted blazer and slim skirt, or tailored pants, which is by far the most versatile in character
- a tunic and skirt suit, in matching or contrasting colors, perhaps black button-front tunic over white skirt, or mixed textures
- a soft-pleated skirt and matching placket-finished shirt as jacket.

The suit should be able to go from day to evening with a simple change of accessories, the opening of a button, the removal of a blouse, or the addition of a camisole or tank top underneath. My own personal favorite is a black double-breasted suit of tropical weight stretch wool gabardine, with peaked lapels and covered buttons, by **BB USA**. It's comfortable and right-everywhere power dressing by day, it's a tuxedo look-alike by night, with no blouse at all or a white crepe jewel neck blouse.

The jeans or khakis are in any shape that suits your body type. I can't even imagine a life-style or a season, except the dog days of summer, where they wouldn't be exactly right for so many things, but it's open season on style. (My own favorite jeans are executed in a trouser style.) These are classics and last forever, so don't go in for faddy overdyes or acid washed treatments. Nothing looks as good as the original indigo denim faded and softened with wear (or stonewashing). Both jeans and khakis mix with every color and every style of look. The important thing to remember, though, is that casual is never a synonym for sloppy. Pair jeans with a sweatshirt when you are doing household chores, certainly, but also team your jeans or khakis with:

ESSENTIAL KHAKI TROUSERS

- a silk shirt and blazer
- a cardigan and shawl on cool days
- a tucked-in tee shirt and a safari jacket on warm days
- that old favorite, a crisply laundered shirt-tail shirt, worn out and loosely belted
- a crew-neck sweater bloused into your pants, pearls, and a shawl.

The classic shirt has no peer in silk. If you are truly lucky, you will find a shirt in a superb medium weight fabric and finished at every turn, preferably with a covered placket front, so that it works both as a blouse and a blouse-jacket with zero bulk. Go for classic details, such as button or French cuffs, convertible notched collar, and classic colors, such as white or cream. This is not the shirt to buy oversize, which limits you to one way of wearing it. Buy it reasonably long, for blousing into pants and skirts, with an easy, body-skimming fit. You'll want to wear it:

- under jackets and cardigans, tucked into pants and skirts
- under dark crew-neck and vee-neck sweaters, to get the punch of white collar and cuffs
- loose over a camisole or tank top, to have bareness by suggestion for casually elegant evenings.

The tee as shirt was made respectable in the sixties (when it was also made legible, but that's another story altogether). Because it is so unexpected under tailored clothes, and yet so understated, it transforms them from ordinary to original faster than you can say Fruit of the Loom. Here's how one woman I know wears her padded-shoulder tee shirts:

THE PERFECT T-SHIRT WITH STITCHED IN SHOULDER PADS AND TINY BOW

- as a blouse to take the starch out of strict suits
- with split skirts and slinky cardigans, bloused and belted, tucked in or out, for a very fluid look
- under sweaters, such as relaxed turtlenecks, to give shoulder definition
- hidden under knit suits, for shoulder definition without seams
- alone, over tapered pants
- alone, over tights, for exercising
- under plain-neck sweaters, as an accent, with the neck edge showing
- under open-neck shirts, especially for walks in the country
- over pants and skirts, with blazers or cardigans
- in summer, as the top half of everything
- over bathing suits
- on cold nights, as a pajama top.

Be sure to fold your tees flat after laundering. You don't have to go so far as pressing them, but you look sloppy if they look rumpled.

The shawl is invaluable for draping over one shoulder with ends flowing loose or held by a loose belt. No matter what you are wearing, the shawl instantly transforms it into chic—it has that bold-stroke effect—and in the offing gives you a long vertical line. And is at the ready to keep you warm. You don't want a shawl to look out of scale on you; go for one a minimum of 50″ square if you are over 5′4″, ends hemmed neat or self-fringed. Or buy huge oblongs or mufflers in stand-out colors and use them as dramatic wraps. For an appealing mid-winter change, or for an evening that will be spent mostly in a car and then indoors, put on an invisible underlayer, wear a suit, and throw a big wool wrap on over it; add gloves. For sheer poetry, and sure chic anytime, put on your simplest dress and get out a long, wide chiffon scarf. Instead of wrapping the oblong around your shoulders from back to front, drape it from shoulder to shoulder across your front, so the ends float behind you as you move, veiling your entrance in a cloud of allure; heads will turn. Wonderful fabrics include wool challis; silk, especially in chiffon for spring and summer; cashmere; and printed rayon georgette, because it drapes like a dream and looks sexy. Use shawls:

- for coverage over anything in cool weather
- for punctuation over a suit

- for poetry over simple dresses, sweater dresses, silk shirts
- for warmth and chic, keep one in the office for chilly days, preferably in cream colored wool (it goes with everything)
- to complete any top and bottom and turn it into an ensemble. A shawl can tie the colors of separates together, or it can be a blast of color on otherwise neutral clothes, or a whisper of hue on whites and pastels.

The scent is your finishing touch; you can't consider yourself dressed without it, no matter where you are going. Every woman needs a scent that works with her own body chemistry, so you will undoubtedly have to do some experimenting to find one that you can wear (lightly) day in and day out, that becomes so identified with you it is like a signature. You can vary your fragrance according to mood, but the best approach is to find a scent you enjoy wearing most of the time—and apply it lightly. Nothing too aggressive; think subtle and intriguing, not obvious and overwhelming. If you are searching for a new scent:

- test one fragrance at a time
- dab a bit into the crook of your elbow or onto the palm of your hand, sites where body warmth will help develop the fragrance fully (if you're shopping, do this on your way into a store, as you pass the cosmetics area)
- after about fifteen minutes, check the fragrance
- repeat as often as you venture forth, until you find a scent you love.

NATTY NEUTRALS

Rule #2. Buy your basic pieces in just one or two neutral colors. First of all, neutrals are always in style; they aren't hot today and then gone tomorrow, just when you want to match up a blouse to a purple skirt. They always look rich, especially when combined monochromatically in variations of tone and texture. They are extraordinarily versatile, and lend themselves easily to being dressed up or down with a change of shoes, bag, scarf, or jewelry. They impose no prior limitations about what can be worn with what, making your capsule wardrobe reach farthest. They simplify dressing—no small consideration at a time when women are juggling multiple roles and always pressed for time. And perhaps most important, they create the essential backdrop against which you splash color and accessories in ways that define your character and spirit.

In fact, for many smart dressers, it is enough that neutrals heighten the impact of color. That allows them to update their wardrobe core of eternals each season in the simplest, strongest, and most economic way possible without having to sit out fashion's trends—they add touches of the season's hottest colors in little but powerfully eye-catching ways. Lime green in a tee shirt under a black suit or over white pants. Or as one color in a vibrant shawl. Or in a pair of cotton socks. Strong purple as a pocket scarf. Or as knitted wool gloves and a fringed muffler. Or an extra jacket in bright orange. And that solves a potential problem of neutrals. Such a strategy allows any neutral to work for any woman any time—if she adds near the face a scarf or blouse or accessory in a complexion-flattering color.

There's no reason to be neutral about neutrals. Beige and black have been traditional neutral colors—but that doesn't mean they are colorless. Black has a chic about it that always makes it right for urban environments and for evening anywhere. (It is *the* wardrobe color of fashion's scribes, and in an ironic turn, at least one fashion advertising firm *requires* its employees to dress in black—every day.) Combined with touches of white it always looks sparklingly fresh—the power of contrast. Or sexy, as in a zebra-striped shawl or chiffon scarf. Or formal; that old tuxedo association. And who said beige has to be boring? Pale beiges such as palomino are rich and luminous on dark-skinned women as well as on the fair-haired and red-haired. Nothing is more luxurious looking than dressing head to toe in differing shades and textures of beige—ivory shirt, tan trousers, camel sweater, brown textured-leather loafers or flats. Taupe gives beige a sophisticated edge. White is another neutral that never looks dull, especially in winter, and lights up a face like no other color can. Navy, once reserved for spring, has become a new all-year neutral, and is *the* reigning fashion neutral of the past year or two; like white, it has snap against most skin tones. Gray has infinite gradations, from incandescent pearl to resonant charcoal.

GOOD LOOKS—NOW!

Rule #3. Buy only what looks good—now. You are building a wardrobe of clothing that you will always want to wear because it looks good and, therefore, makes you feel good when wearing it. So it must fit you and flatter you now. Not as you were last year. Or think you'll be in two months. Life is now. You must look good now. You do this by zeroing in on the right silhouettes for your shape, so that your shape will always look its best in the clothes you have.

LOOSENED UP MATCH-UP

Rule #4. Get rid of restrictive ideas about what's good and what goes with what. There is no law that says jeans can be worn only with a sweatshirt. They're classics—with a shirt, a narrow belt, and a blazer, they have a relaxed chic that is at home anywhere in the world.

Forget about exact color matching. When you build a wardrobe in neutrals, richness comes from wearing different tones and textures of one color—in other words, it's an asset to have clothes that aren't slavish matches.

Matching shoes and handbag is another constricting idea straight out of a 1950s conformist time warp. Women just don't have time for that anymore, and it can look terribly rigid. First, you look best and dressing is easiest when shoe color loosely matches hose and skirt color, in tone if not color. That is one reason why such durable but expensive shoes as alligator pumps have become popular; they go with all bottoms. Second, women don't change bags daily depending on outfit anymore—you're lucky to find one bag (probably carry-all tote or briefcase-pocketbook combo) that transports work and personal items neatly for everyday use; having to change bags frequently would be tremendously disruptive, an unnecessary nuisance. Third, especially for dress or casual wear, where it's most likely to come into play, a shoulder bag in a contrasting color, especially slung across the chest, adds an interesting angle to your body and a good accessory to a neutral wardrobe.

You'll get more play out of your wardrobe if you don't categorize business clothes and dress clothes too exclusively. Take the curse off a strict business suit by adding unexpected flourishes. I love the contrast of a soft-draping cream-colored semisheer shirt worn under a prim suit. Nancye Radmin, founder of The Forgotten Women stores, says that "most women are too narrow-minded about what they can wear." She sees no reason why even such a staple as a gray flannel business suit has to look the same way on every woman who wears it or even the same way on one woman every time she puts it on. "Why not wild it up," she asks rhetorically, "with a silver lurex sweater?" No matter where or when it rears its fresh head, the unexpected is always delightful and appealing.

COLOR—FAST

Rule #5. Add color and flair with accessories. Your style is not in the clothes but in the way you wear them. Although dressing in tone-on-tone neutrals is a time-tested way to achieve understated elegance, there are other times when you simply want more vibrancy and personality. By using color as an accent, you can have a timeless wardrobe and your trendiness, too. Let shawls, gloves, pocket scarves, fabric flowers, mufflers, tee shirts, simple blouses, extra jackets, handbags, even, occasionally, shoes, all serve as color opportunities, whether your interest runs to the color of the moment, jewel brights, muted tones, or pastels. Here's where you can give your personality free reign. Soft pastel chiffon wrapped over the shoulder of a simple white silky tee is refreshingly attractive in the summer and over a white sweater in winter enticing in its softness. Love bold floral prints? Or paisleys or unusual plaids? Throw caution to the wind—literally—and indulge that taste in a shawl. Have a bit of the femme fatale in you? No doubt your neutral will be black, but get a giant red wrap (cashmere is sensational but unnecessary; get **Cashmink**, an I-dare-you-to-tell-the-difference synthetic at an infinitesimal fraction of the price) and fling it over your shoulders; add slinky long red jersey gloves (subtlety isn't your goal here). Love your black leather blouson jacket, but sometimes feel it looks too "hard"? I counteract mine with an eye-poppingly fresh emerald green muffler in meltingly soft wool coiled casually around my neck and a particularly pouchy emerald beret. Sometimes I add green leather driving gloves.

When you're dressed head to toe in navy, a pair of pumps in royal blue brushed leather (better than suede, it's wearable all year; a staple from comfortable **Arche** shoes) looks snappy without being outrageous. If you want to see a taupe suit come to life, add purple pumps; keep everything else taupe-y. Keeping classics fresh with colorful accessories lets you add as much individuality as you want or a situation allows.

PLUS PLUS

Rule #6. To get you virtually every place in style, you'll need to augment your wardrobe with a few other highly versatile pieces. Follow the same pattern in adding these basics, too—select classic styles in neutral colors.

SPLIT SKIRT SOFTLY PLEATED

DIVIDED SKIRT

SLINKY AND SILKY TANKS GO ANYWHERE!

- a split skirt
- a tank top
- a pair of tailored trousers
- a big shirt
- a simple dress
- a seasonless jacket
- a raincoat, unlined or with button-out lining
- a winter coat

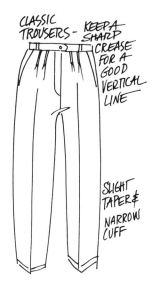

A split skirt could be the most versatile addition to your wardrobe, because it goes everywhere that pants go plus everywhere a skirt belongs. It is softly pleated, and if done in fine, fluid fabrics, has a dressy side, too. When you don't know what the dress code will bring, the split skirt is always right, because it is always chic; get it in black crepe, pair it with a white silk tee, and it has a formal aspect. Another plus: It skirts the hemline issue (and you can safely wear it with knee-highs instead of pantyhose) without compromising on fashionability. Team it with a tank and jacket or just a silk blouse for dress wear, with long sweaters or a tee and cardigan sweater for everyday chic.

A tank top goes under every jacket you own plus on its own (arms permitting) with bottoms to make a bare and dressy look or a bare and sporty look. If your arms aren't terrific, throw on a shirt over the tank and imply bareness. Because its character depends on what it's worn with—dressy under a suit jacket (add earrings but keep your neck bare), sporty over a pair of shorts—the tank works well in versatile fabrics like washable silk (name your color), rayon jersey, silky cotton jersey.

Tailored trousers are indispensable for a professional look in pants. With one simple vee-neck sweater, the addition or subtraction of a silk shirt, a change of belts from tailored leather to clunky gold chains, the use of jewelry or shawls, and shoes from Keds to dress sandals, these pants can accomplish a miraculous metamorphosis from Kate Hepburn sophistication to business-like crispness to sportive relaxation to evening elegance. Lightweight wool gabardine or cotton gab looks and feels good the year round, can be elegant or casual, and lasts forever.

The big shirt in white cotton creates crisp tailored or sporty looks. It goes over your jeans or khakis, with or without a loosely draped belt; solo over tapered or stirrup pants; tucked in under your suit; belted over your black skirt; under your cardigan any way you want; over your tee shirts. At its best in fine cotton, it will do in cotton-poly blend if you don't believe in ironing.

DOUBLE BREASTED BLAZER A TRUE CLASSIC

SHOULDER PADS MAKE THE SHAPE WORK BEST

You don't want it so big it has no shape, just oversize enough to make its point. Make sure its pockets are not so oversize they prevent you from wearing the shirt tucked in.

The jacket in a silhouette that complements your body shape will be worn day in, night out, in three—or if you are lucky—four seasons over everything. This could be a lightweight gabardine blazer in navy, it could be a shirtjacket in taupe suede, or it could be a cardigan jacket in a supple rayon crepe or slubbed viscose and silk. Only if you are under 25 or a student, this jacket could be a jean jacket, earth's first all-season go-with-everything.

A dress for all seasons: mediumweight cotton or cotton/rayon knit or jersey that looks like a long vee neck sweater or a cardigan that didn't know when to stop. Or a ribknit jersey in cotton or lightweight wool (ribknits have flattery, stretch, and movement built in). This could be your little black dress. Perhaps it's a slightly wedge-shaped chemise in beefy cotton jersey. Wear it solo or with a shawl, or under your jacket. This is the kind of item you want for speed dressing, that makes absolutely no demands on you but always looks good. Alternatively, particularly for the pear-shaped, a simple shirtwaist dress in washed silk or dark cotton could be equally versatile—it goes on its own, dressed up with scarves or jewelry, or under sweaters and jackets.

THE GREAT WEDGE DRESS!

ADD ROUNDISH SHOULDER PADS

NOT TOO MUCH BULK JUST ENOUGH FOR EASE

SLEEVES AND HEM ARE TAPERED

SHORTISH LENGTH

LEGS + SHOES DARK

A raincoat is an essential almost everywhere and, if bought with a button-out liner (avoid zip-out liners; the zipper distorts the line of the coat when the lining's not in use), it can do double duty as a winter coat if you live in milder climes. A relaxed trench coat or a balmacaan in tan, navy, or black cotton gabardine is classic, looks best, goes everywhere, and travels well. Be sure it's long enough to go over all you own. By keeping the style classic, you can wear it for years; it thus pays to invest in a good one. Always resist the temptation to get a trendy-looking raincoat; it will look so passé next year you won't want to be seen in it, and if you're like most women, you won't get enough use out of a raincoat to justify buying one each year. Get maximum panache from your classic coat by wearing it with a felt fedora in cool weather.

A winter coat is a must for most women. The best and classiest looking single winter coat you can buy is a balmacaan in wool gabardine or twill. It may cost you a week's salary, but it will pay you back in sleekness, go-with-everything good looks, durability, and, unlike most winter coats, a chameleon-like power to look right with casual clothes, sporty ones, tailored outfits, and casually dressy clothes. Gabardine, being lightweight and supple, can be worn from early fall to mid-spring. And you can wear it while driving a car without feeling like the abominable snowman. Look for a coat with a button-in lining and you will be fortified for the worst winter can deal you. Wear it on the long side. And think shawls.

AN AFFAIR OF THE HEART

Rule #7. Buy only what you fall in love with. If you have reached this far, you have found a foolproof way to take care of basic fashion needs for most situations. Then, as you add to your wardrobe, you can afford to apply the one criterion (in addition to fit and body-type suitability) that guarantees you a wardrobe that will always delight you: Does it steal your heart, capture your spirit, and thus make you feel wonderful? Sooner or later, many women discover that by applying this guideline, even though they never set out to buy something specific, or never know where or when they will happen upon their next purchase, they always have more than enough clothes they love wearing any time, anywhere. And by shopping this way, they are able to sit out a fashion season if the offerings are not to their liking, or they are otherwise preoccupied. Each season, aim to buy one quality outfit that makes you feel great when you put it on. Put some money into one thing, instead of into lots of inexpensive pieces. Over the years, you will acquire a wonderful wardrobe.

Sometimes, it's the most impractical-seeming item that can steal your heart. But being beloved gives it a power to transform the way you feel in it, which makes you eager to wear it; you look for reasons to put it on—over and over again. In the end, it becomes a bargain. Six years ago, I walked into a store where I was helped by a size-six saleswoman wearing a captivating white crop-pants suit, with a boxy cropped top, at once casual, dressy, and starkly simple in a wool-rayon knit. Nothing I tried on that day worked, and on my way out, the saleswoman asked if there wasn't something I wanted. "Sure," I said, going for broke, "what you're wearing." "Why didn't you say so?" she shot back as she reached into some hidden corner and produced the identical item in my size. It looked awful on me: a blessing—it was forbiddingly expensive, especially for something so . . . unclassifiable. Before I knew what I was saying, I asked whether it came in black. Of course, it did. And it looked sensational. Still does. After six years of days at the office, plane and train trips, cocktail parties and dinner parties,

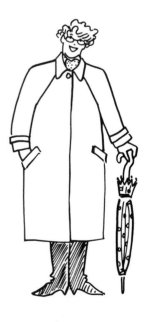

theater-going in New York and London (wrapped in a shawl), strolling in Italy, everywhere in New York, away on weekends to assorted resorts, hotels, and inns, it is still paying off in chic. I love it no less, and I can remember weeks when I wore it at least three days or evenings out of seven. That's what happens when you buy what you love.

The corollary is: Never buy something just because it "goes with" (usually under) something else you already own. Every item in your wardrobe should be able to perform on its own. It should be admirable for its own style and have as much finish as any other item you choose. If you wouldn't select it under other circumstances, don't select it at all. Something else will come along that you'll like better.

FAIL-SAFE

Rule #8. If your closet has ever failed you, it's time to:

- reassess yourself
- reassess your clothes
- reassess the two together.

Start by getting a firm grasp on how you want to look in clothes. It's not enough to have a vague vision; until you can specify it, you won't be able to achieve it without too much wastage. Take some time to find words for the look you admire and the feeling you want to achieve in clothes. If you need some prompting, rummage through fashion magazines and clip the pictures that represent the looks you like, and read the accompanying descriptions. Analyze and describe the feelings of the styles (sit down with a word-finder or thesaurus; it can help you clarify your vision and pinpoint what you want). Put down in words the look and the feeling. Mull them over for a few days; make sure they feel comfortable. Once you know what it is you're after, it's time to go through your closet and analyze everything you own.

First, however, eliminate what doesn't fit. Try on your clothes. Everything. Make a pile of everything that doesn't fit. You will give it away.

Then eliminate what doesn't fit with your newly expressed picture of yourself. Clue: Check items you haven't worn in the past year or more, but are holding on to for some other reason (it cost so much you cringe at the idea of tossing it;

something important happened the one and only time you wore it; you used to wear it so often it is too much of an old friend to bury voluntarily).

Try the clothes you have with items other than those you usually pair them with, to see whether the fault is in the clothes themselves or in a restrictive way you have been looking at the clothes. Add to the give-away pile everything that no longer represents you or for any reason doesn't work. Bundle it up. Put it in a closet near your exit door. If, after a week, you haven't reclaimed anything, give it all away to a woman's shelter or other needy enterprise. Anything you feel so wistful about you've had to snatch out of the pile belongs back in your closet. At least for now. (But ask yourself why you like it, and try to duplicate it in your size or color.)

Rule #9. Plan for life's inevitable emergencies. Plan and try on the clothes you will reach for:

- the day you wake up too late to think about anything except those people already waiting to see you in your office
- the day it is raining hard all day. Hint: Keep your raincoat and fedora on the ready in your coat closet. They are practical and stylish. Under them: Choose clothes that are bright and won't crumple under moisture, hot, or cold. Heavyweight cotton jersey is ideal, all seasons; wear dark opaque pantyhose in the cooler months, dark sheers in the warmer ones
- when a last-minute dinner or party invitation arrives
- when you have to catch a plane in one hour
- the day you're just feeling blah and need the lift of clothes that look chic without your help because you're in no mood to meet any demands. This is your very favorite item of clothing.

Just in case you won't remember under the pressure of circumstances, make a little list of all these emergency groupings, along with accessories, and pin the list inside your closet door. That way, you're always ready to take on the world in style.

Sources of Clothes You May Not Know About

Import stores are inexpensive places for unusual and attractive items that often work well for you. Free-flowing summer dresses in gauzy and colorful Indian cottons and crinkly rayons are mainstays. These fabrics can withstand summer heat—after all, they hail from India, where they know a thing or two about hot-weather dressing. Look for dresses and separates in a heavy cotton hopsacking (heavyweight gauze) that is the trademark of **Sangam Imports.** The clothes are designed for timelessness—and no ironing. The company makes thirty styles, among them a long-sleeve loose-flowing chemise that is extraordinarily versatile—add a hat and go to a lawn party, to a day in town, to the beach (roll up the sleeves), or just hanging loose anywhere. This dress could stand in front of a classroom all day *and* go out to dinner (open the neck button). There's also a dynamite duster known as The Big Coat. Almost everything comes in ten colors a season. And will work for many years. Because the fabric has body, it goes year-round, especially in earth colors and winter brights.

Marimekko is a Finnish design firm renowned for colorfully printed cottons and simple but chic sportswear and dresses made from them. They are sold in stores bearing the Marimekko name, at Crate and Barrel stores, and in other retail outlets in the U.S. Over the years, Marimekko has added knits in fine fibers and simple shapes that lend themselves to style—and to many different body types. The size range is Misses small to large or extra large (18), but the large is often very large indeed. The clothes are distinctive—you will not mistake these for anyone else's designs—but often have a purity of line that most lends itself to individual style. Their fine wool knits are particularly winning.

Laise Adzer is a California-based designer whose trademark is loose, flowing clothes—they come in one size—in a mediumweight woven rayon hopsacking. These clothes represent a distinct point of view and are not for everyone. But they are well-suited to larger bodies because they do not make an issue out of size.

15

Little Things
Mean a Lot—
Accessories

*I*t's no secret that accessories are the great secret of style. What's not so well appreciated is that this is where we, as full-figured women, have a natural advantage. Because what looks best in accessories is what works best for us—the bold strokes, the grand gestures, the really noticeable pieces, items of forthright charm. We can carry them off, give them their due. What might overwhelm a smaller body becomes a statement that reflects well on us.

Accessories do more than pull a look together. They are the smart way to update a wardrobe, and the least expensive way. Updating by accessorization assumes a particularly great importance for full-figured women, because fashion trends are generally not translated as quickly into large sizes as they are into standard sizes. At best, there is a one- or two-season lag. Adding a touch of a beautiful new seasonal color in a bag or shawl or gloves is a way to feel like the parade hasn't passed you by.

Accessories are also the means by which you give a look its distinctive character. In other words, they define your style. They give clothes personality—yours. Accessories are the path to self-expression in clothes. Therefore, accessories should be approached as an adventure in self-invention, a voyage of discovery. They are instruments of amusement, of charm, of spirit, of wit, of elegance, of gaiety, of whimsicality, of cleverness, of romance, of drama, of spontaneity, of sauciness, of creativity—of all the things you are, will be, or can be. Choose them accordingly.

Putting personality in your clothes could be as simple as:

- pinning an extravagant organza flower over the top button of an utterly simple cardigan jacket
- tucking a colorful pair of gloves into a blazer breast pocket
- wearing a large silver bracelet spiraling around each of the close-fitting sleeves of a navy sweater dress
- draping a bright-colored fringed muffler over one shoulder and loosely holding it with a narrow belt
- wearing a floral print necktie (loosely knotted) on a big white silk shirt
- tying an oblong silk scarf to an epaulet and letting the scarf drape front and back
- pinning a giant brooch to your shoulder
- wearing a simple summer chemise and a wide brimmed hat with a long chiffon scarf tied around the crown, ends trailing down your back
- weaving a narrow red velvet ribbon through the links of a gutsy silver chain link necklace, tying the ribbon in a little bow, and wearing it with a black or navy dress
- tying a large silk square, folded in half to a triangle, around your neck and draping the triangle in front
- wearing an armload of wooden bangles with a casual cotton dress
- replacing the row of ordinary buttons on a jacket with classy contrasting ones; black buttons on a white jacket, buttons of bold gold on a plain black suit.

Accessorization is one part invention, one part appropriateness (you wouldn't wear an armload of jangling bracelets to a business meeting), one part daring (being timid doesn't work with accessories—they have to be seen to be appreciated). And one part simplicity. Whatever you do, you want to make a statement—but only one at a time. A huge copper-colored wrap thrown over a brown suit, worn with dark taupe hose and shoes, looks great. Add a copper color hat and shoes and you look overdecorated. Think of accessorization as an improvisation on a single attitude, not an exercise in matching everything up.

Using accessories well takes a certain sense of playfulness. That doesn't mean sticking pom poms on your shoes in a bid for style. It could mean using an old familiar item in a new way. I sometimes take the red button-in lining out of my navy blue twill winter coat and wear it, finished side out, as a long sleeveless tunic over a simple black sweater and skirt. After all, you can be serious without being solemn. Just because something comes prepackaged (coat with liner) doesn't mean that's the way it always has to be worn.

How do you learn the knack? You start with an open mind, take some time by yourself in front of a mirror, and play with new combinations of things you own. And you practice. If you see a look you like in a magazine, try to imitate it until it feels comfortable on you. Play by trying the scarves and jewelry and hats that you own with all your dresses and separates. It takes some practice to see what works, what doesn't achieve the look that you are striving for. The purpose of trying things is to find what works and to rehearse your manner of presentation so that it feels like second nature. And to work the kinks out in advance. You need to know how to keep things in place once you put them on. Because in order to work right, your finish must look effortless. Any bit of self-consciousness—constant adjusting of a hat, tugging at a scarf—will call attention to your problem and make you look as if you are parading around in someone else's get-up. However much time you spend rehearsing, the result should look spontaneous. It may take you a while to practice tossing a scarf over your shoulder to make it look as if it landed there with effortless chic. But effortless it must look—the art that conceals art.

There has to be some harmony in your approach. Even if they match perfectly in color, you can't wear shimmery spandex gloves with a corduroy jacket; one is racy, the other more rustic in attitude; each is so determinedly of its kind that it excludes other possibilities. (Jersey gloves, on the other hand, could look either casual or dressy, depending on how they are worn.) There also needs to be seasonal harmony. Dark suede shoes paired with a breezy cotton skirt will look too heavy. So will heavy metal in the summer.

Put away your serious gold and silver jewelry when the weather gets warm and opt instead for lacquer or woven straw bangles instead of silver ones, for colorfully painted wooden beads instead of gold chains.

Some general approaches to accessorization that always work:

- *Be the things that you are.* Choose accessories that express your attitude. Witty? Think berets, soft hats, and other spirited accessories. Full of coy charm? Look for large collars, add long bias-cut silk scarves as ties. Feeling racy? Look for clothes and accessories with sleek lines; unbutton and unzip; make sure your tapered skirts have slits.

- *Develop a signature look.* It could be an item that you are never dressed without, that becomes identified with you. It could be hats. It could be a collection of animal pins. Or scarves; collect them over the years—they never go out of style (twenty-odd years later, I still own and use the very first thing I ever bought with my own earnings—a white silk twill square from Givenchy with one big black sunflower printed on it). It could be a collection of bangles; one gets lost, but three or four of a kind or related kinds stimulate interest.

- *Think surprise.* Wear a pair of white cotton lace gloves with a summer suit. Indoors, put the gloves in your breast pocket so the fingers are peeking out—subtle but noticeable, and just the right kind of dash for a conservative office. Aim for the touch that tickles, pleases. Go beyond the usual.

- *Forget consistency.* Don't be afraid to change courses from one day to the next, so long as each look makes sense unto itself. One day you may want to dress for all-out sophistication: a long sleeve black sheath, several ropes of gold chains and faux pearls of slightly different lengths, substantial faux pearl button earrings, bright leather gloves, sheer black hose, and black suede pumps. The next day you may want to look more gamine in a big blouson sweater over a silky stitched-down pleated skirt, low heels, a nonbulky scarf loosely coiled around your neck, and a roll-brim hat. When it comes to accessorization, the only consistency should be the regular use of fresh touches and faithfulness to your spirit. And get out of the habit of wearing one outfit the same way every time you put it on. At least promise yourself you'll try it differently each time.

- *Abandon the matching impulse.* It looks too planned and regimental. There's a rulebook somewhere that says to wear an accessory in a color not in your dress you have to use the color at least twice; this is the red-handbag-and-red-shoes-with-navy-suit school of automatic matchup. It ain't necessarily so. First of all, accessories that are related in feeling or tone, rather than matching in color, often produce a richer effect and look more spontaneous and uncontrived. Simulated ivory bracelets and leopard-print anything work well together even though they share no colors; they have a primitive natural link, and colors that blend.

- Second, that leads to the next point: *You will always look better and have more panache if you go for one bigger or more unusual splash rather than two little ones.* Call it impact. A beautiful red shoulderbag slung across the front of a navy jumpsuit (that diagonal shoulder-to-opposite-hip line is exciting all by itself!) could be all the red you'll need; then you can keep the long navy line unbroken with navy hose and shoes. A giant hot pink shawl on a dark dress is a stroke of grand appeal; any other spot of color would be an unnecessary distraction. By the same token, the fingertips of a pair of orange leather gloves poking out of the breast pocket of a dark suit has impact—a touch that draws the eye in—because it is so unexpected. Knowing what is expected, then deliberately violating it in an amusing way (hot-color gloves instead of a sober scarf, plus the loopiness of glove fingers poking out) packs a great deal of appeal; a certain contrariness fashionwise is a good route to style.

- *Don't only think big, think simple.* For sheer flattery, you are always better off going for one substantial item that is linear rather than convoluted. This is why doing nothing more than throwing a large sweep of a bright shawl over a shoulder will always stir more excitement and look so much better on you than matching up your shoes and bag. That doesn't mean you always have to be bold and dramatic, that your approach can't be soft and feminine. Wearing six or seven rings on your fingers may be "feminine" but it looks tacky rather than pretty, and bulks up your hands while remaining inconsequential over all. A luscious long pale aqua chiffon scarf placed around your neck and tied in a big half bow at the side of your face, with the ends flowing, makes a lavishly feminine point with more convincing cachet.

- *Think multiples.* You need impact without being overwhelming. Pinning one little animal brooch to your shoulder—unless it is really big and visible—won't have the impact it takes for a statement; instead, pin on a small herd of them, arranged casually, not in even little rows.
- *Turn necessity into opportunity.* You must wear eyeglasses? Choose frames that are interesting and flattering to your face. (Hint: They should be bigger rather than smaller, though the frames themselves can be quite delicate, if that is what you wish.) Use glasses as a fabulous way to add interest to your face.
- When in doubt, you are always better being underaccessorized than overaccessorized.

SCALE: ONE NOTE

With accessories, scale is everything. A thin gold chain around your neck looks so inconsequential it has a way of emphasizing fleshiness. A gutsier chain of links is more in keeping with your proportions. That doesn't mean everything has to be chunky or clunky, but you want to avoid items that get lost on you. You truly have an advantage over smaller women in that you can wear the stronger, bolder jewelry popular today.

BONANZA

In the past ten years, sales of accessories have doubled. The offerings have multiplied. That makes coordinating an outfit somewhat harder than it used to be. Women of every size are finding that accessories call for a lot more planning—and more drawer space.

Why the boom in accessories? As women increasingly participate in public life, typically in the workforce, they get to exercise their fashion choices regularly. They get practice making good fashion choices, and they choose better clothes. The high price of good clothes forces them to select clothes that are inherently flattering and that lend themselves to variation for frequent use. It's getting to be too expensive to make a mistake. For most American women, fashion took a turn to the more classic in the late 1980s.

Clothes may be getting more classic, but women increasingly are aware of the power of their self-presentation. The very classicism of clothes creates the need for women to find add-on ways to put allure and personality into their dress. The tilt of a hat, the fling of a scarf, a flourish of lace peeking out of a sober suit, the bold color of a glove—accessories are one way an identity can be expressed safely. What's more, their very use adds finish and polish.

For full-figured women, as for all women, accessories are important elements in creating interest in general and in focusing attention on good features. In addition, they are ideal as props for adjusting scale, the impression of overall balance and proportion, for reinforcing the perception that you are the perfect size for you. And of course, they're fun.

There are basically two approaches to accessorizing. The designer-line approach—you buy accessories as extensions of the clothes you are wearing, often from the same designer; these accessories function as accents for a designer's ideas. The approach affords a head-to-toe consistency of look. This, however, is basically fashion, not style. Having a fixed array of accessories to accompany each outfit is an unnecessarily rigid approach to fashion. It gives you little flexibility in altering your look from time to time. And speaking of time, when the outfit goes out of fashion, so does the accessory. There are more serious drawbacks to this approach—it can be quite boring on the one hand (you create a closed system) and very costumey on the other. A woman winds up expressing the designer's personality more than her own. And we haven't even tackled the serious dent this approach can make in your fashion purse.

The second approach to accessories can safely be called the Tiffany approach. You buy accessories like jewels—objects to be worn for their own beauty and style and charm. That does not necessarily mean expensive. Accessories can be classics, suitable for a broad range of wear, adaptable to many kinds of situations, adding glamour and excitement to many kinds of clothes—or they can be touches of throwaway chic, little items with so much verve that they will have served their purpose and provided enough pleasure even if they last only for a season. The thing is, accessories bought for their own charm and style have a way of never going out of style.

While accessory classics can be an investment (a good silver or gold chain necklace, or real pearls costs serious money, but then it lasts forever) you can buy all kinds of accessories with charm and style inexpensively, from shoulder bags to cotton scarves to faux pearls (Barbara Bush has made them acceptable, if boring). The major exception is shoes; cheap shoes cheapen everything they're worn with. Besides, you need the support of really well-made shoes and the breathability of natural materials.

If you like, you can let your accessories change with swings of fashion and whim of mood while your clothes take a more timeless tack. Scout street fairs, import shops, accessory departments for juniors to find accessories with more dash than cash. Then you can discard them, or put them aside for a time with a clear conscience when a fashion has run its course or a color suddenly seems tired. If most of your clothes are in simple shapes and colors, then you can load up on colorful and spirited accessories to vary your look as you feel. These are the elements you will be working with:

BELTS

Every woman needs at least one belt in her wardrobe. It's indispensable for finish, especially when you wear classics. If you have to choose one belt, make it mock crocodile—you get both textural interest and a clean conscience. A belt, especially worn loosely at the waist so that it dips in front, is an excellent way for waistless women to create the impression of a waist. And a belt can be critical in controlling the volume of clothes; blousing a top into a loose belt often helps smooth the middle passage.

If you are long-waisted and narrow on top, you can safely wear a belt at your waist that is two inches wide (match the belt to your skirt or pants). For everyone else, the limit is one inch, and the belt should preferably be in a dark color. Nothing can chop you in half or emphasize a thick waist faster than a thick belt.

But not all belts need be worn strictly at the waist. In addition to narrow leather or skin belts, two other types of belt that look very good, provided they are not pulled tight, are:

CHAIN BELT WORN LOOSE AND DRAPE-Y

- gold chain belts, which are meant to be worn draped just below the waist; they add a dressy touch to simple clothes
- thick draped belts, which are often two to three inches wide and work because they are contoured, with interesting buckles or hitches, and are meant to be slung on the high hip.

Some tips on wearing belts:

- in general, it's wisest to steer a safe course through beltland, sticking to neutrals or tone-on-tones

- when putting on a belt or sash, blouse the top very gently by hunching up your shoulders, then buckling or tying up. Always check your profile in a mirror; if you are busty, you will need to blouse the back a bit more to compensate for the fabric taken up in front
- opt for genuine leather and leather-lined belts; plastic or plastic-lined ones don't let the skin underneath breathe; you wind up with tops that have wrinkles and creases set by perspiration and require constant laundering
- belted jackets and coats should generally be loosely belted; on trench coats and safari jackets, you can double the self-belt around in back and belt it there with just the slightest tautness to suggest the indentation of a waist
- cummerbunds that are on the narrower side make good belts for bottom-heavy and hourglass-shaped figures. Make sure the fabric is soft and self-lined, so it will not be too rigid at the waist, and in case of waistband roll-over, you're safe.

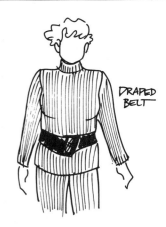

DRAPED BELT

SCARVES

No accessory can do more for you in one stroke than a scarf; nothing adds finish to a look faster, or more definitively, than a scarf. Whether you want a bold effect, a soft one, a flash of flavor, or a pinch of panache, a scarf will do it. Nor is there a safer, surer way to add color or any other kind of variety to a wardrobe. Whatever attitude you want to achieve or effect you want to create, you can do it with a scarf, in the right size, color, print, or texture. In addition, scarves, because they are made to drape, always suggest elegance and, worn right, add linearity to your figure. They are without question the easiest accessory to wear well. If your clothes are mostly in solid colors, you'll want to go to town on scarf prints; nothing has more flair when it comes to accents of color, and in a scarf, even a huge one, no print is too extreme. In fact, scarves are one place it's always safe to be outrageous. For all the glory of prints, don't neglect the impact of one beautiful stroke of color, especially in a long vertical scarf, or the value of white, for pure contrast with dark colors, for the suggestion of formality, and for pure flattery to the face. Never throw a good scarf out. If it feels tired, put it away (clean and pressed) for

OBLONG SHAWL SERAPE STYLE

SHOULDER PADS ARE IMPORTANT WITH SCARVES

BLANKET FRINGE ADDS MOVEMENT

a few years; don't worry, it will look fresh once again. Last year, my old Pucci scarves, unworn for a decade, began looking awfully good again.

Items to invest in:

- oblongs and mufflers, from wool to mohair to silks to cottons and crinkled rayons, for draping over one shoulder; for wearing around your neck with one end tossed over your shoulder; for belting serape style; for wearing loose like an opera scarf; for tying bandolier style down and across your front (a bright tartan would look good); especially in chiffon, for tying in a bow around your neck or around a pony tail; for coiling loosely around your neck, especially on big sweaters and outerwear; and in giant size, for cold-weather wraps. A glittery oblong makes any suit or dress instantly festive
- large (at least 50″–52″) challis squares to be folded in half diagonally or lengthwise and draped over one shoulder atop a blouse and skirt for finish, atop a suit for polish, or over your coat for color and finish
- 36″ squares in silk, cotton, rayon georgette for draping around your neck in myriad ways, filling in awkward necklines, tying over your hair (the Grace Kelly look; add sunglasses), and twisting around your hair
- small neck squares and bandanas for wearing peeking out of the neckline on shirts or filling in awkward necklines (on their own they tend to look out of scale and exaggerate size)
- pocket squares, to tuck in and peek out of pockets
- any scarf made in a fluid, drapey fabric
- ties, in soft patterns or colors, for wearing with closed-neck shirts or dresses
- silk flowers, for pinning on shoulders, at the throat of a blouse or fine jacket.

There are almost infinite ways to wear scarves. Here are some you might not have thought of:

DRAPE A FOLDED SCARF OVER YOUR SHOULDER

PADS HOLD IT UP

- To add interest and excitement to a plain flat neckline, take an oblong scarf of any nonbulky but stiff fabric. I like cotton voile for casual wear, organza or even taffeta, especially Fortuny-pleated taffeta, for dressier wear. Coil the scarf twice around your neck so that the ends wind up in front, tie them once into a half knot so that the ends now stand straight out to each side—then give the scarf almost a quarter turn so that one end shoots off your shoulder more or less parallel to your face, the other falls on the front of your shoulder, and together they form a strong vertical line that pulls attention to your face.

SHOULDER PADS HELP THE DRAPE

- Fold a luxurious looking 36″ silk scarf in half diagonally, place it around your neck, and tie the two ends in front in a half knot about chest level. Put on one or two 24″ strands of pearls. Pull the top end of the scarf over the necklace, so the pearls serve as an attractive anchor. Class with dash.

- Or for an extremely feminine effect without bulky frills, do the same thing using a narrow oblong scarf of lace in white or ecru.

- With an absolutely simple sweater and skirt or dress, take a large chiffon oblong and toss it around your shoulders front to back. Wear it entering a room, with the ends floating behind you. You will look heavenly.

- Twist a 36″ scarf tightly. Holding the ends on top, place it around your head like a headband, knot the scarf securely at the crown of your head, letting the two ends form "rabbit ears," and turn the scarf so that the ends are off center.

- Take the same twisted scarf, loop it twice around one wrist as a bracelet, and knot the ends.

- Fold a 45″ silk square diagonally in half, drape it over one shoulder with the fold toward your neck, then catch the two ends in a little knot at the waistline opposite.

- Make a collar out of any 36″ square scarf. Open the square and fold it into accordion pleats 3″ wide. Place this around your neck with ends even in front. Holding the ends pleated, tie a half knot, then slip the top end over the neckband once again, fanning the ends out to one side. Slip the other end over the neckband, and spread the ends out toward the opposite direction.

CENTER A BIG FABULOUS FLOWER

- To add even more interest to the neckline of a surplice overblouse or sweater, place a long chiffon scarf around your neck and tuck it in so that it lines the neckline all the way around. On the long front diagonal, make sure part of the scarf drapes over the sweater edge.

- Before getting fully dressed, take a 36″ silk square and place it squarely over your chest, print side out. Tie the top ends loosely around your neck in back. Tuck the bottom edge into your panties or pantyhose. Put on a button-front dress or sweater and open it to *there*, or put on a deep vee cardigan, tucking the ends under the neck in back.
- If your coat or outer jacket has epaulets, place a contrasting color wool muffler flat over one shoulder under the strap. Tack it in place. Or change the muffler as you wish (secure it by pinning it from inside your coat). If your coat is red, go for the unexpected: try a bright orange or yellow scarf or both.

JEWELRY

Let's start with the good news. Along with a great shawl, no single accessory item will do as much for a woman as the right earrings, because they focus attention on the face, and specifically on the eyes. The right earrings for a full-figured woman can be defined as those whose scale is perfect, not so tiny they get lost, not so large that they look garish. Size isn't the only criterion. The earrings have to lie close to the ear, so that they call attention to the eyes, but not flat to the face, which draws attention to the neck. And they can't dangle, because, by being so busy in an already crowded area, danglers appear to shorten and widen a thick neck further. That leaves out stud earrings (too small) and dangling earrings (too busy). What's left? "A three-dimensional button earring is a magic earring on larger women," says Carol Goldman, a jewelry designer whose company, **Verve**, produces jewelry scaled to larger women and with a more generous fit.

That said, it's safe to confide that nothing is trickier than steering a correct course through the world of jewelry. Many of the "rules" that work for other women (such as a long strand of beads adds height) turn out not to be so automatic (they don't work if your bust is big, and a single strand could look . . . well, stranded). And if you believe only in the real thing, then you better have very, very deep pockets, because you need jewelry with a strong presence and often, longer lengths; bigger pieces cost more, lots more. Over the course of years, you will want to collect real items—gold and silver bangles and cuffs, pins, and chunky chains; real pearls; rings of substance, and necklaces of precious and semiprecious stones. Very nice if you can get it, but nothing to mourn about if you can't. Because the easiest way to get the look you need is through the use of costume jewelry or a mixture of faux and real, which tends to upgrade everything in the neighborhood.

Earrings that dangle are no-no's for full-figured women not only because they shorten the neck; they also hang next to, and thus accent, the widest part of the face. If you have a long slim face and neck, fine. But otherwise opt for "magic" button earrings. Hoops are particularly troublesome because they repeat the shape of the face and the body. And the "shoulder sweeps" that have swept into fashion over the past two years just drag you down, especially if you have a big bosom as well. Too busy!

Necklaces present some surprises, according to experts.

THE PERFECT EARRING

- Chokers, contrary to what you may have heard, are not automatically taboo, certainly not for bottom-heavy women, who generally can wear whatever they want near the face. Carol Goldman insists that chokers are a bad choice for top-heavy women, because they cut the body off at the neck and emphasize its width. What often makes a choker work, though, is a looser fit; standard size is 16″ to 18″; many women need 20″ to 22″.
- Pearls don't have to be the size of golf balls, but the demure strand you got for your sweet sixteen birthday is not right either. Faux or real, 10 mm is about the right size for classic-looking pearls. You'll look best if you mass three strands of slightly different sizes and lengths, for interest. Or two strands and a substantial gold chain. For frankly fake costume jewelry that intersperses beads with chain, bigger pearls are fine. A good length for a woman of average height is 30″. No matter your height, under no circumstances should long ropes of beads dangle off, or anywhere near, a big bust; they'll only exaggerate its size, especially if they get hooked around one breast. If you have a large bust and must wear a rope of pearls, or want to make the most of a single strand of any beads, at least knot it high on the chest, so it has more "weight" and falls in one straight line (out of harm's way).
- Other necklaces should follow the same length guidelines. Only if you don't have a big bust can you safely wear really long strands of beads, and then, three strands, of slightly

differing lengths, look better than one or two. As for gold and silver chains, they look rich, and at 22″ are just the right size for being seen with suits. But if the chain links don't have substance, you will wind up looking larger. For added richness, I sometimes wear a 22″ chain with a ribbon threaded through it, the color depending on what I'm wearing it with; in the winter, I might use a quarter-inch velvet ribbon in red or black; in the spring, I'm more apt to switch to double-faced satin.

Bracelets should be used in multiples, as in bangles, or gutsy in size, as in cuffs. As for shapes, smooth, domed, angular, geometric, gently curved—all are fine. What you want to avoid is genuine clunkiness; thick wrists widen thick hips. You can carry an armload of assorted silver bangles. But be sure to hold off on other accessories; your bangles become a focal point all by themselves. Again, size is important in getting bracelets to fit right and look right. Standard bracelets, at 7″ to 7¼″ around, are apt not to make it easily over your hand, and if they do, you won't have much play in them. If your hands are big, look for bangles that are 8¼″ around. Unfortunately, Goldman notes, finding good bracelets at a jeweler like Tiffany's can be an ordeal, as many of their bracelets are not even 7″. She notes that it's time jewelers recognized that the more active a woman is, the thicker her wrists.

Wristwatches also should follow scale. A good wristwatch is one of those lifetime investments that always upgrades your look. What you want to avoid are tiny faces with narrow gold or silver straps. Opt instead for a watch in a decent size. But don't get a man's watch; it tends to be just too clunky. For any daytime watch, you can always get a black or brown leather or rich lizard band, since strap manufacturers have long recognized that wrists come in more than one size. Dress watches are another matter. One graceful approach is an oval watch; it covers more of the wrist width without sacrificing delicacy. Look for a simple satin band.

Pins are delicious when grouped for a statement, but a really impressive pin needs the field all to itself. Tiny jewels set into pins tend to disappear on you. Advises Carol Goldman: Go for jewels with emerald cuts. The scale is more in keeping with your body, and they will not get lost on you. Putting a group of pins—they must be related in some visible way—on the shoulder of a simple suit will enliven your whole look and make you appear taller

BRACELETS ARE FAUX-IVORY NEVER REAL IVORY!

GREAT CUFF BRACELETS

because it brings attention upward to your face. If you want to wear a lapel pin, choose one that isn't fussy, that has substantial size, and pin it higher, rather than lower, on your lapel, particularly if you have a big bust; two inches can make all the difference.

Rings, like other jewelry, should not be overly delicate or ornate, nor overly clunky. One or two rings is enough for any woman. More tends to make hands bulky. Again, select stones with emerald cuts.

BROOCH GOES HIGH ON THE LAPEL

HANDBAGS

There's no getting around them; they are absolutely necessary. Used right, they can keep your look linear. Getting a bag big enough to meet your functional needs but contained enough in size so it doesn't add bulk to your body may be cause for rethinking what you carry around with you. Some general guidelines:

- One woman, one bag. Life is complicated enough without having to lug two bags of belongings around with you. More than one bag just drags your whole look down. If you always carry a briefcase and a bag, it's time to get a combination briefcase and pocketbook. Make sure it has a substantial strap to support the weight. The best looking, most durable, most capacious and best scaled bags—and best value for the money—come from **Coach Leatherware.** If you don't need a briefcase but still need more carrying space, then think about consolidating your belongings in one good size tote that contains a purse and other compartments. Get one with long enough straps so that you can carry it on your shoulder.

- The best bags for everyday use are shoulderbags, as they leave your hands free and keep your line longest. But all shoulder-bags are not created equal. First, the length of the strap is critical. It is right when the bag lies close to your body above or below its widest part, never at the full width of the hip or widest body part.

- If you want to sling a bag across your chest, which is not only a safety measure in crowded places but also a good way to add interest, make sure you can adjust the strap longer.

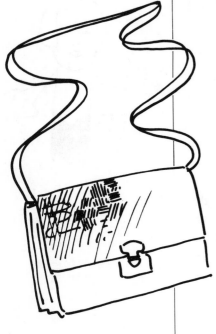

- Never, ever wear a round or pouchy bag—a satchel, a hobo bag, a duffel, a bucket, a saddlebag or whatever name it goes by. It is simply too bulky for your dimensions. Soft-sided pouchy bags have the added drawback of shapelessness. Besides, they make round women look rounder. It's that old story of perception: Never repeat a shape you want to de-emphasize.
- Look for bags that have a distinct shape but not rigid construction. Neat and trim are the descriptives that leap to mind. Just make sure the bag you choose holds all your essentials without awkward bulges; don't be afraid to put it to the test at the sales counter.
- Backpacks look best in the country, in sleek nylon fabrics. For everyday use, especially in leather, they add an awful lot of bulk to bodies, and the straps have a way of pulling at clothes across the chest. They positively weigh down short women. If you can carry it off, and it really is the best solution to your needs, by all means use one.
- This may be strictly a matter of personal opinion, but unless they are taller than they are wide, and slim, quilted Chanel-type bags have a way of looking overstuffed on full-figured women.
- The bag that gets you through the workweek is likely to be in a neutral color that goes with everything, so you don't have to change your bag every day. It is probably not the bag you want to haul around on weekends or wear for special effects.
- For weekend use, definitely go for something smaller and lighter in attitude, but also well scaled and neat of line.
- You can use a bag as a source of color for your whole look. Just keep it the center of interest by making it the only major splash of color you use.
- For all-purpose evening wear, you can't beat a little black suede shoulder bag on a long leather or braided silk strap. But "little" is relative; smaller than your daytime bag, yes; teeny-tiny, no.
- If you choose a clutch bag, be sure to get one that you can hold flat to your body, but is not so wide it chops you down.
- Bags observe seasons, too, both in materials and colors. Nothing seems to weigh a larger woman down more in the

summer than a drab leather pouchy bag. Lighten up at little cost by looking into trim straw carryalls. The neater you look, the cooler you'll feel.

GLOVES

Perhaps the most underestimated contributor to style, gloves not only have a sure way of polishing a whole look, they offer another great opportunity for splashing color onto clothes. And they do it in a risk-free way, that is, without breaking up a vertical body line. Long slinky gloves can also be downright sexy.

- Gloves are not just for warmth. They're for glamour. The least bulky, best-fitting, most versatile glove you can get is medium-weight wool jersey. If you get them long, you can scrunch down the sleeves for everyday use, then wear them in all their slinkiness for dressier occasions. Get them in a bright color and you'll make a strong enough statement to leave the jewels at home. Or get them in black, wear them with black, and pile on your cache of silver or gold bangles.
- Another option for a perfect fit in long slinky gloves—in this case, all glamour and no warmth—is spandex, best in shimmering shades of high-pitch colors or black. Be sure, when your arms make a loud statement, that everything else is kept simple and pure of line.
- Want sportive chic real fast? Put on a pair of driving gloves. There's no law that says they have to be in basic tan pigskin, although those indeed look great with corduroy or khaki pants and sweaters. Get a pair of driving gloves in bright green; wear them with a green muffler against all black.
- Wool or cashmere knit gloves go well with casual sportswear, tend to be cozy in the coldest weather, and fit without problems.
- Daytime suits look best with short leather gloves.
- Gloves with ruffled and other fancy gauntlets work only when the clothing silhouette is straight and simple or the coat silhouette is uncomplicated.

WHITE KID GLOVES

HATS

Hats are literally a way to add inches to your look. And great appeal. Hats have chic. They often have mystery. And they can have tons of charm. There's no reason why you can't wear hats. If you want to instantly understand the power of a hat, put on a fedora the next time it rains, even if you are just going to the supermarket and you have on your scruffiest clothes underneath. Not only will you protect your hair while keeping your hands free (no umbrella), everyone you encounter will assume you are a woman of smart chic—and will treat you that way. Walk tall.

What works, what doesn't:

ROMANTIC HAT
WITH CHIFFON
BOW

- With hats as with all other items, never repeat in a hat shape the body shape you wish to de-emphasize. If your body is round, your best hat will not be a rounded cloche; instead, wear a fedora with a medium-size brim.
- Hats make strong statements by themselves. In the summer, the simple chic of a medium to wide brimmed hat is often accessory enough. In the winter, when you add a brimmed hat, you might need to add a long muffler for a little extra vertical lift; keep the neck area uncluttered.
- On hats with a crown, the crown must be as wide as your face (or your face will look wide by comparison) but no wider.
- The right height of crown is a matter that calls for experimentation on your part, because the shape of the crown plays a strong role in overall proportions. But no crown should ever be taller than your face.
- Don't ever wear a hat that's too tight; not only will you be uncomfortable, the width of the crown will be too narrow for your face.
- The right width brim? You have surprising latitude. It certainly can't be wider than your shoulders. And there is such a thing as too narrow. It partly depends on the height of the crown, its shape, the shape of your face and your body—and the kind of clothes you will be wearing. So always check a prospective hat in a full-length mirror as well as a countertop mirror.
- Berets are delightfully versatile hats so strongly associated with charm that every woman needs at least one. But they can be

hard to wear for a variety of reasons. If they are narrower than your hair, your proportions will be thrown out of balance. If worn straight on, they can create a horizontal line and seem to compress you. So look for slightly enlarged berets, making sure they are made in fabrics that don't slouch too much and collapse on your head. And wear them, and most other hats, perceptibly angled to one side.

JAUNTY BERET

- Caps are cute and very popular, but hard for many full-figured women to wear; they cut down height and they cut down the width of hair above the ears that's often needed to balance body proportions. Opt instead for a spunky and sporty hat with a crown. If it's sun protection you want, get a straw sun visor with a narrow band around your head, which allows you to maintain your hair height and width.

- If you're a skier and ski hats look awful on you because they are brimless knit toques and hug the sides of the head, try turning up the bottom band and doubling it, for extra width. There's always ear muffs.

- Hair bows have just the right proportions, go even more places than hats do, and add great polish to the simplest of outfits. They take a pony tail beyond cute to classy. Wear one . . . but: Lift it up off the nape of your neck, where it will add too much width. And you're better off in a solid color than in funky dots and prints; they get too busy to carry off easily.

HOSE

If you can manage the minor miracle of pantyhose fit (see Chapter 13), you will no doubt want to use pantyhose to maximum advantage. Here's how:

- For the longest look from waist to toe, go for one line of color: Wear pantyhose, whether sheer or opaque, the same color as your skirt *and* shoes; forget about buying pantyhose in your skin tone. At the very least—say, when you're wearing a red, yellow, bright blue, or green skirt—match hose and shoe color, preferably black. The match to clothing does not have to be exact; a whole family of neutrals—taupe, deep sage green, medium gray—all appear to have the same color value and are more or less interchangeable.

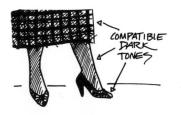

COMPATIBLE DARK TONES

- Always remember that dark tones or values, including the taupe-y neutrals, will slim legs and feet, light tones will appear to widen them.

- A black skirt (or pants!) interrupted by a stretch of beige leg is just too choppy and thus widens you; always select black sheer or opaque hose. Don't think you can get away with even a one-inch gap of beige leg between pants and shoes; it's just as unflattering and ungraceful. Wear black knee-highs or ankle-high hose instead. Or, for a pretty effect, if your ankles permit, wear pearl-gray hose (the eye will see it as white) but only with black patent leather semi-flats. It's that little-girl look that writes its own rules of charm.

- Sheer and opaque hose in black are not only the most flattering to most legs but the most versatile. Black blends with all dark colors, such as navy, burgundy, and brown (the same value), and it subdues bright colors with sophistication.

- Sheer or semi-opaque hose in off-white (avoid stark white unless you're on nursing duty!) work with all light colors. But be careful with off-whites; there are many subtleties of tone. If you are wearing clothes in winter white, or any variation of beige, be sure the off-white you choose has a slightly yellow or beige cast.

- Textured pantyhose are a good way to add sophistication to cool-weather dressing, but the simplest of textures, opaques in a matte finish, can be devilishly hard to find in large sizes. Try the **DKNY** tights; the Tall will comfortably fit an average height woman up to size 20. There's always **Danskin**, which still makes the same tights you wore in ballet school, in your size; they also produce an opaque pantyhose with built-in support.

- Ribbed pantyhose help you add textural interest to dressing in neutral colors. If your calves widen dramatically, however, the vertical ribs will appear to bow as they negotiate the calf area; better to stick to simpler textures. Similarly, other knit-in patterns will be thrown off by—and draw attention to—heavy calves. If you wear ribbed hose, be sure to pair them with mid- to low-heeled shoes; the rule of thumb is: the thicker the stocking, the lower the heel.

- Hose, like other clothes, have seasons. Save your opaques, no matter the color, for cool weather only.
- Can you dispense with hose altogether in the summer? I subscribe to the European school of thought—no pantyhose in the heat, even in the big city. Style has to be rooted in sense. In hot and humid weather, it just doesn't make sense to swath legs, the largest surface area of the body and thus critical for cooling the whole works, in a synthetic film. Nor is it comfortable. And nothing subverts style (or the ability to focus on one's work) more than discomfort. I confess: If I have a heavy-duty business meeting or dressy function, I tend to knuckle under, but not easily.
- Socks are best reserved for use under slacks, and then only if the top of the sock is completely covered when you sit. Again, match sock color to pants and shoes as you would for pantyhose—unless you're using socks for a blast of color. If you wear athletic shoes with skirts and dresses to and from work, you need some form of sock; better a socklet that stops where your shoes stop than anklets or other socks that cut even more of you off.

SHOES

If the rules of proportion require creating the perception of height, then all you need to do is slip into a pair of the highest heels you can find, right? Well, it's not quite so simple. A shoe with a high heel, especially a stiletto, makes you look unbalanced (assuming you could walk in it), as it is out of proportion with your body. You look as if you will topple over.

- To make a long story short, the very best heel height—whether for dress or business—is about 2″ (measured from the center of the heel to the ground) and the very best proportion is a graceful hourglass a little narrower than a true Louis but similarly widened slightly at the base. The proportion is right, the shape is graceful, you get stability and support, and walking is not a hazard to your health.

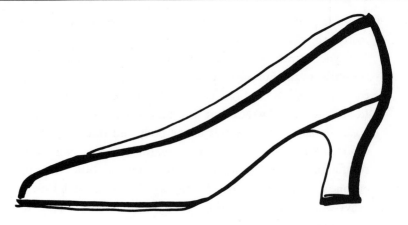

- The shorter you are and the shorter your foot is, the shorter the heel height that's most flattering, that's most supportive, and that maintains your body posture without pitching you forward.
- At the other extreme, true flats also look out of proportion and weigh your whole body down. Worse, they can also make walking cumbersome. The more you weigh, the more flats keep you grounded. The lower your center of gravity, as in the bottom-heavy woman, the less likely flats will look good on you. Instead of a true flat, opt for a semi-flat, with a heel of 1″.
- For most women, the most comfortable heel height for walking is 1½″ to 2″ in height and a bit chunky in width—but the chunkiness looks appropriate on a walking shoe because it supports the function. Search for walking shoes with either real stacked-leather heels (even on most $200 shoes these days the heels are plastic under a veneer of stacked leather) or, even better, molded synthetics that cushion impact. These will make you *feel* like walking.
- Natural materials are essential for uppers and linings on all shoes, but especially for the hard, thin soles on dress shoes and flats. Hard synthetics do not dissipate impact; they build up heat from friction and from enclosing the foot in unbreathable materials. If a woman does any walking at all, the soles of her feet will burn as she puts weight on them. The more weight, or the thinner the synthetic sole, the worse the problem.

- The most flattering dress shoe is a pump with a vee vamp or a tapered U-shaped vamp. It visually lengthens the leg. Slingbacks are good provided you don't have a fleshy heel that widens markedly as you put weight on it (check the back of your foot in a three-way mirror).
- Sandals for all-out dress wear are awfully tricky. Delicate strappy shoes, even if your legs and feet are sensationally shaped, can look out of proportion with your body. The trick is finding sandals with straps that are wide enough to be in scale with your shape, but not clumsy. Unless your feet are long and narrow, a wide horizontal strap across the toes won't solve the problem. If your heels aren't fleshy, a slingback works nicely. If they are, consider a pump, especially one with cutaway sides.
- Black silk pumps often make the most sense as fancy dress shoes, and have the virtue of seasonless appeal. You can get great variety out of pumps by adding clip-on decorations. Soft ribbon bows always look smart and lie flat, for the smoothest line; avoid pom-pom and other strongly dimensional add-ons.
- Shoes with dead-on horizontal straps near the ankle will cut you off and shorten and widen your whole appearance. Shoes with vamps cut straight across will also shorten your leg length and visually widen your feet.
- Leather and suede boots can be very flattering on you provided they leave no part of the leg uncovered between hem and foot and they match the color of your skirt in hue or value.
- The longest look you can get in a shoe is to match the color of your shoes to your stockings and your skirt hem.

TWO-TONE WITH A SLIGHT HEEL

- Always keep your shoes well-polished and in good repair. Sloppy feet can drag a good look down.
- If your feet are even modestly wide, I don't have to tell you that shoe fit is an awful problem. If you wear more than a B width, even the thought of looking for well-styled shoes of high quality can send you into a depression. But it is beginning to get a little easier, as retailers remember their function is customer service and the Western world discovers that active feet are also wider feet. More to the point, feet that taste the comfort of running shoes have a hard time settling for the pinching discomfort of most women's shoes. So the unmistakable stirrings of foot liberation are in the air.

Norm Thompson is a catalogue retailer offering many styles of high-quality casual and daytime dress shoes in true C and sometimes D widths. The company delivers fast and prepays the cost of returns. Write: P.O. Box 3999, Portland, OR 97208, or call 1-800-547-1160.

Strategies for Style

*T*he boom in fashions for larger women has, paradoxically, exposed something of another problem although, in the scheme of things, it is a far better and far more remediable problem than having no clothes to wear. Now that there is plenty to choose from, the effects of the drought years are apt to show: Simply put, full-figured women may not have the years of experimentation and experience in coordinating clothes and putting themselves together that their smaller sisters do. Now that there are choices, it may be even *harder* to develop a distinctive style. Yes, you can wear bright colors. You can wear bold prints. You can wear pleated skirts. You can wear short jackets, low-cut necklines, dramatic sleeves. You just can't wear all of them at one time. Nor should you settle for middle-of-the-road blandness. You have to learn to cut out the fashion background "noise" and find what is right for you. Where do you begin in developing your own style?

- Knowing yourself is the absolute first step.
  Inside and out. Facing the mirror, knowing your strong points, what to accent. Knowing your weak points, what not

to call attention to. Knowing your self, your character. Your personality, its many facets, your many sides. Your spirit. What you like other people to know about you. How you want to be perceived. How you want to feel in clothes. How you live your life. The kinds of situations you regularly meet.

- You also need to know the facts of fashion cold.

Examine fabrics and the effects they create, how they cling or drape, whether they flow or bulk. Understand the different silhouettes and what they do for your figure. What combines well with what. How proportion and scale work on your body. How to create different focal points. Where to put touches of color. Play with the clothes you have and the accessories you own. Take a pin and find the best place on your lapel or shoulder for it. And give yourself plenty of time in stores, to try many things on. That's what fitting rooms are for. No law says you have to buy—until you find something you love. Study what looks good and what makes you feel good, and try to understand what element contributes to the effect you like. Then you are ready to develop your own style personality.

- Define yourself in the language of clothes.

Style is a way of defining yourself in clothes, and the better you know yourself and the clearer your definition of yourself before you get dressed, the more satisfaction you will have with the way you look when dressed. You start by identifying who you are and, through your knowledge of fashion, translate your sense of yourself into a look in clothes. A vague vision of how you want to look in clothes will not help you—that is probably the problem you now have. Until you can specify it (in words or pictures), you won't be able to achieve it, or achieving it will be at enormous expense and wastage, with a closet full of clothes that "don't work" and a few that feel right. No woman can afford that. Look inside yourself (and at the captions of fashion pictures, if you want the vocabulary) and find words that capture your spirit and the feeling you want to achieve in clothes. Then look only for those clothes that express how you see yourself or want to be seen. Since this is not an exercise in fantasy—you need to work with the real stuff—look through fashion magazines, through catalogues. Pay no attention to the size of the models. Study or even clip out the pictures that represent the looks you like.

- Every good artist starts by imitating a master.

Don't be embarrassed to look in magazines for ideas of looks you like. If you can identify in words and in pictures the look and the feeling you want to achieve in clothes, you are off to a good start. Cut out the pictures you like from magazines. Put them in a file near your closet or dresser, or clip them to the inside of your closet door. Start by imitating a look you like. Eventually, you will develop the flair for yourself.

- Experiment. Experiment. And experiment.

Call it play. Set aside private time to try on your clothes; try your accessories with them until you find new combinations that please you, that look interesting. How you go public is a matter of taste. You can rehearse one big fashion change, or you can change the way you dress slowly. Most people are most comfortable going slowly, adding, say, a pocket scarf of color, then adding bigger earrings, rather than radically transforming themselves overnight and shocking those around them. With small steps, you get reinforcement and encouragement as you go. The more compliments you reap—and you will be surprised at how people notice such little touches of color as a pocket scarf—the braver you feel, the greater the incentive to come out of the closet stylewise. This isn't just a fashion issue. In many ways you will be clarifying your sense of yourself.

- Take some chances!

Break out of the mold you are in—and most women are in a mold that has hardened so firmly around them it constricts them. You have to summon up the courage to go out and try things on you've always wanted to wear but were afraid to. Or things you just "know" aren't you. Promise yourself you're just going to try on at least two things—in your correct size, of course—that you never would have tried before. Just do it! You can't develop style without exploring yourself from new angles and without being a bit daring.

- Observe and analyze.

When a well-dressed person catches your eye, make a note of

what she's wearing. Try to figure out what effect has been achieved, what impression has been created, and how, and what you like about it that so pleases you. Do this especially when you travel—en route and at your destination. Travel, particularly long-distance air travel, makes so many demands on style that women who manage to appear fresh and chic while traveling are truly worthy of scrutiny—they have usually stripped style down to its bare essentials without forgetting practicalities. On the streets of other cities and countries, half the fun is the passing fashion parade. By identifying the elements of style, you are in a position to make them your own.

- Give yourself time.

  It takes time to develop style, just as it takes time to know yourself. It takes time for your eye to adjust to seeing yourself in shaped clothes, rather than shapeless ones.

- Keep a perspective that will help you develop your own style and also put style in the proper place in life.

  Style is certainly a means to help us see ourselves more clearly, to express ourselves, to tie us to life and activity. It's serious, but it has to be approached with a lightness of heart. If it gets to be an obsession, then it's time to turn your attention elsewhere. Cultivate a garden. Or help the needy.

- Play to different "audiences."

  Dress for effect. Knowing that style expresses moods and attitudes, you can deliberately create the reaction you want. As the late great designer/writer Elizabeth Hawes put it, "Women who thoroughly understand the art of dressing look at clothes through the eyes of an actress. They think of their clothes not only in connection with themselves, but from the point of view of audience reaction. So a woman who has complete mastery of herself can, by changing her clothes, change the effect she will have on people." Nothing has more of an effect than subtly contradicting expectations—a chiffon scarf with a black leather jacket, for instance.

STYLE "TYPES"

The style personalities women project tend to sort themselves into a few major types. Most women will identify with one type most of the time, and find themselves dressing "in character" at least as often as not. What constitutes a type is a way of putting things together and the color choices, not necessarily the basic elements of a wardrobe. A woman who sees herself as "romantic" could just as likely end up in the same cut of suit as a woman who leans more to the "dramatic"; what is apt to set them apart is the color (pales for a romantic, black or brights for a dramatic), or the style of blouse, or the little touches of accessories. Part of the fun of fashion is knowing that, at the right time, these "types" may all be different facets of one's self, and all can be tried on and enjoyed at one time or another.

- Dramatic—this woman always knows the value of contrast. Clothes may be sleek of line or sweeping in scale—never in between. They are always in black with bright colors and sharp angles. Accessories tend to the big and bold. Most likely to wear a hat. When she errs, she errs on the side of overpowering.
- Classic—this woman always dresses in elegant timeless styles in beautiful fabrics that have an air of femininity-without-frills. They are often in solid colors or graphic prints. Like all sophisticated women, she leans to understatement, but knows that "refined" is never a synonym for "prim." For all the smooth, clean classicism of line, she likes color, especially in accessories. She may err on the side of looking too controlled.
- Romantic—this woman always leans toward the soft pale palette, small prints, soft lines and fluid fabrics, and often prefers sweater sets and softly pleated skirts to other separates, although she prefers dresses to everything else. She's softly feminine, and loves gathers and ruffles. She errs on the side of looking little-girlish.
- The femme fatale—this woman needs no introduction. She's always the one in the leopard print, the snuggest skirt, the shortest hemlines, the highest heels. She enjoys looking frankly sexy, and the world enjoys looking at her. She errs on the side of overdressing.

- Gamine or ingenue—this woman delights by exploiting the appeal of youth and innocence; thus she instinctively knows the value of contradiction in fashion. Her clothes tend to close-fitting, but she also knows how to wear an oversize look. Her hair is always short, with bangs, and emphasizes the eyes. She likes white collars on her dark sweaters, and she likes hats; all her accessories have a crisp feel but can veer into the frankly funky. She errs on the side of overaccessorizing.
- Natural—this woman always looks fresh and very American. She prefers simple, unconstructed clothes—blouses and skirts, perhaps with sweaters—in neutral colors, with minimal accessories. Her outfits are unfussy, and make their point through textural play rather than color contrast. Her idea of power dressing is putting on a blazer. Her glowing skin and beautiful hair are often her most eye-catching accessories. She tends to err on the side of underdressing.

Once you know how you want to look, there are only three invariable requirements for putting any clothes together.

SPIRIT

A handbook of style, any book of style, can at most be suggestive, not definitive. For by its very nature, style is a unique creation, depending, as it does, on individual identity, verve, and the unexpected. It may be no more than the fling of a scarf, the turning of a cuff. To offer as a definition of style suitable for everyone what works for one person is to actually prescribe slavish copying, which is not style at all. The props of style will change from person to person, but one attitude infuses it always—the spirit of self-definition. You define yourself, in part, through how you present yourself. Each time out, you have a fresh shot at it, at finding, revealing another aspect of yourself. When you approach getting dressed with a certain spiritedness, you see it as an adventure, a game with one's self. Perhaps it will help to think of it as tongue in chic. Wit is always a cornerstone of style. Because nothing is more leaden than taking oneself too seriously.

POINT OF VIEW

The second requirement for style is, when you choose an item of clothing you want to wear, you must develop a clear point of view about it. You have invested in simple, timeless clothes, the kinds of clothes that can be worn many ways, for many occasions. In fact, the test of a good item of clothing is that it can lend itself to many points of view, many ways to be worn. A plain white linen shirt dress can be approached, at the most basic level, as dressy, casual, or professional looking, depending on what you pair it with. It can be frankly sexy (neck open down to there, bottom button open, sandals), ladylike (antique brooch at the neck, short off-white gloves, spectator pumps), romantic (worn open, with sleeves folded back, as a duster over filmy beige linen trousers and a languid off-white camp shirt, a sheer voile scarf flowing loosely around the neck). You express the point of view with a few well-chosen accessories that totally and single-mindedly support that attitude. A good basic dress (or jacket or suit) suggests more than one point of view. It's carrying out any one of them—and only one at a time—with consistency that accounts for the success of a look. In getting dressed, your job is to choose from a wealth of possibilities one way that dress could be approached. This time. Next time you may certainly want to wear it differently.

Where do you start with inspiration for a point of view? You can extract cues from the clothes, from your personality, from your mood, from the occasion or from just pure fantasy—the elements of flair.

- An occasion. There's a party for a friend, at her house. It's a very relaxed Saturday night gathering but the air is festive—a belated birthday celebration—and most of the guests know each other professionally. You want to look chic but relaxed. It could be as simple as a pair of tapered black silk pull-on pants, a big white silk shirt worn over them, a large melon-colored organza flower at the neck.

  Or there is a summer afternoon wedding reception on the lawn of the country club. You want to be cool, look airy and light, and leave your hands free for the pleasures of meeting, greeting, and eating while standing and strolling. It could be as easy as a white linen trapeze blouse-jacket over a plain black slim skirt, and a black medium brim straw hat with a colorful chiffon scarf tied around it and flowing down your back. And mid-heel sandals (so as not to tear up the lawn).

- The clothes. You have a taupe suede shirt jacket that is your idea of sportive chic. You love wearing it on weekends in town, with tailored skirts and trousers, and in the country, over sweaters and slacks. Suddenly, you see it next to a blue chambray workshirt and realize it has Western potential. The next time you wear it, you pair it with beige trousers, the chambray shirt, a purple bandana tucked into the open collar, and the concha belt you've had in the back of your closet ever since that trip to New Mexico.

  Or you have just found the greatest sweater jacket a woman could own, a collarless long cardigan in hunter green with a jacquard design in tweedy dark shades. Its deep fall-type tones beg for brown corduroy slacks for casual wear, but the sweater possesses so much rich sophistication you see no reason why you can't wear it as an unmatched suit jacket to the office. You put on a plain black straight skirt, and a drapey, washed silk parchment-color blouse with a large and slightly ruffled collar that lies well away from your face. You add a deep brown oblong georgette scarf under the collar and tie it in a droopy bow. Black opaque hose and basic cordovan wing-tip or plain black low-heel pumps complete the polished effect.

- A mood. You are feeling . . . frisky. You'd like a little excitement, a change of routine, and you wouldn't mind being seen as well as seeing. Yet there is nothing terribly interesting on your calendar. So you call up a friend and cajole her into a spur-of-the-moment expedition to the art galleries in town. You put on a basic black lambswool sweater and knit skirt because you love to wear it, you add black opaque hose and black semi-flats and short black leather gloves—everything clean, simple, and unassuming to this point. Then you wrap yourself in a giant purple wool muffler and anchor it with a simple black shoulder bag. The final touch: a pair of sunglasses—there's nothing like a little mystery to embolden the spirit.

- Personality. You have a soft side that seems to get lost in the crush between raising two small children and managing an office. Next week, you have to make a presentation to be attended by managers company-wide. Top brass will be present, too. You want to look professional, but not boring, and you want to let people know, in a very gentle way, that you are a woman with imagination. Since you will be seen from a distance, you want the sophistication of clothes that are simple of line and well-cut. You already know you're going to put on a very flattering white tunic-length jacket over a slim black skirt. You need your accessories strong and visible, but bold is not the impression you want to make. Finally, you figure it out. You take a Wedgwood blue oblong silk scarf, tie it around your neck into a large half bow, and turn it so the bow is beside your face, the ends flowing loosely.

How much is enough? The minimum you need to establish your point of view. One large silk bow framing the face speaks softly but definitively. A huge wrap and dark eyeglasses have enough presence to stir up all the intrigue you need. A silver belt, a bandana, a workshirt make a subtle Western suggestion; a hat would be one touch too much outside the Lone Star state (unless you are going to a square dance or a rodeo). On a big white shirt, one spirited flower peddles plenty of eye-catching appeal; anything more would dilute the freshness, and subvert the relaxed attitude.

Or approach it from the other direction. You are traveling, and suitcase space is limited. You want to get the most mileage out of what you take. Could you make a whole wardrobe out of a black lambswool vee sweater and slim pull-on skirt? It could look confidently businesslike but not starchy with a 1″ deep brown mock crocodile belt, black or brown mock croc pumps, sheer black hose, and a large shawl in deep gold and black plaid draped over one shoulder. It could be worn off-hand casually, in the city or the country, with a white tee shirt underneath, a plaid wool muffler coiled with ease around the neck, a jean jacket, and for a great line as well as safeguarding possessions, a shoulder bag slung across the body. Finished off with opaque black hose and brown loafer semiflats. Or you could look elegantly sexy for go-to-dinner. Throw onto one shoulder a bright silk or wool muffler and anchor it in front with a gutsy chain belt draped just below your waist. Pull on long black jersey gloves and wear a gold cuff bracelet over one glove. Substantial gold button earrings highlight your face. You finish off with sheer black hose, black suede slingbacks, and a black leather or velvet envelope clutch.

Often enough, women make the mistake of selecting accessories by some scheme—usually color—other than one that develops a single attitude or feeling or point of view. There was a time, years ago, when that was more viable, more likely to meet with success than it is today. Fashion options and accessories were far fewer and demarcations in purpose were far sharper for all items. There were day clothes, cocktail clothes, evening clothes, and, for private consumption, active sport clothes and casual clothes; rarely the twain did meet. It was simply harder to make a mistake. Today, more choices, the proliferation of gradations of purpose and status, the segregation of clothes by "life-style" attitude rather than by function, make style a more subtle achievement—and a more elusive one. The burden of dressing appropriately, to say nothing of style, is now more than ever on the individual.

Understandably, a red scarf stands out on black. But if the scarf is just a little silk square tied around the neck, it is out of scale, too little to establish anything except how little it is and thus, by indirection, suggesting how big the body is. Matching it with red and black suede heels (dressy and racy) and a red leather shoulder pouch (casual, lumpy, and unflattering), as I recently saw a woman do, is to yoke together items that have no fundamental compatibility of line or purpose; as a result, they do not collaborate in creating a coherent impression about the sweater and skirt, or you. Even what they do share (color) is applied too diffusely to make any point—not that contrast by itself constitutes an attitude, an effect, a look. If the object is to make a contrast, one item with more impact (not necessarily bigger but used more eye-catchingly) would be better.

But a point of view would still be needed. Taking a cue from the shoes, though, the wearer could put together a racy little look for a party—simply by adding an alluring lacy red camisole under the sweater and letting its top edge peek into the deep vee neckline. A small black suede shoulderbag or clutch would provide the right finish. The peek-a-boo appeal, by definition, comes from a small but suggestive touch in a place you want to accent.

FOCAL POINT

No matter your "take" or point of view on an outfit, you aren't finished dressing unless you create a focal point, a point of emphasis. Every day, with everything you put on. You concentrate attention on one point, and one point only. Because it stops the eye, the point of emphasis focuses attention on the most important part of the design or the feature you are most interested in accenting. You knowingly, deliberately call attention to your assets. A favorite ploy of designers is to place detail on a dress so that it directs an onlooker's eye to the face; it is important in accessorizing to maintain the built-in lines of emphasis. Having a focal point also implies that one kind of line or color dominates the others in an outfit. A man whose opinion I trust in these matters says: "It's not just a matter of throwing on some significant jewelry. It's putting an exclamation point to what you are wearing."

A flower at the throat, a hat, a silk bow at the side of the neck—all are ways of using accessories to make a focal point of the face, depending on what you are wearing. With a large shawl, the sheer drama of the vertical drape becomes the focal point. Or on a field of black, the peek-a-boo of red camisole draws the eye to the bustline. A focal point is necessary because it brings the onlooker's eye to a rest. And therefore, assuming the focal point is at a flattering place, it diminishes the perception of size. An outfit without a focal point is visually disturbing to an onlooker. And because it gives the eye no place to home in on, it exaggerates size.

Here are a couple of the many other ways to call attention to your face:

- Put an interesting (well-scaled) pin on your shoulder or the upper edge of your lapel.
- Wear glittering boldly sized earrings, not danglers and preferably dimensional.
- Twist a colorful scarf and tie it in your hair with "mouse ear" ends.
- On a perfectly simple and boring single-breasted suit jacket, change the row of buttons to the boldest and most interesting ones you can find.
- Wear sunglasses.
- Wear a white shirt with a crisp collar turned up.

Women err in both directions, when it comes to a focal point. Either they fail to supply one at all, and look unfinished, or they supply too many and look overdone: the highly decorated sweater, the elaborate hairdo, show-stopper earrings. One we read as too uninteresting, the other as too busy. One gives no reason to attract the attention of an onlooker and looks larger than she really is, the other actively confuses the eye and repels attention. A highly decorated sweater (or jacket or dress) makes a statement by itself; everything else should be simple and clean.

BLOCKBUSTER DRESSING

While every good wardrobe starts with a few basic clothes that have great versatility, at some point you will probably acquire a few items that are so resolutely of one attitude that they can be worn only one way. Those are true luxuries, because they don't mix easily and you have to be in the right mood for them; they are not adaptable to your mood. When you do wear them, the polite thing to do is to step quietly (which is to say, simply) out of their way and let them make their statement without competition from you. Most ballgowns (but by no means most evening clothes) fall into this category. Ditto elaborately beaded dresses and jackets. So do some "outrageous" or "conversation piece" accessories; just give them a clean (simple and solid color) and flattering backdrop and let them be their glorious selves. Typical members of this family: huge cuff bracelets, giant colorful shawls, leopard-print shoes—come to think of it, leopard-print anything.

But if you find yourself consistently going for clothes that say it all, you are purchasing a wardrobe of clothes that say too much. Your clothes will either be overdecorated or overtrendy. There will be no room for you to put on your personal stamp—the stamp of style. So look for beautifully cut pieces that leave room for your personality. Style is not in the object but in the wearer.

STRATEGIES—DRESSING UP

Putting a dressy look together is tricky, especially if you are facing a job-related evening. Dressing up is not necessarily a matter of dressing *up*, or adding decoration. It can also be done by letting clothes with simple, flattering, and elegant lines speak for themselves—with the minimum necessary help.

It is not only possible but desirable to approach evening and special occasions the way you approach every day dressing—with clothing in beautiful fabrics in classic and flattering shapes. You can make them say "special" or "evening" by:

- adopting a black-white color scheme. It instantly formalizes anything you don.
- adding glitter. A classic suit or jacket in a glitter fabric will always be in style. Alternatively, you can add glitter in

accessories: sequins, gold, stones real or faux; of course, a little goes a long way. An off-white double-breasted gabardine suit worn with a white silk tank, gold and pearl earrings, a gold necklace, a gold clutch bag, and perhaps a sliver of gold belt has real swank (add white suede shoes and nude sheer hose).

- deploying bareness strategically. Put a tank top under a suit, or under a blouse, and *imply* bareness.
- relying on pale tones in luxurious fabrics. Soft wools, cashmere, silk, fine linen all have an innocent sensuality and look ethereal in off-white, pale gray, barely beige, or the faintest of pinks. They seduce with a whisper.
- or, alternatively, using vibrant color. Jewel tones, like jewels themselves, have an affinity for evening. It is easiest to wear a lot of vibrant color if it's in a matte-finish fabric, like jersey or crepe. Glossy and highly reflective fabrics, like silk charmeuse, work better in smaller touches—the little camisole or tank under a suit, a scarf, a handbag.

Take a simple pair of tapered pull-on pants (evening only) or split skirt (afternoon or evening) in black silk. For an evening out, you can wear either with:

- a white silk tee shirt or other blouse, with or without a cardigan jacket
- a long slinky-slouchy vee-neck cardigan sweater, the neckline filled in with beads or a camisole
- a beaded tunic, or beaded jacket over a tank
- a gold or silver lurex sweater set
- a long scoop-neck or tank-style sweater in pale beige, and a long pale chiffon scarf around your neck
- a long silky sapphire blue shirt.

Formidable? Not at all!

From day to evening. How to make the metamorphosis when you are in the office all day and have a dressy or formal event in the evening? There's always the ploy of dashing home from work early and changing clothes—but that assumes that work and home are near enough. Then, too, you can keep a cocktail dress in your office, hoping for just such a chance to use it. But the approach that makes the most sense, and symbolizes the changed expectations about working women, is to invest in a dressy suit that itself mixes business with pleasure. Your aim should be simple elegance. A neutral-of-your-choice dinner suit with gold or silver accessories. Or a tuxedo suit. Or any suit in wool crepe that is distinguished by draping à la Donna Karan. Not only can most working women take such a suit comfortably from day to evening with a change of accessories, the really smart ones prefer to. A suit signals that they are working women. "Only the wives of executives dress up," one high-powered woman candidly explained to the *New York Times* recently. And it skirts those other pitfalls—you don't want to look like one of the boys, yet looking all-out sexy is for other times and other places, to say nothing of other people.

A good-fitting black suit with a respectably open silk blouse—or even no blouse at all, depending on the cut of the jacket, or if it is a dinner suit—is plenty sexy while above reproach. Men seem to get weak in the knees when seeing women in anything resembling a tuxedo. The change of accessories might include a higher heel or more open shoe, a more open blouse in drapey silk, and strong gold earrings and necklace, or a pearl necklace and bold pin, or perhaps just an opera scarf in the absence of a blouse. A surplice style or a colorful print in silk would be top choices for a blouse, if you wear a blouse.

If there's going to be dancing, you can stick with the dressed-up suit, or take the plunge to a very simple and more covered than bare cocktail dress, with jewelry. It is truly unwise to wear anything low cut to any work-associated event, even if your company schedules an out-of-town outing at a posh resort. Any woman who dresses frankly sexy risks making her male cohorts uncomfortable—and while that doesn't say a lot for them, it could have job repercussions for you. Better to play safe.

STRATEGY: **BARE FLAIR**

In the quest for simple elegance, you rely on the sophistication of a well-cut dress or suit, and let the good lines do the speaking out. In this black jersey dress, for example, the neckline says it all.

Earrings have a "clean" (unfussy) shape but enough presence to highlight the face.

What's not here is at least as important as what is. Bareness is the focal point. Hair doesn't distract from the drama of neckline. *Any* jewelry would spoil the effect.

There's lots of play in neckline due to the give of the fabric. Contours and courage dictate degree of décollétage.

Wide cinch with clean leather closure blends with dress yet adds polish. The trick is a belt long enough so it doesn't cut into flesh.

One bold gold bracelet is a welcome highlight, echoes earrings, and accentuates sexiness of slim sleeves.

A handbag keeps the shoulders beautifully bare. The bag is slim, well-scaled, and lends a bit of textural interest.

Full jersey skirt drapes close to body, flatters most figures. But be sure hem is even all around, not hiked up at back or sides; if so, shorten accordingly.

Sheer black hose maintain line and degree of dressiness.

STRATEGY: **CASUAL CACHET**

Spirit. Attitude. How do you capture it in your clothes? After all, that's what defines style today. Casual clothes allow the most freedom of personal expression. The catch is to look and feel polished but not stiff, to exude ease but not sloppiness. Fit, of course, is critical; it should be relaxed, never tight. And simple shapes, as always, look best. Seek fabrics with texture but no bulk, in related but not matching patterns and colors. Use accessories sparingly but tellingly.

Wit leads the way in a lighthearted hat malleable to mood, definitely there but not overpowering, in a fabric that relates to the coat. A few strategically placed wisps keep hairline looking soft yet not undone.

Loosely tied scarf is perfectly at ease, in scale, and echoes the vertical flow in its own eye-catching pattern without slavishly repeating shirt's.

Panache is built into the fresh striping of the blouse, a neckline that relaxes, a fabric that drapes without cling, and length that allows for comfortable blousing.

A narrow leather belt adds finish without overemphasizing waistline.

Slacks are subtly patterned, finely textured, correctly cut for free movement. Note perfect length.

Unlined raincoat makes a dashing duster with sensational drape and grace of movement. Unexpected touch on rolled-up cuffs recaps informal polish of the whole.

Semi-flat shoes keep the look casual; lightweight oxfords balance menswear theme with femininity.

STRATEGY: **SUITABLE STYLE**

Nothing has as much wardrobe versatility or solves as many wardrobe problems as a suit. And nothing packs as much wardrobe punch as a suit in a vibrant color set against black. Like lipstick red. What we have here is living proof that a suit, even in the absolutely simplest of shapes, doesn't have to be dull. There are many ways to play this suit, many points of view; while it's a stunner by day, it looks great for dinner, with just a change of hose, shoes, and hairstyle, which, after all, won't be tucked under a hat as for day. As shown, the suit works for day, but keep this view of accessorizing in mind any way it's worn: Less is almost always more.

The impeccably neat hairline puts all the panache where it's meant to be—in the hat; its strong color and shape tolerate no fussiness of hairstyle. Yet the pulled-back style is smart enough to go it alone.

A hat full of charm caps the sweet attitude of the suit—gently romantic in an English sort of way. The black-banded bowler, with its well-defined shape and mid-width brim, balances the swing of the jacket.

One big black silk flower adds so much charm because it is unexpected on a workaday suit. Yet it's as bold in scale as the jacket is in tone, and accents the romantic view of the suit.

Played against black, the brilliant color of jacket acts as an accessory in itself. High color in an otherwise classic jacket is always a decorative element. To give color its full impact, other accessories are used sparingly.

The trapeze jacket makes a graceful sweep in motion, yet drapes equally gracefully in repose. The simple and elegant lines continued to below the hip make this jacket workable for any body, and function as the perfect foil for strong color.

The contrast of slim under swing makes this look chic and flattering. Where the skirt should end is not an issue of hemline length but a matter of proportion. A few inches below the knee keeps the attitude romantic.

Densely colored untextured stockings that continue the hue of the skirt create a flattering line. In this case, they are also part of the backdrop against which the bright color works as an accessory.

Sleek, undecorated black pumps (smooth leather or rich suede) complete the long uninterrupted line without distracting the eye.

STRATEGY: **EASY ELEGANCE**

Clothes that are soft, easy, and flattering have a way of never going out of style. And have multiple uses.

With asymmetric fullness, especially above ears, hairstyle balances proportions of face and whole body. Short cut keeps neck uncluttered.

Minimizing bulk at neck maximizes perception of height, keeps top-heavy body in balance. Unexpected touch takes link necklace beyond ordinary—lacing it with velvet ribbon.

Easy-to-wear bloused top skims body in relaxed way, creating smooth, straight line with built-in softness. Silhouette works especially well for big bust.

Drawstring allows as much definition of waist, at whatever point wearer wants, without interrupting flow or overemphasizing waist.

In keeping with soft ease of top, split skirt in beautifully draping crepe falls in smooth line close to body, moves gracefully. Real elegance!

Even though they afford the comfort of pants, soft culottes have all the beauty of a skirt, thus need long, and even, hemline. Despite full coverage, split skirt has own brand of chic, suits all body types.

Dark-tone hose maintain long line from waist to toe, while sheerness suggests dressiness. Opaque hose would make look more casual.

Medium heels flatter legs, highlight slimness under fullness, yet balance full proportions.

STRATEGY: **GRAY FLANNEL GRACE**

A body-skimming dress in any style is a wardrobe asset. This one, in softest wool flannel of medium gray, is stunningly simple for daytime. Given the chic of its good lines, it could be dressed up, too, with silver and lurex accessories, and a neckline revealingly opened.

Simple silver earrings are tailored enough for daytime, well-scaled to subtly emphasize eyes.

Keeping the collar open slightly relaxes the strictness of the look without detracting from propriety.

Raglan shoulders provide room for bust while keeping fit neat. Light pads provide important shoulder line definition.

Built-in counterpoint of trim lines and plush fabric suggests other strict/soft contrasts: A smooth silk men's-style tie against the plush flannel of the dress playfully bends gender while suggesting business appropriateness—and adding some color. Such contradictions are always in style.

Cape front and back give the dress the polish of a suit in one-piece easy dressing.

Sleeves finished on both sides invite rolling up, but note that cuffs work only if sleeves are straight and cuffs are on the small side; too wide and they will shorten the whole body. A simple bangle adds polish and supports the softly tailored attitude.

Combination briefcase-pocketbook holds workday essentials while minimizing clutter. Note substantial strap, in scale with function and body.

This dress could stop at any below-knee length. Dark gray shoes and barely black sheer stockings keep flow vertical.

STRATEGY: **HOT STUFF**

Dressing up in warm weather can be a real challenge. The trick is paring down; you need to rely on the great grace of clean and simple shapes. And while crispness will help you look and feel cool—thus attractive—you still want the flattery of fluidity of line. Think white for freshness, and texture for lots of attitude.

What better proof is there that simplicity is disarming? One long lean cascade of crinkled white fabric. Notice, though, that great drape starts from well-defined shoulders; these are gently but definitively padded.

Cap sleeves broaden shoulder line, essential for establishing proper body proportions and balancing wide hips. Yet they keep the look light and summery.

Bareness of the arms, like bareness anywhere, is appealing, and functions as a decorative element in itself. An array of slim faux ivory bangles calls attention to the arms in a light way without distracting from the bareness.

An off-white shoulder bag in pliable straw adds textural interest, keeps the feeling cool, and echoes the airy softness of the entire look.

Opening the neckline and the skirt hem are subtle ways to add to sexiness without resorting to the heaviness of decoration.

A "tea-length" hemline is not only flattering to fuller legs, it is compatible with the softly fluted edges of the Fortuny-pleated dress.

Sandals are essential for restating the bareness theme; straps are neither too delicate for the body nor too thick for an effect.

17

Style—Capturing the Spirit

Style has always been hard to define because it is the expression of an attitude—a feeling about oneself—more than it is any *object*. It is self-confidence made visible. But it is not complicated to achieve.

Five true tales.

"It was a spring morning in New York and mine was to start with a meeting in midtown, smack in the land of chic. I put on a lightweight black wool suit, with a collarless blouson jacket. To celebrate spring, which New York gets in very small doses, I put on a bright teal silk shirt so that the collar and cuffs were highly visible, and kept the jacket open. Good so far, but I looked unfinished, even with a belt. The unlined jacket was too light to support a major pin, so I took out a long silk scarf that has a touch of teal. But no matter how I tried it, it just bulked up the neck and collar. Then inspiration struck. I pulled the scarf through the jacket's top buttonhole and tied a big colorful bow. Yes! On the way up to my meeting, a woman turned to me and said, 'I love that bow. I've never seen that before. I think I'm going to try that.'" That little flourish passed a powerful test of style—it was unexpected and charming enough to break down the usual barriers between wary strangers on a New York elevator.

"It happened quite by chance. Several items in my wardrobe, all acquired at different times, just seemed to come together once I made a certain purchase. I owned the blouse before anything—a really conventional suit blouse in a lovely, silky fabric (it might even have been polyester, but a gorgeous one!); it had a stock tie which I preferred to arrange in a droopy bow, fell in gathers from a high shoulder yoke, and had gathered sleeves, but all in a very slim, controlled way, in pure cream. Somewhere along the way, I acquired a sweet, collarless smock top—it could be a blouse or jacket—in almost sheer off-white wool. I would never have thought about it over the blouse until one day a pair of black corduroy knickers landed in my closet. I bought them for casual wear with long sweaters, a look I love, but not exactly everyday offerings in large sizes. Their swashbuckling potential drew me to try them with the bowed blouse and, because something more was needed, the smock as jacket. I don't suppose any of it would have worked if I didn't own the only shoes in the world that could possibly handle that combination—black patent monk-strap slip-ons. And, of course, black tights. This was not attire for work or play, but it became my uniform that season for going to performances, to concerts and the theater. It *was* rather theatrical; it always made me feel exciting. I felt taller, more confident, more knowing, more daring. Exciting things seemed to happen to me when I wore it." Clothes occasionally have the power to transform us; the right clothes can strike a note with an aspect of ourselves we seldom get a chance to display otherwise—but oh, when we do! Just by putting them on, some clothes have that kind of perfect pitch, that magical ability to draw out that element of character. Style doesn't just express us; at its very best it reveals us to ourselves, as well as to others.

"There are so many kinds of things I would love to find in larger sizes but can't seem to. One of them is a blouse in a semisheer fabric, one that drapes nicely on the body, goes with a lot of things I own, has a relaxed sexiness about it, but isn't terribly exotic in style. I have for years been keeping an eye out for just such an item. A year ago, just before Mother's Day, I had to scout the lingerie department of a major store in search of a gift. You know how confusing lingerie departments are; I was wandering through the wilderness of nighties searching for the promised land of robes when my eyes fell on what was the top part of some sexy little ensemble—it was white, it was semisheer, it was large, it was a simple blouse style, and, best of all, it had little heart-shaped buttons. Nothing about it specifically said 'bed'; in fact, it looked exactly like the blouse I had been wanting for ages. And it was a lot cheaper than most good blouses. The saleswoman thought I was nuts, buying only the top half of a nighttime ensemble, but I wound up with one great blouse." Style is knowing the possibilities in clothes and deciding for yourself how they are to be worn.

"I guess we all have them—social dates made well in advance; then when the day comes, for whatever reason, you just don't feel up to it. I have finally learned how to cope with them. I put on the simplest all-purpose item of style in my closet—for me, it's black crepe culottes—and a simple blouse. A jacket if it's colder. These clothes are old friends, comfort clothes, the sartorial equivalent of comfort foods. They feel good because they always look good and they so represent 'me' that they perform on my behalf even when I am not up to myself. They don't demand a thing from me. Then I add my favorite finishing piece. I throw around my shoulders a huge wrap in shocking pink silk crepe. I bought it two or three years ago, and I wear it in all seasons. There is something so outrageous about it, yet I am dressed so simply, that it beguiles; it winds up catching people's interest in an admiring way. And that restores my sociability—you can't help but respond." Style, unlike fashion, is not intimidating; it draws the viewer in—and the wearer out!

"I have finally done it. I have acquired a one-dress wardrobe. Last summer I wandered into one of those very inexpensive import shops because something in the window looked like it would fit me. But I wound up being distracted by a dress I might not have otherwise bought if it weren't so cheap I couldn't possibly go wrong. It's crinkled rayon in a long, simple button-front shirt style with cap sleeves. I have no idea what size it really is; it fits; it would fit any woman between size 2 and size 22. I wear it with an armful of light bangle bracelets and it goes out. Because it's got all these little pleats, it's not only flattering, it moves sinuously and dances wonderfully. I put a sweater over it, and it goes anywhere; especially a long pullover, which I belt, and which shortens the dress for street wear. I knot one side of it, and I wear it over my bathing suit. Can you imagine a dress that goes to town in the morning, rolls in the sand at the beach in the afternoon, and goes dancing at night? It travels everywhere in the world, because you roll it into a ball and it comes out fine. I forgot to mention, it's white. 'Impractical,' you say. Yes, but you wash it, wring it out, and it dries fast—looking even better than before. It is whatever I want it to be—and so free in spirit it frees my spirit. I feel great in it." Style is not a price. It is not an age. And it is not a size.

Index